Data Privacy and Security

Legislative Advances and Consumer Protection

snova
New York

Privacy and Identity Protection Series

Guidelines for Digital Identity Verification
Damon Solis (Editor)
ISBN: 979-8-88697-838-4
eBook ISBN: 979-8-88697-929-9

Information Security: Cyberattacks, Data Breaches and Security Controls
Paul Scholz (Editor)
ISBN: 978-1-53615-880-9
eBook ISBN: 978-1-53615-881-6

More information about this series can be found at
https://novapublishers.com/product-category/series/privacy-and-identity-protection/

Ricky K. Segura
Editor

Data Privacy and Security

Legislative Advances and Consumer Protection

snova
New York

Library of Congress Cataloging-in-Publication Data

ISBN: 979-8-89530-730-4 (Hardcover)
ISBN: 978-8-89530-838-7 (eBook)

Published by Nova Science Publishers, Inc. † New York

Contents

Preface

Privacy is a fundamental right. Yet for more than two decades, powerful tech companies have been allowed to set the terms of online interactions. Without meaningful limits on their business practices, they have built systems that invade our private lives, spy on our families, and collect the most intimate details about us for profit. The harms to online privacy are well-documented, including data breaches, unknowingly sharing data with third parties, surreptitiously installing tracking software, misleading users about data collection, and more. As more data is collected on individuals, the harms of abusive data practices become more pronounced.

There is a pressing need to put consumers back in control of their data and protect their privacy. This book addresses these critical issues and explores legislative and regulatory measures to safeguard digital privacy and security.

Chapter 1

Protecting America's Consumers: Bipartisan Legislation to Strengthen Data Privacy and Security*

Committee on Energy and Commerce

MEMORANDUM
June 10, 2022
To: Subcommittee on Consumer Protection and Commerce Members and Staff
Fr: Committee on Energy and Commerce Staff
Re: Hearing on "Protecting America's Consumers: Bipartisan Legislation to Strengthen Data Privacy and Security"

On Tuesday, June 14, 2022, at 10:30 a.m. (EDT), in the John D. Dingell Room, 2123 of the Rayburn House Office Building, and via Cisco Webex online video conferencing, the Subcommittee on Consumer Protection and Commerce will hold a legislative hearing entitled, "Protecting America's Consumers: Bipartisan Legislation to Strengthen Data Privacy and Security."

I. Background

A. Current Law

Unlike other global economic powers, such as the European Union and China, the United States does not have a comprehensive, national data privacy standard. The United States instead relies on sector-specific privacy-related federal statutes that establish varying degrees of protection, impose different collection and use limitations on various entities, and provide consumers with varying degrees of individual rights.[1] These laws include the Health Insurance Portability and

---

* This is an edited, reformatted and augmented version of Subcommittee on Consumer Protection and Commerce, dated June 14, 2022.

[1] Lindsey Barrett, *Confiding in Con Men: U.S. Privacy Law, the GDPR, and Information Fiduciaries*, Seattle University Law Review (Apr. 9, 2019).

In: Data Privacy and Security: Legislative Advances and Consumer Protection
Editor: Ricky K. Segura
ISBN: 979-8-89530-730-4

Accountability Act, which protects information collected by a health care provider;[2] the Family Educational Rights and Privacy Act, which regulates the collection of student data by public school officials and those they designate;[3] the Children's Online Privacy Protection Act of 1998 (COPPA), which covers data for children 12 and under with respect to online services directed to children;[4] the Genetic Information Nondiscrimination Act, which prohibits misuse of genetic data in employment or insurance decisions;[5] and the Gramm-Leach- Bliley Act and the Fair Credit Reporting Act, which apply to financial institutions and credit reporting agencies.[6]

Many different types of data and entities are not covered by those or other sector specific laws. To bridge those gaps, the Federal Trade Commission (FTC) must rely on its unfair or deceptive acts or practices authority under section 5 of the FTC Act.[7] This authority is limited to cases in which (i) the agency can prove substantial, unavoidable injury from conduct not outweighed by benefits to consumers or competition; or (ii) companies fail to live up to their own promises regarding data practices, regardless of whether such practices themselves are harmful.[8] Moreover, there is no federal requirement for entities to make any such promises.[9]

The FTC is also limited in the relief it may obtain. The agency lacks first-offense civil penalty authority, and the Supreme Court held last year that the FTC may no longer rely on section 13(b) of the FTC Act to obtain monetary relief for consumers who have been harmed, meaning most consumers cannot have their money returned even when the FTC is able to prove a violation.[10]

A growing number of states have acted to try and fill the federal void. California, Virginia, Colorado, Utah, and Connecticut have passed comprehensive privacy legislation. These state laws materially vary in their scope, protections, obligations, and enforcement mechanisms.[11]

B. The Need for Regulation

The consequence of the current approach to data privacy is that most companies monitor themselves and may generally collect, use, share, or sell data without having to notify the individuals to whom that data pertains. Once that data is in the hands of third parties it may be further sold, combined, and used.[12] The lack of a federal standard is more pronounced in the increasingly digital world. One 2021 study showed that 70 percent of companies increased their collection of personal consumer data despite 86 percent of consumers citing data privacy as a

---

[2] Health Insurance Portability and Accountability Act, Pub. L. No. 104-191.

[3] 20 U.S.C. § 1232g.

[4] 15 U.S.C. § 6501, et seq.

[5] Genetic Information Nondiscrimination Act, Pub. L. No. 110-233.

[6] 15 U.S.C. §§ 6801-6809; 15 U.S.C. § 1681 et seq.

[7] 15 U.S.C. § 45.

[8] Federal Trade Commission, *FTC Report to Congress on Privacy and Security* (Sept. 13, 2021).

[9] *Id.*

[10] *Id.*; *AMG Capital Mgmt., LLC v. FTC*, 141 U.S. 1341 (2021).

[11] Mayer Brown, *Connecticut Passes Comprehensive Privacy Law: Comparing to Other States* (https://www.mayerbrown.com/en/perspectives-events/publications/2022/05/connecticut-passes-comprehensive-privacy-law-comparing-to-other-state-privacy-laws) (May 11, 2022).

[12] *The State of Consumer Data Privacy Laws in the US (and Why It Matters)*, New York Times (Sept. 6, 2021).

growing concern.[13] Over half of American adults now say they have decided not to use a product or service due to worries over the use of their data.[14]

Online privacy harms are well-documented, including data breaches, providing data to third parties without knowledge, surreptitiously installing tracking software, misleading users about data harvesting, and more.[15] Americans are increasingly distressed by the tradeoff of providing their data in exchange for products and services, with 73 percent now saying this is an "unjustified use" of their information.[16]

As more data is collected on individuals by more products and services necessary for everyday life, the harms from abusive data practices are more pronounced.[17] The coronavirus disease of 2019 (COVID-19) pandemic exacerbated these concerns, particularly for children. One comprehensive study found that 90 percent of remote learning tools recommended by schools tracked students and sent data to advertising companies.[18] Studies consistently show that data is used in ways that disadvantage vulnerable communities and target people of color, often with regard to eligibility for essential products and services such as home loans.[19]

II. Summary of H.R. ____, the "American Data Privacy and Protection Act Discussion Draft"

After failed efforts over many decades, the "American Data Privacy and Protection Act" (the Act) is the first bipartisan, bicameral national comprehensive privacy and data security proposal with support from leaders on the House Energy and Commerce Committee and the Senate Commerce, Science, and Transportation Committee. The Act establishes a national standard to protect consumer data privacy, impose common sense obligations on covered entities, and allow for federal, state, and individual enforcement.

A. Types of Data Covered

Covered data is defined broadly to include any information identifying, linked, or reasonably linkable to an individual or device linkable to an individual. Certain covered data such as health, financial, biometric, genetic, and precise geolocation information is considered sensitive and subject to heightened requirements. The FTC may promulgate regulations to specify additional sensitive data categories to account for technological changes.

---

13 KPMG, *Corporate Data Responsibility: Bridging the Consumer Trust Gap* (Aug. 2021) (https://advisory.kpmg.us/articles/2021/bridging-the-trust-chasm.html).

14 Pew Research Center, *Half of Americans Have Decided Not to Use a Product or Service Because of Privacy Concerns* ((Apr. 14, 2020) (https://www.pewresearch.org/fact-tank/2020/04/14/half-of-americans-have-decided-not-to-use-a-product-or-service-because-of-privacy-concerns/).

15 *6 Examples of Online Privacy Violation*, Cyber News (Apr. 15, 2020).

16 *Americans Widely Distrust Facebook, TikTok and Instagram with Their Data, Poll Finds*, Washington Post (Dec. 22, 2021).

17 *See* note 12.

18 *Remote Learning Apps Shared Children's Data at a 'Dizzying Scale,'* Washington Post (May 24, 2022).

19 *See*, e.g., *Disparity in Home Lending Costs Minorities Millions, Research Finds*, CBS News (Nov. 15, 2019).

B. Entities Covered

Covered entities are also broadly defined and include any entity under FTC jurisdiction as well as nonprofits and telecommunications common carriers. Additional distinctions made within the Act apply to service providers, third parties, and third-party collecting entities, but all are still covered entities subject to the Act with specific heightened requirements or unique standards that apply to their individual business models.

The Act imposes additional requirements on large data holders, defined by meeting revenue or data processing thresholds. Large data holders are considered to have a third-party relationship with any entities within the same corporate structure. Finally, the Act exempts from certain requirements those small and medium-sized covered entities that for the prior three years did not derive more than half their revenue from transferring covered data while earning gross annual revenues and collecting or processing the covered data of individuals, other than for processing payments, below specified thresholds. These small businesses that are not third-party collecting entities are eligible to participate in FTC-approved compliance guidelines.

C. Beyond a Notice and Consent Framework

The Act takes a material step forward in privacy regulation in that it does not rely exclusively on the notice and consent regime generally employed by state privacy laws. Covered entities may not collect, process, or transfer covered data beyond what is reasonably necessary, proportionate, and limited to provide specifically requested products and services or communicate with individuals in a manner they reasonably anticipate. This duty applies irrespective of any consent from an individual. Moreover, covered data must be permanently disposed of or deleted once no longer necessary for the purpose for which it was collected, processed, or transferred. The Act further prohibits the violation of specific loyalty duties and the pay for privacy arrangements that can leave low-income families without access to privacy.

The legislation also includes broad anti-discrimination protections to protect consumers irrespective of consent. It also requires large data holders to submit annual algorithmic impact assessments to the FTC that describe steps the entity has taken or will take to mitigate potential harms from algorithms.

Covered entities must also care for and protect consumers' data by maintaining reasonable data security practices and procedures related to their size, complexity, and covered data activities. There are also requirements to assess vulnerabilities, take preventive and corrective action, evaluate systems, provide training to all employees with access to covered data, and designate an officer or employee to maintain and implement their data security practices. The FTC may promulgate rules to establish data security compliance processes.

D. Protection for Kids

Prior to and throughout engaging in any targeted advertising, covered entities must provide individuals with clear and conspicuous means to opt out of such targeting. Targeted advertising is flatly prohibited for any individual under 17 years of age.

The legislation also creates a new Youth Privacy and Marketing Division at the FTC that is responsible for addressing privacy and marketing concerns with respect to children and minors. The division must submit annual reports to Congress and hire staff that includes experts in youth development, data protection, digital advertising, and data analytics regarding children. Any information related to individuals under 17 is considered sensitive covered data under the Act and therefore subject to heightened restrictions. The risks to those under 17 must be factored into entities' privacy policies, practices, and procedures. Similarly, large data holders must also evaluate their algorithms' unique impacts on children in their algorithm impact assessments. Pre-dispute arbitration agreements and joint action waivers are unenforceable with respect to minors.

E. Individual Data Rights

Under the Act, individuals have the right to access, correct, delete, and export their covered data. Sensitive covered data may not be collected, processed, or transferred to a third party without the individual's express affirmative consent. This consent to transfer data may not be obtained through manipulative means, such as dark patterns. Individuals may opt out of the transfer of any covered data to a third party.

Separately, the FTC must establish an online, public, and searchable registry of registered third-party collecting entities, sometimes called data brokers. Individuals may elect to have all covered data about them held by such entities deleted within 30 days.

The bill also includes a unified opt-out that would be put into place if the FTC finds it feasible. This would allow individuals to exercise that opt-out, as well as the opt-out rights related to targeted advertising and transferring sensitive data to third parties, in a universal fashion that will apply across all covered entities instead of requiring individuals to make these selections with respect to each covered entity. The Act also makes general exceptions to use covered data for limited, specific purposes when the use is necessary, proportionate, and limited to the specific purpose.

F. Transparency and Corporate Obligations

Covered entities must provide privacy policies detailing their activities with respect to covered data in a readily available and understandable manner, including information on where and why covered data is sent, collected, processed, and retained. The policies must also be provided in each language a company operates in. Short-form notices of the covered entity's practices with respect to covered data are also required in some instances.

All covered entities must designate privacy and data security officers to implement privacy and data security programs and ensure ongoing compliance. Large data holders are subject to additional requirements, including annual certifications from their CEO, direct reporting to the CEO, and privacy impact assessments.

G. Enforcement and Relationship to Other Laws

The legislation provides three means of enforcement—the FTC, state attorneys general, and a private right of action. The FTC may obtain civil penalties for all violations of the Act. Any relief the FTC or the Department of Justice obtains enforcing the Act that cannot be provided directly to harmed individuals will be deposited in a Victims Relief Fund and be available to provide relief to individuals harmed by violations under the Act.

State attorneys general may bring cases pertaining to violations of the Act in federal court for injunctive relief; to obtain damages, penalties, restitution, or other compensation; and to obtain reasonable attorney's fees and other litigation costs. States retain all their existing investigatory and administrative powers under state law.

Starting four years after the Act takes effect, persons or classes of persons may bring a civil action in federal court seeking compensatory damages, injunctive relief, declaratory relief, and reasonable attorney's fees and litigation costs for most provisions of the Act. This right does not apply to data minimization, privacy by design, or data security requirements. Pre-dispute joint action waivers for arbitration or administrative proceedings are precluded in all cases.

To bring a private claim, the FTC and the attorney general where a person resides must be notified of the intent to sue and may take up the case if warranted as an intervenor. Improper demand letters seeking monetary payment that do not include a specified disclaimer will prevent suits from proceeding. For claims in which injunctive relief is sought against a covered entity, the Act provides the covered entity a right to cure the alleged violation.

The Act does not limit existing federal law, except where specified. Covered entities subject to and in compliance with the related requirements of specified federal laws shall be deemed in compliance with the related provisions of the Act only to the extent that covered data is subject to the requirements in the other laws. Insofar as covered entities are providers of [broadband internet access service, satellite carriers, or cable operators,][20] no privacy provisions enforced by the Federal Communications Commission shall apply.

State laws covered by the Act are preempted, other than specified state laws. Those laws include general consumer protection laws; civil rights laws; employee and student privacy protections; data breach notification laws; contract and tort law; certain criminal laws; laws on cyberstalking, cyberbullying, nonconsensual pornography, and sexual harassment; laws addressing certain public, financial, and tax records; facial recognition laws; certain surveillance laws; the Illinois Biometric and Genetic Information Privacy Acts;[21] laws addressing medical information; and the right of individuals to sue for data breaches under California law.[22]

H. FTC Structure and Resources

The Act establishes a new FTC privacy bureau to carry out the Act that is comparable to the current bureaus of consumer protection and competition. The new bureau must be fully operational within a year of enactment and include an office of business mentorship to assist

---

[20] This language is bracketed in the discussion draft of the Act.

[21] 740 ILCS 14 et seq.; 410 ILCS 513 et seq.

[22] Cal Civ. Code § 1798.150, as amended.

covered entities with compliance. The Act authorizes the FTC to be appropriated the sums necessary to carry out the Act.

III. Witnesses

The following witnesses have been invited to testify:

Caitriona Fitzgerald
Deputy Director
Electronic Privacy Information Center

David Brody
Managing Attorney, Digital Justice Initiative
Lawyers' Committee for Civil Rights Under Law

Bertram Lee
Senior Policy Counsel, Data Decision Making, and Artificial Intelligence
Future of Privacy Forum

Jolina Cuaresma
Senior Counsel, Privacy & Technology Policy
Common Sense Media

John Miller
Senior Vice President of Policy and General Counsel
Information Technology Industry Council

Graham Dufault
Senior Director for Public Policy
ACT | The App Association

Doug Kantor
General Counsel
National Association of Convenience Stores

Maureen K. Ohlhausen
Co-Chair
21st Century Privacy Coalition

Diversified Reporting Services, Inc.
RPTS GONZALEZ
HIF165170

Hearing on Protecting America's Consumers: Bipartisan Legislation to Strengthen, Data Privacy and Security, Tuesday, June 14, 2022, House of Representatives, Subcommittee on Consumer Protection and Commerce, Committee on Energy and Commerce, Washington, D.C.

The subcommittee met, pursuant to call, at 10:32 p.m., in Room 2123, Rayburn House Office Building, Hon. Jan Schakowsky, [chairwoman of the subcommittee], presiding.

Present: Representatives Schakowsky, Rush, Castor, Trahan, McNerney, Clarke, Cardenas, Dingell, Kelly, Soto, Rice, Craig, Fletcher, Pallone (ex officio); Bilirakis, Upton, Latta, Guthrie, Bucshon, Dunn, Pence, Lesko, Armstrong, and Rodgers (ex officio).

Also present: Eshoo, Rochester, Burgess, and Walberg.

Staff present: Katherine Durkin, Policy Coordinator; Lisa Goldman, Senior Counsel; Waverly Gordon, Deputy Staff Director and General Counsel; Jessica Grandberry, Staff Assistant; Tiffany Guarascio, Staff Director; Perry Hamilton, Clerk; Ed Kaczmarski, Policy Analyst; Zach Kahan, Deputy Director Outreach and Member Service; Mackenzie Kuhl, Digital Assistant; Jerry Leverich, Chief Counsel, Communications and Technology; David Miller, Counsel; Kaitlyn Peel, Digital Director; Caroline Rinker, Press Assistant; Chloe Rodriguez, Clerk; Andrew Souvall, Director of Communications, Outreach, and Member Services; Michele Viterise, Counsel; C.J. Young, Deputy Communications Director; Sarah Burke, Minority Deputy Staff Director; Michael Cameron, Minority Policy Analyst, CPC, Energy, Environment; Nate Hodson, Minority Staff Director; Emily King, Minority Member Services Director; Bijan Koohmaraie, Minority Chief Counsel, O&I Chief Counsel; Tim Kurth, Minority Chief Counsel, CPC; Brannon Rains, Minority Professional Staff Member, CPC; and Michael Taggart, Minority Policy Director.

*Ms. Schakowsky. The subcommittee on Consumer Protection and Commerce will now come to order. Today we will be holding a hearing entitled "Protecting American Consumers Bipartisan Legislation to Strengthen Data Privacy and Security."

Due to the COVID-19 public health emergency, we are still – members can participate both here in our room, and also remotely via online videoconferencing in accordance with the updated guidance from the attending physician. Members, staff, and members of the press can be present in this room without wearing a mask.

For members participating remotely, your microphones will be set on mute for the purpose of eliminating inadvertent background noise. Members participating remotely will need to unmute your microphone each time that you wish to speak. Please note that, once you do unmute yourself, anything that you will say on Webex will be able to be heard over the loudspeaker in the committee room and subject to be heard on Livestream and on CSPAN.

Since members are participating from different locations at today's hearing, we will recognize members such as for questioning, et cetera, by seniority within the subcommittee.

Documents for the record can be sent to Ed Kaczmarski at the email that has been provided through your staff, and all documents will be entered into the record at the conclusion of the hearing.

Before I begin with opening statements, and I will be first, I just want to ask for a moment of personal privilege.

*Voice. Absolutely.

*Ms. Schakowsky. Yeah. I just wanted to acknowledge that we all hold in our hearts our colleague and friend, Sean Casten, who is my colleague from Illinois who lost his 17-year-old daughter yesterday, and I want you to know that the family has asked for privacy.

Sean has not issued a statement yet, and the family has asked for privacy, but I want all of us to hold him and the family in our hearts and send really all of our prayers to the family. So thank you very much for that moment.

So let me begin with five minutes of opening statements.

So today is really a big significant day and a long-awaited day for our subcommittee, the Consumer Protection and Commerce Committee.

We will be considering the bipartisan draft of the American Data Protection and Privacy Act. This is a pitiful – not pitiful – but a pivotal, an important, moment in our journey to ensure that online privacy rights are there for all Americans, and we are definitely on our way.

There are so many people to thank for this. I want to thank the chairman of the full committee, Frank Pallone, for all of his support and leadership on this. I want to thank the ranking member, Congresswoman Rodgers, and we go back quite a long way even before you were the ranking on the full committee working on this and talking about this, and Gus Bilirakis, the ranking member on our subcommittee, for his tireless work.

I also just really want to thank the staff that has put in so much time and energy making this all happen, both the personal staff that we have and the committee staff, for all their great work and for members within the subcommittee outside in the Energy and Commerce Committee and throughout the Congress for input.

The road has been long and sometimes quite bumpy, and we had COVID in between, but here we are today, and we had a wonderful process. I wanted to mention the six roundtables that were put together bringing together all different stakeholders and experts from government, advocacy groups, industry, think tanks, technology experts, and more to meet in these roundtables face-to-face to begin to work out the process, and so this has been super important, and I thank all the participants.

Americans have been demanding that we act. They have often felt helpless online, but now, we are going to be able, I hope, to pass a bill that, on the very first day, we will be able to protect them from the take-it-or-leave-it kind of terms, so that they are able to get what they want, so that they can access all of their data, that they can correct, delete, and transfer their data, that we will provide certainty for the data for the business community, and that we will have space for innovation and protection for small businesses.

We will, hopefully, on day one, be able to increase protection for children, and I want to say a special shout out to Congresswoman Castor for the work that she has done on improving safety for children online, and especially one item anyway, raising the age of protection from 13 to 17.

We want to protect civil rights, and I want to thank Congresswoman Yvette Clarke for her work to help assure that – by making sure that we end discrimination by algorithms, and we are going to make sure that we have accountability for the bad actors. There will be enforcement.

I could go on, but I want to give the remainder of my time to Congresswoman Anna Eshoo.

[The prepared statement of Ms. Schakowsky follows:]

Committee on Energy and Commerce, Opening Statement as Prepared for Delivery of Subcommittee on Consumer Protection and Commerce Chair Janice D. Schakowsky, Hearing on "Protecting America's Consumers: Bipartisan Legislation to Strengthen Data Privacy and Security," June 14, 2022

Today we meet to consider groundbreaking comprehensive federal privacy legislation. With the bipartisan draft of the "American Data Privacy and Protection Act," we have reached a pivotal moment in our landmark effort to enshrine fundamental digital privacy rights for all Americans into federal law.

We live in an increasingly online world, and it is time to pass privacy reform that keeps pace with the speed of technological innovation. I'd like to acknowledge, with immense gratitude, the tireless work of Members on both sides of the aisle—within this Subcommittee and across Congress. This cohesive effort proves, once again, that privacy is *not* a partisan issue.

In particular, I would like to thank Chairman Pallone and Ranking Member McMorris Rodgers for their partnership and Ranking Member Bilirakis for his continued collaboration.

The road has been long—and our journey sometimes grueling—but our work has been fruitful because of our purposeful and inclusive process. Over the last year, we held six roundtables that brought in the expertise of stakeholders from every corner of government, civil society, and industry. The draft we discuss today reflects the ingenuity and wisdom of dedicated public servants, passionate advocates, and tech experts alike.

The "American Data Privacy and Protection Act" will provide relief for consumers who feel helpless online. No longer will consumers be forced to accept take-it-or-leave-it terms in exchange for their privacy. No longer will companies be able to collect endless amounts of data without consumers' consent. And this bill would hold bad actors accountable when they infringe upon consumers' rights.

It will provide regulatory certainty for the business community while taking care to promote innovation and protect small businesses. It will extend critical protections to teens under 17 and bans targeted advertising to this group. These are the kinds of ads that have contributed to the mental health crisis plaguing our young people.

Finally, it will protect Americans from discriminatory algorithms. There is much work before us, and the path forward is clear. I look forward to today's hearing to build on our momentum, years in the making, to pass transformational privacy protections for all Americans.

It's time to return control of their data back to the American people.

* * *

*Ms. Eshoo. Thank you, Madam Chairman.

In 2019, Congresswoman Lofgren and I introduced the Online Privacy Act that academicians have called the most comprehensive privacy bill in Congress. I have a commitment to ensuring that Congress passes strong and enforceable privacy legislation that secures user data, requires companies to minimize collection of personal data, and gives users access to and control of their data.

Federal privacy legislation cannot undermine California's groundbreaking privacy laws and should include protections for small businesses.

So I look forward to working with all of the members on both sides of aisle to produce the strongest privacy protections for the American people. They have waited a long time for it, and I hope that this is the moment where we produce, and I thank you for yielding to me.

*Ms. Schakowsky. So before I yield to my ranking member for his five minutes, let me again for the record, thank all our witnesses for coming today for participating in this hearing, for being here in person, and for us to be able to have time to ask you questions as we move forward.

I am looking forward to a rapid increase in our activity and to get something passed as soon as possible; and at this point, let me yield, now, five minutes for his opening statement to ranking member, Mr. Bilirakis.

*Mr. Bilirakis. Thank you, Madam Chair. Appreciate it. Good morning, everyone.

Thank you, Madam Chair, for holding this important legislative hearing and to our witnesses for your testimony today.

This is an exciting day for the subcommittee as it marks the first time a bicameral, bipartisan comprehensive privacy and data security deal is considered on the congressional docket. This topic has had its ups and downs to get to this point, but I am proud to be here with my colleagues on both sides of the aisle to discuss and improve the America Data Privacy and Protection Act.

I want to thank the chairman of the full committee, of course, the ranking member of the full committee, and of course, my colleague, the chairman of the subcommittee. Thank you very much for giving me the opportunity to have as much input as possible, and I know we are going to go forward.

As a reminder, what we have before us, of course, is a discussion draft which means we should spend our time today learning how we can make it better. And thank you to the witnesses because I know we can make it better. But to be clear, again, this is historic, and we need to keep moving together and build upon a constructive feedback while rejecting tactics that may seek to derail our bipartisan work.

This draft establishes a delicate balance for putting control data back into the hands of everyday Americans while providing businesses with fair rules of the road and preserving their ability to innovate.

I know from my vantage point in Florida, that the travel and tourism industry encounter countless transactions from their visitor interactions, but we know we must be sensitive to those small- and medium-size businesses since they are only using a fraction of data that Facebook or Google do who have legions of lawyers to manage compliance.

For years, I have heard the calls for Congress to urgently enact an national privacy law, so I have a level of skepticism now that, when I hear "Let's take a pause or do it next year," I won't buy that. This is the best committee by far on Capitol Hill in my opinion, and we are up to the challenge.

So hopefully, today's hearing helps shine a light on how this legislation is designed to operate and how we can continue moving the process forward with consensus from both sides of the aisle and both chambers.

We have a broad scope of witnesses for this hearing that can speak to different aspects of the bill, from small businesses and startup technologies to consumer advocates. I know we can bridge any devise we have, and I am thankful for you all being here today.

Today's discussion draft threads the needle, as I said, on many challenges that have acted as barriers to passing a comprehensive privacy and data security bill, including preemption, individual rights to courts, and the role of the FTC; however, just as importantly, this legislation also addresses meaningful policy issues that have been priorities for many members of the Congress on this committee.

Every member on this committee can point to small and mom-and-pop stores in their districts. They can enjoy visiting whether, of course, they can enjoy visiting whether it is a great restaurant with authentic cuisine or a local boutique shop selling homemade goods.

We recognize these businesses don't have infinite resources but still need to collect data in order to make it in today's economy which is very difficult which is why the draft agreement excludes small businesses from certain requirements to lessen the potential burdens they would face, and it provides additional resources for them to help with compliance. I know I don't have too much time here.

The legislation also takes a leap forward in protecting children from malicious online practices. Our draft would ban targeted advertising to children under the age of 17 and show large data holders like Big Tech regularly assess how their algorithms impact and harm children online and classify all data belonging to children under the age of 17 as sensitive covered data which is subject to heightened protections and requirements.

I am pleased to see the language in this draft as protecting children's privacy has long been – this is a priority of mine and other members of the committee, and I want to recognize Congressman Walberg, in particular. He has been working tirelessly on this, and I recognize his bipartisan efforts on this front; and because I don't have any more time, Madam Chair, I will yield back, and I look forward to hearing from the witnesses.

Take care. Thank you.

[The prepared statement of Mr. Bilirakis follows:]

Opening Statement of Republican Leader Gus Bilirakis, Subcommittee on Consumer Protection and Commerce, Legislative Hearing on "Protecting America's Consumers: Bipartisan Legislation to Strengthen Data Privacy and Security," June 14, 2022

Good morning, everyone. Thank you madam chair for holding this important legislative hearing and to our witnesses for your testimony.

This is an exciting day for this Subcommittee as it marks the first time a bicameral, bipartisan comprehensive privacy and data security deal is considered on the Congressional docket. This topic has had its ups and downs to get to this point, but I'm proud to be here with my colleagues on both sides of the aisle to discuss and improve the "American Data Privacy and Protection Act."

As a reminder, what we have before us is a discussion draft, which means we should spend our time today learning how we can make it better. But, to be clear, this is historic and we need to keep moving together and build upon the constructive feedback while rejecting tactics that may seek to derail our bipartisan work. This draft establishes a delicate balance for putting control of data back into the hands of everyday Americans, while providing businesses with fair rules of the road and preserving their ability to innovate. I know from my vantage point in

Florida that the travel and tourism industry encounter countless transactions from their visitor interactions, but we know we must be sensitive to these small and medium sized businesses since they are only using a fraction of data that Facebook or Google do, who have legions of lawyers to manage compliance.

For years I have heard the calls for Congress to "urgently" enact a national privacy law, so I have a level of skepticism now when I hear let's take a pause or do it next year. I won't buy that, this is best committee on Capitol Hill and we are up to this challenge.

So hopefully today's hearing helps shine a light on how this legislation is designed to operate and how we can continue moving the process forward with consensus from both sides of the aisle in both chambers. We have a broad scope of witnesses for this hearing that can speak to different aspects of the bill, from small businesses and startup technologies to consumer advocates. I know we can bridge any divides we have and I'm thankful for you all being here.

Today's discussion draft threads the needle on many challenges that have acted as barriers to passing a comprehensive privacy and data security bill including preemption, individuals' rights to courts, and the role of the Federal Trade Commission (FTC). However, just as importantly, this legislation also addresses meaningful policy issues that have been priorities for many members on this Committee.

Every member on this committee can point to small mom-and-pop stores in their districts that they enjoy visiting, whether it's a great restaurant with authentic cuisine or a local boutique shop selling homemade goods. We recognize these businesses don't have infinite resources but still need to collect data in order to make it in today's economy, which is why the draft agreement excludes small businesses from certain requirements to lessen the potential burdens they would face, and it provides additional resources for them to help with compliance.

The legislation also takes a leap forward in protecting children from malicious online practices. Our draft would ban targeted advertising to children under the age of 17, ensure large data holders like Big Tech regularly assess how their algorithms impact and harm children online, and classify all data belonging to children under the age of 17 as sensitive covered data, which is subject to heightened protections and requirements. I'm pleased to see this language in the draft, as protecting children's privacy has been a long-standing priority of mine that I know we all share, and I want to recognize Congressman Walberg in particular for his tireless bipartisan efforts on this front. This is certainly great progress and I look forward to continuing our work to protect kids' privacy and safety online.

Again, I'm thankful we can hold today's hearing to officially start the process on this bipartisan bicameral legislation, and I'm hopeful with Chairman Pallone's and Leader Rodger's leadership we can get this done. We have a great chance here, and I look forward to a constructive conversation. I yield back.

* * *

*Ms. Schakowsky. Thank you. The gentleman yields back, and now, I recognize the Chair of the full committee, Mr. Pallone, for his opening statement.

*The Chairman. Thank you, Chairwoman Schakowsky.

Today, this subcommittee is taking the significant step of putting consumers back in control of their data and protecting their privacy.

Over the years, the subcommittee, as the chairwoman mentioned, has discussed major breaches and scandals involving the misuse and unauthorized sharing of people's data. We have also talked about how emerging technologies can be used by companies in unintended and potentially harmful ways, including targeting our children.

Our privacy is something we must confront on a daily basis. Almost every company we interact with is conducting surveillance on us. When we visit a single website, many companies are tracking our actions on that site, and we all visit many sites every day.

And that is why there is [inaudible] universal agreement that a national data privacy and security law is urgently needed to protect consumers. More than half of all U.S. adults now say they have declined to try a product or service because they feared how their data might be used or abused if they did so.

And there is simply no real choice when consumers must trade their personal data to use essential services. People cannot navigate the modern world without their smartphone or email address, and with the minimal protections that apply today, most Americans have little reason to think that their data won't be used in unanticipated ways.

Comprehensive national privacy legislation is necessary to limit the excesses of Big Tech and ensure Americans can safely navigate the digital world. For far too many years, Congress has tried and failed to advance comprehensive federal privacy protections; but today, with the American Data Privacy and Protection Act, we have a real chance to begin doing what many in Washington have said was impossible.

So this proposal is the first serious bipartisan, bicameral comprehensive national privacy bill that directly confronts the sticking points which derailed earlier efforts.

The bill presents a fundamental shift in how data is collected, used, and transferred. It rejects the corrosive notice and consent system that has totally failed to protect Americans' data, privacy, and security; and at its core, the draft legislation requires relevant uses of personal data to be reasonably necessary, proportionate, and limited to the services that consumers are requesting.

The bill adds individual rights that allow people to control their data, opt out of targeted advertising, and stop the data from being sold without their permission. Our kids will be protected from abusive advertising and data transfers and businesses will be required to protect consumer data or face real consequences.

I also believe that data privacy rights are civil rights, and this draft legislation ensures that online discrimination is prohibited. It also requires the largest companies to conduct impact assessments on their algorithms, including whether they may harm protected classes.

So to ensure innovation continues, and Big Tech players are not cemented in place, this discussion draft imposes different obligations on different kinds of businesses to reflect their roles in the internet ecosystem. Steps are taken to limit the compliance burden on small- and mid-size businesses without sacrificing consumer protections.

Large data holders like Big Tech face additional requirements and obligations, and data brokers that profit from buying and selling your data are brought out of the shadows.

The bill also provides for robust enforcement by the FTC, state attorneys general, and individuals. It takes a balanced thoughtful approach to existing laws by setting up a strong national framework and preserving room for states to continue protecting their residents where the bill's protections stop.

While Congress is stalled on privacy, the rest of the world has not. The European Union and even China have passed comprehensive privacy laws. American companies have continued to innovate while the federal government has struggled to keep pace, and this bill would immediately reset the global landscape.

So I want to thank Ranking Member Rodgers, Senator Wicker, the Subcommittee Chair Schakowsky, and Ranking Member Bilirakis for their relentless commitment, and it has been relentless to coming to a bipartisan consensus on this discussion draft. I also thank many members of the subcommittee for their tireless efforts as this legislation includes so many proposals from our members over the years.

So today's hearing comes after many hearings and focusing on protecting our privacy online. The draft legislation is the culmination of all that work. I look forward to continuing that process today and keeping the momentum going to finally pass this critical privacy legislation; and with that, Madam Chair, I yield back.

[The prepared statement of The Chairman follows:]

Committee on Energy and Commerce, Opening Statement as Prepared for Delivery of Chairman Frank Pallone, Jr., Hearing on "Protecting America's Consumers: Bipartisan Legislation to Strengthen Data Privacy and Security," June 14, 2022

Today, the Subcommittee is taking a significant step of putting consumers back in control of their data and protecting their privacy.

Over the years, this Subcommittee has discussed major breaches and scandals involving the misuse and unauthorized sharing of people's data. We've also talked about how emerging technologies can be used by companies in unintended and potentially harmful ways, including targeting our children.

Our privacy is something we each confront on a daily basis. Almost every company we interact with is conducting surveillance on us. When we visit a single website, many companies are tracking our actions on that site, and we all visit many sites every day.

That's why there is near universal agreement that a national data privacy and security law is urgently needed to protect consumers. More than half of all U.S. adults now say they have declined to try a product or service because they feared how their data might be used–or abused– if they did so.

There is simply no real "choice" when consumers must trade their personal data to use essential services. People cannot navigate the modern world without their smartphone or email address. And with the minimal protections that apply today, most Americans have little reason to think their data won't be used in unanticipated ways.

Comprehensive, national privacy legislation is necessary to limit the excesses of Big Tech and ensure Americans can safely navigate the digital world.

For far too many years, Congress has tried and failed to advance comprehensive federal privacy protections, but today, with the American Data Privacy and Protection Act, we have a real chance to begin doing what many in Washington have said was impossible.

This proposal is the first serious, bipartisan, bicameral, comprehensive national privacy bill that directly confronts the sticking points which derailed earlier efforts.

This legislation represents a fundamental shift in how data is collected, used, and transferred. It rejects the coercive "notice and consent" system that has totally failed to protect Americans' data privacy and security.

At its core, the draft legislation requires relevant uses of personal data to be reasonably necessary, proportionate, and limited to the services consumers are requesting. The bill adds individual rights that allow people to control their data, opt-out of targeted advertising, and stop their data from being sold without their permission. Our kids will be protected from abusive advertising and data transfers. And businesses will be required to protect consumer data or face real consequences.

I also believe data privacy rights are civil rights, and this draft legislation ensures that online discrimination is prohibited. It also requires the largest companies to conduct impact assessments on their algorithms, including whether they may harm protected classes.

To ensure innovation continues and Big Tech players are not cemented in place, this discussion draft imposes different obligations on different kinds of businesses to reflect their roles in the internet ecosystem. Steps are taken to limit the compliance burden on small and midsize businesses without sacrificing consumer protections.

Large data holders, like Big Tech, face additional requirements and obligations and data brokers that profit from buying and selling your data are brought out of the shadows.

The bill also provides for robust enforcement by the Federal Trade Commission, state attorneys general, and individuals. It takes a balanced, thoughtful approach to existing laws by setting up a strong national framework and preserving room for states to continue protecting their residents where the bill's protections stop.

While Congress has stalled on privacy, the rest of the world has not. The European Union and even China have passed comprehensive privacy laws. American companies have continued to innovate while their federal government has struggled to keep pace. This bill would immediately reset the global landscape.

I want to thank Ranking Member Rodgers, Senator Wicker, and Subcommittee Chair Schakowsky and Ranking Member Bilirakis for their relentless commitment to coming to a bipartisan consensus on this discussion draft. I also thank many members of this Subcommittee for their tireless efforts as this legislation includes so many proposals from our members over the years.

Today's hearing comes after many hearings and roundtables focusing on protecting our privacy online. This draft legislation is the culmination of all that work. I look forward to continuing that process today and keeping the momentum going to finally pass this critical privacy legislation.

* * *

*Ms. Schakowsky. The gentleman yields back.

And now, I recognize for five minutes, Mrs. Rodgers, the ranking member of the full committee.

*Mrs. Rodgers. Thank you, Madam Chair.

One of my top priorities, when I served as the Republican leader of this subcommittee, was enacting a federal privacy standard. This bipartisan, bicameral draft bill, the American Data Privacy and Protection Act, includes policies that have been in the public and received comment over several years.

This is about protecting people from Big Tech, especially our kids, and strengthening America's position in setting global standards. Not China or Europe. It's about promoting American innovation and next generation technologies like AI and AVs.

We must remain focused on creating the best possible standard to protect people's privacy and promote American leadership. This is closest we have come to establishing a national standard, a standard that many said for a long time, is urgently needed. It's the product of years of discussions, negotiations, drafting, stakeholder feedback, and now, committee process, and our work will continue.

Here is a brief overview of the extensive process that has led us to today:

In early 2019, I released my four principles for privacy legislation. Later, Energy and Commerce released a bipartisan staff draft. I was pleased to do that at the time when I was serving with the, now Chairwoman, Jan Schakowsky, and began extensive staff-led conversations to receive feedback.

We've engaged stakeholders through bipartisan discussions and through Republican and Democratic draft bills. That's not to mention the Senate's work and the draft proposals from industry and advocacy groups or the work of the last 20 years. Our draft is the culmination of all this.

I want to join in thanking the chairman, Chairman Pallone, Senator Wicker, Consumer Protection and Commerce leaders, Chairwoman Jan Schakowsky, and our Ranking Member, Gus Bilirakis, for the hard work everyone has done to make it possible. A bicameral, bipartisan draft is finally here, and the door remains open for constructive feedback.

As I said in my 2019 principles to protect privacy and promote innovation, there needs to be one national standard first and foremost. This draft stops an unworkable patchwork of state laws, ensures protections don't change across state lines, and provide certainty to Americans and businesses.

We also need to target data practices from bad actors that cause people harm, for example, because people should know how their data is being collected and shared, this draft requires companies to specify when they are transferring or storing people's data in countries like China, Russia, Iran.

Why are we making sure to target bad actors and practices? Because companies sitting on massive troves of American's data become vulnerable to breaches, hacks, and exploitation.

Instead, we must allow for safe data practices and new innovations that people like. That includes innovations that improve people's lives by saving money and time like real-time updates to avoid traffic and better customer service products.

This principle to prevent real harms from bad actors is especially important for protecting our children and minors no matter where they live. If Big Tech can't target our kids, they can't exploit our kids. Our bill addresses this with heightened requirements for how data of our children is handled, shared, and used.

Additionally, we need to foster stronger and improved data security practices. The American Data Privacy and Protection Act focuses on requiring companies to only keep information they need while encouraging them to take steps to better secure data that is retained.

Finally, a national standard must be workable for small businesses and startups. As we have learned by Big Tech, gaining market share in Europe, large companies can navigate a complicated privacy standard like GDPR or a patchwork of state laws. But smaller businesses cannot afford high-compliance costs and more ineffective regulations, especially with all the challenges they have been facing from the pandemic and inflation.

We're leading the way in this draft bill to unleash the power of small businesses and entrepreneurs, the engines of America's economy. As Chairman Pallone, Senator Wicker, and I said when we released this draft, this is a critical milestone that was years in the making. This is the best opportunity we have had to pass a federal data privacy law in decades.

I look forward to all our continued work together. Let's keep building on these principles and make progress on this draft, so people can trust how their data is being collected and used, and so America wins the future in technological innovations that raise our standard of living and improve people's lives all across the globe.

Thank you. I yield back.

[The prepared statement of Mrs. Rodgers follows:]

Opening Statement of Republican Leader Cathy McMorris Rodgers, Subcommittee on Consumer Protection and Commerce, Legislative Hearing on "Protecting America's Consumers: Bipartisan Legislation to Strengthen Data Privacy and Security," June 14, 2022 as Prepared for Delivery

Thank you, Madam Chair. One of my top priorities when I served as the Republican Leader of this subcommittee was enacting a federal privacy standard. This bipartisan, bicameral draft bill, the American Data Privacy and Protection Act, includes policies that have been public and received comment over several years.

This is about protecting people from Big Tech, especially our kids and strengthening America's position in setting global standards—not China or Europe. It's about promoting American innovation in next-generation technologies like AI and AVs.

We must remain focused on creating the best standard possible to protect people's privacy and promote American leadership. This is the closest we've come to establishing a national standard—a standard that many have said for a long time is urgently needed.

It's the product of years of discussions, negotiations, drafting, stakeholder feedback, and now Committee process. And our work will continue.

Here's a brief overview of the extensive process that has led us to today:

- In early 2019 I released my four principles for privacy legislation;
- Later E&C released a bipartisan staff draft and began extensive staff- led conversations to receive feedback;
- We've engaged stakeholders through bipartisan discussions;
- And through GOP and Democratic draft bills.

That's not to mention the Senate's work, and the draft proposals from industry and advocacy groups or the work from the last twenty years. Our draft is the culmination of all this.

I want to thank Chairman Pallone, Senator Wicker, and our Consumer Protection and Commerce Leaders Jan Schakowsky and Gus Bilirakis for their hard work to make it possible. A bicameral, bipartisan draft is finally here and the door remains open for constructive feedback.

As I said in my 2019 principles to protect privacy and promote innovation, there needs to be one national standard, first and foremost. This draft stops an unworkable patchwork of state laws, ensures protections don't change across state lines, and provides certainty to Americans and businesses.

We also need to target data practices from bad actors that cause people harm. For example, because people should know how their data is collected and shared, this draft requires companies to specify when they are transferring and storing people's data in countries like China, Russia, and Iran. Why are we making sure we target bad actors and practices?

Because companies sitting on massive troves of Americans' data becomes vulnerable to breaches, hacks, and exploitation. Instead, we must allow for safe data practices and new innovations that people like.

This includes innovations that improve people's lives by saving them money and time—like real-time updates to avoid traffic and better customer service products. This principle to prevent real harms from bad actors is especially important for protecting our children and minors, no matter where they live. If Big Tech can't target our kids, they can't exploit our kids.

Our bill addresses this with heightened requirements for how data of our children is handled, shared, and used. Additionally, we need to foster stronger and improved data security practices.

The American Data Privacy and Protection Act focuses on requiring companies to only keep information they need while encouraging them to take steps to better secure data that is retained.

Finally, a national standard must be workable for small businesses and startups. As we've learned by Big Tech gaining market share in Europe, large companies can navigate a complicated privacy standard like the GDPR or a patchwork of state laws. But smaller businesses cannot afford high compliance costs and more ineffective regulations, especially with all the challenges they're facing from the pandemic and inflation. We're leading the way in this draft bill to unleash the power of small businesses and entrepreneurs, the engines of America's economy.

As Chairman Pallone, Senator Wicker and I said when we released this draft, this is a critical milestone that was years in the making. This is the best opportunity we've had to pass a federal data privacy law in decades. I look forward to all our continued work together.

Let's keep building on these principles and make progress on this draft so people can trust how their data is collected and used, and so America wins the future in technological innovations that raise our standard of living and improve people's lives all across the globe.

Thank you, I yield back.

* * *

*Ms. Schakowsky. Thank you. The gentlelady [audio malfunction] – perfect. The gentlelady yields back.

And now, the Chair would like to remind members that, pursuant to committee rules, all members' written opening statements shall be made part of the record.

And now, I would like to introduce our witnesses for today's hearing. We have Bertram Lee, who is the senior policy counsel data decider – is that right? – data decider. Let's see. There it is – data decision maker. That's good. And oh, boy. I have reading issue here. What is this?

*Voice. Artificial intelligence.

*Ms. Schakowsky. I'm sorry.

*Voice. It's artificial intelligence.

*Ms. Schakowsky. Okay. Artificial Intelligence and Future Privacy Forum. Did I get it? Thank you.

Okay. John Miller, who is the senior vice president of policy and general counsel at Information Technology Industry. We have Caitriona Fitzgerald, the deputy director at the – what is it?

*Voice. Electronic [inaudible].

*Ms. Schakowsky. Oh, Electronic Privacy Information Center, EPIC.

We have Douglas Kantor who is the general counsel at the National Association of Convenience Stores. We have Jolina Cuaresma who is the senior counsel, privacy and technology policy at Common Sense Media.

We have the Honorable Maureen Ohlhausen – I get that – Ohlhausen – who is the co-chair of 21st Century Privacy Coalition; Graham Dufault – no – yes, Dufault – sorry – who is the senior director for public policy at ACT The App Association; and we have David Brody, who is the managing attorney, digital justice initiative at the Lawyers' Committee for Civil Rights Under the Law.

So at this time, the chair will recognize each of the members for five minutes, but before we begin, I want to make sure some of you are experienced in testifying here, and I just want to explain the clock system for our witnesses.

There is a timer on your – well not on your screen – but right in front of you. There is a – so as the time winds down to one minute, you will see a yellow mark, and I hope that you will begin to conclude your remarks.

So first, Mr. Lee, you are recognized for five minutes.

Statement of Bertram Lee, Jr., Senior Policy Counsel, Data Decision Making, and Artificial Intelligence Future of Privacy Forum

*Mr. Bertram. Chairwoman Schakowsky, Ranking Member Bilirakis, Chairman Pallone, and Ranking Member McMorris Rodgers, thank you for inviting me today to testify.

My name is Bertram Lee, and I senior policy counsel for Data Decision Making and Artificial Intelligence representing the Future of Privacy Forum.

We commend the committee for holding this hearing and for introducing bipartisan, bicameral privacy legislation. I would like to make four key points:

One, federal privacy legislation is urgently needed.

Two, the American Data Privacy and Protection Act, or ADPPA, is more comprehensive in scope compared to the recently enacted privacy laws in five states; and for your consideration, we have included a chart comparing these state laws to the ADPPA and our written testimony for you today.

Three, the ADPPA compares favorably to global frameworks, including Europe's General Data Protection Regulation, GDPR. And fourth, work remains to be done on specific provisions to ensure that individuals are protected, the bill is workable for business, not for profits and researchers, and that it is harmonized with federal laws.

We are delighted that this committee has produced bipartisan, bicameral federal privacy legislation. We urge Congress to move quickly and thoughtfully as five states have already passed comprehensive federal privacy legislation with likely more to come.

Although state regimes differ, they share several similarities that are important to Congress in pursuit of federal privacy legislation. There is a clear trend. States are making privacy rules whether Congress moves forward or not.

Additionally, key dates are on the horizon for several state laws with both California and Colorado looking to implement rulemaking by July 1, 2023.

Our analysis shows, however, that the ADPPA is more comprehensive in scope than recent state proposals. The ADPPA, compared to its state counterparts, expands civil rights protections against algorithmic discrimination, includes corporate accountability mechanisms not found in state laws, such as the requirement of designating privacy and data security officers as well as executive certifications of compliance, mandates that large data holders provide shortform privacy notices to better inform individuals of how their data will be used, provides pathways for individual redress of privacy violations, creates new data protections for young people 17 and under, as well as broader prohibitions against harmful uses of data, and requires that businesses incorporate privacy-by-design principles in the development of their data processing activities.

The ADPPA also compares favorably to Europe's GDPR in five ways: One, comprehensiveness in terms of data covered, the types of processing covered, and cross-sectoral applicability. Two, individual rights including access, correction, deletion, and portability, as well as a limited right to object. Three, the recognition of special categories of data that merit enhanced safeguards due to their sensitive nature. Four, data minimization for all processing of covered data, including collection and transfers. And five, the ADPPA contains identical standard to the GDPR for what is considered valid consent.

While the ADPPA would be a monumental step forward in ensuring privacy regulations for all Americans, there is still work to be done. We suggest Congress look to add: one, additional funding for the FTC, so that it can fulfill the full mandate of this bill. Two, add more space for iterative processes within the ADPPA, so that it can keep pace with evolving technologies. And three, take a closer look at the intersection of the ADPPA with other federal laws. And four, add more definitional clarity to certain terms in the text.

Again, thank you for this opportunity to testify, and I look forward to your questions.

[The prepared statement of Mr. Lee follows:]

Testimony and Statement for the Record of Bertram Lee Jr., Senior Policy Counsel for Data, Decision Making, and Artificial Intelligence, Future of Privacy Forum, Hearing on "Protecting America's Consumers: Bipartisan Legislation to Strengthen Data Privacy and Security," before the House Committee on Energy and Commerce, Subcommittee on Consumer Protection and Commerce, June 13, 2022

Chairwoman Schakowsky, Ranking Member Bilirakis, Chairman Pallone, and Ranking Member McMorris Rodgers, on behalf of the Future of Privacy Forum, thank you for inviting me to testify today in front of the House Energy and Commerce Subcommittee on Consumer Protection and Commerce. My name is Bertram Lee, and I am Senior Policy Counsel for Data, Decision Making, and Artificial Intelligence at the Future of Privacy Forum (FPF). FPF commends the House Energy and Commerce Subcommittee on Consumer Protection and Commerce for holding this hearing and introducing bipartisan and bicameral privacy legislation.

FPF is a non-profit organization that serves as a catalyst for privacy leadership and scholarship and advancing principled data practices in support of emerging technologies. We are supported by leading foundations, as well as by more than 200 companies and law firms, with an advisory board representing academics, industry, and civil society.[23] We bring together privacy officers, academics, consumer advocates, and other thought leaders to explore the challenges posed by technological innovation and develop privacy protections, ethical norms, and workable business practices.

The four main points we would like to leave you with this hearing are:

1. now is the time for Congress to pass comprehensive privacy legislation;
2. compared to each of the five states that have passed privacy laws since 2018, the American Data Privacy and Protection Act (ADPPA) is more comprehensive in scope, more inclusive of civil rights protections, and provides individuals with more varied enforcement mechanisms;
3. ADPPA compares favorably to global frameworks, including Europe's General Data Protection Regulation (GDPR); and
4. work remains to be done on specific provisions to ensure individuals are protected, the bill is workable for business, not for profits and researchers, and there are not unexpected or undesired consequences. We urge that work to move forward thoughtfully and expeditiously.

FPF applauds Congress for advancing comprehensive privacy legislation. FPF has long recognized the need to enact a baseline, comprehensive federal privacy law that gives individuals meaningful privacy rights and places clear, workable obligations on businesses and other organizations that collect, use, and share personal data. A comprehensive federal law could address the gaps in the current U.S. sectoral approach to consumer privacy, which has resulted in incomplete legal protections. Personal information collected within specific sectors, such as credit reporting, finance, and healthcare, is subject to longstanding federal safeguards. In contrast, commercial data outside of these sectors remains largely unregulated even when the data may be equally sensitive or high-risk.

The ADPPA would achieve this. The legislation would require entities that handle personal data to adopt baseline privacy and security safeguards - including individual rights to access, delete, port, and correct personal data, as well as rights to opt out of targeted advertising and data transfers. The bill would apply to most organizations that handle personal data - commercial entities, common carriers, and non-profits. The ADPPA also includes additional requirements intended to address the unique challenges algorithmic technologies pose to civil rights while promoting the use of technology to identify and mitigate discrimination in appropriate circumstances.

Contemporary data protection is complicated. Any attempt to regulate privacy across diverse sectors of the economy must be approached with care. Bipartisan legislation is an

[23] The views herein do not necessarily reflect those of our supporters or our Advisory Board. See Future of Privacy Forum, Advisory Board, https://fpf.org/about/advisory-board/; Supporters, https://fpf.org/about/supporters/.

excellent opportunity to capture the sense of urgency felt by Congress, individuals, companies, and data protection experts to establish a practical, protective, comprehensive federal privacy regime in the United States. We urge you to move forward quickly and thoughtfully to address stakeholder concerns, reduce the likelihood that legislation impacts individuals and organizations in unexpected and unintended ways, and provide mechanisms to address those unexpected outcomes should they occur. Many of the contentious issues regarding data protection legislation can be addressed through careful drafting and consideration of the available legal, technical, and policy tools. Congress has an opportunity to meet the challenges posed by contemporary information-driven business practices with legislation that protects consumers and provides much-needed clarity to businesses about their obligations.

I. Now Is the Time for Congress to Pass Federal Privacy Legislation

Congress should advance a baseline, comprehensive federal privacy law. This was true when Future of Privacy Forum CEO Jules Polonetsky testified to it in the Senate in 2019, and it is even more true today. As he indicated, the impact of data-intensive technologies on individuals, and marginalized communities in particular, is increasing every day as the pace of innovation accelerates. Each day's news brings reports of a new intrusion, new risk, further harm, or another boundary crossed. Sometimes it's a company doing something that consumers or critics regard as "creepy;" sometimes, it is a practice that raises serious risks to our human rights, civil liberties, or our sense of autonomy. There is a growing public awareness of how data-driven systems can reflect or reinforce discrimination and bias, even inadvertently.

For many people, personal privacy is a deeply emotional issue, and a real or perceived absence of privacy may leave them feeling vulnerable, exposed, or powerless. For others, concrete financial or other harm may occur; a loss of autonomy, a stifling of creativity due to feeling surveilled, or the public disclosure of highly sensitive information like individuals' financial data or disability status are just some potential consequences of technology misuse, poor data security policies, or insufficient privacy controls.

Now more than ever before, Congress has the opportunity to pass a law that will shape these developments to mitigate the risks of data for society. Delaying Congressional action means that businesses will inevitably continue to develop new models, build infrastructure, and deploy technologies without the guidance and clear limits that only Congress can set forth. This creates real economic costs that will only increase the longer we go without a statutory standard.

Current business practices and new technologies are being shaped by laws worldwide, while the U.S. approach to data protection remains outdated and insufficient. The continuation of cross-border data flows, which are crucial to the United States' leadership role in the global digital economy, is under stress. This may put U.S. companies, from financial institutions to cloud providers, at a disadvantage. Congress must ensure that the U.S. is not left behind as the rest of the world establishes trade and privacy frameworks that will de facto define the terms of international information and technology transfers for decades to come.

The United States currently does not have a baseline set of legal protections that apply to all commercial data about individuals regardless of the particular industry, technology, or user base. For the past decades, we have taken a sectoral approach to privacy that has led to the creation of federal laws that provide strong protections only in certain sectors such as surveillance, healthcare, video rentals, education records, and children's privacy. As a result,

U.S. federal laws currently provide strong privacy and security protection for information that is often particularly sensitive about individuals but it leaves other – sometimes similar – data largely unregulated aside from the Federal Trade Commission's (FTC) Section 5 authority to enforce against deceptive or unfair business practices.

The U.S. has not always lagged behind its major trade partners in privacy and data protection policymaking. In fact, the central universal tenets of data protection have U.S. roots. In 1972, the Department of Health, Education, and Welfare formed an Advisory Committee on Automated Data Systems, which released a report setting forth a code of Fair Information Practices.[24] These principles, widely known as the Fair Information Practice Principles (FIPPs), are the foundation of not only existing U.S. laws but also many international frameworks and laws, including GDPR.[25] And while GDPR is the most recent influential international data privacy and protection framework, the U.S. should look for interoperability with and insights from the OECD Privacy Guidelines[26] and the Asia-Pacific Economic Cooperation (APEC) framework and Cross-Border Privacy Rules (CBPRs).[27]

The U.S. has a shrinking window of opportunity to regain momentum at both the national and international levels. If we wait too long, more countries and states will act, which will have an immediate impact on new technologies and business initiatives and ultimately reduce the impactof any federal law.

II. Compared to Recent StatePrivacy Laws, ADPPA Is More Comprehensive

Five states recently established comprehensive privacy laws. Some are fairly similar, although with key distinctions. Others have striking differences - for example, California's approach is significantly different from the other four states in both form and structure.

Although these state regimes differ, they share several similarities that are important to Congress' pursuit of federal privacy legislation:

---

[24] Records, Computer, and the Rights of Citizens: Report of the Secretary's Advisory Committee on Automated Personal Data Systems, U.S. Dept. of Health & Human Services (1973), https://aspe.hhs.gov/report/records-computers-and- rights-citizens.

[25] Regulation (EU) 2016/679 of the European Parliament and of the Council of 27 April 2016 on the protection of natural persons with regard to the processing of personal data and on the free movement of such data, and repealing Directive 95/46/EC (General Data Protection Regulation), https://eur-lex.europa.eu/eli/reg/2016/679/oj.

[26] Organization for Economic Co-operation and Development, Privacy Guidelines, https://www.oecd.org/internet/ieconomy/privacy-guidelines.htm.

[27] APEC has 21 members comprising nearly all of the Asian-Pacific economies, including the United States. The CBPR system—endorsed by APEC member economies in 2011 and updated in 2015 attempts to create a regional solution across 21 member economies, whose governments are at different stages of compliance with the APEC Privacy Framework. In the United States, the Federal Trade Commission has agreed to enforce the CBPRs. Eight APEC countries have formally joined the CBPR system—United States, Canada, Mexico, Japan, Singapore, Taiwan, Australia and the Republic of Korea. In the recent United States-Mexico-Canada Agreement (USMCA), which Congress is reviewing as it considers ratification, the three countries promote cross-border data flows by recognizing the CBPR system as a valid data privacy compliance mechanism for data-transfers between the countries. See Cross-Border Privacy Rules System, http://cbprs.org/. Also relevant for the Committee's reference is Convention 108 of the Council of Europe, an international data protection treaty that has been signed by 54 countries to date, not including the United States.

1. First, these laws have been enacted since 2018, and the most recent state legislative sessions across the U.S. - whether they resulted in bill passage or not - included more activity on data protection bills than any in recent memory. There is a clear trend - states are making privacy rules whether Congress moves forward or not.
2. Second, key dates are on the horizon for several of the state laws. The California Privacy Protection Agency (CPPA) is in the midst of an important rulemaking to clarify rights and obligations under the CPRA, with additional regulatory and enforcement activity expected over the next twelve months. The Colorado Attorney General is crafting rules to implement the Colorado Privacy Act, with a regulations deadline of July 1, 2023.
3. Third, individuals and businesses are acting now in response to the states' laws. Individuals in California are clicking CPRA-required "do not sell" links on websites and filing "data subject access requests," which the CPRA requires companies to honor in many cases. The California Attorney General has initiated enforcement actions against entities the AG alleges do not comply with the law and the Virginia Attorney General is poised to do the same under Virginia's privacy law in six months.[28] And companies are dedicating substantial resources to build compliance programs in light of these new regimes.
4. Fourth, state bills are not coalescing around a single de facto national standard. The first-enacted law - California - did not result in a string of states adopting identical or nearly identical laws. While there are real similarities between, e.g., the Virginia and Colorado laws, there are also important differences between the Virginia, Colorado, Utah, and Connecticut regimes. And many pending state bills are different still. The lack of state-to-state uniformity is resulting in different rights for individuals and different obligations for businesses.

Taken together, these four factors should encourage Congress to move quickly toward a common, workable national standard. By analyzing the approaches taken by state lawmakers, including what protections they provide, how they are structured, and where compromises were achieved, many lessons can be learned to inform Congress' work on a comprehensive federal bill.

In the addendum to our testimony, we offer a comparison of key ADPPA provisions to different state laws. Our analysis demonstrates that the ADPPA is more comprehensive in scope, more inclusive of civil rights protections, and provides individuals with more varied enforcement mechanisms than recent state laws:

1. ADPPA expands civil rights protections against algorithmic discrimination, whereas state laws have sought to codify existing civil rights protections.
2. ADPPA includes corporate accountability mechanisms not found in the state laws, such as the requirement of designating privacy and data security officers and executive certifications of compliance.
3. In addition to requiring traditional privacy policies, ADPPA requires certain large data holders to provide 'short form' privacy notices to better inform individuals of how their data will be used and their rights, a provision not found in any state law.

---

[28] https://oag.ca.gov/privacy/ccpa/enforcement.

4. ADPPA provides pathways for individual redress of privacy violations in some circumstances, whereas state laws have left enforcement almost exclusively to government agencies.
5. ADPPA creates new protections for youth data, including a prohibition on targeted advertising to minors under the age of 17, as well as including broader prohibitions against harmful uses of data.
6. ADPPA requires that businesses incorporate privacy-by-design principles in the development of their data processing activities to an extent not found in existing state laws.

1. Civil Rights Protections and Algorithmic Discrimination

ADPPA, unlike any state privacy law, extends longstanding civil rights protections that prohibit discrimination in the enjoyment of public accommodations by protected class (race, gender, sexual orientation, etc.) to the provision of online products and services. This includes, for example, protections against price discrimination in digital marketplaces and content monetization based on an individual's race, gender, or similar trait. The ADPPA would prohibit both direct, intentional discrimination and disparate impact (neutral practices that have a disparate discriminatory impact on a protected class).

ADPPA would also require large data holders who collect, process, or transfer covered data to conduct yearly algorithmic impact assessments. Additionally, a covered entity, as defined by the bill, must conduct an algorithm design evaluation, including any training data used to develop an algorithm, if it uses an algorithm in whole or in part to collect, process, or transfer covered data.

2. Corporate Accountability Requirements

The ADPPA requirement for privacy and data security officers at companies is a major step toward formalizing data protection accountability mechanisms in the U.S. Leading organizations have appointed compliance experts to these roles and dedicate substantial resources to building effective privacy programs. Global privacy regimes encourage or require this sort of institutional commitment to data protection. But these roles and programs are not universal, and recent state privacy laws do not incentivize or require organizations to appoint privacy and data security officers to the extent of ADPPA. The ADPPA requirements are consistent with emerging trends in FTC enforcement actions and settlement agreements, which routinely require companies to adopt "comprehensive privacy and/or security programs."

For years, many have asked that privacy and data security be a part of the corporate governance structure for companies.[29] By mandating that corporate governance structures take into account privacy and data security concerns, privacy, and data security professionals are better able to help ensure not only compliance with ADPPA but also build public trust.[30] We have already seen great strides in privacy and data security becoming an integral part of the

---

[29] https://www.ftc.gov/business-guidance/blog/2021/04/corporate-boards-dont-underestimate-your-role-data-security-oversight; https://hbr.org/2000/11/chief-privacy-officer; https://www.avertium.com/blog/chief-privacy-officer-enterprises-c-level-leadership-personal-data-privacy.

[30] https://www.forbes.com/sites/blakemorgan/2020/06/22/50-stats-showing-why-companies-need-to-prioritize-consumer-privacy/?sh=46c2bd037f61.

corporate governance infrastructure. However, placing legal obligations on companies to do so ensures better privacy and data security practices globally.

3. Short Form Privacy Notices

Large entities' provision of simple, understandable short-form privacy notices in addition to full privacy policies is a major help to consumers. Experts have long understood that consumers are unable to meaningfully review and understand all the privacy policies governing personal data on all the digital services they use.[31] And the terms of most policies likely create additional challenges. In many cases, even privacy professionals struggle to understand the jargon and legalese associated with current privacy policies. Short form privacy notices put consumers in a better position to understand how their data is being used, where it goes, and what policies companies have in place in order to better protect their data.

Addressing the widespread problems of targeted advertising is also critically important. Digital ads can play a key role in supporting media and services, but from publishers to advertisers to consumers, everyone agrees the current ecosystem is unsustainable. A path that ensures competition, prevents discrimination, and supports individual rights without requiring complicated choices by consumers is needed.

4. Individual Redress and Expanded Consumer Rights

ADPPA's inclusion of individual redress mechanisms, on top of regulatory enforcement, goes beyond what existing state privacy laws provide, and thus provides greater protections for consumers. The history of civil rights enforcement shows that individual redress can ensure accountability, particularly for individuals from traditionally marginalized communities. At the same time, ADPPA seeks to prevent bad faith litigation and provide small businesses the right to cure.

Similar to most U.S. laws and proposals (including the CCPA), ADPPA would prohibit retaliation against individuals who exercise their privacy rights, meaning a covered entity could not deny service to individuals who choose to opt out of certain data sharing or decline to waive their privacy rights, while preserving loyalty programs that provide free or discounted products and services in exchange for an individual's continued business.

5. Data Protection for Children and Restrictions against Harmful Data Uses

The ADPPA would create additional federal data protections for minors, prohibiting collection of personal information from those under age 17 without affirmative express consent, barring targeted advertising to individuals under 17, and conditioning data transfers regarding individuals between 13 and 17 years old on express consent. ADPPA would also create a new Youth and Privacy Marketing Division at the FTC that would be responsible for enforcement.

The bill takes an approach to child privacy that FPF has long recommended - it grants important protections to young people aged 13-17 while declining to extend parental access provisions to teens. These protections are increasingly important as more teens use digital services, but the parental access provisions COPPA provides to children can raise privacy and safety issues when applied to teenagers.

---

[31] In 2012, Prof. Lorrie Faith Cranor and Aleecia McDonald, privacy experts and researchers at Carnegie Mellon, estimated that reading every privacy policy that the average American encounters in a year would take 76 work days. Given the increased integration of technology into everyday life, it is likely that number has increased greatly in the decade since the study. https://www.theatlantic.com/technology/archive/2012/03/reading-the-privacy-policies-you-encounter-in-a-year-would-take-76-work-days/253851/.

Overall, these ADPPA's protections are more comprehensive than those set forth in recent state laws, either in terms of the ADPPA's substantive provisions, coverage ages, or the investigative and enforcement resources provided.

The ADPPA would also provide heightened protections for other types of sensitive consumer data, including government-issued identifiers, genetic information, biometric data, and intimate photos and videos. The sensitivity of data is often contextual, and state law approaches to regulating it have met with varying degrees of success. Some laws regulating sensitive data have failed to account for evolving technologies, leaving novel data sets under regulated. Other state laws concerning sensitive data have been critiqued for inadvertently imposing burdensome requirements on emerging technologies that pose few privacy risks. The ADPPA provides a regulatory mechanism for recognizing new categories of sensitive data under the law; it would also be helpful to include a mechanism to provide additional clarifying guidance regarding the scope of the definitions for sensitive data categories.

6. Privacy by Design and Data Minimization

The ADPPA's privacy by design provision would require covered entities to "establish and implement reasonable policies, practices, and procedures" regarding data processing. Covered entities would be required to mitigate risks, including to individuals under 17, in their design, development, and implementation of products and services. This would include implementing meaningful safeguards and training to facilitate compliance with all privacy laws, in alignment with guidance from the Federal Trade Commission over time.

Privacy by Design is a key feature of many global data protection regimes, including the GDPR ("Data Protection by Design and by Default"),[32] and provides an important safeguard that goes beyond notice and choice. Among its core principles are user-centric design, visibility, transparency, and privacy as a default setting.[33] Supporters of Privacy by Design also argue that it encourages state-of-the-art privacy engineering, and the development and use of privacy-enhancing technologies (PETs).

III. Comparing ADPPA to GDPR and Global Data Privacy and Protection Frameworks

Commerce, data flows, business practices, and privacy compliance regimes are increasingly global. As Congress crafts federal privacy legislation, it should consider how individuals' rights and organizations' obligations would interact with global privacy regimes. These intersections have implications for how individuals understand and avail themselves of rights to access and control personal data, how privacy safeguards are implemented by organizations, and how enforcement actions proceed against those who misuse personal information. A successful federal regime would ensure that user rights are robust, understandable, and consistent, while companies are governed by clear rules that do not subject them to conflicting legal obligations across borders. It would also ensure that Americans enjoy the same or greater level of protection for their data privacy rights as do individuals from outside the US covered by comprehensive data privacy frameworks like the GDPR.

---

[32] Article 25.

[33] Ann Cavoukian; https://iapp.org/media/pdf/resource_center/pbd_implement_7found_principles.pdf.

Any new privacy law creates risks - risks of uncertainty and unintended consequences for individuals and organizations, risks of inconsistent legal obligations to businesses, and more. New privacy frameworks generate opportunities to align obligations with existing regimes so that individuals understand their rights and companies have clear, consistent responsibilities. Congress also has the opportunity to help ensure that organizations subject to other global regimes - including Europe's GDPR - can utilize or build on years of previous compliance work.

Similarities to GDPR

ADPPA compares favorably to GDPR in a number of respects. For example, ADPPA matches GDPR in defining a broad scope of covered data and in providing Americans individual data privacy rights like access, correction, deletion, and portability in relation to their personal information handled across sectors.

Under both ADPPA and GDPR, commercial entities and not for profits would have obligations to protect and restrict the processing of all personal information that can identify a person, directly or indirectly. That includes, for example, the wide range of information about our personal devices that may not be attached to our name, but can nonetheless be used for targeted and micro-targeted advertising, the creation of detailed profiles of our lives, and behavior, and in some cases used to discriminate against people in pricing, messaging, and opportunities.

Understanding how ADPPA fits into global frameworks helps support consistent protections for individuals and ensures businesses and not for profits of every size can compete in international markets.

Given the importance of the United States data protection framework to the global economy, we encourage policymakers to consider the interoperability of this legislation with the GDPR. As drafted, the legislation has a more streamlined overall approach compared to the GDPR, which is stronger in some aspects and more limited in others. There are also several ways in which this legislation could be better aligned with the GDPR to enable easier compliance for entities that may be subject to both.

The key areas where the ADPPA aligns with the GDPR are:

1. *Comprehensiveness in terms of data covered, types of processing covered, and cross-sectoral applicability,* with the caveat that the ADPPA is more limited in comparison. While it largely applies across industries and to non-profits, it does not apply in the public sector.[34] The ADPPA also does not cover publicly available personal information and employee data, as the GDPR does. Otherwise, its definition of covered data is just as broad, including the "identifiability" standard by reference to unique identifiers, just like the GDPR. Its definitions of collection, processing, and transfers are also as broad as the GDPR definition of "processing."
2. *The existence of individual rights, including access, correction, deletion, and portability, as well as a limited right to object.* The rights of individuals to control their own information are an essential element of the GDPR and the rights provided by the ADPPA measure up well to it. However, the GDPR right to object is broader in scope, as it applies to any processing of personal data conducted on the basis of the legitimate

[34] The 1974 Privacy Act applies to federal agencies, and states have passed comparable laws.

interests of the covered entity, and is not limited only to transfers and targeted advertising.

3. *The recognition of special categories of data that merit enhanced safeguards due to their sensitive nature.* Both GDPR and ADPPA prohibit the processing of specific categories of sensitive data, with exceptions based on consent and other limited grounds. However, ADPPA is more comprehensive in terms of the categories of sensitive data it protects and is also more protective than the GDPR since it has more limited exceptions allowing the processing of such data.
4. *Requiring data minimization for all processing of covered data, including collection and transfers.* Just like in ADPPA, the data minimization principle underpins all processing of personal data under the GDPR. Moreover, there are instances of the principle of purpose limitation that surface in ADPPA, similar to how it manifests as an overarching principle in the GDPR.
5. *The identical standard for valid consent under GDPR and ADPPA - "freely given, specific, informed and unambiguous" - as well as the similar requirements against bundling of consent* for different acts and practices ensure that individual consent is meaningful and not a "tick the box," "take it or leave it" exercise. The right to withdraw consent also has an identical standard under the two frameworks - it must be as easy to withdraw consent as it is to give consent. This provides a strong safeguard for individuals in relation to how their personal information is collected and used. At the same time, it streamlines compliance for those entities covered by both frameworks.

IV. Recommended Revisions and Additions

A comprehensive federal privacy law would be a monumental step towards ensuring that all Americans have meaningful privacy rights across all business sectors that use personal data. But it is hard to craft a privacy law that is clear, consistent, and interacts harmoniously with existing legal frameworks and evolving technologies and business practices. More work remains to be done to ensure that ADPPA appropriately protects individuals, is workable for businesses, and there are not unexpected or undesired consequences. Below are four recommendations that would improve ADPPA:

1. Funding for the FTC

The FTC would need substantial additional funding to effectively enforce ADPPA, as well as to comply with additional requirements ADPPA places on the Commission. The bill would provide the Commission with the authority to enforce privacy requirements that are more specific than the FTC's current general authority to combat "unfair and deceptive" business practices. With greater specificity comes greater demand for capable technologists, lawyers, and other experts to ensure the Commission is effectively executing Congress' mandate. In addition to this heightened need for general investigation and enforcement resources, ADPPA includes specific provisions that would require the FTC to promulgate new regulations regarding certain bill provisions and to create a "Youth Privacy and Marketing Division," headed by a Director. Rulemaking and the establishment of a new division should be supported by additional funding for the Commission; these activities require support beyond the general increase in authority, investigative activities, and enforcement actions contemplated by ADPPA.

Fully staffing and funding the FTC is critical for ADPPA to live up to its promise as a thoughtful and powerful privacy law that would bring critical privacy protections to all Americans. A fully functioning FTC is critical to ADPPA's success.

2. More Iterative Processes

Portions of the bill provide for limited FTC rulemaking, but several key provisions do not include mechanisms to update the law in light of rapidly evolving technologies and business practices. The impact of technological change has long bedeviled authors of privacy laws. In 2012, Congress amended the Video Privacy Protection Act to account for the shift from physical video stores to online video delivery - a shift that was unforeseeable in 1988 when the law was passed, download speed typically topped out around 2,400 baud, and it would have taken approximately 100 hours to download a single feature film even if one were available.

Congress and state lawmakers have turned to various mechanisms to address the legislative challenges posed by evolving technology, including targeted rulemaking authority regarding specific statutory provisions, administrative safe harbors, and other methods. California's and Colorado's recent privacy laws authorize rulemaking as a mechanism to provide certainty on definitions, take account of newly-discovered or developed categories of sensitive data, and promote the development of novel privacy-enhancing technologies. Sections that might benefit from iterative mechanisms might be the definition of sensitive data and the recognition that certain types of privacy-enhancing technologies may change.

3. Intersection with Other Federal Laws

The ADPPA takes a practical approach to preserving longstanding federal privacy laws (COPPA, FERPA, HIPAA, etc.). Individuals and companies have established understandings of rights and responsibilities under these laws, and the ADPPA largely preserves these frameworks. However, any comprehensive privacy bill can generate unexpected outcomes when it intersects with decades-old statutes, regulations, agency guidance, and interpretive jurisprudence. We recommend that Congress analyze the intersection of these laws from a compliance standpoint and create more clarity when appropriate so that consumers and businesses can better understand how the ADPPA intersects with specific provisions of the existing federal privacy regimes.

For example, the ADPPA preserves the COPPA statute and rule, but the ADPPA includes a limited private right of action that COPPA lacks. Under one interpretation, this could produce a counterintuitive result, with teens granted an enforcement mechanism against unlawful data processing that would be unavailable to children.

Another potential anomaly could arise from the inclusion of childrens' data in the ADPPA's "sensitive covered data" category. The provisions for processing "sensitive covered data" do not include a knowledge standard. This is unsurprising, because nearly all of the sensitive data categories can be identified by examining the data. For example, few compliance experts are likely to mistake a list of account login credentials or genetic data for other, less sensitive data.

However, the fact that data was collected from a child may not be obvious on its face or easily distinguishable from data collected from adults. And the ADPPA places substantively different obligations on entities that serve targeted advertising or engage in onward data transfers involving adults' versus childrens' data. Those who process data from minors or from "general audience" products and services will likely benefit from greater clarity on this point.

Additionally, in order to prevent unintentionally amending U.S. surveillance laws and to allow for both clarity for covered entities with respect to compliance and to better protect civil liberties, we would suggest that this section expressly reference compliance with due process along with state and federal law as a precondition for law enforcement data access. Such language is also necessary for other sections that reference law enforcement access (Sec. 102(a)(3), (5), and (6); Sec. 203(d)(3)(vi)). Failure to address this could also create jurisdictional friction with the judiciary committees in both houses.

4. Definitional Clarity

Several ADPPA definitions could benefit from clarification, either through statutory revision, regulatory explication, or judicial interpretation. When ADPPA definitions are intended to align with similar terms in other legal frameworks, those links could be made explicit in the legislative history, subsequent rulemaking, or informal guidance from the FTC. There would be a particular benefit in identifying circumstances in which ADPPA terms align with existing federal sector laws or with the GDPR; both could be helpful from a compliance standpoint and give much-needed clarity to the bill. For example, given the centrality of the term, we recommend aligning the definition of "covered data" with "personal information" in the GDPR while providing clarifying, non-exhaustive subsections to ensure that the definition includes, *but is not limited to*, persistent identifiers, device identifiers, pseudonyms generated through probabilistic tracking, and so forth. This is but one example of many where revised definitions could help from a compliance, enforcement, and consumer rights standpoint.

We also recommend that Congress consider expanding the research exception for ADPPA. The current exception for IRB-approved research is much more limited than as defined under the Common Rule, which allows for "systematic, generalizable studies," i.e., not only research that is in the "public interest." Data driven research is the lifeblood of public health, clinical research, and has been proposed as one part of a practical approach to platform accountability. An expanded research exception, aligned with research best practices and subject to common sense ethical review and privacy safeguards, would be welcome.

Additional clarity on the distinction between data controllers and processors is needed. Most data protection laws, including the GDPR, establish a clear distinction between data controllers (that determine the purposes and means of processing) and data processors (that process data solely on behalf of a controller – for example, cloud storage and other service providers).

Typically, processors are not expected to comply with the majority of business obligations but are expected to assist controllers in compliance and may not process data further for secondary uses. In most other global frameworks, including the GDPR, as well as in some of the state laws in the US, the relationship between controllers and processors is governed by a Data Processing Agreement - a contract where the obligations of each are laid out, confidentiality obligations are established, as well as rules about what happens to personal information once the relationship between controllers and processors ends. In contrast, the current Draft applies obligations broadly to all "covered entities," with only limited exceptions for service providers. It also does not include the obligation for covered entities and service providers to enter an agreement. The definitions are likely to create conflict when obligations of the service providers are in conflict with restrictions of certain controllers.

Conclusion

Now is the time for Congress to pass comprehensive privacy legislation. The impact of data-intensive technologies on individuals and marginalized communities is increasing every day as the pace of innovation accelerates. Congress has the opportunity now to pass a law that will shape these developments to maximize the benefits of data for society while mitigating risks. Delaying Congressional action means that businesses will inevitably continue to develop new models, build infrastructure, and deploy technologies without the guidance and clear limits that only Congress can set forth.

Compared to each of the five state privacy laws passed since 2018, the American Data Privacy and Protection Act (ADPPA) is more comprehensive in scope, more inclusive of civil rights protections, and provides individuals with more varied enforcement mechanisms; ADPPA compares favorably to global frameworks, including the GDPR. This is a monumental feat that should be celebrated by all involved. Of course, work remains to be done on specific provisions to ensure individuals are protected, the bill is workable for business, and there are not unexpected or undesired consequences. We again ask that Congress move forward thoughtfully and expeditiously to find common ground on these critical issues.

Again thank you for the opportunity to testify, and I look forward to answering your questions.

Addendum

Please see disclaimers contained in relevant footnotes

Table 1. Comparative chart (between the American data protection and privacy act, California privacy rights act, and other comprehensive state privacy laws)[35]

	ADPPA	California Privacy Rights Act[36]	Other Laws (Colorado, Connecticut, Virginia, and Utah)[37]
Covered Entity Threshold (*the requirements for an entity to be subject to the law*)	Either: • Collects, processes or transfers covered data and is (i) subject to FTC Act; (ii) a common carrier under title II of the Communications Act of 1934; or (iii) a non-for-profit organization; OR	Either has: • Annual revenue >$25 million; • Annually buy, sell, or "share" personal information of 10,000+ consumers; OR • Derive 50% annual revenue from selling or sharing personal data for behavioral advertising	• Most require controlling or processing personal data of over 100,000 state residents; OR • Derive 50% of annual revenue from the sale of personal data and control/process personal data of 25,000 state residents

35 This chart focuses on high-level details of what is and is not in the proposed bill and state laws. It is not designed to reflect subtle distinctions between these proposed and codified laws.

36 The California column reflects the provisions of the CPRA, which will go into effect on January 1st, 2023, and will replace the currently enacted CCPA. Certain aspects of California law are being clarified through rulemaking.

37 Colorado, Connecticut, Virginia, and Utah are included in the same column because these states share similar structural frameworks. Despite this similarity, the laws of these states contain significant variations in consumer rights and business duties.

Table 1. (Continued)

	ADPPA	California Privacy Rights Act[38]	Other Laws (Colorado, Connecticut, Virginia, and Utah)[39]
	• Any entity or person that controls, is controlled by, is under common control with, or shares common branding with an entity that meets the above requirements.		
Scope/Coverage *(features affecting which entities have obligations under the law)*	• Extends to non-profits and common carriers • Includes limited small business carve-outs	• Does not extend to non-profits • Includes small business carve-outs	All laws contain small business exemptions. Most do not extend to non-profits (except Colorado)
Consumer Rights			
Access *(ability to request what data an entity has)*	Yes	Yes	Yes
Correction *(right to correct inaccurate data held by an entity)*	Yes	Yes	Yes (Not Utah)
Deletion *(right to request deletion of personal data held by an entity)*	Yes	Yes	Yes
Portability *(ability to receive a copy of data and transfer in*	Yes	Yes	Yes
readable format to another entity)			
Opt-In Consent *(an individual must affirmatively consent for an entity to collect or use certain data)*	For: • Sensitive covered data • Adolescent data transfers (13–17); • Retention of data beyond its processing purpose; Service provider transfers of covered data to other entities.	For: • Sale or sharing of adolescent data (13–15); • Inconsistent secondary use Does not require opt-in consent for collection or processing of sensitive data.	All other state laws require opt-in consent for *sensitive data* and inconsistent secondary uses of data (except Utah). Connecticut requires opt-in consent for sales and targeted advertising using adolescent data (13-15).
Opt-Out Rights (*the right of an individual to cease being subject to certain processing activities)*	For: • Targeted advertising • Data transfers	For: • Data sales and sharing (including cross-context behavioral advertising)	All other states permit opt-out targeted advertising and data sales.

[38] The California column reflects the provisions of the CPRA, which will go into effect on January 1st, 2023, and will replace the currently enacted CCPA. Certain aspects of California law are being clarified through rulemaking.

[39] Colorado, Connecticut, Virginia, and Utah are included in the same column because these states share similar structural frameworks. Despite this similarity, the laws of these states contain significant variations in consumer rights and business duties.

	ADPPA	California Privacy Rights Act[40]	Other Laws (Colorado, Connecticut, Virginia, and Utah)[41]
	• Does not require for automated decision-making or profiling	• Right to 'limit the use and disclosure of sensitive personal data' • Future rulemaking on automated decision-making and profiling.	Utah is the only state that does not permit individuals to opt-out for profiling
Global/Unified Opt-Out *(Automated exercise of opt-out rights through user-enabled signals)*	Required if found feasible by FTC within 18 months	Yes	Included in Colorado and Connecticut; excluded in Virginia and Utah
Business Obligations			
Privacy Notices *(information provided about an entity's actions taken with respect to personal data)*	Yes, plus short-form notices for 'large data holders'	Yes, but no short-form notice requirement.	All require privacy notices, but do not require short-form notices.
Data minimization *(the requirement to limit data collected and retained as necessary for the purpose)*	Yes	Yes (pending regulations)	Most state laws have limited minimization principles connected to privacy notices.
Privacy by Design (*requirement for entities to consider privacy risks in the design, development, and implementation of products)*	Yes	No	No
Prohibited processing activities (*prohibits the collection and use of certain data unless the purpose falls within an exception, including affirmative express consent)*	Yes, including • SSNs • Precise geolocation information • Biometric information • Password • Non-consensual intimate images • Genetic information • An individual's aggregated internet search or browsing history • An individual's physical activity information from a smartphone or wearable device, with exceptions.	No	No

40 The California column reflects the provisions of the CPRA, which will go into effect on January 1st, 2023, and will replace the currently enacted CCPA. Certain aspects of California law are being clarified through rulemaking.

41 Colorado, Connecticut, Virginia, and Utah are included in the same column because these states share similar structural frameworks. Despite this similarity, the laws of these states contain significant variations in consumer rights and business duties.

Table 1. (Continued)

	ADPPA	California Privacy Rights Act[42]	Other Laws (Colorado, Connecticut, Virginia, and Utah)[43]
Data security provisions (*requiring entities to implement certain security measures)*	Yes, additional obligations for 'large data holders'	Yes	Yes
Civil Rights Provisions and AI (*providing that data processing cannot discriminate against protected classes)*	Yes, plus requires algorithmic impact assessments and design evaluations.	Limited to complying with existing laws. Does not require algorithmic assessments.	Most state laws have civil rights provisions limited to complying with existing laws. None require algorithmic assessments.
Privacy Impact Assessments (*technical assessment to identify and document privacy risks for systems and processes)*	Yes (applicable to 'large data holders')	Yes (assessments required for risky processing activities)	Yes (assessments required for risky processing activities). Not required in Utah.
Specific 'Data Broker' Requirements (*requirements for entities that collect data from secondary sources, aggregate, and sell the data to other entities)*	Yes, requires "third-party collecting entities" to register with the FTC and honor a "Do Not Collect" mechanism.	No	No
Non-retaliation for exercise of consumer rights (*an entity may not deny products or services, or charge different prices, based on whether individuals exercise privacy rights)*	Yes	Yes	Yes (limited in Utah)
Enforcement			
Private Right of Action *(right of individuals to bring suits for violations)*	Yes, for most provisions	Only for data breaches or business violation of security measures	No
Regulatory Enforcement *(regulatory body or executive agency responsible for enforcing the law))*	FTC & State Attorneys General	Attorney General and California Privacy Protection Agency	Typically State Attorney General (and District Attorneys in Colorado).

[42] The California column reflects the provisions of the CPRA, which will go into effect on January 1st, 2023, and will replace the currently enacted CCPA. Certain aspects of California law are being clarified through rulemaking.

[43] Colorado, Connecticut, Virginia, and Utah are included in the same column because these states share similar structural frameworks. Despite this similarity, the laws of these states contain significant variations in consumer rights and business duties.

	ADPPA	California Privacy Rights Act[44]	Other Laws (Colorado, Connecticut, Virginia, and Utah)[45]
Regulatory Rulemaking *(ability of regulatory bodies or executive agencies to create rules; and the scope of this authority)*	Yes, fairly broad authority for the FTC for identified provisions	Yes for identified provisions	Except Colorado, no other state law contains rulemaking provisions.
Enforcement of Arbitration Agreements (*provisions relating to the validity of pre-dispute agreements requiring individuals to arbitrate any potential claims and waive judicial redress)*	Yes - Entities may generally have pre-dispute arbitration agreements with individuals over 18 years old. Individuals under 18 years old cannot be subject to arbitration agreements or joint action waivers.	Unclear - the law generally states that agreements to limit consumer rights are unenforceable, however Courts have granted motions to compel arbitration of asserted CCPA class action claims where terms and conditions contained arbitration provisions.	No
Safe Harbors and Defenses (*compliance mechanisms that prevent or provide protection against enforcement actions)*	Yes - technical compliance programs and commission approved compliance guidelines.	No	No

*Ms. Schakowsky. Thank you.

And now, Mr. Miller, I recognize you for five minutes.

Statement of John Miller, Senior Vice President of Policy and General Counsel, Information Technology Industry Council

*Mr. Miller. Chairwoman Schakowsky, Ranking Member Bilirakis, Chairman Pallone, Ranking Member McMorris Rodgers, and distinguished members of the subcommittee, on behalf of the Information Technology Industry Council, or ITI, thank you for the opportunity to testify today.

As senior vice president of policy and general counsel, I lead ITI's trust data and technology policy team, including our strategy and advocacy on privacy, cyber security, and data policy globally.

ITI represents 80 leading global companies from every corner of the information and communications technology sector, and privacy has been a longstanding policy priority for ITI and our members as foundational to establishing consumer trust.

---

44 The California column reflects the provisions of the CPRA, which will go into effect on January 1st, 2023, and will replace the currently enacted CCPA. Certain aspects of California law are being clarified through rulemaking.

45 Colorado, Connecticut, Virginia, and Utah are included in the same column because these states share similar structural frameworks. Despite this similarity, the laws of these states contain significant variations in consumer rights and business duties.

ITI commends Chairman Pallone, Ranking Member McMorris Rodgers, and Senator Wicker for your work on the American Data Protection and Privacy Act discussion draft. We have for several years shared your goal of an acting comprehensive privacy legislation in 2019 releasing our fair privacy framework to serve as a roadmap for a federal law.

Today, multiple U.S. states and over 140 countries have passed privacy legislation, while until now, we have continued to lag in making appreciable progress at the federal level. ITI recognizes maintaining this current path is unsustainable, and we are hopeful the draft can provide the much-needed impetus to change this trajectory.

In terms of both its scope and potential impact, the draft could foreshadow an inflection point on par with Europe's General Data Protection Regulation or the California Consumer Privacy Act due not only to the robust protections it aspires to achieve for Americans, but also for its wide ranging and potentially disruptive impact on companies across every sector of the U.S. economy, including longstanding business models that have helped fuel the internet's development and corresponding economic growth.

This draft deserves to be thoughtfully considered by all stakeholders as the most credible bipartisan and bicameral effort yet to advance comprehensive federal privacy legislation in the United States, and we look forward to continuing to constructively engage with the subcommittee as the bill moves forward, but a clear-eyed view should acknowledge the bill is not perfect and needs improvement in several key areas.

First, the definition of "sensitive covered data" is overly broad in numerous respects. Perhaps the most problematic subsection appears to subject all online activity relating to individuals to opt-in consent rendering many critical internet functions difficult if not impossible to perform in areas ranging from routine browsing to preventing cyber-attacks.

Sensitive covered data is also very [inaudible] defined in several other respects, including sweeping in telephone numbers, texts, emails, and voicemails also subjecting these and other data categories to express opt-in consent. The definition should be recalibrated to better align it with other privacy laws.

Second, the draft does not carefully distinguish between the different types of entities that use data or their obligations. In particular, the draft does not clearly differentiate the responsibilities of covered entities or data controllers and service providers or data processors.

This so-called controller processor distinction is made clear not only in the GDPR, but in all five state laws. Given the complex and variable relationships between entities using data, it is essential to clearly delineate between the roles and responsibilities of controllers and processors for a privacy law to function effectively, including to apportion potential liabilities, and the draft should be modified to more clearly define these entities, rather than lumping them in their obligations together.

Third, we have concerns that, as presently drafted, the definition of "targeted advertising" would prevent the ad-supported internet business model from continuing. Any federal privacy law should protect the privacy of Americans, but also, seek to preserve data innovation in the business models that have helped power the growth of the internet economy.

We suggest changes to bring the definition of "targeted advertising" more in line with the definitions included in recent state privacy laws which struck the right balance to enable internet companies to reasonably advertise to users on their own sites while protecting their privacy interests.

My written testimony also suggests revamping other provisions including as related to algorithms and cyber security.

With respect to the approach to enforcement, the draft contains multiple prongs providing strong redress and enforcement, including robust FTC rulemaking, enforcement authorities, and resources as well as enforcement by state attorneys general.

In light of the already strong FTC and AG enforcement provisions in the draft, it is reasonable to ask whether including a private right of action is necessary to ensure a robust enforcement. While we appreciate the efforts to narrow the PRA, our members remain concerned the provision remains too broad and misses the mark as currently drafted. Amongst other reasons, the combination of unclear definitions with the availability of attorneys' fees, it seems like a recipe for a flood of lawsuits.

Finally, regarding preemption, we appreciate the draft expresses the intent to preempt state privacy laws covered by the provisions of the bill, [inaudible] questions regarding how the draft rationalizes its execution of preemption given the lengthy savings clause include some laws that appear to be covered by the draft, but not others.

We all agree we need to get privacy legislation done, but we should also agree we need to get privacy legislation right.

Thank you for the opportunity to testify today, and I look forward to your questions.

[The prepared statement of Mr. Miller follows:]

Written Testimony of John S. Miller, Senior Vice President of Policy and General Counsel Information Technology Industry Council (ITI), before the Committee on Energy & Commerce Subcommittee on Consumer Protection & Commerce, United States House of Representatives, Protecting America's Consumers: Bipartisan Legislation to Strengthen Data Privacy and Security, June 14, 2022

Chairwoman Schakowsky, Ranking Member Bilirakis, Chairman Pallone, Ranking Member McMorris Rodgers, and Distinguished Members of the subcommittee, thank you for the opportunity to testify today. I am John Miller, Senior Vice President of Policy and General Counsel at the Information Technology Industry Council (ITI).[46] I lead ITI's Trust, Data and Technology Policy team, driving ITI's strategy and advocacy on privacy and data protection, cybersecurity and supply chain resiliency, government access to data, digital platforms, artificial intelligence, data policy, Internet of Things, cloud computing, and other technology and digital policy issues. I have developed deep expertise on privacy, data protection, and data security policy and legal issues over the past sixteen years, including advising governments and policymakers on these issues, both domestically and globally, at a large multinational technology company as well as at ITI.

ITI is the premier advocate and thought leader in the United States and around the world for the information and communications technology (ICT) industry. We represent leading

---

[46] The Information Technology Industry Council (ITI) is the premier global advocate for technology, representing the world's most innovative companies. Founded in 1916, ITI is an international trade association with a team of professionals on four continents. We promote public policies and industry standards that advance competition and innovation worldwide. Our diverse membership and expert staff provide policymakers the broadest perspective and thought leadership from technology, hardware, software, services, manufacturing, and related industries. Visit https://www.itic.org/ to learn more.

companies from across the ICT sector, including hardware, software, digital services, semiconductor, network equipment, cybersecurity, Internet companies, and other organizations using data and technology to evolve their businesses.[47] Privacy is a longstanding ITI policy priority, as protecting privacy is integral to establishing and maintaining the consumer trust that is integral to our members' businesses. Consumer trust is a key pillar of innovation, and the industry I represent today recognizes it must do everything it can to deepen that trust and make sure we meet our customers' expectations when it comes to protecting their privacy and personal data.

ITI commends Chairman Pallone, Ranking Member McMorris Rodgers, and Senator Wicker for your work on the American Data Protection and Privacy Act (ADPPA), the discussion draft that is the subject of today's hearing. The technology sector has for several years shared your goal of enacting comprehensive federal privacy legislation, and the ADPPA represents welcome and tangible progress toward that goal. In terms of both its scope and potential impact, the draft bill represents not only a significant contribution to the evolving domestic and global conversation on privacy legislation, but arguably an inflection point on par with Europe's General Data Protection Regulation (GDPR) and the California Consumer Privacy Act (CCPA), due not only to robust protections it aspires to achieve for the American people but also for its wide-ranging and potentially disruptive impact on businesses across every sector of the U.S. economy and data innovation, including longstanding business models that have helped fuel the internet's development and corresponding economic growth. The ADPPA deserves to be taken seriously and thoughtfully considered by all stakeholders as the most credible bipartisan and bicameral effort yet to advance comprehensive federal privacy legislation in the United States, but we also need to acknowledge the bill needs substantial improvement, and we look forward to continuing to constructively engage with you and your staff as the bill moves forward.

ITI has long called for federal privacy legislation and shares many of the committee's concerns and priorities regarding individuals' personal data use and protection. In 2019, we released our *Framework to Advance Interoperable Rules (FAIR) on Privacy*.[48] Our FAIR Privacy framework seeks to move the conversation forward on federal privacy legislation by offering a flexible model that enhances transparency, increases consumer control, establishes company accountability, promotes data security, and calls for meaningful enforcement, oversight, and redress mechanisms. It is also important to note that we drafted the FAIR Privacy framework against the backdrop of Europe's GDPR having recently come on line, the CCPA's passage into law, and while many other comprehensive privacy bills were being considered in major global markets and several U.S. states. ITI's FAIR Privacy framework aspires not only to serve as a roadmap for a federal law in the United States but to create alignment with the privacy protections of other privacy regimes across the globe, enable interoperability with these global approaches, and avoid a fragmented approach to privacy at the U.S. state level.

Unfortunately, in the ensuing three years we have observed several more U.S. states and markets passing their own privacy laws including Colorado, Virginia, Utah, and Connecticut, as well as the passage of an additional law in California, the California Privacy Rights Act (CPRA), which amends CCPA and will come into force in 2023. Additionally, Brazil, China

[47] See ITI membership list at: https://www.itic.org/about/membership/iti-members.

[48] Framework to advance Interoperable Rules on Privacy https://www.itic.org/public-policy/FINAL FrameworktoAdvanceInteroperableRules(FAIR)onPrivacyFinal_NoWatermark.pdf.

and over 140 other countries have passed privacy legislation, while the United States has continued to lag on making appreciable progress on a privacy law at the federal level. The technology sector recognizes maintaining the status quo and this current path is unsustainable. First, it leads to uneven and confusing protections for individuals in the United States that vary from state to state, and which are not on par with the protections of their peers globally. Second, the feared increasingly fragmented regulatory landscape is fast becoming a reality that exhausts resources and disproportionately impacts U.S. businesses. And finally, with every day that goes by without a federal law, the stature of the United States as a leader on the global privacy stage is diminished. We are hopeful the ADPPA can provide the much-needed impetus to change this trajectory.

I will focus the balance of my written testimony on three areas: (1) briefly reviewing the core elements of ITI's FAIR Privacy and noting where ADPPA positively aligns, while also flagging important divergences; (2) assessing some of the most significant areas where we believe ADPPA must be strengthened, including clarifying several key definitions and improving and refining other portions the discussion draft; and (3) evaluating the polarizing provisions on preemption and a private right of action.

I. ITI's FAIR Privacy Framework and the ADPPA

ITI's FAIR Privacy framework sets forth specific ideas to advance the privacy rights of individuals and makes explicit the responsibilities of tech companies in using personal data while acknowledging the many different contexts in which individuals and companies interact with data. It proposes establishing context-based individual control rights for consumers to ensure meaningful transparency and a clear understanding of their choices relative to the use of their personal data.

Our FAIR Privacy framework also clearly defines an entity's responsibilities around handling personal data to hold them accountable, thereby ensuring companies use personal data responsibly and transparently. However, it also allows for variance in those obligations based on the extent to which an entity determines the purposes for and manner of use of personal data and makes certain that accountability obligations travel with data transferred to other entities' (such as service providers) for their own use. Finally, and importantly, ITI's FAIR Privacy framework seeks to protect individuals' privacy while avoiding the onerous process requirements that can degrade the user experience, inject unnecessary costs into the ecosystem, or otherwise deter continued innovation and the participation of small- and medium-sized enterprises in the digital economy.

The ADPPA shares many similarities to ITI's FAIR Privacy framework, although there are also important differences. Like ITI's framework, the discussion draft establishes robust individual control rights, putting consumers in the driver's seat when it comes to their personal information and giving them the right to expressly and affirmatively consent to the use of their sensitive personal data. However, the definition of sensitive data in the ADPPA is not only broader but in important respects less clear than that which we contemplated (or exists in other comprehensive privacy laws).

Like ITI's FAIR Privacy framework, the ADPPA requires companies to maintain robust data security programs and employ data minimization practices. ITI's framework seeks to ensure that such security programs and minimization practices are calibrated to not only the size of companies but a series of factors and considerations appropriate to the manner, purposes and context by which companies use personal data, and while the ADPPA acknowledges many of these same context-specific considerations, it additionally layers several prescriptive security requirements on all companies, which they may be inadvertently barred from implementing due to other provisions in the bill, and includes a minimization requirement that can be read expansively to prohibit all forms of processing not falling under a permitted purpose.

And like ITI's FAIR Privacy framework, the ADPPA calls for strong accountability and oversight. However, while our framework similarly called for an oversight body such as the Federal Trade Commission (FTC) to be appropriately resourced including with the technical capacity needed to regulate effectively to protect individuals, for companies to maintain records pertaining to their use of data, risk assessments, and security programs so that they are auditable in the event incidents do occur, and for individuals to have the right to redress mechanisms that ensure their rights are adequately protected, the ADPPA goes significantly further, imposing unnecessary and unprecedented prescriptive requirements on companies to perform algorithmic impact assessments and design evaluations, and elevating a broad private right of action in a manner that may make it the preferred form of redress.

I will discuss the principal issues touched on in this section in more depth below.

II. Recommendations to Strengthen the ADPPA

One of the most critical parts of any bill is the "definitions" section, and the ADPPA is no exception. The scope of the protections bestowed to individuals, obligations imposed on companies and the potential impact of the enforcement provisions all flows from these key provisions. In our view, there are several key definitions in the discussion draft that must be clarified and tightened up to ensure that the bill achieves what should be its primary purpose of protecting individuals' privacy and personal data without unnecessarily undermining data innovation.[49] I highlight a few of the most problematic definitions below as well as a couple of other important provisions in the discussion draft that we believe must be recalibrated (please do not consider this an exhaustive list).

A. "Sensitive Covered Data"

The definition of "sensitive covered data" under Section 2(22) is overly broad in numerous respects and out of step with sensitive data definitions in similar laws at the U.S. states and globally, render many critical internet functions difficult if not possible to perform, and is in some ways inconsistent with other provisions in the discussion draft.

Perhaps the most problematic section is 2(22)(A)(xi), which includes "information identifying an individual's online activities over time or across third party websites or online services," thus seemingly subjecting all online activity relating to individuals to opt-in consent. This broad definition, would, for instance, render routine browsing activities performed by users difficult, arguably requiring them to provide opt-in consent every time they logged into a search engine. Perhaps more concerningly, this provision would effectively eliminate the

---

[49] While I will offer constructive feedback aimed at improving a few specific provisions in the discussion draft, I want to make it clear that this is not an exhaustive list, and that we will offer additional written feedback to staff including technical edits as we continue to receive and consolidate feedback from ITI members.

ability of companies to perform the cybersecurity analyses necessary to prevent cyber-attacks (including those required by the data security provisions in the bill), or act as content delivery networks, or do many other things requiring the processing of unique identifiers such as IP addresses (i.e., information identifying an individual's online activities) necessary for these functions.

One recommended improvement to section 2(22)(A)(xi) would be to replace the "or" in the language cited above with an "and" so that this subpart of the definition would read: "information identifying an individual's online activities over time and across third party websites or online services."

Beyond "online activities," what qualifies as "sensitive covered data" is in numerous other respects very broadly defined and would include any telephone number, text, email, voicemail, or phone or text logs, amongst other things. The discussion draft thus greatly expands the definition of what is considered sensitive data in existing prominent global privacy laws and U.S. state laws. The implications of this expansion are at least twofold: first, it elevates several seemingly "ordinary" categories of personal data (such as telephone numbers which are publicly available in phone books) to be on par with obviously sensitive data such as social security numbers, health or biometric data; second, requiring affirmative express consent to collect, process, or transfer all sensitive covered data would extensively impact many companies who may simply be unable to comply with these provisions. For instance, given many service providers are business-to-business (B2B) companies that may not have direct relationships with or access to consumers so as to be able to obtain the required consent, the result of the overbroad sensitive data definition is to create an unworkable situation where a service provider could be held liable for a covered entity's failure to appropriately gain consent, including in instances where a consumer decides to do something as ordinary as changing their phone number.

We recommend recalibrating the definition of sensitive covered data in the discussion draft to better align it with the definitions of "sensitive data" in other privacy laws.

B. "Covered Entity" and "Service Provider"

One of the reasons ITI built context into our FAIR Privacy framework was because while each one of our eighty companies uses data every day, they each use data differently, both in their internal operations in how they interact with their different types of customers, and in how they use data to innovate and continue to drive their businesses forward. Each one of those eighty companies also have a unique business model and will experience the impacts of the ADPPA differently should it become law. The same is true of every other U.S. business, because data is important to all of them, and the multiplicity of ways that companies use data is matched by the potential impacts the ADPPA would have on their businesses, their technology products and services, their employees, and their customers.

While the bill makes an effort to distinguish the responsibilities of entities based on their size (e.g., by creating separate obligations for "large data holders" and an exception for "small data" entities), it does not carefully distinguish the obligations of the different types of entities that use data. In particular, it does not clearly differentiate the responsibilities of "covered entities" (or what are commonly referred to as "data controllers" under the GDPR, or entities that determine the purposes for which and the means by which data is processed) and "service providers" ("data processors" under the GDPR, or entities that processes personal data only on behalf of a controller). The so-called data controller/data processor distinction is made clear not only in the GDPR but in other comprehensive privacy legislation globally and in the United States (indeed, the distinction is clear in all five U.S. state bills).

Given the complex and variable relationships between entities in the data ecosystem, it is essential to clearly delineate between the roles and responsibilities of covered entities/controllers and service providers/processors for a privacy law to function effectively. For example, there are times when a company will act as a covered entity/controller that is deciding the means or purposes of managing and processing data, while at other times, that same company will act as a service provider that is processing data on behalf of a covered entity/controller solely at their direction and under a contract. Covered entities and service providers should both be regulated under the ADPPA (or any federal privacy law), but it is imperative for the law to assign the appropriate role-based obligations to controllers and service providers so as to apportion their responsibilities and potential liabilities clearly.

Unfortunately, the discussion draft does not clearly delineate between "covered entities" in sec. 2(9) and "service providers" in sec. 2(23), and in fact the definitions could be read as imposing greater obligations on the service providers, flipping the typical controller/processor paradigm, even though the processors often lack access to data they do not control. We recommend the discussion draft be modified to define these terms more crisply in line with other major privacy legislation or at least try to distinguish the obligations of "covered entities who are not acting as service providers" rather than lumping these different entities together.

C. "Covered Data"

Amongst other things, several aspects of the definition of "employee data" as defined under "Covered Data" under Section 2(8)(C)) should be clarified. First, the definition should be further strengthened to include information that laws require employers to collect about employees, such as diversity data.

Second, employees should not be able to demand deletion of such data if employers collect it pursuant to legal obligations. Third, subpart (ii) of the definition of Employee Data assumes that the business contact details of an employee will be provided to the employer. In practice, it is often the other way around with employers providing business contact details to the employee.

D. "Targeted Advertising"

As stated above we believe the ADPPA or any comprehensive privacy law should have a dual objective - protecting the privacy of Americans while also preserving data innovation, including the business models that have helped the internet thrive and powered the growth of the global internet economy.

We have concerns that as presently drafted, the definition of "targeted advertising" in sec. 2(26) would simply preclude the ad-supported internet business model to continue, as publishers would not be able to use their knowledge of the preferences and interests of their users to show ads. We would suggest changes that would bring the definition more in line with the definition of "targeted advertising" that was included in recent privacy laws passed by Virginia, Colorado, Utah, and Connecticut. The definitions in those states struck the right balance to enable internet companies to reasonably advertise to their users on their sites while protecting their privacy interests.

We recommend limiting the definition of "targeted advertising" in sec. 26(A) to the use of data collected over time *and* across third party websites or online services. This edit would be consistent with the approach taken in the state bills and also consistent with a similar edit we suggested making to the "sensitive data" definition as related to "online activity." We additionally recommend revisiting the exceptions in the definition under sec. 26(B)(ii) for first party advertising and sec. 26(B)(iii) for contextual advertising as they seem unnecessarily limiting given the trust relationship companies typically have established with users of their own sites or apps.

Beyond the critical definitions reviewed above, there are other provisions in the discussion draft that the committee should consider revamping, including those relating to algorithms and cybersecurity.

E. Algorithmic Impact Assessments and Design Evaluations

With respect to Algorithms and Civil Rights under Section 207, ITI shares the firm belief that building trust in the era of digital transformation is essential and agrees there are important questions that should be addressed regarding the responsible development and use of algorithms. We are also aware of existing concerns regarding potential negative outcomes related to the use of algorithms and are participating in related existing efforts underway at the Department of Commerce around AI risk management, explainability and mitigation of AI bias at the National Institute of Standards and Technology (NIST) and privacy and civil rights at the National Telecommunications and Information Administration (NTIA). We encourage the Committee to consider these ongoing federal workstreams as a potential guide to future legislative efforts rather than prematurely including in the discussion draft prescriptive requirements to conduct algorithmic design evaluations and impact assessments, which are unprecedented not only in privacy laws globally but even laws more squarely focused on related topics such as artificial intelligence.

F. Cybersecurity Exceptions

While the legislation is appropriately focused on consumer privacy rights, including data security, the combination of vague definitions and somewhat haphazardly aggregated general exceptions in section 209 could easily implicate all sorts of enterprise focused, B2B activity that could have serious unintended consequences, particularly on cybersecurity.

For example, large swaths of internet and network telemetry used for real-time cybersecurity defense and security automation activity could be considered covered data (and potentially sensitive covered data due to the geolocation provision). Additionally, as mentioned above, given IP addresses, a foundational data point of cybersecurity vulnerability management, are considered a unique identifier despite being publicly available information and thus also categorized as sensitive covered data requiring consent, the ADPPA as drafted could create substantial headwinds for routine, enterprise- focused cybersecurity activity.

We suspect cybersecurity activity is not intended to be negatively impacted by this legislation. While section 209 does include a general exception "to detect or respond to a security incident or fulfill product or service warranty," and another "to protect against fraudulent or illegal activity," the exceptions as written do not clearly include cyber defense activity where large swaths of network data are analyzed in real-time for the purpose of preventing security incidents.

We would encourage the Committee to explicitly include security incident *prevention* in the exception, amongst other changes. Detecting or responding to a security incident means the incident is already happening, and we want to ensure we do all we can to enable companies to protect consumers by preventing an incident in the first place.

III. Evaluation of ADPPA's Enforcement Provisions and Preemption

As the committee considers our recommendations for improvement, I would urge you to not lose sight of the fact that edits to specific provisions should not be considered in isolation, and that you should stay focused on how these provisions interrelate to and impact each other. In other words, a change to one section may well have an impact on a host of other sections. That is certainly the case when it comes to some of the key definitions, but also to other sections such as the enforcement provisions.

As mentioned above, ITI is on record in our FAIR Privacy framework as supporting strong redress and enforcement as essential to protecting American citizens' privacy rights. The discussion draft contains multiple prongs providing strong redress and enforcement, including robust FTC rulemaking and enforcement authorities including the establishment of a new bureau dedicated to enforcing the ADPPA (sec. 401) and enforcement by state attorneys general (AG) (sec. 402). These authorities must be evaluated in the context of the existing FTC and AG enforcement regimes, which are substantial and, by way of comparison, do not need to be built from the ground up as has been the case with other privacy regimes that have recently come on line (such as Brazil's LGPD).

Of course, the discussion draft notably includes a Private Right of Action (PRA) (sec. 403), and reasonable minds can disagree as to whether a PRA is necessary in light of the other strong enforcement provisions. While we appreciate staff's efforts to narrow the PRA provision, our members remain concerned that it is too broad and will not appreciably limit a likely wave of litigation, for at least three reasons. First, while it is true neither punitive nor statutory damages are permitted under the PRA, the availability of attorney's fees could encourage the filing of borderline meritorious cases by specialized attorneys charging exorbitant hourly rates. Second, while plaintiffs must provide 60 days' notice to the FTC and/or AGs to allow them to take over a case, the somewhat illogical result this approach may lead to may be that the *less* meritorious cases are the ones that will be pursued by private litigants in court. Third, and perhaps most importantly, the previous section summarized several key definitions in the discussion draft that are broad and/or unclear such as the key terms "sensitive data" and "covered entity"/"service provider" - the problems with these unclear terms will only be exacerbated by the availability of a PRA because lawsuits will inevitably be required to clarify which entities have what obligations under the law unless the definitions are substantially tightened.

The goal of the ADPPA or any privacy law should not just be to protect American citizens' privacy, but to do so in a way that does not unnecessarily hamstring U.S. businesses and continued data innovation. In the context of the discussion draft when considered as a whole, the PRA as currently drafted misses this mark. The committee should consider other reasonable limits on a PRA in order to allow consumers the ability to enforce their rights without subjecting industry to broad class action liability in lawsuits where there is no demonstrable harm to consumers. For instance, section 303 grants the FTC authority to issue regulations to establish a process for the proposal and approval of technical compliance programs for covered entities. The FTC, State AGs and courts must consider a covered entity's history of compliance with these programs in actions brought pursuant to sections 401-403. One idea worth considering is whether section 303 could be further strengthened, such as by considering whether submitting to a technical compliance program might be considered as a "safe harbor" to guard against the potential abuse of the PRA provision.

We stand ready to work with Committee staff to explore whether the PRA can be meaningfully cabined in this or other ways so as to reasonably maintain individuals' ability to pursue their rights without unnecessarily damaging businesses and the American economy.

With respect to preemption, ITI has long advocated for the inclusion of preemption in any federal privacy law, and we appreciate the ADPPA expresses the intent to preempt state consumer privacy laws covered by the provisions of the bill (sec. 404(b)). It appears the intent of the preemption clause is to be broadly preemptive subject to the specific exceptions in the savings clause. To clarify this intent, it would be helpful to note that the bill preempts not just laws that are specifically "covered by the provisions of this Act" but all laws "relating to the subject matter covered by this Act" minus the explicit exceptions.

Regarding the exceptions, the lengthy list of state laws that is preserved seems to include some laws that are at least in part covered by the ADPPA (e.g., Illinois' Biometric privacy law (BIPA)), but not other similar laws (e.g., Texas' biometric privacy law.) At a minimum, we would like to better understand the Committee's rationale for preempting some specific existing state privacy laws and not other similar laws.

The discussion draft explicitly preserves state consumer protection laws of general applicability in section 404(b)(2)(A), and we note the bracketed language there, which would prohibit pleading the fact of a violation of the ADPPA as an element of a violation of state consumer protection laws. These brackets should be removed because without this limitation the preemption clause would be rendered somewhat meaningless.

Conclusion

ITI and our member companies appreciate the committee's attention to this matter and its effort to develop a compromise solution to advance comprehensive federal privacy legislation. We share the committee's goal of enacting comprehensive federal privacy legislation, and we are committed to working with the Committee, others in Congress and the stakeholder community to find common ground. This is a highly complex bill impacting every American citizen's privacy rights and nearly every American company's ability to operate and innovate. We all agree we need to get privacy legislation done. But we should also all agree need to get privacy legislation right, because the stakes are too high.

If we take a clear-eyed view of the ADPPA, we must acknowledge that the bill is not perfect. But we must also fairly acknowledge the discussion draft represents arguably the best chance we have ever had to move the ball forward on federal privacy legislation to prove to American citizens and the world that the United States takes privacy seriously and protects it in a way that maintains American companies' continued leadership in driving innovation globally.

As ITI continues to gather feedback on the discussion draft of the ADPPA from its member companies, we look forward to sharing that feedback with the committee. Thank you again for the opportunity to testify today, and I look forward to your questions.

*Ms. Schakowsky. Thank you.

And now, I recognize Ms. Fitzgerald for five minutes for your statement.

Statement of Caitriona Fitzgerald, Deputy Director, Electronic Privacy Information Center

*Ms. Fitzgerald. Chairwoman Schakowsky, Ranking Member Bilirakis, Chairman Pallone, and Ranking Member McMorris Rodgers, members of the subcommittee, thank you for your leadership on the American Data Privacy and Protection Act, for holding this important hearing, and for the opportunity to testify today.

I am Caitriona Fitzgerald, deputy director at the Electronic Privacy Information Center, or EPIC. EPIC is an independent non-profit research center established in 1994 to protect privacy, freedom of expression, and democratic values in the information age.

For over 20 years, EPIC has been calling on Congress to pass comprehensive federal privacy legislation. Unfortunately, for the past two decades, powerful technology companies have been allowed to set the terms of our online interactions. These companies have more economic and political power than many countries.

In the absence of a federal privacy law, they have been allowed to deploy commercial surveillance systems that collect and can modify every bit of our personal data. Through a vast opaque system of databases and algorithms, we are sorted into winners and losers based on who we are, where we go, what we made, what we search for, and more.

These monitored surveillance systems are too complex and opaque for the vast majority of Americans to understand or control. We do not need any more evidence that self-regulation doesn't work. It has put us in this crisis, and it is just going to get worse and worse until a strong privacy law is passed, and the longer Congress delays, the harder it will get to reign in these harmful business practices.

And the investigative journalists at The Markup have exposed some of the worst data abuses happening today. For example, when they scanned hundreds of sensitive – of websites on sensitive topics – they discovered an alarming amount of tracking, including a state agency page on how to report child abuse was sending data about its users to ad tech companies.

The Mayo Clinic was using keylogging to capture health information that individuals typed into forms for appointments or clinical trials. Even if they closed out the form without hitting submit, that was saved in a folder that was titled "webforms for marketers."

Buzzfeed recently reported that users of the app pray.com were surprised to learn that the company was releasing information about them to third parties including Facebook. They knew they could be targeted with ads based on the content they engaged with on pray.com and users rightly felt that this went against the private personal nature of prayer.

Nearly every week, there is new story about location data being packaged and sold. A top catholic church official was recently forced to resign after a catholic media site outed him using cell phone data to show that the priest was a regular user of Grindr and visited gay bars.

Trackers collect millions of data points each day that are then sold or transferred to data brokers who combine them with other data sources linked to us to build invasive profiles which are then made available for sale.

Often, these profiles are used to target people with ads that stalk them across the web; and in other cases, the profiles are fed into secret algorithms that are used to determine interest rates on mortgages and credit cards or deny jobs, depriving people of opportunities and perpetuating structural inequalities.

Even our children are not safe from unfettered data collection and processing or profiling. The Markup recently released an extensive investigation of software used in K to 12 schools, and one company PowerSchool was found to be using algorithms that relied on free and reduced lunch status to predict a student's future success and provide teachers with graduation risk scores as early as seventh grade.

These industries and systems have gone unregulated for more than two decades and this is where it has left us. The system is broken. Technology companies have too much power, and individuals too little, but it does not have to be this way. We can have a strong technology sector in the United States while protecting personal privacy. We need to retake control of our personal information from the entities that want to hoard our data and monetize it.

And the American Data Privacy and Protection Act does this by focusing on data minimization which shifts the obligation to protect privacy away from individuals, and instead, requires companies to limit their collection and use of personal data.

Now, the U.S. is in data privacy crisis. You all know that. There is work to be done on the bill, but the American Data Privacy and Protection Act presents Congress with the opportunity, right now, to reclaim privacy as a meaningful right and reestablish America as a global leader on privacy. We need Congress to move strong privacy legislation forward this session to stop the very real harms that are happening online every minute of every day.

It is time to change the business models that have led to today's commercial surveillance systems. Please do not let this moment pass. The time to act is now.

Thank you for the opportunity to testify today, and I look forward to your questions.

[The prepared statement of Ms. Fitzgerald follows:]

Statement of Caitriona Fitzgerald, Deputy Director, Electronic Privacy Information Center (EPIC), Hearing on "Protecting America's Consumers: Bipartisan Legislation to Strengthen Data Privacy and Security," before the House Committee on Energy & Commerce, Subcommittee on Consumer Protection and Commerce, United States House of Representatives, June 14, 2022

Chair Schakowsky, Ranking Member Bilirakis, and members of the Subcommittee, thank you for holding this hearing and for the opportunity to testify today on the American Data Privacy and Protection Act. My name is Caitriona Fitzgerald, Deputy Director at the Electronic Privacy Information Center, or EPIC. EPIC is an independent nonprofit research organization in Washington, DC, established in 1994 to protect privacy, freedom of expression, and democratic values in the information age.

For more than two decades, powerful tech companies have been allowed to set the terms of our online interactions. Without any meaningful restrictions on their business practices, they have built systems that invade our private lives, spy on our families, and gather the most intimate details about us for profit. These companies have more economic and political power than many countries and states. Through a vast, opaque system of databases and algorithms, we are profiled and sorted into winners and losers based on data about our health, finances, location, gender, race, and other personal characteristics and habits. The impacts of these commercial surveillance systems are especially harmful for marginalized and multi-marginalized communities, fostering discrimination and inequities in employment, government services, health and healthcare, education, and other life necessities.

But it does not have to be this way – we can have a strong technology sector in the United States while protecting personal privacy. We need to retake control of our personal information from the entities that want to collect it, use it, and disclose it for any and every purpose they choose. We do not need any more evidence that self-regulation by technology companies does not work. The result of lack of regulation is clear and it has put us in this crisis. The longer Congress delays, the more difficult it will be to rein in these harmful business practices. It is long past time to establish comprehensive protections for privacy and civil rights online. Congress must act now to reclaim privacy as a meaningful right and to protect personal data. The American Data Privacy and Protection Act presents Congress with the best opportunity it has had in decades to stop the very real harms that are happening online every minute of every day.

In my testimony I will discuss the crisis we face today due to the lack of a comprehensive U.S. privacy law, how the American Data Privacy and Protection Act addresses that crisis, and some opportunities to improve the bill.

A. The United States' Data Privacy Crisis: Surveillance Capitalism Run Wild

The United States now faces a data privacy crisis. The lack of a comprehensive U.S. privacy law has allowed abusive data practices to flourish, threatening our rights and institutions. Robust data protection standards are essential to ensure the preservation of human rights and dignity and the healthy functioning of our democracy.

Due to the failure of policymakers in the United States to establish adequate data protection standards, online firms have been allowed to deploy commercial surveillance systems that collect and commodify every bit of our personal data.[50] The platforms and data brokers that track us across the internet and build detailed profiles to target us with ads also expose us to ever-increasing risks of breaches, data misuse, manipulation, and discrimination.[51]

The notice-and-choice approach to privacy regulation that dominated the United States' response to this uncontrolled data collection over the last three decades simply does not work. The focus on notice has led to longer and more complicated privacy policies that users do not read and could not change even if they did. And modern surveillance systems, including the schemes used to track our digital and physical activities across the web and across devices, are too complex and opaque for the vast majority of internet users to understand or control.

BuzzFeed recently reported that religious social networking service and app Pray.com was collecting detailed information about its users, including the texts of their posts, and linking it

---

[50] *See generally* Shoshana Zuboff, *The Age of Surveillance Capitalism* (2019).

[51] *See* Consumer Fed. of America, *Factsheet: Surveillance Advertising: How Does the Tracking Work?* (Aug. 26, 2021), https://consumerfed.org/consumer_info/factsheet-surveillance-advertising-how-tracking-works/.

with information obtained from third-parties and data brokers.[52] Pray.com was also releasing detailed data about its users with third-parties, including Facebook, meaning "users could be targeted with ads on Facebook based on the content they engage with on Pray.com — including content modules with titles like 'Better Marriage,' 'Abundant Finance,' and 'Releasing Anger.'"[53] Users of the app called these practices "exploitative," "manipulative," and "predatory," and said they went against the private nature of prayer.[54]

In 2020, The Markup found that one-third of websites surveyed contained Facebook's tracking pixel, which allows Facebook to identify users (whether or not they are logged into Facebook) and connect those website visits to their Facebook profiles.[55] The Markup also scanned hundreds of websites on sensitive topics and discovered an alarming volume of tracking, including:

- A state agency page on how to report child abuse sending data about its visitors to six ad tech companies;
- WebMD and Everyday Health sending visitor data to dozens of marketing companies; and
- The Mayo Clinic using key logging to capture health information individuals typed into web forms for appointments and clinical trials, regardless of whether the individual even submitted the form or not—information which was saved to a folder titled "web forms for marketers/tracking."[56]

These trackers collect millions of data points each day that are sold or transferred to data brokers, who then combine them with other personal data sources to build invasive profiles. Often these profiles are used to target people with "personalized" advertisements that stalk them across the web. In other cases these profiles are fed into secret algorithms used to determine the interest rates on mortgages and credit cards, to raise consumers' interest rates, or to deny people jobs, depriving people of opportunities and perpetuating structural inequalities.[57]

B. Data Minimization Is Critical in Limiting Unfettered Data Collection

The ubiquitous online surveillance described above causes substantial and widespread privacy harms. Data minimization offers a solution. Data minimization sets limits on processing which

---

52 Emily Baker-White, *Nothing Sacred: These Apps Reserve The Right To Sell Your Prayers*, BuzzFeed (Jan. 25, 2022), https://www.buzzfeednews.com/article/emilybakerwhite/apps-selling-your-prayers.

53 *Id.*

54 *Id.*

55 Julia Angwin, *What They Know... Now,* The Markup (Sept. 22, 2020), https://themarkup.org/blacklight/2020/09/22/what-they-know-now.

56 Aaron Sankin & Surya Mattu, *The High Privacy Cost of a "Free" Website*, The Markup (Sept. 22, 2020), https://themarkup.org/blacklight/2020/09/22/blacklight-tracking-advertisers-digital-privacy-sensitive-websites.

57 *See Protecting Consumer Privacy in the Age of Big Data*, 116th Cong. (2019), H. Comm. on the Energy & Comm., Subcomm. on Consumer Protection and Comm. (Feb. 26, 2019) (testimony of Brandi Collins-Dexter, Color of Change), https://energycommerce.house.gov/sites/democrats.energycommerce.house.gov/files/documents/Brandi%20Collins%20Dexter%2002.26.2019.pdf.

requires data to be used *specifically* to deliver the goods and services that an individual has requested, consistent with the consumer's expectations. Companies complying with data minimization requirements must also delete personal information when it is no longer needed to serve the purpose for which it was collected.

Section 101 of the American Data Privacy and Protection Act establishes limits on the unfettered processing of personal data by requiring that entities only collect, use, and transfer data that is reasonably necessary, proportionate, and limited to: (1) provide a specific product or service requested by the individual or (2) a communication reasonably anticipated within the context of the relationship, with some exceptions specifically spelled out in section 209. The adoption of data minimization techniques consistent with this rule is essential to data protection across the board.[58]

Data minimization is essential for both consumers and businesses. Data minimization principles provide much needed standards for data security, access, and accountability, assign responsibilities with respect to user data, and restrict data collection and use. Indeed, a data minimization rule can provide clear guidance to businesses when designing and implementing systems for data collection, storage, use, and transfer. And data security will be improved because personal data that is not collected in the first place cannot be at risk of a data breach.

Data minimization is not a new concept; it just needs to be applied as a rule to all personal data collection online. Privacy laws dating back to the 1970s have recognized and applied this concept. The Privacy Act of 1974, a landmark privacy law regulating the personal data practices of federal agencies, requires data minimization. Each agency that collects personal data shall "maintain in its records only such information about an individual as is relevant and necessary to accomplish a purpose of the agency required to be accomplished by statute or by executive order of the President."[59]

The recently passed update to the California Consumer Privacy Act also includes provisions requiring a limited form of data minimization.[60] The European Union General Data Protection Regulation (GDPR) requires companies, among other things, to minimize collection of consumer data to what is "[a]dequate, relevant, and limited to what is necessary in relation to the purposes for which they are processed."[61] This means that many companies that would be covered by this bill are already complying with data minimization rules for users in other jurisdictions.

Human beings are more than data points to be sold to advertisers and data brokers. We all deserve privacy and autonomy with respect to our personal information. Individuals should be allowed to browse the internet or scroll through their favorite apps without worrying whether companies will use their own data in ways they do not anticipate. Data minimization offers a practical solution to a broken internet ecosystem by providing clear limits on how companies can collect and use data. EPIC encourages the Subcommittee to retain the data minimization

---

[58] *See* EPIC & Consumer Reports, *How the FTC Can Mandate Data Minimization Through a Section 5 Unfairness Rulemaking* (Jan. 2022), https://epic.org/documents/how-the-ftc-can-mandate-data-minimization-through-a-section- 5-unfairness-rulemaking/; *see also* Access Now, *Data minimization: Key to protecting privacy and reducing harm* (May 2021), https://www.accessnow.org/data-minimization-guide/.

[59] 5 U.S.C. § 552a (e)(1).

[60] Cal. Civ. Code § 1798.100(c).

[61] Regulation (EU) 2016/679 (General Data Protection Regulation) Art. 5 § 1(c).

provisions in section 101 of the bill and to pair them with a duty of loyalty that will require companies to act in the best interest of the individuals whose data they collect.[62]

C. Some Forms of Sensitive Data Uses Deserve Even Higher Protections

Some types and uses of data are especially sensitive and warrant even stricter regulation. For instance, biometric, genetic, and precise geolocation data are inherently sensitive. But even information about the products people buy and the services they search for can qualify as sensitive if used to make inferences about individuals' health, religious beliefs, economic situations, and other characteristics.

Nearly every week there is a new story about how precise location data is being packaged and sold to the highest bidder. Location data can be combined with other data to reveal an individual's movements or to track them in real time, which can pose a significant threat to physical safety. Location data can also reveal sensitive information about individuals including their religious affiliation, their personal and political beliefs, their sexual orientation, their health status, or other sensitive categories. Despite common assurances from companies, precise location data is not "anonymous" and can in many cases be linked back to an individual. Last year, a top Catholic Church official was forced to resign after a Catholic media site used cellphone data to show that the priest was a regular user of the queer dating app Grindr and visited gay bars.[63] Both Google[64] and location data firms[65] have been found harvesting users' locations even after they have opted out. The Centers for Disease Control paid $420,000 to access one year of location data from data broker SafeGraph to track patterns of tens of millions of Americans during the COVID-19 pandemic.[66]

Health data is another category of data that requires heightened protection. Many people assume that the health data they enter in apps is protected by the Health Information Portability and Accountability Act (HIPAA), but it is frequently not. HIPAA only covers health care providers, health insurers, and health care clearinghouses. Last year, Flo Health, the developer of a popular fertility-tracking app, settled a Federal Trade Commission complaint alleging that the company shared health information of its users with outside data analytics providers, including Facebook and Google, after promising such information would be kept private.[67] But the only reason the FTC was able to bring a case against the company is that Flo Health misled users in its privacy policy, stating that the company and app would not share users' health

---

62 *See* Neil M. Richards & Woodrow Hartzog, *Legislating Data Loyalty*, (June 8, 2022). 97 Notre Dame L. Rev. Reflection 356 (2022), https://papers.ssrn.com/sol3/papers.cfm?abstract_id=4131523.

63 Michelle Boorstein et al., *Top U.S. Catholic Church official resigns after cellphone data used to track him on Grindr and to gay bars*, Wash. Post (July 21, 2021), https://www.washingtonpost.com/religion/2021/07/20/bishop- misconduct-resign-burrill/.

64 Ryan Nakashima, *Google tracks your movements*, like it or not, Assoc. Pres (Aug. 13, 2018), https://apnews.com/article/north-america-science-technology-business-ap-top-news-828aefab64d4411bac257a07c1af0ecb.

65 Joseph Cox, *Location Data Firm Got GPS Data From Apps Even When People Opted Out*, Vice (Oct. 25, 2021), https://www.vice.com/en/article/5dgmqz/huq-location-data-opt-out-no-consent.

66 Joseph Cox, *CDC Tracked Millions of Phones to See If Americans Followed COVID Lockdown Orders*, Vice (May 3, 2022), https://www.vice.com/en/article/m7vymn/cdc-tracked-phones-location-data-curfews.

67 *In re Flo Health, Inc.*, FTC File No. 192-3133 (June 2021), https://www.ftc.gov/legal-library/browse/cases-proceedings/192-3133-flo-health-inc.

details with anyone. If Flo Health had simply disclosed these practices in their privacy policy, there would be no federal law expressly prohibiting the company from transferring users' sensitive fertility data to marketers and third parties.

The American Data Privacy and Protection Act rightly recognizes that some sensitive categories and uses of data deserve stricter controls and would halt some of these dangerous business practices. Section 204 requires that, on top of meeting the data minimization threshold, a covered entity may not collect, process, or transfer an individual's sensitive personal data without affirmative express consent. And for some categories of data—including precise geolocation data, social security numbers, biometric information, and genetic data—section 102 prohibits transfers outright or restricts them to very limited circumstances.

The concern with sensitive data is that it can easily be misused and causes significant harm if breached. U.S. privacy law should strictly limit the collection, use, and transferring of sensitive data.

D. Algorithmic Oversight is Particularly Important in Mitigating Harms to Marginalized Communities

The use of artificial intelligence and other automated systems to make decisions about individuals poses significant risks to fundamental rights. Public and private actors are increasingly relying on automated decision-making tools to determine eligibility for jobs, education, housing, parole, bail, credit, insurance, healthcare, and government services.[68] The error, bias, and discriminatory patterns embedded in these systems perpetuate systemic inequality,[69] yet neither public agencies nor private companies are typically required to evaluate the impacts and biases of these systems before they use them.

Indeed, many automated decision-making systems have been deployed by both government agencies and private companies with little to no oversight, despite questions regarding their effectiveness.[70] A 2019 National Institute of Standards and Technology ("NIST") study of facial recognition tools—which are typically "AI-based"[71]—found that the systems were up to 100 times more likely to return a false positive for a non-white person than for a white person.[72] Specifically, NIST found that "for one-to-many matching, the team saw higher rates of false positives for African American females," a finding that is "particularly important because the consequences could include false accusations."[73] A separate study by Stanford University and MIT, which looked at three widely deployed commercial facial

---

[68] Danielle Keats Citron & Frank Pasquale, *The Scored Society: Due Process for Automated Predictions*, 89 Wash. L. Rev. 1 (2014).

[69] *See* Rashida Richardson, *Racial Segregation and the Data-Driven Society: How Our Failure to Reckon with Root Causes Perpetuates Separate and Unequal Realities*, 36 Berkeley Tech. L.J. 3 (2022).

[70] David Freeman Engstrom, Daniel E. Ho, Catherine M. Sharkey, & Mariano-Florentino Cuéllar, *Government by Algorithm: Artificial Intelligence in Federal Administrative Agencies* 6 (Feb. 2020), https://www-cdn.law.stanford.edu/wp-content/uploads/2020/02/ACUS-AI-Report.pdf.

[71] Nat'l Inst. Standards & Tech., *Face Recognition Vendor Test (FRVT) Part 3: Demographic Effects* 14 (Dec. 2019), https://nvlpubs.nist.gov/nistpubs/ir/2019/NIST.IR.8280.pdf.

[72] Nat'l Inst. Standards & Tech., *NIST Study Evaluates Effects of Race, Age, Sex on Face Recognition Software* (Dec. 19, 2019), https://www.nist.gov/news-events/news/2019/12/nist-study-evaluates-effects-race-age-sex-face-recognition-software.

[73] *Id.*

recognition tools, found an error rate of 34.7% for dark-skinned women compared to an error rate of 0.8% for light-skinned men.[74] A review of Rekognition—an Amazon-owned facial recognition system marketed to law enforcement—revealed indications of racial bias and found that the system misidentified 28 members of U.S. Congress as convicted criminals.[75] This type of facial recognition is used in public benefit verification, job applicant screening tools, remote test proctoring systems, and numerous other sensitive contexts.

Consumers are often surprised to learn that decisions impacting their lives[76] were made using algorithms. In healthcare settings, consumers have been shocked to discover that data collected by their essential health equipment was used to make reimbursement decisions.[77] Insurance firms have fed patients' financial investment data, car ownership records, cell phone numbers, and property records into algorithms to predict health outcomes and generate health risk scores.[78]

Even our children are not safe from having decisions made about them by opaque algorithms. The Markup recently released results from an extensive investigation of software used in K-12 schools. One company, PowerSchool, was found to be using algorithms that relied on indicators of family wealth, such as free and reduced lunch status, to "predict" a student's future success and provide teachers with graduation risk scores as early as seventh grade.[79] PowerSchool claims to have data on 75% of K-12 students in North America.[80]

The Markup also examined Naviance software, which is used by approximately two- thirds of high school students in the U.S. to research and apply to college. Naviance was found to gather data on students as they used the software and to allow colleges to target students with paid advertisements promoting enrollment.[81] The Markup obtained contracts showing that numerous universities, including the University of Kansas, University of Southern Maine, and

---

74 Joy Buolamwini & Timnit Gebru, *Gender Shades: Intersectional Accuracy Disparities in Commercial Gender Classification,* Proceedings of Machine Learning Research 81:1–15 (2018), https://www.media.mit.edu/publications/gender-shades-intersectional-accuracy-disparities-in-commercial-gender- classification/.

75 Russell Brandom, *Amazon's facial recognition matched 28 members of Congress to criminal mugshots*, The Verge (July 26, 2018), https://www.theverge.com/2018/7/26/17615634/amazon-rekognition-aclu-mug-shot- congress-facial-recognition.

76 *See* Genevieve Smith & Ishita Rustagi, *When Good Algorithms Go Sexist: Why and How to Advance AI Gender Equity*, Stan. Soc. Innov. Rev. (Mar. 31, 2021), https://ssir.org/articles/entry/when_good_algorithms_go_sexist_why_and_how_to_advance_ai_gender_equity ("A husband and wife compared their Apple Card spending limits and found that the husband's credit line was 20 times greater. Customer service employees were unable to explain why the algorithm deemed the wife significantly less creditworthy.").

77 *See* All Things Considered, *How Insurers Are Profiting Off Patients With Sleep Apnea*, NPR (Nov. 21, 2018), https://www.npr.org/2018/11/21/670142105/how-insurers-are-profiting-off-patients-with-sleep-apnea ("And that's when he realized that the machine was actually spying on him and tracking his sleep habits and sleep patterns. And the irony is he wasn't able to use the machine because he didn't have the new mask and yet they hadn't been sending the new mask because they said he wasn't using the machine.").

78 *See* Marshall Allen, *Health Insurers Are Vacuuming Up Details About You—And It Could Raise Your Rates*, ProPublica (July 17, 2018), https://www.propublica.org/article/health-insurers-are-vacuuming-up-details-about-you- and-it-could-raise-your-rates.

79 Todd Feathers, *This Private Equity Firm Is Amassing Companies That Collect Data on America's Children*, The Markup (Jan. 11, 2022), https://themarkup.org/machine-learning/2022/01/11/this-private-equity-firm-is-amassing-companies-that-collect-data-on-americas-children.

80 *Id.*

81 Todd Feathers, *College Prep Software Naviance Is Selling Advertising Access to Millions of Students*, The Markup (Jan. 13, 2022), https://themarkup.org/machine-learning/2022/01/13/college-prep-software-naviance-is- selling-advertising-access-to-millions-of-students.

the University of Massachusetts Boston used the software to target their enrollment ads only to white students.[82]

These data practices threaten individual privacy and civil rights, and companies have proven time and again that they cannot police themselves.[83] The provisions of the American Data Privacy and Protection Act that extend civil rights protections online and provide oversight of algorithms are vital to protecting the public, especially marginalized individuals and communities.

The American Data Privacy and Protection Act sets accountability and transparency requirements for automated decision-making tools by requiring Algorithmic Impact Assessments and Algorithm Design Evaluations, which can provide meaningful oversight if done right.[84] EPIC does recommend adding more robust requirements to the impact assessments under section 207 so they do not simply become box-checking exercises.[85] Compelling businesses to explain how each algorithm was developed, the training data, and the anticipated purposes and capabilities would make these assessments more effective.

Unless express, binding limits on the use of AI are established *now*, the technology will quickly outpace our collective ability to regulate it. Effective algorithmic impact assessments with strong oversight are critical to protect against discriminatory uses of data and ensure fairness in decision-making.

E. Strong Enforcement Is Critical to Privacy Protection

Robust enforcement is the bedrock of effective privacy protection. This means both a private right of action and enforcement by authorities at the federal and state levels—including the authorities that are best suited to tackle data protection.

1. A Private Right of Action

A private right of action is a crucial tool to supplement administrative enforcement, and we applaud the drafters of this bill for coming to a workable compromise on a private right of action. If a company violates federal privacy law, affected individuals and groups of individuals should be able to pursue meaningful redress from that company on their own. While government enforcement is essential, the scope of data collection online is simply too vast for one entity—or even 50 entities—to regulate. Individuals and groups of individuals who use online services are in a good position to identify privacy issues and bring actions to vindicate their interests. In the absence of a private right of action, there is a very real risk that companies will not comply with the law because they think it is unlikely that they will be caught or fined.

---

[82] *Id.*

[83] *See generally* Ari Ezra Waldman, *Industry Unbound* (2021) (demonstrating that many privacy impact assessments conducted under GDPR have become little more than checkbox forms).

[84] *See* Ari Ezra Waldman, *Power, Process, and Automated Decision-Making*, 88 Fordham L. Rev. 613, 624 (2019), https://ir.lawnet.fordham.edu/cgi/viewcontent.cgi?article=5633&context=flr ("Procedural requirements like algorithmic impact assessments, source code transparency, explanations of either the result or the logic behind it, and a human in the loop who can hear someone's appeal move opaque automated systems closer to more familiar, and more accountable, decision-making regimes").

[85] *Id.* at 628 (citing Lauren Edelman, *Working Law: Courts, Corporations, and Symbolic Civil Rights* 100-50 (2016)).

Private enforcement ensures that data collectors have strong financial incentives to meet their data protection obligations.

Many privacy laws include a private right of action, and these provisions have historically made it possible to hold companies accountable for their privacy violations. Though the American Data Privacy and Protection Act does not include statutory damages, in the past Congress has frequently included statutory damages in privacy statutes to avoid protracted disputes over quantifying damages. This is important because it is often difficult to assign a specific economic value to the harm caused by a privacy violation.

For example, when Congress passed the Cable Communications Policy Act in 1984, it established privacy rights for cable subscribers and created a private right of action for recovery of liquidated damages of $100 per for violation or $1,000, whichever is higher.[86] The Video Privacy Protection Act specifies liquidated damages of $2,500.[87] The Fair Credit Reporting Act affords individuals a private right of action that can be pursued in federal or state court against credit reporting agencies, users of credit reports, and furnishers.[88] In certain circumstances, individuals can also recover attorney's fees, court costs, and punitive damages. The Driver's Privacy Protection Act similarly includes a private right of action.[89] The Telephone Consumer Protection Act allows individuals who receive unsolicited telemarketing calls to recover actual monetary loss or up to $500 in damages per violation.[90]

The statutory damages set by federal privacy laws are not large in an individual case, but they can provide a powerful incentive in large cases and are necessary to ensure that privacy rights will be taken seriously by businesses that process personal data. EPIC encourages the Subcommittee to add statutory damages to the private right of action in section 403.

2. Federal Agency Enforcement

Federal agency enforcement is also critical. EPIC has long advocated for the creation of a standalone Data Protection Agency,[91] but establishing a bureau within the Federal Trade Commission is a step in the right direction, provided Congress allocates adequate resources to the new bureau so the FTC can carry out all the regulatory and enforcement obligations required of the Commission in this bill.

We applaud the provisions in the American Data Privacy and Protection Act giving the FTC first-time civil penalty authority. Existing law severely constrains the Commission's power to impose financial consequences on companies that violate civil and privacy rights. Unless a company is already under an FTC consent decree, the Commission can generally only obtain civil penalties if a business violates a cease-and-desist order or a trade regulation rule, both of which require a lengthy administrative process. Enabling the Commission to seek civil penalties against first-time violators will be a powerful deterrent against exploitative data practices and a key tool for holding lawbreaking companies accountable.

---

[86] 47 USC § 551(f).

[87] 18 USC § 2710(c)(2).

[88] 15 U.S.C. §§ 1681n-1681o.

[89] 18 U.S.C. § 2724.

[90] 47 USC § 227(c)(5).

[91] *See Big Data: Privacy Risks and Needed Reforms in the Public and Private Sectors*, 117th Cong. (2021), H. Comm. on H. Admin. (Feb. 16, 2022) (testimony of Caitriona Fitzgerald, EPIC), https://epic.org/wp-content/uploads/2022/02/EPIC-HouseAdmin-Feb2022.pdf.

Rulemaking authority is also a cornerstone of effective data protection. Although the right to privacy is timeless, the ways that companies seek to use personal data and the technologies that process it are rapidly changing. Safeguarding the right to privacy in the internet era requires clear, detailed, and up-to-date rules developed with the benefit of public participation and agency expertise. It is critical that Congress give the FTC the authority to implement the American Data Privacy and Protection Act through public rulemaking processes. Rulemaking authority will enable the Commission to clarify the obligations of covered entities and the rights of individuals, to update those rules as technology and circumstances evolve, and to effectuate the purposes of the Act with input from all stakeholders.

As drafted, the Act includes FTC rulemaking authority to define new categories of sensitive covered data responsive to emerging privacy threats; to establish processes for access, correction, and deletion requests by individuals; to create a global mechanism enabling individuals to opt out of certain abusive data practices industry-wide; and to implement the Act's data security requirements. We support these provisions and urge Congress to ensure that the FTC has the power to implement other critical components of the Act through rulemaking, including the data minimization, duty of loyalty, and preemption sections.

3. Enforcement by State Attorneys General and Agencies

State Attorneys General have historically played a strong role in privacy enforcement, largely stemming from their consumer protection watchdog role.[92] The American Data Privacy and Protection Act rightly preserves and expands this critical enforcement role for state Attorneys General. The bill should also recognize that states may have specialized privacy enforcement agencies and should not limit authority specifically to the "attorney general of a State or the chief consumer protection officer."

F. It Is Time for the United States to Reclaim Its Role as a Global Leader for Privacy Protection

It is long past time for the United States to enact a comprehensive privacy regime and reclaim our role as a global leader in protecting individuals' fundamental rights to privacy and data protection.

Many who read about emerging privacy threats today think of how they will be analyzed under Europe's General Data Protection Regulation or even the emerging regulatory frameworks being developed in California, Colorado, and other states. But it was the United States Congress that stepped forward in the 1970s to tackle the emerging issues of records, computers, and the rights of citizens;[93] to address the threat of unfair and inaccurate consumer profiles; and to call for closer study of how to protect personal privacy in an information society.[94] And many decades before those more modern laws were passed, the very concept of

---

[92] Danielle K. Citron, *The Privacy Policymaking of State Attorneys General*, 92 Notre Dame L. Rev. 747 (2017), https://scholarship.law.nd.edu/ndlr/vol92/iss2/5/.

[93] U.S. Dep't of Health, Educ. & Welfare, Records, Computers, and the Rights of Citizens (1973), *available at* https://epic.org/documents/hew1973report/.

[94] U.S. Privacy Protection Study Comm'n, Personal Privacy in an Information Society (1977), *available at* https://archive.epic.org/privacy/ppsc1977report/.

privacy as an individual right was pioneered here in the United States by Louis Brandeis and Samuel Warren[95] and ultimately developed and implemented through state common law.[96] Even in the earliest days of the development of our federal communications regulations, privacy was recognized as a critical right and enshrined in statute.[97]

Indeed, the United States' leadership on privacy and legislation to preserve the security of electronic communications helped usher in the personal computing and internet revolutions that made possible so many aspects of our modern society. And yet at critical points in the development and deployment of these powerful technologies over the last three decades, Congress failed to modernize our critical legal infrastructure. Instead, the United States sat by as other countries took a proactive approach to reining in the harmful business practices and threats to individual rights that have emerged in the internet era.

The hands-off and self-regulatory approaches to regulating privacy and data collection practices have failed. But in many cases the hard work of consumer protection agencies, state attorneys general, and consumer advocates have held back some of the most egregious data abuses. And state lawmakers filled the gaps with new laws addressing emerging data protection problems. Now it is time for Congress to give federal and state authorities and consumer advocates the tools they need to protect privacy rights online.

The United States is uniquely positioned to tackle these hard problems. Despite having a strong rights-based approach and broad geographic impact, Europe's General Data Protection Regulation has faced criticism for its indeterminacy and a lack of strong enforcement.[98] That is why it is critical for Congress to establish clear and comprehensive rules backed by robust enforcement to protect Americans online and reestablish the U.S. as a global leader in both privacy protection and technological innovation.

Conclusion

Privacy is a fundamental right, and it is time for Congress to act to protect the privacy rights of all Americans. The bipartisan American Data Privacy and Protection Act presents Congress with the best opportunity it has had in decades to stop the very real data abuses and privacy harms that are happening every minute of every day. EPIC urges Congress to not let this moment pass without enacting strong protections for Americans' privacy. We need comprehensive data protection legislation, robust enforcement, and ample resources to ensure privacy, equality, and security in our online world.

Thank you for the opportunity to testify today.

Ms. Schakowsky. Thank you.

And now, Mr. Kantor, I recognize you for five minutes.

---

95 Samuel D. Warren & Louis D. Brandeis, *The Right to Privacy*, 4 Harv. L. R. 193 (1890).

96 William L. Prosser, Privacy, 48 Calif. L. Rev. 383 (1960).

97 *See* 47 U.S.C. § 605(a).

98 *See, e.g.*, Ilse Heine, Ctr. for Nat'l Sec. Studies, *3 Years Later: An Analysis of GDPR Enforcement* (2021), https://www.csis.org/blogs/strategic-technologies-blog/3-years-later-analysis-gdpr-enforcement.

Statement of Doug Kantor, General Counsel, National Association of Convenience Stores

*Mr. Kantor. Well, thank you for having me on the panel today. Thank you all, and I, in particular, want to thank the chairs and ranking members of the full and subcommittee for your dedication to finding a compromise on this issue. It is one that has bedeviled generations of law makers and generations of outside groups trying to find a national privacy law, and it is a significant moment that we have a bipartisan compromise.

I am here on behalf of the National Association of Convenience Stores as well as the Main Street Privacy Coalition. I represent lots of regular old brick and mortar businesses. I think, I am the only person at the table who does.

One of the things that we urge in the midst of these discussions is, that our focus on the internet and on technology companies not distract us from the fact that any legislation in this area will regulate everyone, including those boring old brick and mortar businesses, and it needs to work for everyone.

That's a difficult thing to do given how incredibly different the business model of a corner convenience store is from the largest most defistocated (sic) technology companies in the nation and in the world that this bill will get at.

One of the ways that is really important, and this was pointed out by ITI in their testimony as well, is figuring out that relationship between covered businesses, many of them brick and mortar businesses like I represent, and service providers in the bill. That is often the big technology companies.

We think there are some innovations in this bill that are extremely helpful that is, it spells out in statute what the various responsibilities are of those entities. Some previous bills had left those things to contract, and that is just a prescription for saying, "The bigger company with more market power will decide who is liable and how these responsibilities get doled out."

We appreciate that you have avoided that pitfall. We do think that there is more that can be done in this bill to spell out those responsibilities, so that it is clear everybody needs to comply with each part of the bill, and in particular, sections 203 and 204 which spell out consumer rights.

There are ways in which some of these big technology companies as service providers will not need to fulfill those responsibilities and that responsibility may fall on the brick and mortar business or other consumer-facing business and that liability, we don't think is right; and frankly, we don't think for consumers that they should be put in the position of not getting the rights that it looks like they should have in the bill because those service providers can hide behind the customer-facing business.

A similar area that we worry about a lot is the need to cover a group of entities that are outside of the jurisdiction of this committee. That is financial services companies, and we exchanged data – our members do – with financial services companies of all kinds millions of times every day. Just the convenience store industry does a hundred and sixty-five million transactions a day. That is a lot of data.

To make sure people are protected, those financial services companies need to be covered by the bill, and we urge the committee to work with the financial services committee and eventually with the Senate banking committee to make sure those companies are covered, otherwise, we can't do our job fully to work with them and make sure that all of those types of data – some of which is the most sensitive data we have – is covered by the bill, and people's rights are afforded there.

We also think there is more that we can do with respect to the preemption provision of the bill. Courts are loathed to preempt state laws, and one of the reasons they often in the case law don't preempt state laws is where there are a lot of exceptions to a preemption provision, and we think there is case law that can give good guidance to show how to make it follow what we believe is the author's intent to preempt state privacy laws.

We are also concerned like many business folks about private rights of action, and in particular, I will note how that might interplay with other parts of the bill here like the pricing loyalty provision of the bill that appears to try to save customer loyalty programs.

Lots of our folks like these programs. Their customers love them – buy five cups of coffee, get one free, get a free ice cream on your birthday. Everybody likes that stuff. We don't want to get rid of those, and we are concerned that, in particular, based on the lawyers committee testimony in reading of the Private of Action provisions, some of those programs and other just discounts in sales could be put at risk.

So we look forward to working with you on all of those items and appreciate all the work that has gotten us here today.

Thank you.

[The prepared statement of Mr. Kantor follows:]

Testimony of Doug Kantor, General Counsel, National Association of Convenience Stores, before the Subcommittee on Consumer Protection and Commerce of the U.S. House of Representatives, Committee on Energy & Commerce, Hearing on "Protecting America's Consumers: Bipartisan Legislation to Strengthen Data Privacy and Security," June 14, 2022

Thank you for providing me with the opportunity to testify on data privacy and security.

I am testifying today on behalf of my association, the National Association of Convenience Stores (NACS), as well as a coalition that we helped found to try to address these issues, the Main Street Privacy Coalition (MSPC). NACS is an international trade association representing the interests of the convenience industry. In the United States, the industry includes more than 148,000 stores employing 2.3 million people. It is truly an industry of small business with a full 60 percent of the industry comprised of single-store operators. The industry handles about 165 million transactions each day – a number equivalent to about half of the U.S. population. The large volume of data exchanged through those transactions is just one aspect of the business that requires the use and exchange of data to facilitate commerce.

The MSPC is comprised of a broad array of 19 national trade associations that together represent more than a million businesses that line America's Main Streets. From retailers to Realtors®, hotels to home builders, grocery stores to restaurants, gas stations to travel plazas, and self-storage to convenience stores, MSPC member companies interact with consumers day in and day out. Our members' businesses can be found in every town, city and state in our nation, providing jobs, supporting our economy and serving Americans as a vital part of their communities. Collectively, the industries that MSPC trade groups represent directly employ approximately 34 million Americans and constitute over one-fifth of the U.S. economy by contributing $4.5 trillion (or 21.8%) to the U.S. gross domestic product.[99]

I. Executive Summary

NACS and the MSPC have long advocated for a uniform national privacy law. Having data privacy and security laws that create clear protections for Americans while allowing our members' businesses to serve their customers in the ways they have come to rely upon is a key goal. Achieving that goal, however, has been elusive. One of the challenges that has been central to this effort is that the overwhelming focus on the data practices of technology companies by many participants in public debates about privacy should not blind us to the fact that privacy law needs to work for Main Street. We appreciate our discussions with the Committee on these questions to date and hope that those discussions will continue as work is done to improve the draft legislation before the Committee.

Given the diverse and complex ways that data is used in our modern world, it helps to have principles to guide efforts to find effective ways to regulate in this area. We think adhering to the following seven principles can help achieve the best public policy results in this area.

- Establish Uniform Nationwide Rules and Enforcement for Data Privacy
- Ensure Industry Neutrality and Equal Protection for Consumers Across Business Sectors
- Impose Direct Statutory Obligations (Rather than Contractual Requirements Alone) for All Entities that Handle Consumer Data
- Preserve Customer Rewards and Benefits
- Achieve Transparency and Customer Choice
- Ensure Accountability for Business's Own Actions
- Include Reasonable Data Security Requirements

The American Data Privacy and Protection Act (ADPPA or the Act) represents an important milestone on the road to achieving a national data privacy standard that meets these principles. We see the intent in the Act to work toward each of the principles set forth above. We also see a number of areas in which additional work will be important to ensure that the Act fulfills the policy goals intended by its authors.

Among the most impactful areas in which we see the benefits of additional work on the bill include the need to cover all industry sectors and participants that interact with data covered by the Act. Currently, the Act creates a rule whereby financial services firms subject to a law that does not have privacy requirements that give consumers credible protection are deemed to be in compliance with the Act. There needs to be a plan to work with the House Financial Services and Senate Banking Committees to rectify that issue and cover financial services companies in the Act.

Additional work should also be done to ensure that the vast category of "service providers" that do the bulk of the work of collecting, processing, transmitting, storing, and transferring

---

[99] Information on the MSPC including a full list of its members can be found at https://mainstreetprivacy.com/about/.

data in our modern economy are fully responsible for their role in such work and required to comply with every aspect of the Act as they are able. The Act has language in some areas to advance this goal, but also has language that creates uncertainty which can and should be addressed. More importantly, each of the privacy laws enacted in four States the past two years require service providers to be responsible for protecting consumers' data to a greater extent than this Act, and we urge the Committee to match or exceed those protections.

How any data privacy law handles the questions of whether and on what basis individuals may be able to bring lawsuits against businesses under the law, as well as whether and how a federal law preempts state laws, will be controversial at every stage of the legislative process – and for many years following the passage of any such law. Those two issues have long blocked progress on other aspects of privacy legislation. We appreciate that the work and dedication of the staff and Members of this Committee to put forward a bipartisan legislative draft is allowing all of us to focus on other issues. But, these two issues merit additional attention and we believe changes are in order to ensure that the Act creates a scheme that works for consumers and businesses – and follows the intended goals of the authors.

We also see ways for the language of the Act to be modified to ensure that consumers continue to get the benefits that they have come to expect from the business community and our economic system. These include access to loyalty discounts and rewards that Main Street businesses provide as well as competition on prices and product and service offerings that is enhanced by many forms of advertising that are broadly accepted by consumers.

In addition, there are a number of areas in which additional interpretive and substantive issues can be addressed through continued collaborative work on the Act. We appreciate the effort and dedication it took to get us to a hearing on a bipartisan draft of privacy legislation and the opportunity you have afforded us to be part of that process. We look forward to continued efforts to get us to our shared goal of a uniform law that works for American consumers and businesses alike.

II. Key Principles Essential to Privacy Legislation

The exchange of data is central to much of the world's commerce. Simply to ensure that business occurs as intended on a daily basis requires large volumes of data to be used and exchanged by a multiplicity of different actors. The ways in which this happens is incredibly diverse across the economy and therefore quite complex. That diversity and complexity is one of the reasons that writing legislation to cover privacy is so challenging.

Take just one simple example that illustrates the complexity of this topic. When a consumer walks into a convenience store to buy some bubble gum and uses a credit or debit card, simply to ensure that can happen the card data must go from the store's terminal over another company's data lines to a payment processor and/or the store's bank and then over more data lines (which may or may not be owned by the same company) to a payment card network (such as Visa or Mastercard) and then over more data lines to the bank that issued the consumer the credit or debit card . . . and then the entire process happens again in reverse. All of that happens in seconds (or fractions of a second) so that the consumer can walk out of the store with gum.

Later, for most transactions, the data travels through a similar process to ensure that the funds are properly settled in the right account.

That is just one of the most common examples which happens millions of times each day all over the nation and must happen for some of our most basic needs for goods and services to be met. There are innumerable other ways in which data is exchanged that are also necessary for our economy to operate in the ways that we have come to expect. And, of course, there are other ways in which data is exchanged and used that raise questions about what we should and should not allow – and the degree of control that all of us as individuals should be in a position to exercise regarding how our data is used.

To make sense of privacy policy in light of the vast number of complex data-sharing activities that happen on a regular basis, it helps to have some guiding principles. Once you lose sight of those, it is easy to lose your way in this area.

In our view, those principles should be:

- *Establishing Uniform Nationwide Rules and Enforcement for Data Privacy* – Congress should create a sensible, uniform federal framework for data privacy regulation that benefits consumers and businesses alike by ensuring that sensitive consumer information is protected in a consistent manner regardless of the state in which a consumer resides. Preempting state laws by enacting a set of nationwide rules for all businesses handling consumers' personal data is necessary to achieve the important, national public policy goal of uniform consumer privacy protections.
- *Industry Neutrality and Equal Protection for Consumers Across Business Sectors* – Federal data privacy frameworks and legislation should apply requirements to all industries that handle personal data and not place a disproportionate burden on certain sectors of the economy while simultaneously alleviating other sectors from providing equal protection of consumer data. An equivalent data privacy standard should apply, regardless of whether a business directly collected data from a consumer or obtained it in a business-to-business transaction.
- *Direct Statutory Obligations (Rather than Contractual Requirements Alone) for All Entities that Handle Consumer Data* – Effective consumer protection regulations cannot be achieved by relying on some businesses to regulate the conduct of other businesses through contracts alone. Data service providers and other third parties need direct statutory obligations to ensure they comply with relevant privacy laws, particularly those offering transmission, storage, analytical processing or other consumer data services for thousands of small businesses.
- *Preservation of Customer Rewards and Benefits* – Any federal data privacy framework should preserve the ability of consumers and businesses to voluntarily establish mutually beneficial business-customer relationships and set the terms of those relationships. Federal law should include safe harbors to ensure that consumers can purchase, or otherwise obtain, the goods and services they want by taking advantage of benefits, incentives or enhanced services they earn from being loyal customers, even if other customers choose not to engage in such programs.
- *Transparency and Customer Choice* – Consumers deserve to know what categories of personal data businesses collect and how that data is generally used. These policies should be clearly disclosed in company privacy policies readily accessible to consumers. These obligations should apply to all businesses handling consumers'

personal data, including service providers, third parties, and financial services businesses.

- *Accountability for Business's Own Actions* – Privacy law should not include terms that could potentially expose businesses, including contractors and franchises, to liability for the actions or noncompliance of a business partner. Those business partners should be responsible for their own compliance and any resulting liability. In particular, consumer-facing businesses should not be unfairly saddled with liability if other types of businesses do not fulfill their own obligations under the law.
- *Data Security Standards* – A federal data privacy law should include a reasonable data security standard for all businesses handling consumer data, as well as a uniform process for businesses suffering a data security breach to notify affected individuals. Currently, consumer-facing industry sectors are required to comply with 54 state and U.S. territorial laws on data breach notification requirements, and nearly half of the states have enacted data security laws. However, financial institutions and service providers are often exempt from these state breach notice requirements. All businesses handling consumers' data should be required to protect personal data and provide notice of their own security breaches when they occur.

Collectively, these principles can keep us on track to privacy law that is comprehensive and beneficial for consumers and businesses alike.

One of the things that has come along with the remarkable technological advances of the past generation, however, is a growing sense that the cost of many technologies is individuals' privacy. That concerns us and it is important that consumers trust our members and other businesses with which they deal. But, in constructing policy to deal with concerns regarding the tech sector, we should take care not to forget about Main Street businesses. The folks we represent can sometimes be ignored if the only construct that is considered is how commerce takes places on the Internet or through a mobile application.

Many in other industry sectors (particularly the technology and telecommunications sectors) will argue that their operations are so specialized that they should be exempted from certain requirements in privacy legislation. We are one of the few groups that will say the opposite – we are not special. We know that the Main Street businesses we represent will be covered by any privacy legislation. That is as it should be. Our members accept this responsibility because they value customer trust and consumer protection. But, every business sector should be covered by, and subject to, data privacy law and each business handling consumers' data should be responsible for doing what it can to protect privacy in accordance with the law – and should not be able to push liability for what it can do onto another business that is not in a position to do that on its behalf.

Unfortunately, shifting liability onto other businesses is precisely the tack that many businesses that consider themselves "service providers" take when advocating on these issues. They want Main Street businesses that deal directly with consumers to take the responsibility for what those "service providers" do. If we allow that to happen, consumers will be left with gaps in their privacy protection and Main Street will be saddled with liability that it has no practical way to avoid.

III. The American Data Privacy and Protection Act

The ADPPA represents an important milestone on the road to achieving a national data privacy standard. Gaining bipartisan agreement on a privacy proposal is incredibly difficult. By doing that, the Act makes important progress toward our goal of national policy. It is clear that the authors of ADPPA share many of the principles outlined above for privacy legislation. There also remain a number of parts of the Act on which we hope to work with the Committee to make improvements to ensure that it succeeds in meeting our principles. And, there remain areas of the Act that raise questions regarding how the provisions will apply. We hope this testimony can serve as a helpful roadmap to work through all of these issues.

Protecting Consumers across Business Sectors

Ensuring that consumers are protected regardless of the business sector that has or handles their data is fundamental to ensuring we have effective privacy laws. The limits of committee jurisdiction, however, can get in the way of achieving this goal. But, those limitations can be overcome.

The Energy & Commerce Committee does not have jurisdiction over financial services firms. Those firms argue that they should be exempt from any new privacy regime because they are covered by the privacy provisions of the Gramm Leach Bliley Act (GLBA). That argument withers in the face of even the slightest scrutiny. Virtually no one involved in serious privacy discussions today would consider GLBA to be an adequate model for privacy legislation. GLBA, enacted in 1999, requires that covered businesses send customers a written privacy policy once per year and provide them with a limited ability to opt-out of third party marketing. That is it.

GLBA does not require the notice to be available at other times (such as on a website) and it does not require providing consumer rights like access to information and an ability to correct or delete information. GLBA does not include prohibited uses of data and it does not require affirmative consent by consumers even for some of the most questionable uses of sensitive data that might be engaged in by financial services firms.

GLBA isn't sufficient to protect consumer privacy and, frankly, isn't very relevant to the debate around privacy legislation today. There should be a plan to work with the House Financial Services Committee and Senate Banking Committee to ensure that entities subject to GLBA will be fully subject to the provisions of the Act and any new privacy law. It would be indefensible if a new federal law passed that provided consumers more privacy rights when they go to the dry cleaner than when they go to their bank. We look forward to working with the Committee to address this in the Act.

Accountability for Business's Own Actions and Direct Statutory Obligations

One of the areas of recent privacy legislation that has proven challenging is the treatment of service providers. Some of the difficulty may be due to our assumptions about businesses across the country. We often think about the large businesses with which we deal directly on a day-to-day basis. But, the vast majority of Main Street businesses across the nation are small businesses. These small businesses must deal with a number of service providers including telecommunications firms, data cloud storage firms, data and payment processors, website-hosting firms, advertising firms, financial institutions, and many more. In contrast to Main

Street businesses, these service providers are often large national or international businesses with many small business clients.

In fact, with regard to Internet access and other services, Main Street often has very limited choices of service providers in the marketplace. The Federal Communications Commission has reported that nearly half of all Americans have only one choice of high-speed broadband provider. The size disparities between Main Street businesses and service providers, and the lack of market choice leads to contracts of adhesion that disadvantage Main Street and often assign liability in ways that are not fair. Contracts are not an effective way to protect consumer privacy because they allow large businesses to game the system and ultimately mean that consumer rights are only protected if small businesses are willing to sue the large businesses in the face of violations. Typically, smaller businesses aren't willing to do that due to resource constraints and their need to continue to do business with the service provider in question.

Those that argue we should not worry as much about service providers – including telecommunications and technology companies – as we do about businesses with direct consumer relationships are ignoring what we know about privacy. Large businesses providing the communications and technology services that we take for granted today have a history of using private data in ways that most consumers would find objectionable. For example, Verizon agreed to pay a $1.35 million settlement to the Federal Communications Commission because it was inserting tracking cookies into data packets in order to track consumers across the Internet.[100] Main Street businesses often use service providers like Verizon to offer their customers wi-fi and other communications services. But those Main Street businesses would have no better luck determining whether Verizon was committing privacy violations of this sort than individual consumers would. That is just one of many examples of questionable privacy activities by companies that may be considered service providers within this legislation that Main Street businesses are not in a position to know about.[101]

We appreciate that the ADPPA has made important progress on aspects of these relationships. The Act imposes statutory obligations rather than relying on contracts. That is a key point.

It also requires service providers to comply with consumer requests when they are received from other businesses. But, more needs to be done to ensure this part of the Act fulfills its purpose. For example, the language of the Act is unclear regarding when a service provider must fulfill a consumer request and when it must only provide assistance to another business.

More work is required to ensure these responsibilities are clear. The goal should not be controversial. Service providers should be required by law to do what they are in a position to do to ensure that consumer rights are protected. The same should be true of businesses that deal

---

[100] Karl Bode, "Verizon Strikes $1.35 Million Settlement with FCC Over its Use of Stealth 'Zombie Cookies'" *techdirt* (March 7, 2016) (available at https://www.techdirt.com/2016/03/07/verizon-strikes-135-million-settlement- with-fcc-over-use-stealth-zombie-cookies/).

[101] *See, e.g.*, "A Look at What ISPs Know About You: Examining the Privacy Practices of Six Major Internet Service Providers," Federal Trade Commission (Oct. 2021) (available at https://www.ftc.gov/reports/look-what-isps-know- about-you-examining-privacy-practices-six-major-internet-service-providers); Karl Bode, "Verizon didn't bother to write a privacy policy for its 'privacy protecting' VPN," *Vice* (Aug. 6, 2018) (available at https://www.vice.com/en/article/a3q4gz/verizon-didnt-bother-to-write-a-privacy-policy-for-safe-wi-fi-privacy-protecting-vpn); Julia Angwin, "AT&T Helped U.S. Spy on Internet on a Vast Scale," New York Times (Aug. 15, 2015) (available at https://www.nytimes.com/2015/08/16/us/politics/att-helped-nsa-spy-on-an-array-of-internet-traffic.html).

directly with consumers. But, neither category of business should be liable for the other's failure or refusal to follow the law.

The material difference between service providers and consumer-facing businesses really boils down to a procedural matter – namely, the fact that consumer requests to exercise their rights should go to the consumer-facing business first. Other than that, both categories of business should be required to fully follow the law and not be exempt from entire sections of the bill.

That means service providers should be subject to all sections of the bill, including sections 203 and 204, to ensure that there are no gaps in the privacy coverage that consumers receive. The language in section 302 exempting them from compliance with sections 203 and 204 should be removed so that there is no question that service providers must comply with the law – with the only distinction being that in most instances they would receive consumer requests from consumer-facing businesses and would respond to those consumer-facing businesses rather than responding to consumers directly.

In addition, the ADPPA (at section 302) imposes a due diligence requirement on consumer-facing entities in working with service providers and third parties that it does not impose on those service providers and third parties. Given the size, sophistication, and market power differences, if any due diligence were justified it would be more likely to run in the other direction. The typical single-location corner convenience store or coffee shop does not have the resources or expertise to conduct due diligence on the privacy policies and practices of corporate giants like Verizon, Comcast, Microsoft, and many others on which their businesses rely. The fact that each single store operator would have to conduct such due diligence on multiple large companies – Internet service providers, data storage companies, payment processors and more – makes it more unachievable even for larger businesses. In our view, the due diligence requirement should be removed as it is inconsistent with the disparities in size and resources we see among most of these businesses across the nation.

Uniform Nationwide Rules and Enforcement

An important justification for a federal privacy law is that it can provide clear and consistent rules for consumers and businesses regardless of where they are located or operate across the nation. We appreciate that the Act includes language seeking to achieve this goal.

The number and range of exceptions to the preemption provisions of the Act, however, raise troublesome questions regarding the scope of the Act's preemptive effect. Case law in this area indicates that too many exceptions to federal laws attempting to preempt state law can undermine the intent and preemptive effect of the federal law entirely and reduce it to a scheme that simply preempts conflicting state laws (much like any federal law does based on the Supremacy Clause of the Constitution).[102]

In addition to the general question of whether the preemption provision of the Act will be effective, the exception for the California law on data breach notification raises additional questions. That part of the California law includes an ability for individuals to file lawsuits for noncompliance which would not need to adhere to the procedural requirements of the ADPPA.

[102] *See, e.g., Williamson v. Mazda Motor of Am., Inc.*, 562 U.S. 323 (2011); *Sprietsma v. Mercury Marine*, 537 U.S. 51 (2002); *Geier v. American Honda Motor Co.*, 529 U.S. 861 (2000); *Beyond Systems, Inc. v. Keynetics, Inc.*, 422 F.Supp.2d 523 (D. Md. 2006).

It is not clear to what extent that may create a loophole that could be exploited in a way that is contrary to the intentions of the Act's authors.

The exception in the preemption provision for violations of common law also creates a risk of inconsistent standards applying in different jurisdictions across the nation.

The enforcement provisions of the Act, of course, have been a focus of attention. We support allowing enforcement by the Federal Trade Commission (FTC) and state attorneys general.[103] Many businesses, however, are wary of allowing individuals to file lawsuits to enforce a privacy law. Our members share those concerns which stem from the complexity of achieving compliance with privacy laws as well as from experience with large volumes of questionable legal claims that have proliferated in other areas of the law. For example, Main Street businesses have received many demand letters from lawyers alleging violations of telemarketing rules, ADA website accessibility requirements, and patent laws. All too often, potential litigants are able to exploit the knowledge that obtaining legal representation and defending against a claim under a complex federal law is expensive. Those costs can lead businesses to agree to settlements of even non-meritorious claims simply to avoid litigation.

While the Act requires individuals to file with the FTC and state attorneys general 60 days prior to filing litigation, it appears that regardless of how those authorities evaluate the merits of those claims the individuals would still be able to pursue litigation. That raises questions about the purpose and effectiveness of the 60-day waiting period. This is an area of the Act that we think needs additional work.

Consumer Transparency and Choice

The Act lays out important consumer rights including the right for consumers to access their data, get mistakes corrected, and have data deleted. The Act also requires privacy policies to give consumers information regarding items including the categories of data collected, purposes of processing such data, and the categories of other entities receiving data. All of these are important rights that we support.

We do think there should be some recognition that certain data that relates to consumers is business data that should not be subject to deletion. Data that helps businesses track products sold, exchanged or returned by consumers, products under warranty, and other transaction information are important for businesses to maintain their operations, customer service, and inventory tracking. Financial records of businesses necessary for accounting, tax compliance and the like, for example, also should not inadvertently be subject to a consumer deletion request.

Preservation of Customer Rewards and Benefits

The Act seeks to address questions that have arisen in the context of state privacy laws regarding the viability of customer loyalty and rewards programs. Those programs offer customers things like free or discounted items after a certain number or dollar value of purchases. Of course, in order to provide those types of rewards, businesses must have a way to keep a count of the purchases made by those customers. But, State laws requiring that customers must be treated the same, even if some of them choose to prevent a business from

---

[103] We would note that the authority of the FTC to seek fines under the Act, potentially before providing necessary clarity regarding requirements and what constitutes a violation of law, raises concerns.

tracking their purchases, created the possibility that offering other customers who voluntarily signed up for loyalty or rewards programs any price discounts would violate the law.

It is clear that Americans overwhelmingly want these programs to remain legal.[104] Generally, the states that most recently have passed privacy laws have all found ways to sufficiently preserve these programs.

The right principle to apply in this area is that consumers should not face retaliation for exercising their rights under privacy laws. The language of the Act might not get us to that principle. Rather than focusing on retaliation, section 104 of the Act requires "loyalty . . . with respect to pricing." This is a concept that does not exist today. If a sales price only applies to customers who have signed up for a rewards program, does that fulfill "loyalty" to the customers who decline to give their consent to enter the rewards program?

There is a rule of construction in the Act that is clearly intended to preserve these rewards programs. But, that language is made less clear by the way the section is positioned as requiring loyalty to all customers on pricing. And, the rule of construction is conditioned on the reward being given "in exchange for an individual's continued business." Typically, these programs are rewards for past business – not exchanges for future business (that is just a desired outcome). The rule of construction in the Act is also conditioned on the rewards program complying with all of the other requirements in the Act and regulations. That language is unnecessary and raises an interpretive question as to whether things in the Act that would not otherwise apply to the rewards program would now apply.

Getting this right is an important aspect for consumer acceptance of any new privacy regime.

More broadly, the Act recognizes that privacy should not unnecessarily hold up the normal and uncontroversial workings of commerce. Section 209 of the bill includes a number of helpful provisions to protect against negative outcomes. For example, that section provides a general exception to requirements in the bill for the data exchanges necessary to complete transactions and deal with "billing, shipping, and accounting."[105] There are similar exceptions allowing for data to be used to undertake system maintenance, inventory management, prevent fraud, deal with security incidents, and the like. The exceptions enumerated in this part of the bill are needed.

We do recommend, however, that section 209 make clear exactly the parts of the bill to which these exceptions apply. We would expect, for example, that these exceptions would override the need for any affirmative consent of consumers under sections 202 and 204, as well as for minors in section 205. We would also expect these exceptions to override the right to deletion in section 203. A number of other such questions arise throughout the bill. Given those questions, it would improve the bill to include a clear statement of the provisions of the bill to which the provisions of section 209 apply.

In addition, an area in which there are complex relationships among companies exchanging data includes advertising. Some of this is necessary as smaller businesses in particular must use service providers to help them keep up with their large competitors on marketing activities.

---

[104] According to a survey conducted by Bond Brand Loyalty Inc., 79% of consumers say loyalty programs make them more likely to continue doing business with brands that offer them and 32% of consumers strongly agree that a loyalty program makes their brand experience better. Bond Brand Loyalty Inc., *The Loyalty Report* (2019) *available at* https://cdn2.hubspot.net/hubfs/352767/TLR%202019/Bond_US%20TLR19%20Exec%20Summary%20Launch% 20Edition.pdf.

[105] ADPPA section 209(a)(1).

Those small businesses cannot replicate the in-house advertising operations the many large businesses have.

There are, of course, legitimate concerns about how data is used in advertising. At the same time, that advertising fuels a significant amount of U.S. commercial activity and provides people information they want and need regarding available product and service offerings as well as pricing information. The economy would not be nearly as price-competitive without a healthy advertising sector and current price competition clearly benefits consumers. The breadth of the definition in the Act of sensitive data (including, in particular, that it does not include clear exceptions for the use of data when it is not linked to a specific individual) paired with some of the affirmative consent requirements in the Act may lead to difficulties for some of the types of advertising that are expected and helpful to people. This is an area that is complex and we welcome the opportunity to further explore it with the Committee.

The provision in section 302 of the Act requiring consent of the individual before a service provider can share data with another service provider will lead to problems with certain types of first-party advertising and other uses of customer data that are not controversial and do not require affirmative consent. There are often multiple service providers involved in making advertising happen and it should not require specific individual consent to ensure that those businesses can share the tasks involved in providing these and other services. As long as all of the service providers in the data chain must fully comply with the Act, consumers will remain protected.

Data Security Standards

The Act includes provisions relating to data security and we appreciate that the legal standard it sets is one of reasonableness. That is the appropriate standard and one we have long advocated. The generality of that standard is necessary due to the tremendous diversity among organizations that will be subject to the law. And, having that standard take account of factors like the size and complexity of the entity and the sensitivity of the data it handles makes sense.

We would recommend, however, that there be changes to the "specific requirements" in section 208 of the Act. Requiring those specifics overrides the helpful flexibility of the reasonableness standard. The requirements also override considerations like the size and complexity of the business being regulated. The specifics are, in short, both too lenient and too strict. For large, sophisticated businesses that many of us picture when thinking about privacy, the specific requirements in section 208 are minimal measures. Clearly, we should expect these things to take place.

For many small businesses, however, the specific requirements elevate form over substance and are overly burdensome. As noted previously, the vast majority of Main Street businesses are small and the specifics mean that the FTC cannot fully take into account size and complexity when considering data security. For example, in many single store operations – like a convenience store or restaurant – the owner of the business may work behind a counter serving customers for long hours every week. Does it really help anyone for that individual owner to formally designate "an officer, employee, or employees to maintain and implement" data security practices? It is clear that owner is the person responsible. Requiring that designation to be formally made will not improve data security and, at worst, will serve as an easy "gotcha" for lawyers to look for when filing individual lawsuits. The other specific requirements could serve the same unfortunate purpose of providing a litigation checklist rather than materially advancing the data security provided by these small businesses.

In our view, these issues could be addressed by removing the specific requirements or simply making them examples of things that could be done if they are reasonable based on the size and complexity of the entity and the other considerations laid out in section 208. While there is an exception in the Act for businesses that handle smaller amounts of data, we are concerned that it is too stringent to allow many businesses to qualify – though that provision may provide another avenue to address some of these concerns.

We note that the Act does not include data breach notification requirements. It has been our position that the burdens of varying state requirements are particularly acute in this area. When companies suffer data breaches, they often need to hire counsel to advise them on the varied timeframes and requirements around the manner of notification in different states. This is an area that would benefit from uniformity.

It is also an area in which coverage of entities subject to the Gramm Leach Bliley Act would be particularly helpful. Many state laws exempt GLBA entities on the mistaken notion that they are subject to federal data breach notification requirements. They are not. GLBA recommends that notice should be provided following a data breach, but it does not require it.[106] That ought to be remedied in any privacy bill.

Other Issues

There are a number of other issues that would benefit from additional work through the legislative process. Some of the most impactful topics that merit attention include:

- *Definition of covered entity* – Currently, the way a covered entity is defined in section 2(9) of the Act includes that an entity that "shares common branding with another covered entity." Many franchisees and franchisors share common branding but are distinct companies. Similar arrangements are common to about half of the convenience industry. While the major integrated oil companies own just 0.2 percent of motor fuel outlets, about half of them use the branding of an oil company or refiner. The owners of these retail outlets are independent businesses, typically small businesses, that have an arm's length contract allowing them to display that branding. If those companies are deemed to be the same covered entity, then they will each be liable for the privacy practices of the oil brand or franchisor as well as all of the other branded outlets or franchisees. That is not a tenable outcome and we don't believe that was the intended outcome of the authors of the Act. But, this is an important issue and one we are eager to fix in the next iteration of the Act's language.
- *Definition of large data holder* – The Act treats large data holders differently than other businesses regulated under the bill in several respects. That definition, therefore, should avoid sweeping small- and medium-sized businesses within its bounds. The provision at section 2(17)(B)(ii) regarding the number of individuals' sensitive data

---

[106] GLBA instructs various agencies to establish security guidelines, not regulations, to implement the directives in GLBA. Gramm-Leach-Bliley Financial Services Modernization Act, Title V of the Financial Services Modernization Act of 1999, Pub. L. No. 106-102, 113 Stat. 1338 (Nov. 12, 1999) (*codified at* 15 U.S.C. §§ 6801, 6809, 6821, and 6827). When designing security controls, financial institutions need to "consider" a data breach response plan but are not required to develop a data breach response program or notify consumers after a breach. *Interagency Guidelines Establishing Information Security Standards*, 66 Fed. Reg. 8616 (Feb. 1, 2001) and 69 Fed. Reg. 77610 (Dec. 28, 2004) promulgating and amending 12 C.F.R. Part 30, app. B (OCC); 12 C.F.R. Part 208, app. D-2 and Part 225, app. F (Board); 12 C.F.R. Part 364, app. B (FDIC); and 12 C.F.R. Part 570, app. B (OTS).

that it handles creates a risk that those small- and medium-sized businesses could be viewed as large data holders simply because their business depends on having a large number of small-dollar transactions with customers. We think this issue could be addressed by making clear that transaction data does not count toward the large data holder definition. This would be consistent with the concept in section 209 providing that transaction data is subject to a general exception from some requirements in the Act and with the exemption for those with small amounts of data in section 208.[107]

- *Privacy policies* – Everyone will have an interest in businesses doing more on privacy over time and improving their policies. Language in section 202(d) of the Act, however, might create a disincentive to doing that. It references the need for affirmative express consent when a material change is made to a privacy policy. But, that requirement seems to extend even to changes that under the Act would not otherwise require affirmative express consent. That will create a strong reluctance for businesses to update and change their policies, even in consumer- friendly ways, because policies or actions that are viewed as not requiring affirmative consent will be transformed into ones that do. We recommend making clear that such affirmative consent only attaches when the change to the policy implicates affirmative consent under the Act.
- *Restricted practices* – In general, we have always been open to making clear that some data practices should be prohibited. This can provide clarity for businesses and consumers and allow other commerce to take place without as much friction. The Act includes a recitation of such practices in section 102. We see some areas within that section which could be improved. For example, the use of social security numbers needs exceptions allowing that data to be used for prospective employees for the purpose of conducting background checks. It also appears that there should be an exception for current employees (unless section 102 will be limited to covered data).
  - Another example is the use of the term "authentication." That is a term of art with respect to payments, but it's not clear how broad the term is intended to be in the Act – particularly because the term is used at multiple points in the Act. Defining that term could help avoid confusion.
  - Smaller businesses rely on service providers to do what some of their competitors are able to do in-house. One of those things is providing advertising to their own customers. That type of advertising is something that American consumers expect. The use of their data, including such things as past purchases or parts of their history browsing a retailer's website, generally are not controversial when they involve that retailer using the information to market directly to their own customers. But, as noted, these retailers don't have the technological sophistication to do all of that themselves (or the employees to do the work of putting together even basic advertising like direct mail).
- *Sensitive Covered Data* – The Act includes credit and debit card numbers in its definition of "sensitive covered data." But, the last four digits of those numbers are printed on receipts and used to help facilitate product returns and track the status of

[107] It is worth noting that without this change, large numbers of businesses could be deemed both large data holders under the definition in section 2 and simultaneously fall within the small data exception in section 209 of the Act.

purchases in other ways. The definition should make clear that the last four digits of payment card numbers do not constitute "sensitive" covered data.

* * *

We appreciate the dedication of the Members and staff in getting us to this point and the opportunity to discuss these issues with you. A bipartisan draft of federal privacy legislation marks a significant milestone on the journey to get a federal law. There remain many areas on which we look forward to working with the authors to make changes to improve the legislation and clarify how it will work.

*Ms. Schakowsky. Thank you so much for your testimony.

And now, Ms. Cuaresma, you are recognized for five minutes.

Statement of Jolina Cuaresma, Senior Counsel, Privacy and Technology Policy, Common Sense Media

*Ms. Cuaresma. Good morning, Chair Pallone, Ranking Member McMorris Rodgers, Chair Schakowsky, and Ranking Member Bilirakis, and of course, the members of the subcommittee. Thank you for inviting me here today to testify on this bipartisan and bicameral legislative proposal to strengthen data and privacy security.

I am Jo Cuaresma, Senior Counsel for Privacy and Tech Policy at Common Sense Media, America's leading organization dedicated to helping kids and families harness the power of media and technology as a powerful force in kids' lives.

I have a 20-year legal career spanning private practice, the government, and academia. I focus at the intersection of administrative law, technology, and consumer protection. Most importantly, I am a mom to a teenager in high school. On behalf of Common Sense and its cofounder and CEO, Jim Steyer, I strongly urge this committee, your counterpart in the Senate, and this Congress, this year to pass a strong data privacy bill, one that includes strong protections for minors.

All consumers, but especially our kids and teens, deserve privacy and protection from online harms. Tech firms should be constrained in their wild west data collection practices and be required to provide clear and conspicuous notices, so that individuals can make real choices about their online activities without penalty. Companies should also know that they will be held accountable for violating a national privacy law.

The American Data Privacy Protection Act draft lays the groundwork for achieving these goals. It establishes important data protections with regards to civil rights, and it seeks to minimize the collection and sharing of data which we have long maintained as the very first step to reducing online harms to our kids and teens.

We understand that this draft is a compromise as it must be. At the same time, we do urge this committee to seriously consider the changes that we are proposing. Internet regulations are long overdue. Current law fails to protect children.

Youths spend increasing amounts of time on sites that automatically capture data. Our research shows that screen use is up 17 percent for tweens and teens just since the pandemic. At the same time, youth are pressured to share sensitive data about themselves on platforms by their own peers.

The APPA draft contains much needed consumer protections. For example, it prohibits firms from collecting, processing, and transferring sensitive covered data without first obtaining an individual's opt-in consent.

It also mandates that tech firms minimize their data collection to what's reasonable. It grants the FTC and state AGs the authority under the statute, and it establishes a private right of action. It raises the age of covered children to under 17. It bans behavioral advertising to minors, and it establishes the Youth Privacy and Marketing Division.

Still, there are changes needed to help achieve your goals. We need to cover all minors under the draft's privacy protections. We need to substantially increase FTC's staff and its funding.

And lastly, and most importantly for children, we need to change the knowledge standard by closing the loophole enabling companies to evade complying with children's protections. Firms should have the legal obligation to use the information they have, not just in their marketing departments, but also, in their legal divisions.

I would, however, want to think the bipartisan leaders for this draft to not including the knowledge standard in the data and kids' data given the definition in 204 – sorry – given the definition in 204 for "sensitive covered data."

I want to thank you, and I look forward to your questions.

[The prepared statement of Ms. Cuaresma follows:]

Written Testimony of Jolina C. Cuaresma, Senior Counsel, Privacy and Technology Policy, before the House Energy and Commerce, Subcommittee on Consumer Protection and Commerce, Hearing on "Protecting America's Consumers: Bipartisan Legislation to Strengthen Data Privacy and Security," June 14, 2022

I. Introduction

Good morning, Chair Pallone, Ranking Member McMorris Rogers, Chair Schakowsky, Ranking Member Bilirakis, and members of the Subcommittee. I am Jolina Cuaresma, Senior Counsel for Privacy and Technology Policy at Common Sense Media. Thank you for inviting me to testify this morning on this bipartisan legislative proposal that seeks to strengthen data privacy and security.

On behalf of Common Sense Media, and its Co-Founder and CEO Jim Steyer, I believe that this committee, your counterpart in the Senate, and this Congress should do everything within your power, this year, to reach a historic agreement on comprehensive data privacy legislation, including strong protections for minors. We believe that the American Data Privacy Protection Act Draft (ADPPA Draft) lays the groundwork for achieving this goal. It is bipartisan and bi- cameral. It establishes important data protections with regard to civil rights.

And it seeks to minimize the collection and sharing of minors' data, which we have long maintained is the first and most important step to reducing online harms to kids and teens.

We understand that this draft reflects a compromise, as is necessary in the legislative arena, and we appreciate how hard members of the House and Senate, on both sides of the aisle, have worked to get to this point. At the same time, it is our expectation that the Committee will seriously consider changes that we, and other organizations, are proposing to help this legislation better achieve its stated objectives. But there is no question that now is the time, once and for all, for Congress to come together to pass a strong national data privacy and security bill.

II. My Professional Background and Common Sense Media

I have undergraduate degrees in Finance and Economics, a J.D., and an LL.M in Advocacy. My background in business includes earning the highest distinction from GE's Financial Management Program. I have a 20-year legal career that spans private practice, government, and academia. While an enforcement attorney, and later a regulatory counsel, I represented clients in matters involving the U.S. Department of Justice, the Securities Exchange Commission, FINRA, and the Consumer Financial Protection Bureau. As a federal regulator, I conducted investigations and brought enforcement actions, helped build the nation's first supervisory program over non- depository institutions, and had a lead role drafting regulations under the Dodd-Frank Act. While in academia, I helped run the Federal Legislation Clinic at Georgetown Law Center, where I also taught classes on statutory implementation. Along with other Georgetown and MIT professors, I co-taught a joint legislative drafting course where teams of law and computer science students resolved public policy concerns arising from the use of emerging technologies.

Since 2017, I have been an adjunct professor at University of California, Berkeley School of Law, where I teach a seminar on regulatory oversight. Beginning in 2019, I have served as a co- author for two consumer protection treatises that are published by Thomson Reuters. Over the course of my career, I have worked on matters involving constitutional law (e.g., separation of powers and fourth amendment jurisprudence) and a range of federal law (e.g., securities, corporate governance, and consumer protection).

I am privileged to now use my background on behalf of Common Sense, America's leading organization dedicated to helping kids and families harness the power of media and technology as a positive force in kids' lives. We reach 125 million households annually with our age-appropriate media ratings and reviews, and our award-winning Digital Citizenship Curriculum is the most comprehensive K-12 offering of its kind in the education field. We have more than 1.2 million registered educators using our digital citizenship resources, and more than 70% of U.S. schools are Common Sense Media members. Our curriculum teaches kids, parents, and educators how to make smart and responsible choices online.

Common Sense also plays a leading role on online privacy and security issues by communicating directly with leaders of American tech firms at the highest levels. And our policy advocacy and research departments are widely regarded as independent and trusted voices for kids on privacy, platform accountability, and connectivity issues. Common Sense has been honored to appear as a witness before this Committee on several occasions for both the majority and the minority.

As an attorney working at a children's advocacy organization and as a mom, my job responsibilities dovetail with my parental duties. As a single parent to a teenager who uses social media platforms, I could not be a more committed member of Common Sense's policy advocacy program with its track record of championing federal and state laws that protect children.

It is my privilege to use this background to offer the following analysis and comments on the ADPPA Draft. In my testimony today, I outline sections of the draft that provide much-needed data protections and merit Congress' approval, and I also discuss areas of the draft that require strengthening in order to better achieve your stated objectives.

III. The ADPPA Draft Is a Significant Step Forward from the Status Quo

Internet regulations are overdue and the ADPPA Draft contains a number of much-needed consumer protections. For example, section 204 prohibits firms collecting, processing, and transferring "sensitive covered data" without first obtaining an individual's affirmative consent. If enacted, the section would establish an opt-in regime for a broad scope of sensitive information. Notably, the legislative proposal defines the term "sensitive covered data" to include no fewer than 16 categories of information. It also anticipates technological advancements. Section 2(22)(B) grants the Federal Trade Commission (Commission) rulemaking authority to define any additional category of sensitive data that should be similarly protected.

Moreover, the ADPPA Draft makes it mandatory for tech firms to minimize their data collection to what is "reasonabl[e]" and to disclose their data use practices. The legislative proposal also grants both the Commission and state attorneys general enforcement authority under the statute.

For purposes of my testimony here today, I will limit my comments to the sections of the ADPPA Draft that are most relevant to children and teens.

A. Kids and Teens Are Entitled to Online Protection and Safety

Stronger privacy protections are not the only thing needed to make the internet safer and healthier for minors, and Common Sense believes Congress should address other aspects of platform accountability as well. But stronger privacy protections are the first step and a key step to reducing well-known online harms to minors.

Children should be allowed to grow up, to go from tweens to teenagers to young adults, without worrying about a permanent record of typical youthful indiscretions or the collection of their every thought and "like." Yet, our youth spend increasing amounts of time on sites that automatically capture their data, while at the same time they face pressure to share extremely personal and sensitive information about themselves and their peers, and to view this as common. One survey found that almost 25% of minors, ages 9 to 12, and about 33% of those aged 13 to 17, believe that sharing sexually explicit content was normal for their age group.[108]

---

[108] Self-Generated Child Sexual Abuse Material: Youth Attitudes and Experiences in 2020, Thorn and Benenson Strategy Group, (Nov 2021).

In addition to inappropriate sharing, kids and teens are routinely exposed to harmful content. Consider these sobering statistics that describe the current world in which our children live.[109]

- *By the time a child reaches 13, an ad tech firm has compiled over 70 million data points on that child.* The information, which includes the websites visited, what content was viewed, and for how long, is used to sort kids into target ad groups.
- *In 2019, Facebook categorized nearly 1 million kids under 18 as being interested in alcohol and 740,000 as interested in gambling.* This reflects that the company's business model is based on child exploitation and subjecting kids to harmful content.
- *During the first year of the pandemic, 85% of YouTube videos included ads targeting kids aged 0 to 8.* One in five of these videos were not age appropriate and contained images of drugs, alcohol, violence, or sexual content.

The statistics around child sexual abuse are sickening, made even more so because some tech firms profit from it.[110]

- One in four children between the ages of 9 and 17 have had a sexual encounter with an adult online. Roughly one in five are between the ages of 9 and 12.
- In a single year, from 2019 to 2020, "self-generated" child sexual abuse online content jumped 80%. An overwhelming majority of these victims are girls ages 11 to 13 who have frequently been coerced into sharing images or videos of themselves on live streaming sites.

When tech firms are willing to profit from child sexual exploitation, it should come as no surprise that they are willing to place "profits over people." This is not hyperbole. Meta Whistleblower Frances Haugen, who has testified in the House and the Senate, risked her own personal safety to provide uncontroverted evidence that we cannot trust firms to regulate themselves. She provided countless documents making clear that senior corporate leadership knew their social media platforms, Facebook and Instagram, routinely exposed teens to harmful conduct.[111] Despite this, in an effort to increase ad revenue, the company changed its algorithms in 2018 to boost user engagement. How did it do this? By increasing the promotion of harmful content such as "civic misinfo, civic toxicity, health misinfo, and health antivax content."[112] This is just one important reason why reducing the amount of minors' online data that is collected and shared can reduce some of the online harms they experience today.

---

[109] Katie Joseff, *Behavioral Advertising Harms: Kids and Teens, Common Sense Media*, Common Sense Media (Feb. 2022); Katie Joseff, *List of Social Media Harms*, Common Sense Media (Dec. 2021).

[110] *Id.*

[111] *Facebook Knows Instagram is Toxic for Teen Girls, Company Documents Show*, WALL ST. J. (Sept.14, 2021) (reporting that one in five teens say that Instagram makes them feel worse about themselves); *Teen mental health deep dive*, WALL ST. J. (Sept. 29, 2021) (reporting that internal research reflected that among teens who reported suicidal thoughts, 13% of British and 6% of American teenagers traced the desire to kill themselves to Instagram).

[112] *Five points for anger, one for a 'like': How Facebook's formula fostered rage and misinformation*, WASH. POST (Oct. 26, 2021).

B. Current Law Fails to Provide Children Commonsense Protections

In 1998, when Congress passed the Children's Online Privacy Protection Act (COPPA), kids did not have the social media that they have today. Friendster did not come online until 2003, followed by Facebook in 2006, Instagram in 2010, and Snapchat in 2011. COPPA was seven years old before people shared videos online — YouTube did not launch until 2005 — and twenty years passed before short-form videos exploded in popularity with TikTok's release in 2018. Nearly 25 years have passed since COPPA's enactment, and during this time, the exponential growth in computing power has allowed these social media companies and other firms to collect ever larger data sets containing millions of data points about individuals, leading us into the era of "Big Data."[113]

Yet, during all this time, Congress has not provided children new privacy and safety protections. For years, civil society groups, parents, and lawmakers have tried to pressure tech companies to change their practices. Lawmakers' attempts at passing commonsense legislation have come in fits and starts. House and Senate subcommittees and committees have held hearing after hearing about online harms to children.[114] Kids and teens, and their families, are fed up with waiting any longer.

C. While This Bipartisan Legislative Proposal Offers Sorely-Needed Commonsense Protections for Children and Teens, Key Sections Must Be Strengthened

1. Obtaining Privacy Protections for Kids under 17 Would Be a Watershed Moment

As mentioned above, the ADPPA Draft creates an opt-in regime for "sensitive covered data,"[115] which is defined to include over a dozen protected categories, including any "[i]nformation of an individual [under the age of 17]."[116] For years, children's advocacy groups, including Common Sense, have argued that all data about minors is sensitive, and we urge the committee to modify the bracketed to text to the age of consent to include all 17 year olds. If enacted, this

---

[113] *Big Data: A Tool for Inclusion or Exclusion?*, Federal Trade Commission Report (Jan. 2016) (last visited June 12, 2022). Big data has often been characterized as having volume (refers to the vast quantity of data), velocity (refers to the speed at which new data can be accumulated), and variety (the breadth of data), with each growing at a rapid rate. *Id.*

[114] *See e.g.*, *Kids Online During COVID: Child Safety During an Increasingly Digital Age*, Before the Subcomm. on Consumer Protection and Commerce, 116 Cong. (2021); *Holding Big Tech Accountable: Targeted Reforms to Tech's Legal Immunity*, Before the Subcomm. on Communications and Technology, 117 Cong. (2021); *Toxic Marketing Claims and Their Dangers*, Before the Subcomm. on Consumer Protection, Product Safety, and Data Security, 117 Cong. (2021); *Protecting Kids Online: Facebook, Instagram, and Mental Health Harms*, Before the Subcomm on Consumer Protection, Product Safety, and Data Security, 117 Cong. (2021); *Protecting Kids Online: Testimony from a Facebook Whistleblower*, Before the Subcomm on Consumer Protection, Product Safety, and Data Security, 117 Cong. (2021); *Protecting Consumer Privacy*, Before the Comm on Commerce, Science, and Transportation, 117 Cong. (2021*); Protecting Kids Online: Snapchat, TikTok, and YouTube*, Before the Subcomm on Consumer Protection, Product Safety, and Data Security, 117 Cong. (2021); *Protecting Kids Online: Instagram and Reforms for Young Users*, Before the Subcomm on Consumer Protection, Product Safety, and Data Security, 117 Cong. (2021); and *Disrupting Dangerous Algorithms: Addressing the Harms of Persuasive Technology*, Before the Subcomm on Communications, Media, and Broadband, 117 Cong. (2021).

[115] Section 204 requires a tech firm to obtain an individual's affirmative express consent before collecting, processing, or sharing any "sensitive covered material," which is defined to include information belonging to "individuals under 17." It is unclear, however, whether the legislative proposal contemplates allowing a 15-year-old individual to provide consent. Moreover, the ADPPA Draft does not make clear whether it or COPPA would control for individuals under 13. We encourage the committee to address these issues.

[116] Section 2(22)(A)(xv).

section would provide a substantial upgrade to COPPA, where protections end when a child turns 13.

2. Prohibiting Targeted Advertising Is a Key Component to Protecting Kids' Online Safety

With few limitations, companies can track and profile children and teens and subject them to behavioral ads that are often disguised as other "real" online content.[117] I know that Adtech firms have long tracked nearly every aspect of my teenager's online activities. They collect seemingly mundane information: the strike of a key or a click of the mouse as she uses her laptop, cross tracking the information to the taps and swipes when she's on her smartphone. Given my daughter's age and her internet usage, a *single* Adtech firm likely has upwards of 100 million data points. And there are many such firms, and each with the same goal: to make predictions about kids based on the large data sets collected. With artificial intelligence (i.e., machine learning), firms identify patterns in my child's online activity and use them to build a behavioral profile on her. Then using automated algorithmic decision-making,[118] a computer determines the digital ads it believes are more likely to pique her curiosity. Whether she clicks on an ad or not – that is just another data point collected and analyzed to make further refinements to her profile.

The *human brain is not fully developed until 25*. This means that my teen's *prefrontal cortex* — the part of her brain that controls emotional maturity, self-image, and judgment — has another decade or so to go. Until then, neuroscience finds that she is not yet mature enough to make informed decisions and she shouldn't be subjected to targeted marketing. As a lawyer, there is limited legal recourse in shielding her from companies' invasive practices. As a mom, I know that my other options — repossess her laptop and phone, change the WiFi password — are impractical and feel punitive. They risk isolating her from friends. Moreover, the Adtech firms would still collect millions of data points, even if she to use the internet only for schoolwork. Her teachers don't use textbooks; instead, they post class materials to the course website, where they also provide links to other online resources. The pandemic further accelerated the widescale adoption of using the internet for nearly every aspect of learning. When her public school adopted remote-learning, teachers began requiring students to upload homework assignments to the Ed tech platform Canvas. And even with the move back to in-person learning, the practice didn't return to handing in assignments in class.[119]

Given the lack of real options, a ban on marketing to kids in the ADPPA Draft is a welcomed development.[120] Section 205(a) provides:

> A covered entity shall not engage in targeted advertising to any individual under the age of 17 if the covered entity has [actual knowledge] that the individual is under [that age].

---

[117] Under the Children's Online Privacy Protection Act, a company must obtain a parent's consent before collecting, using or disclosing the personal information of children online.

[118] An "algorithm" is basically a precise set of instructions or procedures to achieve a given task. An "automated algorithm," does not require human involvement to complete.

[119] With the increasing use of Ed tech apps in the classroom, the Commission recently issued a policy statement reminding firm of their obligations under COPPA. *See* Press Release, Federal Trade Commission, *FTC to Crack Down on Companies That Illegally Surveil Children Learning Online* (May 19, 2022) (last visited June 12, 2021).

[120] As the level of knowledge a tech firm must have under section 205(a) of the ADPPA is enclosed in bolded brackets, my observation is subject to change. *See infra* section IV. A (discussing the "actual knowledge" standard).

However, whether this ban would effectively protect children turns on the definition of "targeted advertising" under section 2(26). Notably, section 2(26)(A) establishes the category of online ads that cannot be marketed directly to children while section 2(26)(B) lists the categories of ads that companies may continue to use.

Section 2(26)(A) defines "targeted advertising" to mean:

> [D]isplaying to an individual . . . an online advertisement that is selected based on known or predicted preferences, characteristics, or interests derived from . . . data collected over time or across third party websites or online services about the individual.

Accordingly, the ADPPA Draft would make third-party advertising unlawful. However, this outcome is unclear based on the ad categories "not include[d]" as unlawful under section 2(26)(B)(i)-(iii):

i. advertising or marketing to an individual in response to the individual's specific request for information or feedback;
ii. first-party advertising based on an individual's visit into and purchase of a product or service from a brick-and-mortar store, or visit to or use of a website or online service that offers a product or service that is the subject of the advertisement; [or]
iii. contextual advertising when an advertisement is displayed online [that is related to/based on] the content of the webpage or online service on which the advertisement appears.

Here, section 2(26)(B)(ii) makes clear that the ADPPA Draft makes evident that first-party advertising is lawful. Section 2(26)(B)(iii) permits contextual advertising, but such advertising can be both first- and third-party. Additionally, as drafted, section 2(26)(B)(ii) may also permit first- and third-party.

The text of sections 205(b) and 2(26)(B) of the ADPPA Draft presents an opportunity to provide children with meaningful protections. However, we encourage the committee to clarify whether the legislative proposal contemplates a total ban of third-party advertising or whether the ban is limited in scope.

3. The Dedicated Group within the Federal Trade Commission Would Provide Kids and Families Enhanced Protection but Only if the Agency Is Properly Funded and Staffed

The ADPPA Draft section 205(c) would establish a new department within the Commission, the "Youth Privacy & Marketing Division," (Youth Division) whose sole responsibility is to "address[] the privacy of children and minors, and [the] marketing directed at children and minors." This is a marked improvement over what we have today: no regulatory resources committed entirely to protecting children online.

The ADPPA Draft recognizes the importance of having a dedicated team that focuses entirely on protecting our youth online. Standing up a Youth Division will become increasingly critical to protecting kids and teens from the next wave of emerging technologies. On the horizon is the metaverse, which Mark Zuckerberg describes this way during a *Facebook 2Q2021 earnings call:*

> It's a virtual environment where you can be present with people in digital spaces. You can think of it as an embodied internet that you are inside of rather than just looking at. This is going to be the successor of the mobile internet.

In other words, the metaverse will become as ubiquitous as the internet, which still lacks safeguards. It is hard to imagine children facing *graver dangers* in the near future. Privacy harms in the metaverse are particularly alarming because these platforms record children's nonverbal biometric data, such as facial and eye movements. This information enables Ad tech companies to track and target individuals' physical desires for commercial exploitation.[121] Common Sense's own research shows that by spending just 20 minutes in a virtual reality (VR) simulation, individuals involuntarily feed the platform nearly two million unique recordings of their body language. The safety of kids and teens is even more at risk in the universe, where there are virtual strip clubs, sexual grooming, simulated sex acts, and rape threats. With the immersive nature of VR, our youth may experience heightened trauma. The Youth Division must protect our children from existing harmful online content as well as those in a virtual world that is fast approaching.

It is unclear, however, what a new division at the Commission would have the authority to do. Section 205(c) does not identify the scope of what actions it may undertake when "addressing" children's privacy or marketing. If the ADPPA Draft were passed, without any changes specifying the team's authorities, the statute is unlikely to withstand judicial scrutiny on nondelegation grounds.[122] As drafted, it would be no surprise if the Supreme Court were to strike the provision.[123]

It is also clear that the Commission does not have the bandwidth to create this new division given existing resources. To date, Congress has already tasked the agency with enforcing *82 other laws,* including the prohibition against unfair and deceptive acts and practices under Section 5 of the Federal Trade Commission Act. Moreover, by legislative design, the Commission is the only independent federal agency tasked with protecting American consumers *and* promoting competitive markets across the economy. This is a critical mission made more difficult to accomplish by the ever-growing mismatch in resources between the Commission and tech companies.[124]

The important new protections under the proposal would be undermined if Congress failed to provide the Commission the additional resources necessary to carry out these new responsibilities. It is well documented that the agency is now and has been for years underfunded and understaffed. As internal email communications show, in addition to a hiring

---

[121] Katie Joseff and Nelson Reed, *What are Kids Doing in the Metaverse?*, Common Sense Media (Mar. 23, 2022).

[122] Under Article I of the Constitution, "All legislative powers" is vested in Congress. Courts have interpreted this to mean that Congress cannot delegate its authority to other entities, such as regulatory agencies, including the Commission. This judicial interpretation, known as the nondelegation doctrine, was last used to strike down a statute in 1935. To avoid a similar fate, any congressional policy decisions must be reflected in ADPPA's statutory text and Commission need only "fill up the details" to implement the statutory program.

[123] In 2019, Justices Gorsuch and Thomas along with Chief Justice Roberts approved reinstating the nondelegation doctrine while Justice Alito expressed interest in doing so. *Gundy vs. United States*, at No. 17-6086 (U.S. June 20, 2019) (last visited June 12, 2022). Justice Kavanaugh would likely agree based on his rulings as a judge on the D.C. Circuit Court of Appeals. *PHH Corp. v. Consumer Fin. Prot. Bureau*, 839 F.3d 1, 12 (D.C. Cir. 2016). Based on her confirmation hearings, Justice Barrett is an originalist, and likely to support this doctrine.

[124] In fact, the largest Big Tech companies enjoyed revenues in 2021: $117.9B at Meta (parent company of Facebook and Instagram), $257.6B at Alphabet (parent company for Google and YouTube), $378.3B at Apple, and $168B at Microsoft.

and pay freeze, the Commission brought fewer cases. It makes little sense to task the Commission with implementing another statutory program, especially one as important and as online privacy, without a substantial increase to the agency's budget.[125]

IV. Additional Discussion of Changes to the ADPPA Draft Are Needed to Ensure Reasonable Protections for Children and Teens.

A. The Knowledge Standard Must be Changed by Closing the Loophole Enabling Companies to Evade Complying with Children's Protections

Putting aside that brain development continues well past the teen years, the *U.S. Surgeon General Dr. Vivek Murthy's warning* about our youth mental health crisis underscores the urgency to ban targeted advertising. During the height of the pandemic, our children were not "homeschooled." We sat them down, placed a computer monitor inches from their face, told them to go online for long stretches of time. Our children were "internet-schooled." They deserve and are entitled to strong online protections. Now, more than ever.

The ADPPA Draft brackets the term "actual knowledge" in section 205(a)'s ban on targeted ads. "Actual knowledge" is the same term found in COPPA, the statute enacted decades before TikTok. Tech platforms are subject to COPPA only when they have "actual knowledge" of an individual's age, making it child's play to evade the statute's compliance requirements. In other words, COPPA does not penalize a tech firm for burying its head in the sand.

Under today's legal framework, websites and apps may turn a blind eye when young people use their services because COPPA does not make it mandatory for firms to make good faith attempt to determine a user's age. At the same time, tech platforms claiming the lack of "actual knowledge" have business models that succeed only when kids use their websites. The most prominent example is *YouTube*.[126] While touting its popularity with children to prospective advertisers, the company argued that it was not subject to COPPA requirements because it is a "general-audience" site. It refused to acknowledge that portions of its platform, such as toy review videos, were clearly directed to kids under 13.

To be clear, we are not advocating for strict liability. As children's privacy advocates, we are not interested in encouraging nor do we believe it is necessary for companies to collect even more information. Instead, we ask that this legislative proposal acknowledge that firms collect millions of data points already, and that such data informs them of the age of its users. Put simply, we ask that firms have a legal obligation to use that information, not just in its Marketing Division but also in its Legal Division.

---

[125] *Letter to the Appropriations Committees*, Common Sense Media (May 16, 2022).

[126] Earlier this year, in March 2022, the Commission ordered WW International (formerly known as Weight Watchers) to destroy the algorithms or AI models it built using personal information collected through its Kurbo healthy eating app from young kids without obtaining parental consent. WW International and Kurbo had marketed the app for use by children as young as eight years old. If the ADPPA Draft were enacted with the "actual knowledge" standard, the Commission would spend its limited resources investigating and bringing actions against wrongdoers view penalties as the cost of doing business.

B. The Private Right of Action Waiting Period Should Be Shortened and Simplified so Consumers Can Obtain Deserved Relief

We are encouraged that like other federal consumer protection statutes, the ADPPA Draft provides for a private right of action (PRA). However, we raise a few concerns for the committee's review.

We are unaware of Congress delaying the enforcement of its statutory mandates for more than two years. To be sure, there are consumer protection statutes that establish a PRA that becomes effective after the statute's enactment date. These statutes, however, provide that the period between the effective date of the PRA (along with other provisions of the statute) and the statute's enactment date ranges from 120 days to eighteen months.[127] Shortening the waiting period would better align the ADPPA Draft to other consumer protection statutes of its kind.

In addition, certain aspects of the ADPPA Draft's enforcement framework may prove burdensome for harmed consumers. For example, section 403(a)(3) requires individuals to first notify the Commission and the state attorney general of their intent to file a PRA. They must wait 60 days to provide these offices time to evaluate whether to bring a government action. When the Commission opts to enforce the statute, individuals are unlikely to recover compensatory damages.[128] And while there are other sections that merit the committee's review, we recognize that establishing a PRA framework is a step in the right direction. Market forces may work better when individuals use their own resources, not taxpayers, to obtain compensatory relief.

C. Increased Funding and Staffing for the Commission Is Essential

As stated above in section III (C) (3), the Commission is outmatched relative to the size of the companies it must regulate and number of laws it is tasked with enforcing. Congress has an obligation to the consumers on whose behalf it is drafting this legislation to also ensure that the Commission receives a robust and sustained increase in appropriations and staff slots.

---

[127] The Gramm-Leach-Bliley Act, (Financial Services Modernization Act of 1999), represents the last time Congress acknowledged privacy concerns regarding consumer information. It went into effect "120 days after the date of the enactment of this Act." (Pub. L. No. 106-102, 113 Stat. 1385). The Fair Credit Reporting Act took effect "upon the expiration of one hundred and eighty days following the date of its enactment." (Pub. L. No. 91-508, 84 Stat. 1136). The Fair Debt Collection Practices Act took effect "upon the expiration of six months after the date of its enactment." (Pub. L. No. 95-109, 91 Stat. 883). When the Equal Credit Opportunity Act was first enacted, it took effect "upon the expiration of one year after the date of its enactment." (Pub. L. No. 83-495, 88 Stat. 1525). Similarly, the ECOA Amendments of 1976 took effect "12 months after the date of enactment." (Pub. L. No. 94-239, 90 Stat. 255). Like the ECOA, the Consumer Leasing Act took effect "one year after the date of its enactment." (Pub. L. No. 94-240, 90 Stat. 261). The Electronic Fund Transfer Act took effect "upon the expiration of eighteen months from the date of its enactment, except that sections 909 and 911 [took] effect upon the expiration of ninety days after the date of enactment." (Pub. L. No. 95-630, 92 Stat. 3741). Section 909 pertains to consumer liability for unauthorized transfers while section 911 deals with the issuance of credit cards.

[128] *See AMG Capital Mgmt., LLC v. Fed. Trade Comm'n*, 593 U.S._ (2021) (holding that section 13(b) of the FTC Act does not extend the Commission's authority to obtaining monetary relief for victims). Since the Court's decision, the Commission is limited to seeking injunctive relief against wrongdoers. Until Congress passes legislation restoring the agency's authority, individuals can only obtain monetary damages against wrongdoers as long as the Commission does not seek to enforce matter itself.

Conclusion

Americans are sick and tired of having their online data and the data of their children mined and used for profit. Poll after poll shows overwhelming majorities of voters from both parties supporting new privacy protections and holding social media firms accountable. Without action from Congress, consumers are powerless against the data practices of large companies.

This year and this Congress must be the time and the place when children, teens, and all consumers are finally treated with the respect they deserve for their data. People are entitled to protection from online harms and the ability to operate in an environment that reduces the harmful impacts of online existence. Tech firms' notices must be clear and conspicuous so individuals can make choices about their online activities without penalty. This is true for all consumers but is especially needed now because of the increased online harms being experienced by children and teens.

The fact that the Committee is holding this hearing on your bipartisan and bicameral draft is an important sign that there is still time and still the will to reach a data privacy agreement. We know there is hard work ahead. Common Sense Media is committed to being a resource to you during this next phase and we again strongly encourage you to consider the changes recommended here and to reach an agreement on online data privacy and security that includes strong protections for minors.

*Ms. Schakowsky. Thank you so much.

And now, let me recognize Ms. Ohlhausen for your five minutes.

Statement of Maureen K. Ohlhausen, Co-Chair, 21st Century Privacy Coalition

*Ms. Ohlhausen. Great. Chair Schakowsky, Ranking Member Bilirakis, Chair Pallone, Ranking Member McMorris Rodgers, and other distinguished members of the subcommittee, thank you for the opportunity to testify at this important hearing.

My name is Maureen Ohlhausen, and I am the co-chair of the 21st Century Privacy Coalition and a partner at the law firm Baker Botts. I also had the pleasure of serving as an FTC commissioner and acting chairman, and I am testifying today on behalf of the coalition.

I would like to begin by commending the authors of thisbipartisan, bicameral discussion draft. The coalition has advocated for comprehensive national privacy legislation for nearly a decade, and we have always believed that such legislation needs to be bipartisan to be successful.

This discussion draft shows that there is potential for a bipartisan path forward on this urgently needed legislation. The discussion draft incorporates a number of elements that the coalition perceives as foundational in privacy legislation.

First, it is stronger and more comprehensive than existing state laws addressing issues such as transparency, consent, and other consumer rights, data security, and civil rights protections.

Second, the legislation does abase the FTC as the principal agency responsible for enforcing the new law with the assistance from state attorneys general.

Third, it provides a national framework that preempts state laws, regulations, and other requirements. In the absence of such a framework, consumers and businesses today are required to navigate a tangled web of confusing and often inconsistent data privacy requirements from various levels of government.

Fourth, the discussion draft, at least partially, recognizes not only that the FTC is the agency with the greatest experience to enforce this new law, but that legacy privacy requirements in the Communications Act must be preempted.

It embraces a more holistic and modern approach to protecting consumer privacy based upon the type of information collected, used, or shared rather than the legacy regulatory history of the entity collecting, using, or sharing such information.

We believe, however, that the draft needs to be improved before any additional action is taken on the legislation. The draft raises several concerns that warrant further consideration.

First, though the draft would preempt the FCC's privacy and data security authority with respect to broadband and video services. It stops short at preempting the same authority with respect to voice services.

Congress should provide a holistic set of requirements governing the privacy associated with voice-related information whether through traditional voice or over-the-top services. It does not benefit consumers to impose different requirements that depend upon an entity's legacy regulatory history.

Second, while the bill appropriately seeks to replace the FCC's traditional oversight of video privacy requirements with equivalent protections that would be enforced by the FTC, the language used in the bill far exceeds the requirements of the Cable Act and equivalent satellite protections as well as the reasonable obligations and standards incorporated into recent state privacy laws.

These requirements have worked well for over five decades to protect consumers while fostering innovation for cable customers. The same is true for voice information, and the bill should be revised to permit consumers to benefit from the high level of service and customized packages they have come to expect.

Third, the bill should better reflect a risk-based approach based on the nature of the relevant information and how it is used. We are concerned that the bill creates uncertainty for routine operational uses of information that are necessary to serve customers and operate a business.

Fourth, the draft seemingly provides broad state preemption, but includes various exemptions that may unduly limit its application. In past hearings before Congress, witnesses from industry, academia, and civil society have urged the adoption of a national privacy standard that would prevent an inconsistent patchwork of state regulation. Permitting states to adopt privacy-specific laws even after this law passes would be highly problematic.

Thank you, again, for the opportunity to participate in today's hearing. It is critical that Congress enact privacy legislation this year to address the growing patchwork of state laws, that we also urge the committee to keep working to improve the bill, especially in the areas I have addressed in my testimony.

Thank you.

[The prepared statement of Ms. Ohlhausen follows:]

Hearing on "Protecting America's Consumers: Bipartisan Legislation to Strengthen Data Privacy and Security," Testimony of Maureen K. Ohlhausen, Co-Chair, 21st Century Privacy Coalition House Committee on Energy & Commerce, Subcommittee on Consumer Protection and Consumer June 14, 2022

Introduction

Chair Schakowsky, Ranking Member Bilirakis, Chair Pallone, Ranking Member McMorris Rodgers, and other distinguished Members of the subcommittee, thank you for the opportunity to testify at this important hearing examining how to better protect consumer privacy. My name is Maureen Ohlhausen, and I am co-chair of the 21st Century Privacy Coalition ("Coalition"),[129] as well as a partner at the law firm Baker Botts L.L.P. I had the pleasure of serving as a Federal Trade Commission ("FTC") Commissioner (2012–2018) and Acting Chairman (2017–2018). I am testifying today on behalf of the Coalition.

I would like to begin by commending the authors of the bipartisan, bicameral discussion draft that is the subject of today's hearing. The Coalition has advocated for comprehensive national privacy legislation for nearly a decade, and we have always believed that such legislation needs to be bipartisan to be successful. This discussion draft shows that there is potential for a bipartisan path forward on this urgently needed legislation.

The Coalition appreciates that the authors and many Members of Congress are committed to enacting federal legislation. All of us share a desire for strong consumer privacy protections that apply uniformly throughout the nation based on the sensitivity and use of the data, and which allow consumers to continue to benefit from services and technologies on which we have come to rely even more heavily during this pandemic. We want consumers to enjoy confidence that their personal information is not subject to varying protections from state to state, or even within a state, regardless of the entity that collects such information.[130] Federal legislation should also provide strong enforcement that protects consumer data that could result in harm if misused or disclosed, while also allowing companies the flexibility to develop innovative new products that consumers want.

---

[129] The member companies/associations of the 21st Century Privacy Coalition are AT&T, Comcast, Cox Communications, CTIA, DIRECTV, NCTA – The Internet and Television Association, T-Mobile, USTelecom, and Verizon.

[130] *See* Memorandum from Public Opinion Strategies and Peter D. Hart to the Progressive Policy Institute, Key Findings from Recent National Survey of Internet Users (May 26, 2016), https://www.progressivepolicy.org/wp-content/uploads/2016/05/Internet-User-National-Survey-May-23- 25-Key-Findings-Memo.pdf (finding that 94% of consumers favor such a consistent and technology-neutral privacy regime, and that 83% of consumers say their online privacy should be protected based on the sensitivity of their online data, rather than by the type of Internet company that uses their data). *See also* https://www.progressivepolicy.org/press/press-releases/press-release-consumers-want-one-set-rulesprotecting- information/ ("Ultimately, consumers want to know there is one set of rules that equally applies to every company that is able to obtain and share their data, whether it be search engines, social networks, or ISPs, and they want that data protected based on the sensitivity of what is being collected' said Peter Hart.").

The Legislation Has Many of the Elements Necessary for a National Privacy Framework

The discussion draft incorporates a number of elements that the Coalition perceives as foundational in privacy legislation. First, it is stronger and more comprehensive than existing state laws, addressing issues such as transparency; consent and other consumer rights; data security; civil rights protections; and the relationship between companies, their affiliates, their vendors, and third parties. Second, the legislation designates the FTC as the principal agency responsible for enforcing the new law, and permits State Attorneys General to assist the FTC with its enforcement.

As the former Acting Chair of the FTC, I am particularly appreciative that this draft also provides the FTC with several sorely-needed enforcement tools, such as civil penalty authority for a first violation of the Act, limited APA rulemaking authority, the ability to provide restitution to consumers harmed by violations, and jurisdiction over common carriers. The FTC has brought hundreds of privacy- and data security-related enforcement actions, covering both on- and offline practices and fast-evolving technologies,[131] and is well-suited to draw on its experience and knowledge in the field to vigorously enforce the law, while still allowing consumers to enjoy the benefits of the many innovative products offered in today's dynamic marketplace. This legislation would empower the FTC with more-effective enforcement tools to protect consumers from violations.

Third, the discussion draft provides a national privacy and data security framework that preempts state laws, regulations, and other requirements. In the absence of such a framework, consumers and businesses today are required to navigate a tangled web of confusing, and often inconsistent, data privacy requirements from various levels of government. American consumers and businesses deserve the clarity and certainty of a single federal standard for privacy. That is why state preemption must be an essential component of national legislation.

Fourth, the discussion draft at least partially recognizes not only that the FTC is the agency with the greatest expertise to enforce this new law, but that legacy privacy requirements in the Communications Act must be preempted. This would allow the FTC to take a more holistic and modern approach to protecting consumer privacy based upon the type of information collected, used, or shared, rather than the legacy regulatory history of the entity collecting, using, or sharing such information.

Areas in Which the Bill Needs Improvement

We believe, however, that the discussion draft needs to be improved before this subcommittee or the Energy & Commerce Committee takes any additional action on the legislation. The draft raises several concerns that warrant further consideration. First, though the draft would preempt

---

[131] *See, e.g.*, FED. TRADE COMM'N, FTC'S USE OF ITS AUTHORITIES TO PROTECT CONSUMER PRIVACY AND SECURITY (2020), https://www.ftc.gov/system/files/documents/reports/reports-response-senate-appropriations-committee-report-116-111-ftcs-use-its-authorities-resources/p065404report privacydatasecurity.pdf; *Oversight of the Federal Trade Commission: Strengthening Protections for American's Privacy and Data Security: Hearing Before the S. Comm. on Commerce, Science, and Transportation*, 116th Congress (2019-2020) (statement of the FTC), https://www.ftc.gov/system/files/documents/public_statements/1578963/p180101testimonyftcoversight20200805.pdf.

the Federal Communications Commission's ("FCC") privacy and data security authority with respect to broadband and video services, it stops short at preempting the same authority with respect to voice services.

In today's converged, digital world, consumers utilize traditional voice services as well as over-the-top services and applications to engage in voice communications. Congress should provide a holistic set of requirements governing the privacy associated with voice-related information. It does not benefit consumers to impose different requirements that depend upon an entity's legacy regulatory history.

Second, while the bill appropriately seeks to replace the FCC's traditional oversight of video privacy requirements with equivalent protections that would be enforced by the FTC, the language used in the bill far exceeds the requirements of the Cable Act and equivalent satellite protections, as well as the reasonable obligations and standards incorporated into recent state privacy laws. The cable and satellite privacy requirements have worked well for over five decades to protect consumers, while also fostering innovation in new features and services for cable customers.

If not changed, the video provisions of the bill could result in significant disruption to operational, marketing, and advertising practices that have long served consumers well in the television marketplace. It is critical that Congress not upend the balanced structure and requirements of the Cable Act and its satellite corollary. Some modest tweaks to the draft could achieve this important result.

The same is true for the inclusion of voice information in the bill. In addition to addressing the regulatory disparity in the treatment of voice service providers I mentioned earlier in my testimony, the bill's language needs to be revised to permit consumers to benefit from the high level of service and customized packages they have come to expect.

Third, the bill should be refined so it better reflects a risk-based approach based on the nature of the relevant information and how it is used. This would be consistent with well-established principles of privacy laws and the FTC's privacy enforcement practices. We are concerned that the bill creates uncertainty for routine operational uses of information that are necessary to serve customers and operate a business. For example, our companies provide a suite of communications services, often in a bundled package. Our customers benefit when we are able to use information we collect in the course of serving them to market services, packages, or pricing that better suit their needs. Such first-party marketing should be included in Section 209's general exceptions.

Fourth, the draft ostensibly provides broad state preemption, but includes a number of exceptions to such preemption that may unduly limit its application. In past hearings before Congress, witnesses from industry, academia, and civil society have urged the adoption of a national privacy standard that would prevent an inconsistent patchwork of state regulation.[132]

---

[132] *See Protecting Consumer Privacy in the Era of Big Data: Hearing Before the Subcomm. on Consumer Protection & Commerce of the Comm. on Energy & Commerce*, 116th Cong. (2019) (statement of David F. Grimaldi, Jr., Exec. Vice President, Public Policy, Interactive Advertising Bureau) (stating a privacy framework should "reduce consumer and business confusion by preempting the growing patchwork of state privacy laws"); *id.* (statement of Roslyn Layton, Visiting Scholar, American Enterprise Inst.) (calling for a "single standard of data protection" and a "technology neutral national framework with a consistent application across enterprises."); *id.* (statement of Denise E. Zheng, Vice President, Tech. & Innovation, Business Roundtable) ("Legislation should eliminate fragmentation of privacy protections in the United States by harmonizing approaches to consumer privacy across federal and state jurisdictions through a comprehensive national law that ensures consistent

Establishing a truly national framework must be a core component of federal privacy legislation. Permitting states to adopt privacy-specific laws even after this law passes would be highly problematic. In addition, we are concerned about the meaning of the term "electronic surveillance" in the context of this bill, which is undefined and could be interpreted by states very broadly. The predictable outcome would lead to confusion and litigation, both of which the legislation should strive to avoid.

Fifth, the discussion draft would ban joint-action waivers in arbitration agreements, which would have the practical effect of making arbitration unavailable to millions of consumers with individualized claims who lack the resources to pursue such claims in court.

Conclusion

Thank you again for the opportunity to participate in today's hearing. I again applaud the authors of this bill and both Commerce Committees for the hard work that has gone into developing a comprehensive national privacy law. We view this draft as progress toward that goal, but also believe improvements are necessary to achieve the bill's underlying purposes.

It is critical that Congress enact privacy legislation this year to address the growing patchwork of state laws, though we also urge the Committee to keep working to improve the bill, especially in the areas I have addressed in my testimony. The Coalition appreciates the opportunity to continue to work with the bill's authors and the Committee to achieve bipartisan consensus on national, technology-neutral privacy legislation that provides clear protections for consumers, articulates specific limits on companies' ability to collect, use, and share sensitive personal information, and grants the FTC the explicit authority necessary to enforce a new law. I look forward to your questions.

*Ms. Schakowsky. Thank you.

And Mr. Dufault, you are recognized for five minutes.

Statement of Graham Dufault, Senior Director for Public Safety, Act – The App Association

*Mr. Dufault. Thank you, Chairwoman Schakowsky, Ranking Member Bilirakis, Chairman Pallone, Ranking Member McMorris Rodgers.

My name is Graham Dufault, and I am senior director for public policy at ACT, The App Association. The App Association is the leading trade group representing small software and mobile device companies in the app economy which accounts for about $6.3 trillion globally and supports about 5.9 million jobs here in the U.S. alone.

---

privacy protections and avoids a state-by- state approach that leads to consumer confusion and makes compliance nationwide very challenging.").

Additionally, testimony from Nuala O'Connor, then CEO of the Center for Democracy and Technology, described CDT's model baseline privacy legislation, which includes preemption of state privacy laws. *See* Center for Democracy & Tech., Federal Baseline Privacy Legislation Discussion Draft (Dec. 5, 2018), https://cdt.org/wp-content/uploads/2018/12/2018-12-12-CDT-Privacy-Discussion-Draft-Final.pdf.

We applaud this subcommittee and its counterparts for bringing us closer than we have ever been to a federal privacy law.

Consumers want to leverage software and connectivity to access better services from healthcare and education to payments and productivity, but we have heard loud and clear that consumers are sick of finding out that their data has been misused for unexpected and ulterior purposes and that harms accrue from those misuses.

This draft takes us one step closer to a federal regime that enables consumers to access digital tools that they want in the manner they expect.

For our member companies, a federal privacy law must accomplish two overarching goals: Number one, the bill must enhance consumers' trust in software-driven goods and services, so the requirements must be meaningful; and number two, the bill must provide legal certainty for small companies like our members.

The draft bill we consider today, the American Data Privacy and Protection Act, provides the framework we need to achieve these goals at this moment – and I trust measures are pending in both chambers – that could threaten to completely undo the current data privacy and security protections that consumers enjoy in the mobile space, so this privacy draft is an especially welcome developed.

But even though this effort is one we encourage; we urge the subcommittee to consider the following:

First, the private right of action or PRA. This enforcement mechanism in the draft is a powerful one. It authorizes private litigants to seek injunctions against covered entities for all but a few violations of the Act, but appropriately, there are safeguards.

A litigant must first notify the FTC and their state AG before bringing a claim, and then, issue a demand letter clearly identifying the violation at issue. Then, the way we understand it is that, the target generally has the right to cure the violation within 45 days. These protections help, but we urge the negotiators to work with us to perfect this language.

Second, the preemption provision. The overarching paragraph preempts state laws that are covered by the provisions of the Act. Then, there are 16 or so exemptions to the main paragraph, and these make the Court's job more complicated when interpreting Congress's intent in this space. So on this, we hope to work with negotiators to finetune that language as well.

Third, the compliance programs. The draft appropriately authorizes the FTC to approve small business compliance programs that meet or exceed the requirements in the draft. Small software and connected-device companies want to comply with strong privacy and data security laws, and they can.

Compliance programs help ensure that they have the resources to do so, and they send a signal of quality to the market.

Fourth, data minimization and consumer rights. We have been calling for Congress to provide rights for consumers to access, delete, and correct data about themselves, and we also support sensible limits on collection and processing. We believe these consumer protections would benefit small businesses as well, and we think the negotiators have struck a reasonable balance on these sections of the draft.

But compromise for the sake of compromise is meaningless. What are really trying to accomplish with the privacy bill? From our perspective, a privacy bill is necessary to ensure people's data works for them, not against them, and our member companies need a straightforward federal regime that makes way for an innovation on privacy.

Take Tampa Bay's Thinkamingo, for example. Thinkamingo serves student-age kids from all over the country with apps that help their creative writing and other skills. It would be subject to the draft bill in its commonsense updates regarding adolescents aged 13 to 17, but also, the Children's Online Privacy Protection Act as a service for children, limitations on cross-app tracking, and parental control – or it benefits from device-level privacy features like on-device processing and limitations on cross-app tracking and parental controls, and we want to make sure the federal law supports these innovations.

Inevitably, the world under the draft would be complex for our members, but that's true of the status quo too and imagine how much worse it would be with 50 different iterations of these moving pieces.

This is why we need a federal privacy law to be as clear as possible. It must limit openings for opportunists to take advantage of and profit from our member companies confusion; but above all, a federal privacy law must support and enhance the trust consumers have in the software that increasingly powers healthcare, financial services, education, and entertainment and so many other aspects of our lives.

We urge Congress to seize this moment confidently but carefully. We appreciate being a part of this process, and I look forward to your questions.

[The prepared statement of Mr. Dufault follows:]

Protecting America's Consumers: Bipartisan Legislation to Strengthen Data Privacy and Security, Testimony of Graham Dufault, Senior Director for Public Policy, ACT | The App Association, before the U.S. House of Representatives, Committee on Energy and Commerce, Subcommittee on Consumer Protection and Commerce

Executive Summary

ACT | The App Association (the App Association) is the leading trade group representing small mobile software and connected device companies in the app economy, a $6.3 trillion global ecosystem[133] led by U.S. companies and employing 205,360 people in Illinois and 237,090 in Florida.[134] Our member companies create the software that brings your smart devices to life. They also make the connected devices that are revolutionizing healthcare, education, public safety, and virtually all industry verticals. They propel the data-driven evolution of these industries and compete with each other and larger firms in a variety of ways, including on privacy and security protections.

We applaud this Subcommittee for its lead role in the 117th Congress' unprecedented progress toward a comprehensive federal privacy regime clarifying and enhancing the privacy and data security authorities of the Federal Trade Commission (FTC or Commission). Congress has never been closer to a compromise bill that would set a single, national set of rules for data privacy and security across all 50 states and the territories, while better protecting consumers

[133] ACT | THE APP ASSOCIATION, APP ECONOMY FAST FACTS (May 2022), *available at https://actonline.org/wp- content/uploads/About-the-App-Economy.pdf.*

[134] ACT | THE APP ASSOCIATION, STATE OF THE U.S. APP ECONOMY: 2020 (7th Ed.), *available at* https://actonline.org/wp-content/uploads/2020-App-economy-Report.pdf.

and limiting unnecessary compliance costs and legal gamesmanship. We are especially pleased that Congress is taking meaningful steps toward a federal privacy framework, which policymakers should pursue to the exclusion of antitrust proposals that would manifestly weaken data privacy and security protections for your constituents.[135]

Here is a summary of our takeaways regarding the draft American Data Privacy and Protection Act (ADPPA):

- Preemption, Sec. 404(b)
  - The overarching preemption language is reasonably strong, but a small tweak could enhance its effectiveness. Similarly, each exception to it could threaten its integrity and some of the exceptions would allow laws that fail to strike a reasonable balance to stand.
- Private right of action, Sec. 403
  - The right to sue for a violation of ADPPA is broad, applying to any person or class of persons, for an injury associated with a violation of ADPPA or regulations under it. It is also powerful, offering compensatory damages or injunctions as available remedies. However, we appreciate the guardrails in this draft, which we believe would help deter nuisance lawsuits and sue- and-settle business models that fail to benefit consumers while taxing small companies.
- Small business treatment
  - Although some of ADPPA's provisions may be unnecessarily broad or subject covered entities and even consumers to undue risks, we believe the bill takes a balanced approach to small businesses, applying certain requirements only to large data holders and providing a safe harbor for small businesses under a certain threshold.

I. Preemption and Private Right of Action

A) Preemption, Sec. 404(b)

We have advocated for a federal privacy framework to include a preemption provision expressly preempting state laws for years now and appreciate that ADPPA includes one. The Information Technology and Innovation Foundation (ITIF) recently estimated the costs on businesses if 50 states enacted their own separate privacy regimes.[136] The study projected an annual cost of $98 to $112 billion for out-of-state companies, with $20 to $23 billion of that cost landing on small firms like App Association members. If we sound like a broken record on preemption, it is because these costs are avoidable and not necessary to meaningfully protect consumers from data privacy and security harms.

---

[135] *See* Letter from Morgan Reed, president, ACT | The App Association, to Majority Leader Chuck Schumer and Minority Leader Mitch McConnell, United States Senate, Re: Open App Markets Act (S. 2710) and American Innovation and Choice Online Act (S. 2992) Would Create Unacceptable New Threat Vectors in Mobile Ecosystems (Mar. 8, 2022).

[136] INFO. TECH. & INNOVATION FOUNDATION, THE LOOMING COST OF A PATCHWORK OF STATE PRIVACY LAWS (Jan. 2022), *available at* https://cdn.sanity.io/files/03hnmfyj/production/2ecc8714efc329b2494f47cede821a40c9a0e6d5.pdf.

The overarching preemption language is reasonably strong, providing that no state or political subdivision of a state may "adopt, maintain, enforce, prescribe, or continue in effect" any law or provision having the force and effect of law, "covered by" the provisions of ADPPA or regulations promulgated under it. This construct should capture the general-applicability privacy laws that would create the most significant confusion, conflict, and compliance issues we have urged Congress to avoid as states enact slightly differing privacy requirements. However, we would recommend that the negotiators amend the provision to preempt any state provision "related to" the provisions of ADPPA. The Supreme Court has interpreted the "covered by" construct more narrowly than "related to," such that courts have upheld state laws directly regulating the subject of a federal law with "covered by" preemption language.[137] A strong, federal privacy law that comprehensively regulates data privacy and security activities should supersede state laws that address the same conduct, even if they have a narrower scope or more detailed requirements.

The 16 exceptions to the preemption provision make the "related to" construct especially important. Nonetheless, the negotiators should consider removing some of them because ADPPA is unlikely to preempt many of the laws the exceptions intend to address, so the exceptions may serve only to unintentionally except laws that should be preempted. Despite the established precedent on "related to" versus "covered by," courts have approached preemption of state laws in unpredictable ways, so we believe an express preemption provision is necessary to realize Congress' intent for a federal privacy framework to be the law of the land. Unfortunately, each exception creates additional risks that a court might expand its breadth to cover state laws and requirements that Congress never meant to except from preemption. For example, the exception for "laws that address health information" may be read to except a more general privacy law that happens to address health information not otherwise subject to the Health Insurance Portability and Accountability Act (HIPAA)—a category of state requirement the bill probably intends to preempt. A broad reading of that exception, or another like it, might result in the state patchwork Congress seeks to avoid. ADPPA appropriately addresses healthcare data and subjects it to heightened requirements, including opt-in consent. As we noted in a letter to this Committee last year,[138] privacy abuses like the one at issue with the FTC's *Flo* settlement—which involved health data not otherwise covered by HIPAA—is one of the most important reasons for Congress to establish a federal privacy law.

Some of the specific laws that appear in the exceptions may also fail to strike the thoughtful balance the negotiators have in this draft.[139] We urge the negotiators to consider strengthening Sec. 404(b)(1) to preempt state provisions "related to" ADPPA's provisions and remove some of the exceptions in 404(b)(2)—or at least make one of those changes or the other. Arguably, many of those exceptions are unnecessary, especially if the negotiators keep the "covered by"

---

[137] *See CSX Transportation, Inc. v. Easterwood*, 507 U.S. 658, 664 (1993) (interpreting a "covered by" preemption clause); *Morales v. Trans World Airlines, Inc.*, 504 U.S. 374, 382 (1992) (interpreting a "relating to" preemption provision).

[138] Letter from Morgan Reed, president, ACT | The App Association, to The Honorable Frank Pallone, Chairman, House Committee on Energy and Commerce, and The Honorable Cathy McMorris Rodgers, Republican Leader, House Committee on Energy and Commerce (Feb. 17, 2021).

[139] CLIFFORD CHANCE, THE COMING WAVE OF BIOMETRIC CLASS-ACTION SUITS, attorney advertising (Mar. 2021), *available at* https://www.cliffordchance.com/content/dam/cliffordchance/briefings/2021/03/The-Coming-Wave-of-Biometric-Class-Action-Suits.pdf.

language (which, all else equal, federal courts will likely interpret to let a broader class of state laws stand than if the provision used a "related to" construct).

Lastly, we agree with the bracketed text in Sec. 404(b)(2)(A), clarifying that a common law claim may not cite a violation of ADPPA as an element of liability. This language would help prevent private causes of action ADPPA does not intend to create in Sec. 403 or except from preemption in Sec. 404(b)(E).

B) Private Right of Action, Sec. 403

The negotiators have arrived at a reasonable compromise on this provision, which provides a good basis for further potential improvement. The private right of action (PRA) in ADPPA would apply to the entire Act and its regulations—except for data minimization, privacy by design, or data security requirements—and to any person or class injured by a violation. This provides especially broad coverage in terms of both which kinds of violations can give rise to a PRA and which categories of consumers may bring a PRA. For example, the PRA in this draft is available for almost all violations of the ADPPA and is not limited to a subset of injury types from a violation. Similarly, Sec. 404(b) prohibits pre-dispute arbitration agreements in certain circumstances (for example, with respect to individuals under the age of 18). Finally, the PRA in ADPPA would make powerful remedies available to individuals. In addition to compensatory damages, an individual litigant could seek and obtain an injunction for a violation of ADPPA or any of its regulations. The threat of an injunction can lead to much higher settlements because a putative defendant may be induced to pay an amount just under the cost of not being able to do business at all (e.g., the business's entire revenue amount for the duration of an injunction). As a corollary, injunctions can also be attractive for opportunistic trial attorneys to engage in a pattern of suing and settling for frivolous reasons unrelated to protecting consumers because of their potentially higher payouts.

ADPPA's PRA includes a few safeguards that would mitigate the potential for the PRA to impose undue costs on covered entities, and we appreciate the negotiators' thoughtful approach in this regard. For example, before bringing a claim, an individual litigant would first have to notify the FTC and a state attorney general's (AG's) office, giving the enforcement agencies 60 days to determine whether to take on the complaint. If the agencies have declined to act on the complaint, then the individual or class may proceed with a demand letter to a target. Pursuant to Sec. 403(d), the demand letter must include a passage guiding the target to the FTC's website for further information, and pursuant to 403(c)(1) must also identify the specific provisions of the Act the target is alleged to have violated. Upon receipt of the demand letter, a small business target (or if an injunction is sought, any covered entity target) has a right to "cure" the alleged violation, "in the event a cure is possible." Under 403(c)(2), if the target "demonstrates it has cured the noticed violation or violations and provides the person . . . an express written statement that the violation or violations has been cured and that no further violations shall occur, an action for injunctive relief may be reasonably dismissed."

The safeguards here provide some meaningful protection from harassing and low-value lawsuits. However, we urge the negotiators to consider a few potential improvements.

First, the PRA could be limited to a narrower subset of violations of the law. For example, a PRA may not be as helpful to remedy failures to respond to a request to correct but may be appropriate to address data security lapses (provided that the preemption exception for California's privacy law is removed). Second, the effect of the cure in 403(c)(2) may be unintentionally limited to providing for the reasonable dismissal of injunctions only, even if the target is a small business under 209(c). We believe this may be inadvertently narrow, given that 403(c)(1) provides a right to cure for injunctive relief *or* for presumably any relief sought against a small business under 209(c). We recommend the negotiators amend 403(c)(2) to read (new text in bold), "an action for injunctive relief or, with respect to an action against a covered entity that meets the requirements of section 209(c) of this Act, an action for any relief provided in section 403(a)(2), shall not be permitted and may be reasonably dismissed." Without a change along these lines, the legislation might unintentionally limit the effect of a cure for small businesses—and adding "shall not be permitted" could strengthen the provision and give courts more cover for dismissal.

Third, we urge the negotiators to consider limiting the PRA to a subset of injury types. For example, instead of any injury giving rise to a PRA, it could be limited to "substantial" privacy harms resulting from a given violation, providing a more meaningful deterrent to lawsuits that impose disproportionate costs on small companies for relatively minor issues. Lastly, negotiators could require private litigants to show that covered entities possessed some level of scienter (or consciousness) of the alleged violation. This additional safeguard would help protect small businesses from facing private lawsuits involving good faith or inadvertent lapses that result in little or no harm to individuals.

II. Consumer and Civil Rights

One of our primary asks of Congress has been for a federal privacy bill to include a set of consumer rights, "implemented in a way that avoids additional compliance layers without enhancing consumer understanding and trust."[140] The balance the negotiators struck with ADPPA is a solid foundation. However, we have some constructive feedback for the negotiators to consider as they continue their work.

A) Consumer Rights, Sec. 202

Sec. 202(b)(9) would require covered entities to disclose "whether or not any covered data collected by the covered entity is transferred to, processed in, or otherwise made available to" China, Russia, Iran, or North Korea. We share the concerns with foreign adversaries' access to and exploitation of Americans' data. Even so, the location of data may provide less valuable insights into the risk than whether foreign adversaries are able to access it. For example, if a company is based in such a country—and therefore subject to the adversary's national security and surveillance laws—then even if the data is stored outside that country, we should worry about its access to Americans' data stored by that company. Meanwhile, an American app company may be barred under U.S. law from cooperating with foreign adversary investigators, illustrating that the location of the data alone is instructive but not as dispositive of a foreign adversary's access to it than whether the company is based in that country. There do not appear to be any restrictions on the app company from caveating the 202(b)(9) disclosure to accurately reflect why it may need to process data in China or another of those countries—and therefore

---

[140] *See* ACT | THE APP ASSOCIATION, PROTECTING CONSUMER PRIVACY GROWS SMALL BUSINESS (May 2022), *available at* https://actonline.org/wp-content/uploads/Protecting-Consumer-Privacy-Grows-Small-Business95-1.pdf.

clarify that such processing should present no additional risk to Americans. Clarifying this in the bill or report language may help ameliorate any unintended consequences of the provision.

B) Civil Rights, Sec. 207

This section includes a requirement for covered entities to conduct either an "impact assessment" (if they are large data holders) or an "algorithm design evaluation" if a non- large data holder develops the algorithm itself. We urge the negotiators to consider couple of factors on these provisions. First, the impact assessment provision applying to large data holders might inadequately protect sensitive information related to the algorithm, its training, and its use. Sec. 207(c)(3)(C)(ii) allows the covered entity to redact "trade secrets," but there may be other information that, if it lands in the wrong hands, may pose unintended consequences. Similarly, the requirement to allow access to any Member of Congress may inadvertently result in sensitive non-public information being published or placed in the hands of an entity that may seek to harm the individuals to which it pertains. Accordingly, we encourage the negotiators to reconsider allowing such access to any congressional office and to impose safeguards on access to impact assessments in the hands of the FTC (e.g., by providing an exemption from the Freedom of Information Act (FOIA)). Second, we urge the negotiators to consider amending Sec. 207(c)(3)(B) so that it reads "to the extent practicable" instead of "possible." Hiring an external firm to evaluate an algorithm may impose costs on small firms developing lower-risk algorithms that are not justified by the benefits. Accordingly, we also urge the negotiators to amend 207(b)(5)(B) so that it reads "shall exclude" instead of "may exclude." This change would appropriately require the FTC to exclude low and minimal risk algorithms from the requirements' coverage, instead of leaving it to the agency's discretion.

We appreciate that this provision appropriately scopes the role of the FTC to one in which the agency assists other agencies in enforcing other existing civil rights laws, where applicable. We have urged this approach in the past and appreciate that the negotiators have adopted it with the ADPPA draft. However, the PRA also applies to this section, so individuals may sue for a violation of it. Sec. 207(a)(1) would broadly prohibit collecting, processing, or transferring covered data in a manner that "discriminates or otherwise makes unavailable the equal enjoyment of goods or services on the basis of race, color, religion, national origin, gender, sexual orientation, or disability." Since other laws address these forms of discrimination (although perhaps not explicitly as it relates to transferring or processing data in a manner that results in discrimination), it is unclear to what extent a PRA for such discrimination would be duplicative of those other civil rights laws. Protecting civil rights is rightfully a priority for the negotiators, but we urge caution as to how opportunistic litigants may widen or contort a broad prohibition like the one in 207(a)(1). For example, the Virginia Consumer Privacy Act and the Connecticut consumer privacy law both prohibit processing personal data in violation of state and federal laws that prohibit unlawful discrimination against consumers.[141] This approach could more directly address the problem without inadvertently broadening liability beyond its intended scope. We look forward to working with the negotiators to better understand how they intend for it to be enforced.

---

[141] *See* Va. Code Ann. 59.1-571 – 59.1-581 (2021); Connecticut State Senate, Substitute Senate Bill No. 6, Pub. Act No. 22-15 (2022 Sess.), *available at* https://www.cga.ct.gov/2022/ACT/PA/PDF/2022PA-00015- R00SB-00006-PA.PDF.

III. Definitions

A) Sensitive Covered Data, Sec. 2(22)

ADPPA requires covered entities to obtain express, affirmative consent for collecting and processing sensitive covered data, so the definition should not extend to substantially all data. There are a few categories of data that we urge the negotiators to consider removing from the definition of sensitive covered data:

- Sec. 2(22)(i) – This provision appropriately includes Social Security numbers (SSNs), other government identification, etc., but the exception for "required by law" to be displayed may be narrow. This exception should be broadened to include such information that is "lawfully made available publicly," or a similar construct that would remove publicly available government identification information from sensitive covered data.
- Sec. 2(22)(vii) – This provision appropriately includes the content of certain personal communications, but also certain metadata associated with those communications. We believe it may be unnecessary to include "any information that pertains to the transmission of voice communications," as it could sweep in more metadata than the provision intends.
- Sec. 2(22)(xii) – This provision includes "calendar information" and related pieces of information. This may unintentionally add unnecessary friction where, for example, an app seeks to add or export an event to or from a separate app, and we urge the negotiators to remove it.
- Sec. 2(22)(xiv) – This provision covers viewing habits. It may also unintentionally add friction where a consumer intends to provide access to their streaming viewing information in the course of using a streaming service.

B) Biometric Information, Sec. 2(3)

The definition of "biometric information" in ADPPA includes "facial or hand imagery," which are broad concepts that may sweep in more than the negotiators intend. For example, modern smart devices often use this kind of imagery to authenticate users each time they want to access their device or an app. Requiring opt-in consent for each use could in many cases add needless friction for authentication uses, even if more sensitive uses (such as one-to-many identification) might generally warrant opt-in consent.

C) Covered Data, Sec. 2(8)

The definition is a thoughtful one that appropriately excludes de-identified data, employee data, and publicly available information and we appreciate that ADPPA endorses a privacy by design approach. However, we urge the negotiators to consider whether the draft could clarify that when a covered entity designs secure systems that put data in control of the user in a manner that shields it from the covered entity's access, the draft avoids unnecessarily subjecting such data to opt-in consent and other requirements.

IV. Other Provisions

A) Data Minimization, Sec. 101

We applaud the negotiators for adopting a workable data minimization framework. The provision would prohibit collections, processing, or transfer beyond what is reasonably necessary, proportionate, and limited to products and services requested by the individual or communications anticipated within the context of the relationship. We had advocated for negotiators to avoid the approach of barring all processing unless a lawful basis exists and ADPPA's framework fortunately takes the more flexible approach. We also appreciate that instead of rules, ADPPA requires the FTC to issue nonbinding guidance, which will help inform covered entities without subjecting them to more complex forms of liability.

B) Data Protections for Children and Minors, Sec. 205

We welcome provisions to strengthen privacy protections for children and adolescents beyond the Children's Online Privacy Protection Act (COPPA). We appreciate the goals of the negotiators in addressing targeted advertising to minors and agree that Congress should address the issue. However, we note that there may be constitutional implications for an outright ban on certain kinds of advertising. Experience has shown that bans on advertising, even to minors, have had difficulty standing up to First Amendment scrutiny,[142] and there may be less constitutionally fraught ways of dealing with the issues the negotiators seek to address. We would welcome the opportunity to work with the negotiators on this provision.

We also appreciate that Sec. 205(d) would require the FTC's Inspector General to issue a report on COPPA's safe harbors. The safe harbor program plays a vital role in enabling small businesses to appropriately protect kids online and helps send a signal to parents that an appropriate third party has reviewed and certified an app or other service's compliance. This Subcommittee's rigorous oversight could help strengthen and improve the program and we welcome this scrutiny.

C) Small Business Provisions, Secs. 209(c), 304

Sec. 304 appropriately provides a safe harbor for small businesses adhering to compliance programs that "meet or exceed" the ADPPA's requirements, with a reasonable threshold described at 209(c). Notably, 209(c)'s threshold is pegged at $41 million in annual revenue or processing data on 100,000 or fewer *individuals*—as opposed to devices—per year on average over the most recent three-year period. We appreciate the negotiators' recognition that the number of connected devices per household has doubled over the past few years and therefore a threshold based on number of devices may be a less accurate reflection of the breadth of a company's impact on consumers. The safe harbor would ensure that App Association members are rightfully viewed as—and held accountable for—complying with a federal framework, while alleviating liability concerns and compliance burdens.

---

[142] *See Reno v. ACLU*, 521 U.S. 844 (1997).

V. Oppose Antitrust Proposals That Prohibit Privacy and Security

Pending legislation in both chambers—the American Innovation and Choice Online Act (S. 2992/H.R. 3816) and the Open App Markets Act (S. 2710/H.R. 7030)—would prohibit key privacy and security measures that protect consumers on their mobile devices. For example, mobile software platforms (app store/operating system combinations) recently introduced additional controls for smartphone owners, enabling them to limit the ability for one app to track their activities across other apps. Apple's version of the feature is called AppTrackingTransparency (ATT), which has been available for about a year[143]—and Android's, called Privacy Sandbox, was announced in February.[144]

Controls like ATT and Privacy Sandbox address a notoriously intractable information asymmetry problem with online services—that the behavioral advertisers building profiles on people know a lot more about what they're doing than consumers themselves. The information asymmetry problem is a common form of "market failure," if it leads to consumers not understanding an economic bargain and therefore may distort the market. But in this case, the market itself has produced solutions that consumers seem to use, as statistics indicate that 75 to 90 percent of consumers[145] are opting out of cross-app tracking. ATT and Privacy Sandbox are a good start, but we still need a federal privacy law. Controls like this should be available in other marketplaces, not just on smartphones. H.R. 3816 and H.R. 7030 would essentially prohibit ATT and Privacy Sandbox, so we urge members of this Subcommittee to oppose the bills for the same reasons as supporting privacy legislation.

Certainly, free online services and ad-supported apps are important options. Some of our member companies offer ad-supported apps and many of them benefit from knowing whether an ad they've purchased was successful. However, an ecosystem in which that overarching model is the *only* choice—and that unshackles abuses in data collection—obviously fails to serve most consumers, at least the large majority who have opted out of cross-app tracking. And advertising is not valueless, nor is it inherently less effective, with the introduction of more effective consent mechanisms. Of course, the corollary to the notion that consumers care about privacy is that they are willing to pay for it. For example, one white paper found a 0.3 percent increase[146] in the likelihood that an iOS app would be paid or offer in-app payments after Apple rolled out ATT. Even so, the fact that this effect is infinitesimal pokes a hole in inflated rhetoric around ATT's competition foreclosure effects, and it also suggests the direct costs of privacy controls are, thus far, insubstantial (even if consumers *are* willing to pay more for privacy).

If Congress wants to improve the competitive prospects of nascent and smaller competitors in the app economy, diminishing the value of the app stores by steamrolling their privacy features is not a welcome solution. Rather, we believe this Subcommittee's and its counterparts'

---

[143] Anthony Ha, "Apple's App Tracking Transparency feature has arrived – here's what you need to know," TECHCRUNCH (Apr. 26, 2021), *available at* https://techcrunch.com/2021/04/26/apples-app-tracking-transparency-feature-has-arrived-heres-what-you-need-to-know/.

[144] Anthony Chavez, VP, Product Management, Android Security & Privacy, "Introducing the Privacy Sandbox on Android," The Keyword blog (Feb. 16, 2022), *available at* https://blog.google/products/android/introducing-privacy-sandbox-android/.

[145] Manoj Balasubramanian, "App Tracking Transparency Opt-In Rate – Monthly Updates," Flurry (May 2, 2022), *available at* https://www.flurry.com/blog/att-opt-in-rate-monthly-updates/.

[146] Reinhold Kesler, "The Impact of Apple's App Tracking Transparency on App Monetization," Work in Progress (Apr. 14, 2022), *available at* https://www.dropbox.com/s/miom2cdoub8241w/ATT_Paper_Kesler.pdf?dl=0.

work on ADPPA and similar measures could uplift the value of all the other distribution options, including the open internet, by subjecting the broader ecosystem to a set of national requirements. That way, consumers think about digital goods and services as privacy protective whether they are obtained through a mobile software platform or on an HTML website. We would prefer the route of enhancing the value of all the competitive alternatives rather than destroying one of them.

Conclusion

As a key negotiator in the bicameral, bipartisan effort to enact federal privacy reform, this Subcommittee's work must be commended, and we hope our input is a constructive addition to the negotiators' work. We look forward to further assisting these efforts as the process unfolds.

Appendix: App Economy Innovators in Your Districts

Tech driven small businesses are the backbone of innovation, driving solutions that power how we live, work, and play through safe, secure, connected technology. Below you will find companies in corresponding congressional districts for each member of the Subcommittee on Consumer Protection and Commerce. These companies are not only driving innovation across the app economy, but they're also creating jobs and opportunities in your communities, taking your district, and our nation, further into the 21st century workforce as global leaders.

Majority

Rep. Jan Schakowsky, Chair (IL-09)
Company: Kidz Learn Applications
The one-woman team at Kidz Learn Applications has been developing iOS and Android mobile apps that provide educational content to children for the past decade. Kidz Learn Applications has developed more than 20 apps with lessons ranging from math to vocabulary and even created a guide for educational, kid-friendly places in New York City for a day of fun for kids and adults alike.

Rep. Bobby Rush (IL-01)
Company: Duality Accelerator
Founded just last year, Duality Accelerator is a 12-month program based in Chicago that helps early-stage software and hardware startups to reach a viable stage of business. Their first cohort consisted of six companies engaging in quantum technology, and they have partnered with entities such as the Universities of Illinois and Chicago as well as Argonne National Laboratory and the Chicago Quantum Exchange.

Rep. Kathy Castor (FL-14)
Company: Accusoft
Located in Tampa with 170 employees, Accusoft, originally founded as Pegasus Imaging Corporation in 1991, focuses primarily on content processing through image and document cleanup while providing application programming interfaces (APIs) and barcode collection through mobile apps. They also provide digital conversion tools that turn paper document and paper-based processes (often found in legal, financial, and health transactions) into customized digital processes based on each client's unique needs.

Rep. Lori Trahan (MA-03)
Company: Fisheye Software
Founded in 1997 and located in Maynard, Fisheye Software focuses on building enterprise-level software that makes complex systems easier to understand. They provide services to a number of clients, both in the government and commercial systems, contributing to anything from data archiving to air traffic control or missile defense systems.

Rep. Jerry McNerney (CA-09)
Company: CloudKrest Technology Solutions
Cloudkrest is a two-person digital marketing solutions company located in Stockton and has been in business since 2017. Cloudkrest is focused specifically on web design, app development, digital branding, and content creation with customers both local and international.

Rep. Yvette Clarke (NY-09)
Company: Stellar Health
Since Stellar Health's founding in 2018, this Manhattan-based healthcare technology company has rapidly grown to nearly 200 employees and is providing connected health solutions to patients everywhere. Stellar Health helps provide providers with targeted recommendations to deliver value-based improvements to care and financial performance to hospitals. This means that through Stellar Health's services, patients receive care faster and at a lower cost throughout the care chain.

Rep. Tony Cárdenas (CA-29)
Company: Swift 200
Located in Panorama City, Swift 200 is a custom software development firm that works to solve a wide range of problems for clients of varying sizes within the app economy. From content marketing and search engine optimization (SEO) to web and mobile application development, Swift takes projects from idea to reality.

Rep. Debbie Dingell (MI-12)
Company: Arbormoon Software Inc.
Founded in 2004, the eight-person team at Arbormoon Software focuses almost entirely on mobile app development, whether it be iOS or Android. Based in Ann Arbor, they have created apps for the University of Michigan as well as SiriusXM, Peterbilt, local radio stations, and a number of other small businesses and startups local to the area.

Rep. Robin Kelly (IL-02)
Company: Pathfinder
Based in Kankakee and founded in 2020, Pathfinder is a full-service creative marketing agency that helps their clients tell stories through web and mobile solutions. Having grown to nearly 100 employees in less than two years, their offerings include web development, graphic design, photography, and other digital marketing offerings.

Rep. Darren Soto (FL-09)
Company: Yac
Originally founded as "Yelling Across Cubicles"—because it was essentially built as a digital walkie talkie to be used in the workplace—Yac was founded in 2019 and located in Kissimmee. Since then, Yac has grown to include other functionality including asynchronous meetings, voice messages, screensharing, and shareable links, all focused on making remote work more collaborative.

Rep. Kathleen Rice (NY-04)
Company: AppSoft Technologies, Inc.
Located in Garden City and founded in 2015, AppSoft Technologies creates mobile applications for entertainment and gaming audiences. AppSoft Technology is singularly focused on creating mobile apps that are geared towards video games, esports news, and information. They also acquire existing games and redevelop or otherwise improve them.

Rep. Angie Craig (MN-02)
Company: Avionte Staffing and Recruiting Software
Avionte Staffing and Recruiting Software, located in Eagan, provides solutions for payroll, attendance, and billing, as well as customer relationship management, new job applications, and onboarding capabilities. Since opening their doors in 2005, they have served more than 900 customers and nearly 25,000 users across the United States and Canada.

Rep. Lizzie Fletcher (TX-07)
Company: For All Abilities
For All Abilities is a software platform that helps companies address and provide for their employees with disabilities. The platform assesses employees and then prescribes and trains them to use individualizes supports and accommodations that meet ADA requirements.

Rep. Frank Pallone, Ex officio (NJ-06)
Company: DealerApp Vantage
DealerApp Vantage, located in Piscataway, is the nation's leading native mobile app development company that specializes in automotive dealers. They have mobile app solutions aimed to fit all budgets and sizes, from small business, single roof top dealerships to some of the largest auto groups in the United States.

Minority

Rep. Gus Bilirakis, Ranking Member (FL-12)
Company: Thinkamingo
Since 2011, Tampa-based Thinkamingo has been a husband-and-wife team working together to build family friendly, education-focused mobile apps. Their apps range from interactive dice meant to take young writers to inspired story tellers to imagination- driven spy kits complete with virtual disguises, including a voice changer.

Rep. Fred Upton (MI-06)
Company: SPARK Business Works
Founded nearly five years ago and headquartered in Kalamazoo, with two other offices in the state, SPARK Business Works is a custom software development and design firm. They stand prepared to help businesses of any size create an effective online presence that aims to improve each client's unique needs for the connected customer experience.

Rep. Bob Latta (OH-05)
Company: Spoke Design LLC
Spoke Design helps businesses of all sizes build their brand and digital presence through their full-service design and web agency. Founded 13 years ago in Toledo, Spoke offers full-stack development as well as thoughtful user experience and interface design.

Rep. Brett Guthrie (KY-02)
Company: BEHAVR
Founded in 2016, BEHAVR is creatively utilizing virtual reality technology to help revolutionize the way that people handle anxiety-related disorders. Based in Elizabethtown with a team of over 50 employees, BEHAVR helps treat stress, fear, and anxiety through the use of gradual exposure to the situations that provoke the negative emotions.

Rep. Larry Bucshon (IN-08)
Company: Gropod
Located in Evansville and founded in 2016, Gropod is working to help people grow their own food through technology in order to create a more sustainable world and allow people to increase their food independence. With 12 employees, Gropod is building hydroponic farming systems that can grow anything from lettuce and other vegetables to any number of fruits or spices.

Rep. Neal Dunn (FL-02)
Company: TechFarms
TechFarms, founded in 2015 and located in Panama City Beach, has a singular mission: create a more technology-focused and vibrant entrepreneurial ecosystem in northwestern Florida. The team at TechFarms has created a collaborative coworking space for local business owners with the goal of lifting up the whole community.

Rep. Debbie Lesko (AZ-08)
Company: No Boundaries Marketing Group
The 10-person team at No Boundaries Marketing Group works to simplify digital marketing and advertising for small to medium-sized businesses. They were founded in Surprise in 2019 and provide search engine optimization (SEO) as well as other strategic, digital, and traditional marketing services.

Rep. Greg Pence (IN-06)
Company: Accutech Systems Corporation
Located in Muncie and founded in 1987, Accutech provides software solutions and services to those in the financial industry. Accutech's solutions include a wealth management platform and mobile applications that make opening an account easy, as well as a business intelligence dashboard.

Rep. Kelly Armstrong (ND-AL)
Company: Bushel
Located in Fargo and founded in 2017, Bushel leverages technology to help serve participants in the grain industry through mobile applications, websites, and other elements of digital infrastructure. Bushel provides a number of solutions and products that aim to help those in the grain industry create a more streamlined workflow.

Rep. Cathy McMorris Rodgers, Ex Officio (WA-05) Company: Gestalt
Founded in 2017, Gestalt is a 15-person team working to bring healthcare into the 21st century by replacing microscopes and glass slides with automated, electronic, and digital workflows. They provide services related to pathology in the medical field to professionals as well as those in education or academic research.

*Ms. Schakowsky. Thank you.

And now, last, but not least, Mr. Brody, you are recognized for five minutes.

Statement of David Brody, Managing Attorney, Digital Justice Initiative, Lawyers' Committee for Civil Rights under Law

*Mr. Brody. Thank you, Chair Schakowsky, Ranking Member Bilirakis, Chair Pallone, Ranking Member McMorris Rodgers and members of the committee. Thank you for the opportunity to testify today on bicameral, bipartisan legislation to strengthen data privacy and civil rights.

My name is David Brody, and I lead the Digital Justice Initiative at the Lawyers' Committee for Civil Rights Under Law. The Lawyers' Committee uses legal advocacy to achieve racial justice fighting inside and outside the courts to ensure that black people and other people of color have voice, opportunity, and power to make the promises of our democracy real.

Our Digital Justice Initiative works at the intersection of racial justice, privacy, and technology to address predatory data practices, discriminatory algorithms, and other online harms that disproportionately affect people of color.

If a business posts a sign that says, "Whites only," it should not matter if it is written in ink or pixels, the discrimination is the same, the harm is the same, and the legal consequences should be the same.

We care about data privacy because it ensures that who we are cannot be used against us unfairly. Privacy rights are civil rights. Every individual deserves the full measure of freedom in their engagement with an online- and data-driven world – both freedom to and freedom from – freedom to define yourself, freedom to organize and advocate for what you believe, freedom to learn, freedom to play, freedom to start a business or find new opportunities, freedom to be let alone.

Advancing racial justice and equity in the digital world also requires ensuring freedom from discrimination. Everyone has a right to engage in online economy free from algorithmic bias, digital redlining, and pervasive surveillance.

Passing comprehensive privacy legislation such as the American Data Privacy and Protection Act would significantly advance these freedoms. The proposed bill includes many strong and protective provisions as well as some areas where we hope the legislation can be improved.

First, the bill would prohibit discriminatory uses of personal data and require companies to test their algorithms for bias. Online and offline restricting access on the basis of protected characteristics should not be allowed. Algorithms are not magic. They are the product of the humans who build them and the quality of their data inputs.

The data fed into an algorithm – where someone lives, their job and credit history, their associations, their wealth, and their health – these data are themselves intertwined with generations of discrimination in housing, employment, education, banking, insurance, and criminal justice.

Absent responsible design and safeguards, an algorithm can mistake the consequences of racial discrimination and equality for the preferences of the user and produce digital redlining. The provisions in this bill would promote the responsible use of algorithms.

Second, the bill would require companies to collect and use only as much personal data as is reasonably necessary and proportionate to provide the services that consumers expect, reducing the amount of unnecessary personal data floating around online, reduces the potential risks from abuse, data breaches, and other harms.

Identify theft and fraud, for example, disproportionately impact communities of color; and for this reason, I agree with my colleague, Mr. Kantor, that financial services should be covered by this bill.

However, there are parts of the bill that need improvement. Most importantly, the narrow private right of actions severely curtails the ability of individuals to have their day in court if their rights are violated.

Almost every major civil rights law includes a robust private right of action, so that individuals can vindicate their own rights in recognition that, historically, governments have not always protected everyone equally. The bill has procedural hurdles that will punish everyday consumers trying to get relief or sometimes even ask for a refund. If we are to have the rule of law, we must allow the law to rule.

In addition, Federal Communications Commission displacement should be limited to provisions directly related to privacy and ensure that it doesn't break other aspects that are important to the functioning of the FCC.

Decades ago, we decided as a nation that our polity is stronger when everyone has a fair chance, and Congress passed the Civil Rights Act of 1964 to prohibit segregation in interstate commerce. Since then, the internet and other novel technologies have created the risk of new forms of redlining and discrimination.

It's time to build upon our civil rights infrastructure to ensure that everyone has equal opportunity on the internet and fair access to the information, goods, and services it enables. Let's work together and get this done.

Thank you. [The prepared statement of Mr. Brody follows:]

Statement of David Brody, Managing Attorney of the Digital Justice Initiative, Lawyers' Committee for Civil Rights under Law, U.S. House Committee on Energy and Commerce Subcommittee on Consumer Protection and Commerce

I. Introduction

Chair Schakowsky, Ranking Member Bilirakis, and Members of the Committee, thank you for the opportunity to testify today on bipartisan, bicameral legislation that seeks to strengthen data privacy, security, and civil rights. My name is David Brody, and I am the Managing Attorney of the Digital Justice Initiative at the Lawyers' Committee for Civil Rights Under Law ("Lawyers' Committee").

The Lawyers' Committee uses legal advocacy to achieve racial justice, fighting inside and outside the courts to ensure that Black people and other people of color have voice, opportunity, and power to make the promises of our democracy real. Our Digital Justice Initiative works at the intersection of racial justice, technology, and privacy to address predatory commercial data practices, discriminatory algorithms, invasions of privacy, disinformation, and online harms that disproportionately affect Black people and other people of color, including people with intersectional identities, like immigrants, women of color, and LGBTQ people of color.

If a business posts a sign that says "Whites Only," it should not matter whether it is written in ink or pixels. The discrimination is the same. The harm is the same. And the legal consequences should be the same. We care about data privacy because it ensures that who we are cannot be used against us unfairly. Privacy rights are civil rights.

Every individual deserves the full measure of freedom in their engagement with an online and data-driven world—both freedom to and freedom from. Freedom to define yourself. Freedom to organize and advocate for what you believe. Freedom to learn. Freedom to play. Freedom to start a business or find new opportunities. Freedom to be let alone.

Achieving racial justice in a digital world also requires advancing freedom from discrimination and inequity. Everyone has a right to engage in the online economy free from algorithmic bias, digital redlining, and pervasive surveillance.

We are encouraged by the American Data Privacy and Protection Act, a bipartisan and bicameral effort to safeguard data privacy and civil rights online. Passing comprehensive privacy legislation would be a major advancement for the public good. The proposed bill includes a number of provisions that would protect the rights of all Americans, and some areas where we hope the legislation can be improved.

First, the bill would prohibit discriminatory uses of personal data and require companies to test their algorithms for bias. We know from years of reporting and research that algorithms used for advertising and eligibility decisions frequently produce discriminatory outcomes and restrict access to housing, employment, credit, healthcare, education, and other businesses. This discrimination disproportionately impacts Black and Brown communities, as well as other marginalized and disenfranchised groups.[147]

Second, the bill would require companies to collect and use only as much personal data as is reasonably necessary to provide the services that consumers expect, and to safeguard that data. Reducing the amount of unnecessary personal data floating around online reduces the potential for that data to be abused. Identity theft and fraud disproportionately impact communities of color, and low-income consumers are less likely to have the resources to bounce back after being ripped off.[148]

Third, the bill would give individuals transparency into and control over how their data is used. Requiring disclosure of data practices—including revealing with whom a company shares your information—is essential to identifying and mitigating discriminatory practices. The bill also empowers individuals with the ability to access, correct, and delete their own information.

However, there are parts of the bill that need improvement. Most importantly, the narrow private right of action severely curtails the ability of individuals to obtain relief from a court when a company violates the Act. A right without a remedy is no right at all to people who have been wronged. The current proposal inserts several procedural hurdles that will not reduce litigation costs but will block injured individuals from being able to have their day in court—such as traps designed to trip up individuals who do not use magic words when asserting their rights. If we are to have rule of law, we must allow the law to rule. In addition, the bill gives many new responsibilities and authorities to the Federal Trade Commission, as it should. It is imperative for Congress to ensure that the FTC also receives all of the resources it needs to successfully execute this new mission.

Almost sixty years ago, we decided as a nation that our polity is stronger when everyone has a fair chance. Congress passed the Civil Rights Act of 1964 to prohibit segregation in interstate commerce. The internet and other novel technologies create new challenges to the prevention and elimination of redlining and discrimination. It is time to build upon our civil rights infrastructure to ensure that everyone has equal opportunity on the internet and fair access to the information, goods, and services it enables.

---

[147] *See* JANE CHUNG, RACISM IN, RACISM OUT: A PRIMER ON ALGORITHMIC RACISM, PUBLIC CITIZEN 10 (2022), https://www.citizen.org/article/algorithmic-racism/; YESHIMABEIT MILLNER AND AMY TRAUB, DATA CAPITALISM AND ALGORITHMIC RACISM, DATA FOR BLACK LIVES AND DEMOS (2021), https://www.demos.org/sites/default/files/2021- 05/Demos_%20D4BL_Data_Capitalism_Algorithmic_Racism.pdf.

[148] FED. TRADE COMM'N, SERVING COMMUNITIES OF COLOR: A STAFF REPORT ON THE FEDERAL TRADE COMMISSION'S EFFORTS TO ADDRESS FRAUD AND CONSUMER ISSUES AFFECTING COMMUNITIES OF COLOR (2021), https://www.ftc.gov/system/files/documents/reports/serving-communities-color-staff- report-federal-trade-commissions-efforts-address-fraud-consumer/ftc-communities-color-report_oct_2021-508-v2.pdf.

II. Lack of Privacy and Online Civil Rights Protections Adversely Impacts Communities of Color

Privacy legislation is a civil rights issue because it can help ensure that people's identities and characteristics cannot be used against them unfairly. Strong legislation can secure for everyone the "inviolability of privacy" that is "indispensable to preservation of freedom of association."[149] Such protections can empower communities of color and open doors for marginalized populations. It can also provide clarity to businesses and level the playing field for entrepreneurs.

However, there is currently no comprehensive federal privacy law. Existing anti-discrimination laws have many gaps and limitations as well. Some exclude retail or have unresolved questions as to whether they apply to online businesses. Others apply to specific sectors, like housing and employment, but may not cover new types of online services used to match individuals to these opportunities. To give a few examples, under current federal law it would be legal for an online business to charge higher prices to women or to refuse to sell products to Christians.[150] A service provider could use discriminatory algorithms to look for workers to target for recruitment so long as the provider does not meet the definition of an "employment agency" under Title VII.[151] And it is wholly unclear whether existing laws will apply at all to discrimination in many new online-only economies related to online gaming, influencers, streamers, and other creators.

As a result of gaps in federal law, individuals currently have little recourse against discriminatory algorithms and AI models used in commercial data practices that reinforce the structural racism and systemic bias that pervade our society. Tech companies can misuse personal data, intentionally or unintentionally, to harm marginalized communities through deception, discrimination, exploitation, and perpetuation of redlining. Absent updated and robust anti-discrimination protections, online businesses can deny service on the basis of race or ethnicity, provide subpar products based on gender or sexual orientation, charge higher rates based on religion, or ignore the accessibility needs of persons with disabilities.

This dynamic is deeply contrary to cornerstone principles and promises of equal access and a level playing field for everyone. Without strong privacy and online civil rights protections, discrimination will continue to infect the digital marketplace. Not surprisingly, extensive documentation cited below demonstrates that consumers of color continue to receive worse treatment and experience unequal access to goods and services due to discriminatory algorithms and exploitative data practices.

In advertising, for example, Facebook (now known as Meta) allowed discrimination in the targeting and delivery of ads for housing, credit services, and job openings based on race, sex, and age. The company was eventually forced to change its ad targeting system as part of a legal settlement,[152] but was still charged with engaging in race discrimination by the Department of

---

[149] *NAACP v. Alabama*, 357 U.S. 449, 462 (1958).

[150] *See* 42 U.S.C. §§ 1981, 2000a; *Shaare Tefila Cong. v. Cobb*, 481 U.S. 615 (1987).

[151] Aaron Rieke and Miranda Bogen, *Help Wanted: An Examination of Hiring Algorithms, Equity, and Bias*, UPTURN (2018), https://www.upturn.org/reports/2018/hiring-algorithms/.

[152] Barbara Ortutay, *Facebook to overhaul ad targeting to prevent discrimination*, ASSOCIATED PRESS, March 19, 2019, https://www.apnews.com/38c0dbd8acb14e3fbc7911ea18fafd58.

Housing and Urban Development.[153] Similar practices have been the target of investigations, including at Twitter and Google.[154] In fact, Meta *literally* engages in redlining—it allows advertisers to select which zip codes to include or exclude from receiving an ad, and draws a red line on a map showing the excluded neighborhoods.[155] Academic research suggests that Facebook uses ad delivery algorithms that reproduce discrimination even when the advertiser did not intend to discriminate, including again in the housing, credit services, and employment contexts.[156]

In the job application and screening process, predictive artificial intelligence ("AI") tools can cement and reflect biases.[157] Amazon used a hiring algorithm for years that automatically penalized resumes for including the word "women's" and gave lower priority to applicants who had graduated from two all-women's colleges.[158]

Too often, a consumer's identify will determine which products they get offered.

A Berkeley study found that biases in "algorithmic strategic pricing" have resulted in Black and Latino borrowers paying higher interest rates on home purchase and refinance loans as compared to White and Asian borrowers. These pricing disparities are commonly driven by machine learning algorithms that target customers based on their personal data. The difference alone costs Black and Latino customers $250 million to $500 million every year.[159]

Retail websites have been found to charge different prices based on the demographics of the user.[160] For example, an online shopper's distance from a physical store, as well as distance from the store's competitors, has been used in algorithms setting online prices, resulting in price discrimination. Because of historical redlining and segregation, and the lack of retail options in many low-income neighborhoods, this resulted in low-income communities of color paying higher prices than wealthier, whiter neighborhoods when they shopped online.

---

[153] Tracy Jan and Elizabeth Dwoskin, *HUD is reviewing Twitter's and Google's ad practices as part of housing discrimination probe*, WASH. POST, March 28, 2019, https://www.washingtonpost.com/business/2019/03/28/hud-charges-facebook-with-housing- discrimination/.

[154] *Id.*

[155] "[Facebook] has provided a toggle button that enables advertisers to exclude men or women from seeing an ad, a search-box to exclude people who do not speak a specific language from seeing an ad, and a map tool to exclude people who live in a specified area from seeing an ad by drawing a red line around that area." Charge of Discrimination, *U.S. Dept. of Hous. and Urban Dev. v. Facebook, Inc.*, FHEO No. 01-18-0323-8 at 4 (Mar. 28, 2019), https://www.hud.gov/sites/dfiles/Main/documents/HUD_v_Facebook.pdf; Brief of *Amicus Curiae* Lawyers' Committee for Civil Rights Under Law in Support of Plaintiff's Opposition to Facebook's Demurrer to First Amended Complaint, *Liapes v. Facebook*, No. 30-CIV-01712, at 10 (Calif. Super. Ct. 2021), https://lawyerscommittee.org/wp-content/uploads/2021/03/Leave-and-Amicus- Combined.pdf.

[156] Louise Matsakis, *Facebook's Ad System Might be Hard-Coded for Discrimination*, WIRED, April 6, 2019, https://www.wired.com/story/facebooks-ad-system-discrimination/.

[157] Aaron Rieke and Miranda Bogen, *Help Wanted: An Examination of Hiring Algorithms, Equity, and Bias*, UPTURN (2018), https://www.upturn.org/reports/2018/hiring-algorithms/.

[158] Jeffrey Dastin, *Amazon scraps secret AI recruiting tool that showed bias against women*, REUTERS, Oct. 9, 2018, https://www.reuters.com/article/us-amazon-com-jobs-automation-insight- idUSKCN1MK08G.

[159] Laura Counts, *Minority homebuyers face widespread statistical lending discrimination, study finds*, HAAS SCHOOL OF BUSINESS AT THE UNIVERSITY OF CALIFORNIA, BERKELEY (Nov. 13, 2018). http://newsroom.haas.berkeley.edu/minority-homebuyers-face-widespread-statistical-lending- discrimination-study-finds/.

[160] Jennifer Valentino-DeVries et al., *Websites Vary Prices, Deals Based on Users' Information*, WALL ST. J., Dec. 24, 2012, https://www.wsj.com/articles/SB10001424127887323777204578189391813881534.

Communities of color are targeted by predatory and low-quality for-profit online colleges.[161] Ashford University, a for-profit, mostly online University, deliberately sought to place their ads in front of Black, Latino, low-income students who are first in their family to attend college.[162] This targeting is as successful as it is predatory. Black and Latino students are overrepresented at Ashford as well as at other for-profit schools generally.[163] Once these students attend for-profit Universities online, they are trapped with higher levels of debt and loan defaults than students at public, non-profit schools. Roughly 70% of Black Americans who borrow money to attend Ashford or other for-profit colleges end up defaulting on that loan within ten years.[164]

Consumer financial discrimination is also common online. Google's search engine previously served ads for payday loans when a user ran searches for terms associated with financial distress such as, "I need money to pay my rent."[165]

Algorithms that set car insurance rates charge communities of color higher premiums than predominantly White neighborhoods with the same risk levels.[166]

The common denominator in all of these examples is sloppy or abusive use of personal data. By prohibiting discriminatory data use and requiring companies to test their algorithms for bias, many of these harms can be prevented.

III. The American Data Privacy and Protection Act

The "American Data Privacy and Protection Act" would establish a national data privacy and data security framework. We are pleased to see that it prioritizes civil rights protections that address data-driven discrimination. The draft legislation is the first major comprehensive privacy proposal to gain bipartisan and bicameral support. We are encouraged by the progress of this legislation, and want to address this Committee on four important pieces of the legislation: the civil rights protections included, the importance of the bill's data minimization standards, how transparency empowers individuals, and the critical need for a more robust and effective private right of action.

A. Welcomed and Needed Civil Rights Protections

The time has come to enact a comprehensive consumer privacy law that safeguards civil rights online. We are encouraged by the strong civil rights section of the American Data Privacy and

---

[161] *See* Genevieve Bonadies et al., *For-Profit Schools' Predatory Practices and Students of Color: A Mission to Enroll Rather than Educate*, HARVARD L. REV. BLOG (July 30, 2018) https://blog.harvardlawreview.org/for-profit-schools-predatory-practices-and-students-of-color-a- mission-to-enroll-rather-than-educate/; Larry Abramson, *For-Profit Schools Under Fire For Targeting Veterans*, NPR, Apr. 9, 2012, https://www.npr.org/2012/04/09/150148966/for-profit-schools- under-fire-for-targeting-veterans.

[162] *Id.*

[163] *Id.*

[164] *Id.*

[165] Aaron Rieke and Logan Koepke, *Led Astray: Online Lead Generation and Payday Loans*, UPTURN (2015), https://www.upturn.org/reports/2015/led-astray/.

[166] Julia Angwin et al., *Minority Neighborhoods Pay Higher Car Insurance Premiums Than White Areas With the Same Risk*, PROPUBLICA, April 5, 2017, https://www.propublica.org/article/minority- neighborhoods-higher-car-insurance-premiums-white-areas-same-risk; Sarah Jeong, *A.I. Is Changing Insurance*, NEW YORK TIMES, April 10, 2019, https://www.nytimes.com/2019/04/10/opinion/insurance-ai.html.

Protection Act especially the language that seeks to change the status quo for Americans harmed by discriminatory algorithms, advertising, and retail discrimination. Existing civil rights laws do not cover the entirety of the discriminatory harms people routinely experience online.

We welcome the civil rights provisions of the "American Data Privacy and Protection Act" that will prohibit many common forms of online discrimination. The bill prohibits using personal data to discriminate based on protected characteristics. This would prohibit targeting or delivering ads based on protected characteristics, such as race, sex, or religion. It would also apply to discriminatory algorithms and technologies that use them, such as commercial use of a biased facial recognition system.[167] The bill allows companies to process protected class data for the purpose of self-testing to root out discrimination, as well as to diversify a pool of applicants, candidates, or customers. The anti-discrimination provision would also preserve free speech; it does not apply to non-commercial activities or to private clubs or groups, which are the same exceptions in the Civil Rights Act of 1964.

In addition, the bill requires impact assessments for the algorithms employed by companies, as well as pre-deployment algorithmic design evaluations. We have seen algorithms reproduce patterns of discrimination in employment recruiting, housing, education, finance, mortgage lending, credit scoring, healthcare, vacation rentals, ridesharing, and other services.[168] The bill requires the assessments to test for discrimination in these types of economic opportunities, as well as to explicitly test for disparate impacts on the basis of protected characteristics. We hope that these assessments will help companies identify biases and problems in their algorithms before they are implemented and cause harm.

The civil rights provision in the bill will also apply to social media platforms. These protections should help increase fairness in recommendation algorithms that have been shown to disadvantage creators and influencers of color.[169] These provisions are critical in addressing civil rights online. We are encouraged by the digital access rights and transparency requirements that will help identify discriminatory practices, and we urge this Committee to include strong civil rights protections in legislation going forward.

B. Important Data Minimization Standards

Pervasive access to peoples' personal data, often obtained without the knowledge or consent of the individual, can lead to discriminatory, predatory and unsafe practices. Companies should not collect or use more personal info than is necessary to do what the individual expects them to do. Beyond basic cybersecurity and legal obligations, companies also should not use personal data for secondary purposes that an individual does not expect, or has not consented to. The reason is simple: personal data collected by companies can proliferate in a way that maximizes risk for the individual and for society at-large. Clear baseline protections for data collection,

---

[167] Kashmir Hill, *Flawed Facial Recognition Leads To Arrest and Jail for New Jersey Man*, NEW YORK TIMES, December 29, 2020, https://www.nytimes.com/2020/12/29/technology/facial-recognition- misidentify-jail.html.

[168] Civil Rights, Civil Liberties, and Consumer Protection Organizations Letter to the FTC, August 4, 2021, https://www.lawyerscommittee.org/wp-content/uploads/2021/08/FTC-civil-rights-and-privacy- letter-Final-1.pdf.

[169] Reed Albergotti, *Black Creators Sue YouTube, Alleging Racial Discrimination,* WASH. POST, June 18, 2020, https://www.washingtonpost.com/technology/2020/06/18/black-creators-sue-youtube-alleged-race-discrimination/; *Twitter finds racial bias in image-cropping AI*, BBC, May 20, 2021, https://www.bbc.com/news/technology-57192898.

including both primary and secondary uses of data, should be enacted to help cage risk, and prevent harms.

Fraud and identity theft disproportionately harm Black and Brown communities. This Act reduces the amount of data that will fall into the wrong hands and be used illicitly for fraud and identity theft. Data breaches are often especially problematic for people of color living on fixed or low incomes.[170] Companies track cell phone location data without consent and sell this data to debt collectors and other predatory actors, which disproportionately harms low income Black and Brown communities.[171] This bill's data minimization requirements will restrict data collection and use to purposes necessary for providing services expected by an individual and restricts secondary uses or data sharing without explicit opt-in consent.

Personal data are the fuel of online commerce. They can be used for good—to create new products, conduct beneficial research, mitigate disparities, or tailor experiences that consumers want. They can also be abused—to steal someone's identity, exclude someone from opportunities, target someone for harassment or abuse, engage in predatory practices and scams, or to reinforce the legacies of segregation and redlining.

Keeping data collection, use, and sharing limited to what is reasonably necessary and proportionate to provide expected services is essential to keeping consumers safe. Just like combustible fuel, an overflowing or leaking data ecosystem is a dangerous situation.

We are encouraged that the Act imposes a baseline duty on all covered entities to collect or use covered data only as needed and appropriate, and is not a "notice and consent" regime in which any practice is allowed so long as a consumer consents after being presented with lengthy and legalistic privacy notices. Such data minimization efforts can reduce risks of abuse and harm from data breaches. In contrast, notice and consent has repeatedly been shown to be a failure. Just as we do not expect consumers to understand how every aspect of their car engine works, we likewise should not expect them to understand how the online data ecosystem works. With a car, consumers expect that when we drive it off the lot it will be safe and function correctly, and that if it does not they will have recourse.

Consumers should expect no less from digital products either.

C. How Transparency Empowers Individuals

Transparency about how companies collect and use data will ultimately shed light on discriminatory practices. Providing individuals with understandable, easy to read, privacy policies detailing data collection puts the individual in the driver's seat. This transparency, coupled with giving users the ability to access, correct, or delete their data, lets individuals make empowered choices. They can choose to access and correct their data, opening pathways to self-sufficient fixes for inaccurate background check reports, which disproportionately harm Black and Brown Americans.[172] Giving individuals the power to delete their data empowers

---

[170] Kori Hale, *T-Mobile's hack of 50 million users leaves black community at risk*, FORBES, September 9, 2021, https://www.forbes.com/sites/korihale/2021/09/10/t-mobiles-hack-of-50-million-users-leaves-black-community-at-risk/?sh=48fc391b7435.

[171] Joseph Cox, *I Gave a Bounty Hunter $300. Then He Located Our Phone,* VICE NEWS, January 8, 2019, https://www.vice.com/en/article/nepxbz/i-gave-a-bounty-hunter-300-dollars-located-phone-microbilt-zumigo-tmobile.

[172] Christina Stacy & Mychal Cohen, Urban Inst., *Ban the Box and Racial Discrimination: A Review of the Evidence and Policy Recommendations*, 17 (2017), https://www.urban.org/sites/default/files/publication/88366/ban_the_box_and_racial_discrimi nation_4.pdf (finding that inaccuracies in criminal record data especially harm

them to protect themselves. They can reduce their data footprint, or take away their data from insecure third parties, minimizing the risk of fraud, identify theft, and exploitation.

Currently, data brokers continually collect and amass data for sale. Some may not be accurate. This data is then used to conduct background checks for employment, housing, and other services, as well as for credit scoring. Inaccuracies disproportionately harm people of color, as well as those who have a conviction or arrest record. This bill rectifies that harm by creating a data broker registry, reporting requirements and a national opt-out registry. In addition, the bill requires businesses—including data brokers—to minimize the data they collect, restricts selling such data to third parties without consent, and provides individuals with a right to access, correct, or delete their data.

D. Need for a More Robust Private Right of Action

As encouraged as we are about some provisions of this Act, we know that data privacy legislation will only live up to its promise if it is able to be readily enforced. As currently written, the "American Data Privacy and Protection Act" has reasonably good enforcement mechanisms for the Federal Trade Commission and State attorneys general, but a narrow and limited private right of action for individuals. We have concerns that without a stronger private right of action, it will be difficult for individuals to vindicate their own rights and address the harms we have documented.

The best way for an individual to safeguard their rights is to be able to seek a remedy to the injury they suffer themselves, in a court of law. As currently written, the private right of action in the Act is weak and difficult to enforce. The private right of action will not come into force until four years after the Act becomes effective. Despite the real and pervasive harms rampant on the internet, real people will be asked to wait years to have wrongs against them addressed, while faceless and anonymous entities causing harm can continue to flourish. Once a private individual is allowed to bring suit, they are still limited in the remedies they can seek. Under the current language of the Act, remedies are limited to compensatory damages, injunctive and declaratory relief, and attorney's fees and costs. There is no provision for punitive or statutory damages, which have served as an effective deterrent for especially harmful actors under other legal regimes—not even nominal damages are allowed.

In addition, there are numerous procedural pitfalls designed to trip up individuals on their way to the courthouse, some of which may be unconstitutional violations of free speech or due process. First, the bill bars *anyone* from making *any* request for money to a covered entity until certain narrow conditions are met—and those conditions may never occur.[173] Besides being an unconstitutional prior restraint on speech, this would cause huge unintended consequences—consumers could not request refunds and businesses would be unable to invoice each other. It would effectively shut down interstate commerce if a court loyally applied the plain meaning of the text. It would also severely jeopardize the ability to recover compensatory damages. Moreover, it would impede the ability of businesses to settle disputes without having to engage in more costly litigation. If the goal of this provision is to deter the trial bar, that will also fail as smart attorneys can easily circumvent it.

---

people of color, because they represent a disproportionate share of U.S. arrests and are thus more likely to have missing information regarding the outcome of a case).

[173] *See* Sec. 403(a)(3)(B) of the bill, titled "Bad Faith."

Second, the bill includes an onerous "right to cure" that does nothing that is not already accomplished by existing civil procedure and standing rules—other than impose new hurdles to get to court.[174] It ostensibly gives covered entities a window to cure an injury before an individual could bring a case seeking injunctive relief.

However, Article III standing and equitable relief jurisprudence *already* provide this offramp: a defendant can always cease an ongoing harmful practice and if there is no risk of recurrence, then claims for injunctive relief are moot and get dismissed. All this new provision does is risk creating new substantive hurdles to otherwise meritorious cases—it will increase litigation costs while providing no benefit.

Third, the bill plays "gotcha" games designed to trick everyday consumers into forfeiting their rights. A "demand letter" provision requires that an individual must use a specific sentence—magic words—in their *first* communication to a covered entity asserting a violation of their rights.[175] If the individual fails to do so, they forfeit their rights. What average consumer is going to know to do this when contacting customer support to dispute an issue and try to assert their rights?

Consumers may forfeit their rights without ever knowing, and the covered entity will be free to continue its unlawful practices. In addition, this provision appears to be a substantive due process violation: the provision says that one individual's failure can cause an entire class of individuals to forfeit their rights.

Finally, the private right of action does not apply to the data minimization section of the bill, which is the core protection for consumers. This means individuals will not be able to sue when a company fails to comply with their most basic requirement to only process personal data in a manner that is necessary and proportionate.

We support removing the barriers in the private right of action as the clearest way to ensure that the promises made elsewhere in this bill materialize for all who access the digital world.

Conclusion

The "American Data Privacy and Protection Act" is a promising piece of legislation aimed at solving long lingering critical problems. We appreciate this Committee's attention to the issue and the opportunity to testify on how to strengthen privacy protections for individuals and curb data-driven discrimination. The Lawyers' Committee looks forward to working on a bipartisan bias to advance this legislation over the finish line, ultimately securing long overdue data privacy and online civil rights protections for all Americans, particularly people of color who are most often targeted for harm in the digital world.

* * *

*Ms. Schakowsky. Thank you.

---

[174] *See* Sec. 403(c) of the bill.

[175] *See* Sec. 403(d) of the bill.

We have concluded, now, with the witnesses' opening statement. At this time, we will move to member questions. Each member will have five minutes to ask a question and to get the answer, and I will begin.

Let me just first share a couple of visions of what the world will be like after this privacy bill gets passed, and I want to thank our witnesses both for the encouragement that you have given us, but also, the recommendations that you have made.

But what I am looking for is on day one, that consumers will have, certainly, in general, control over their personal data. That they won't have to read stacks of privacy policies and be a lawyer to understand their rights and what they are agreeing to.

Companies will only be able to collect the minimum amount of data that is necessary for that transaction, and that data won't be sold to data brokers and anyone else without expressed consent from consumers.

Mr. Lee, I want to begin with you, and I am wondering if you, briefly, could just say how does this bill on day one make the internet a safer place for consumers across the country?

*Mr. Lee. Thank you for the question, Chairwoman Schakowsky.

And the ADPPA would make the internet safer for people day one by doing four things: One, mandating data security requirements for companies. Right now, that is not a mandate, and mandating data security requirements helps with a litany of other data harms that we're seeing across the board.

Two, including corporate accountability mechanisms such as designating privacy and data security officers. Three, creating significant protections from marginalized communities through the civil rights and algorithmic impact assessments. And lastly, requiring that business incorporate privacy-by-design principles for the development of their data processes and activities.

And none of these four points that I have made are in any other state provision or any other state bill and would go so far beyond what we currently have right now.

*Ms. Schakowsky. Thank you. And Mr. Lee, this bill protects children, people of color, and other marginalized communities online. Can you explain those protections a little bit?

*Mr. Lee. Chairwoman, I would love to.

The bill would make the internet safer for marginalized communities and really all Americans by prohibiting discriminatory practices, mandating algorithmic impact assessments, particularly, for large data holders which is incredibly important as we currently do not understand, and I think, a lot of the large data holders don't really fully understand the impact that their algorithms have, particularly, on all communities.

And just for reference, for civil rights, civil rights protects the majority of Americans, and we need to think about that when we're thinking about what the impact of these algorithms are having on all Americans. And the FTC showed that identify theft disproportionately impacts marginalized communities. Data minimization plays a key role in making sure marginalized communities are safer online.

And lastly, there is broad consensus that AI and algorithms, when not tested, were designed with marginalized communities in mind, can have deleterious effects on broad communities at large, and really, it is intersectional because it is not just the protected classes of communities highlighted in the bill, but there are carryover effects, particularly, in communities where there is high rates of disability, communities where there is high rates of economically disadvantaged people.

This is true across the board, and AI has an impact on all of those communities.

*Ms. Schakowsky. Thank you.

Mr. Brody, kind of along the same lines, this bill makes promises to Americans about the privacy of their data. Can you explain the enforcement mechanisms that will ensure consumers are protected and that the companies live up to their promises?

*Mr. Brody. Absolutely. Thank you for that question.

This bill has a three-legged stool of enforcement. So first, it empowers the FTC with a range of authorities including a new privacy bureau and a new kids division as well as some rulemaking authorities and broad enforcement power for the FTC.

Second, it provides state attorneys general with the ability to fully enforce the law which is extremely important because state AGs tend to be more connected to their communities and the needs of their citizens of their state, and they can fill gaps when the FTC, due to limited resources, may not be able to address all the issues.

And third, it includes a private right of action which is especially important for individuals to be able to vindicate their rights and have their day in court.

The FTC and state AGs are not always going to have the resources or ability to get to every single harm, and that's why it is important for individuals to be able to go to court and seek relief. It's especially important for civil rights violations as almost every major civil rights law has a private right of action in recognition that people of color and marginalized communities need to be able to go to the judicial branch for relief.

*Ms. Schakowsky. Thank you. And my time has expired, and now, I recognize the ranking member for his five minutes of questions.

*Mr. Bilirakis. Thank you, Madam Chair. I appreciate it very much.

As I mentioned in my opening statement, I am pleased to see this draft established meaningful protections for children while they navigate on the online ecosystem; however, I understand one job remains in how we determine whether an online user is an adult or a child.

Thinking in terms of fantasy football league, I used to play quite a bit. I don't have time anymore. How do you determine someone is a child versus an adult? You could be age 15 or 55 and have the same interest here. Of course, the kids beat us every time. I am concerned about how much and what kind of information we may condone to guess a user's age.

So Mr. Dufault, what is your opinion on an actual knowledge standard for covered entities when prohibiting certain practices like targeted advertising or transferring sensitive data as opposed to a constructive standard?

*Mr. Dufault. Well, thank you for the question, Ranking Member Bilirakis.

I think that the actual knowledge standard is one that can be workable. I think, it is a reasonable compromise, and the problem becomes one of evidence as you highlighted whether or not you have the right evidence to show whether or not a company knew for sure that somebody was under a certain age.

Under COPPA, under a certain age, a company will have to get verified parental consent that they have permission to collect data about that child and the way that is accomplished is a few different ways. Oftentimes, the company will have the user go through a certain test that only an adult would reasonably know what the answers are to, and there are other ways in which they try to accomplish that, like, having the adult send a credit card number or call an 800 number or things of that nature.

That kind of evidence can be a little bit difficult to collect in a way that doesn't cause a whole lot of friction, and so it becomes an issue of trying to figure out whether or not that person is under a certain age with specificity and constructive knowledge could actually sort of exacerbate that question because it would bring in other kinds of concepts and whether or not other sort of pieces of evidence might be offered.

So I think, we have to first figure out what kinds of evidence qualify for actual knowledge before we think about expanding it, and I think, technology has helped us do a little bit better job, figure out whether or not somebody is of a certain age, and parental controls at the platform level have been very helpful in identifying parents and children and those relationships that exist.

And I think that the law just probably needs to keep up with those innovations and those methods by which you can check somebody's age.

*Mr. Bilirakis. Thank you very much.

*Mr. Dufault. Yeah.

*Mr. Bilirakis. Mr. Kantor, your businesses have many types of customers, and I would be interested in your insight here. There certainly is a difference between kids' data that small local stores may receive, and kids' data that TikTok or Instagram collects.

Do you see this as an area that should only be reserved for the largest data holders. Please – and try to be as brief as you can, too, but I know this is a very important topic. Please. Thank you.

*Mr. Kantor. So actually, our view is that we got to make the bill work for everybody. We don't, actually, think segregating by size is something that is necessary if you do this right. I completely agree with Graham with respect to the idea that actual knowledge is an important standard here because you often don't know who you are dealing with online, and that may be misleading in certain ways.

Every spring, I used to shop online for little league baseball bats. Was I an adult? Was I a kid? I loved it, but – so those things can sometimes lead us to incorrect conclusions.

So we think, as long as you do it right, our members can comply whether they are small or large but getting it right is tough.

*Mr. Bilirakis. Thank you very much.

Next question is for Ms. Ohlhausen. I would greatly appreciate your insight on this question of course, so give me your opinion on this particular topic. In addition, I want to ask you about the new bureau and office of business mentorship championed at the FTC and the language is in the draft.

Can you elaborate on how a new bureau with an office specifically dedicated to business mentorship will allow for greater instruction and compliance amongst covered entities. In my opinion, it's a win/win. But please, if I can get your opinion quickly, I would appreciate it.

*Ms. Ohlhausen. Yes. So the FTC has a long history of engaging in business education, and it has been a very useful investment by the agency because really everyone is better off if that business knows how to comply with the rules, and they comply with it, and then, consumers aren't harmed, and the FTC doesn't have to use enforcement resources.

So I think it's a very excellent investment that will pay a lot of dividends for the FTC to have an office that really continues this mission that it has done an excellent job pursuing previously.

*Mr. Bilirakis. Very good. Thank you. I yield back, Madam Chair. Thank you for the extra time.

*Ms. Schakowsky. The Chair recognizes Chairman Pallone for five minutes.

*The Chairman. Thank you, Chairwoman.

Our bill has strong data minimization as a base along with important data protections for individuals, kids, and small businesses layered on top. So in this way, our bill goes further to protect consumer privacy online than the notice and consent regimes that, you know, seem to be more – that are more common right now.

So I want to ask a series of questions, but if you could, you know, maybe, limit your response to a minute.

Ms. Fitzgerald, as you point out in your testimony, the concept of data minimization has been around for some time, but why is it important to include data minimization in any comprehensive privacy bill?

*Ms. Fitzgerald. Yeah. Thank you, Chairman Pallone.

Data minimization is absolutely critical because it makes privacy the default. You know, it takes the onus off individuals to protect their privacy, and instead, requires companies to be the one to think about how to limit the collection and use of personal data, and that means that a collection and use will warrant, you know, it will better align with what consumers expect.

*The Chairman. And from the consumer perspective, how is this distinguished from a structure that relies primarily on notice and choice?

*Ms. Fitzgerald. Notice and choice doesn't protect privacy. You know, just requiring companies to tell us about all the ways they have used our data in a long privacy policy that no one reads doesn't protect privacy, and a lot of these services have become so central to our lives that there is no choice but to, you know, accept the terms and opt in.

Data minimization instead requires the companies to limit the data that is – you know, limit their collection to what's reasonably necessary for the service.

*The Chairman. Yeah. And I agree. I mean, notice of choice basically is just you give notice, and then you go and do what you want.

*Ms. Fitzgerald. Right.

*The Chairman. How this bill's data minimization provision is more privacy protective than other privacy laws and proposals that you have seen?

*Ms. Fitzgerald. Yeah. The ADPPA's, you know, focus on data minimization is what really sets it apart from state laws that have recently been passed, you know, many of the proposals we have seen in Congress over the last few years, it really just sends that strong message that privacy is the default going forward.

For users, it means that privacy doesn't mean this pop up that, you know, says, "Accept," and everyone just clicks it to make it go away. It means, that the onus is on the company, and that surveillance is no longer the norm.

*The Chairman. All right.

Now, this bill is also the first of its kind in that it includes strong civil rights protections to prohibit discrimination online.

So let me ask Mr. Brody, how would the civil rights protections in the bill help to protect Americans against discrimination online?

*Mr. Brody. So this bill has very strong civil rights protections. First, it has a antidiscrimination provision that prohibits covered entities from processing personal data in a manner that discriminates in the provision of goods and services on the basis of protected characteristics, things like race and sex, religion.

And then, it also has robust algorithmic bias assessment requirements. So large companies will be required to assess their algorithms to test what kinds of impacts they are having to see if they are causing disparate impacts on the basis of protected characteristics or impeding access to critical services like housing, jobs, credit.

They will also be required to evaluate the design of their algorithms before they are deployed, and that is key.

We need to make sure that the test subjects are not the general public, and that algorithms are tested to make sure they are safe and effective before they are deployed.

*The Chairman. Thank you. Now, let me get one more question. This is to Ms. Cuaresma. In the State of the Union Address, the President specifically talked about protecting children and teens online noting how this group has been negatively impacted by the conduct of social media companies.

So if I could ask you how does this legislation address some of the difficulties for teens using online social media?

*Ms. Cuaresma. Sure. Thank you, Chair.

So it does it in two ways. They are both in sections 204 and 205. The definition of "sensitive covered data," it includes children under the age of 17.

So I want to thank this committee for not including the actual knowledge standard under the [audio malfunction] the sections with respect to sensitive data.

The other section is in 205 which talks about targeted advertising. So we are going – as long as you pass this bill, which I hope you will, we are going to be able to prohibit companies from advertising to our kids under the age of 17; however, we do need to fix the actual standard knowledge in that, and I do understand how difficult it is to know how old somebody is.

And here is the thing. As Common Sense Media, we don't want you to ask us or ask our children for more information.

All we are saying is, "Look, if you have it, and you are using it as part of your marketing proposals in saying, 'Hey, you want to use our platform'," – because we know that our audience watches videos targeted to them, and you know what?

You should also have to use it in your legal divisions.

Thank you for your question.

*The Chairman. All right. Thanks so much. Thank you, Madam Chair.

*Ms. Schakowsky. The gentleman yields back, and now, I recognize the ranking member of the full committee, Mrs. Rodgers.

*Mrs. Rodgers. Thank you, Madam Chair.

Before I start, I would like to insert into record previous coalition letters from a range of groups that have written us over the past three years to act on comprehensive privacy legislation.

*Ms. Schakowsky. Without objection.

*Mrs. Rodgers. Thank you.

[The information follows:]

* * *

STATE OF CALIFORNIA
Gavin Newsom, Governor

CALIFORNIA PRIVACY PROTECTION AGENCY

2101 Arena Blvd
Sacramento, CA 95834 www.cppa.ca.gov

June 13, 2022

The Honorable Jan Schakowsky, Chair
The Honorable Gus Bilrakis, Ranking Member
Committee on Energy and Commerce
Consumer Protection & Commerce Subcommittee
United States House of Representatives
Washington, DC 20510

Subject: California Pre-emption in the American Data Privacy and Protection Act

Dear Chair Schakowsky and Ranking Member Bilrakis,

Thank you for your work on consumer privacy, as demonstrated by Tuesday's hearing on "Protecting America's Consumers: Bipartisan Legislation to Strengthen Data Privacy and Security" and the release of the American Data Privacy and Protection Act Discussion Draft (ADPPA). As the Executive Director of the California Privacy Protection Agency (CPPA), I write to clarify how the ADPPA affects Californians and our agency. Californians currently have important rights under the California Consumer Privacy Act (CCPA) as amended by the California Privacy Rights Act (CPRA), which would be taken away by this measure, and would not be replaced with an equivalent federal right.

The ADPPA as written, similar to Consumer Online Privacy Rights Act proposal of June 8, 2022, proposes to pre-empt nearly all provisions of the California Privacy Protection Act, and would significantly weaken the privacy protections that 40 million Californians—one in eight Americans— currently enjoy. ADPPA seeks to replace stronger provisions with weaker ones. It proposes to subject the global opt out of the transfer of information to third parties to a feasibility study, and limit protections over deceptive interfaces that subvert consumer intent, known as "dark patterns." It also seeks to remove the existing "floor" on the CCPA: importantly, the CCPA as amended by the California Privacy Rights Act cannot be weakened. Finally, in seeking to pre-empt our expert agency, it would significantly reduce privacy enforcement capabilities. These points will be explored in more detail below.

In 2018, the California State Legislature unanimously approved the CCPA, which grants Californians certain inalienable rights with respect to consumer privacy, including the right to access, delete, and stop the sale of personal information. These are rights that Californians have enjoyed since the measure went into effect on January 1, 2020, and that have been actively enforced by the Attorney General since July 1, 2020.[176] In November 2020, California voters approved Proposition 24, the California Privacy Rights Act, which expands and further enshrines these protections, and adds new ones, including a data minimization provision, a rulemaking to provide an opt out of automated decisionmaking, and the ability to limit the use of sensitive information. These provisions will become operative on January 1, 2023.

[176] State of California Department of Justice, CCPA Enforcement Case Examples, https://oag.ca.gov/privacy/ccpa/enforcement.

The initiative also created and funded an expert agency, the California Privacy Protection Agency, with a primary focus on privacy and data protection. The initiative enlists our agency to issue implementing regulations and, along with the Attorney General, to enforce these rights. Not only does the CPPA provide administrative enforcement under California law, but it has audit authority as well. Privacy- specific staffing is projected to match what currently exists at the Federal Trade Commission.

ADPPA would strip Californians of these rights and protections, as it proposes to pre-empt the California Consumer Privacy Act, § 1798.100 et seq., except for a single provision, § 1798.150, the private right of action in the event of a negligent data breach. The bill also proposes to pre-empt our agency's enforcement. In the current draft, the Agency likely would not be able to enforce the federal bill with respect to violations involving Californians—which would compromise consumer privacy further, given the CPPA's unique capabilities in this area.

Because the CPRA was passed by initiative, and the initiative holds that amendments to the act be in furtherance of the privacy intent of the measure, California enjoys a floor of privacy protections that cannot be weakened. This provision allows the California State Legislature, with the Governor's approval, to amend the law to strengthen privacy protections, but does not allow the measure to be weakened by future amendments that are incompatible with the purpose and intent of the act: to strengthen consumer privacy. However, ADPPA proposes to eliminate those protections.

Additionally, while ADPPA includes concepts similar to those in the CCPA as amended by CPRA, the federal proposal as written seeks to reduce privacy protections that Californians currently enjoy, including a prohibition on manipulative "dark pattern" interfaces in opting out of data sales and a requirement that businesses honor browser privacy signals as an opt out of sale. These are just two examples of ways in which ADPPA is weaker. These weaker provisions, together with the elimination of the CCPA's "floor" on privacy protections and the CPPA's enforcement capacity, would lower the bar on privacy protections for Californians.

While we appreciate the work that has been done on ADPPA, it is important that no rights are taken away. I would be pleased to connect with you and any of your colleagues to discuss California's approach and the impact of this measure on California and the California Privacy Protection Agency.

Respectfully submitted,

Ashkan Soltani
Executive Director
California Privacy Protection Agency

cc: Members, Consumer Protection & Commerce Subcommittee
The Honorable Nancy Pelosi
The Honorable Anna G. Eshoo
The Honorable Doris O. Matsui
The Honorable Raul Ruiz
The Honorable Scott H. Peters
The Honorable Nanette Diaz Barragan

* * *

June 13, 2022

The Honorable Jan Schakowsky
Chair
House Committee on Energy & Commerce
Subcommittee on Consumer Protection & Commerce
Washington, D.C. 20515

The Honorable Gus Bilirakis
Ranking Member
House Committee on Energy & Commerce
Subcommittee on Consumer Protection & Commerce
Washington, D.C. 20515

RE: June 14 "Protecting America's Consumers: Bipartisan Legislation to Strengthen Data Privacy and Security" Hearing

Dear Chair Schakowsky and Ranking Member Bilirakis:

The Confidentiality Coalition thanks you for holding a hearing on, "Protecting America's Consumers: Bipartisan Legislation to Strengthen Data Privacy and Security."

The *Confidentiality Coalition* is composed of a broad group of hospitals, medical teaching colleges, health plans, pharmaceutical companies, medical device manufacturers, vendors of electronic health records, biotech firms, employers, health product distributors, pharmacies, pharmacy benefit managers, health information and research organizations, and others, committed to advancing effective patient privacy and security protections. Our mission is to advocate policies and practices that safeguard the privacy and security of patients and healthcare consumers while, at the same time, enabling the essential flow of patient information that is critical to the timely and effective delivery of healthcare, improvements in quality and safety, and the development of new lifesaving and life-enhancing medical interventions.

Accessing and sharing health data allows healthcare providers to deliver quality care and enables patients to become more engaged in their health decisions. While the Health Insurance Portability and Accountability Act (HIPAA) safeguards a specific subset of "protected health information" (PHI) and applies only to traditional healthcare entities and their business associates, a vast amount of health-related information does not fall within the HIPAA regulatory framework and is largely unprotected from misuse. The COVID-19 public health emergency (PHE) has led to significant amounts of personal health information collected outside the HIPAA regulatory structure. This information should be afforded privacy and security protections that align with HIPAA. Creating protections for this information will build public trust in data collection and sharing so that the information can be used to improve health outcomes and create conveniences for consumers.

The Confidentiality Coalition thanks you for your work on the bipartisan, bicameral "American Data Privacy and Protection Act." This bill provides a meaningful step to ensure that patients can receive robust privacy protections for their personal information and as we evaluate it, and assess its interaction with HIPAA covered information, we look forward to working with the Committee on the protection of healthcare information. As the Committee continues its work on this and other legislation, we encourage you to recognize the need to protect health data not covered by HIPAA. The Confidentiality Coalition has developed *"Beyond HIPAA"* principles to govern the sharing of this information. These principles emphasize harmonization with HIPAA's privacy and security rules. They also advocate for individual authorization processes (including revocation of authorization) for use and disclosure of identifiable health information not covered by HIPAA. Furthermore, Coalition members support limits on the use of identifiable data beyond the expressed purpose for which authorization was given. Developing legislative and regulatory solutions to protect consumers' health information not covered by the HIPAA rules will build trust in data collection, give stakeholders better certainty about how to protect such information, and ultimately help improve health outcomes.

The Confidentiality Coalition looks forward to working with you on steps to improve privacy protections for non-HIPAA health data. Please contact me at tgrande@hlc.org or 202-306-3538 with any questions.

Sincerely,

Tina O. Grande
Chair, Confidentiality Coalition and
Executive VP, Policy, Healthcare Leadership Council

June 13, 2022

Chairman Frank Pallone
House Energy and Commerce Committee
2125 Rayburn House Office Building
Washington, D.C. 20515

Ranking Member Cathy McMorris Rodgers
House Energy and Commerce Committee
2322 Rayburn House Office Building
Washington, D.C. 20515

Chairwoman Jan Schakowsky
Consumer Protection and Commerce Subcommittee
House Energy and Commerce Committee
2125 Rayburn House Office Building
Washington, D.C. 20515

Ranking Member Gus Bilirakis
Consumer Protection and Commerce Subcommittee
House Energy and Commerce Committee
2322 Rayburn House Office Building
Washington, D.C. 20515

Dear Chairs Pallone and Schakowsky, and Ranking Members McMorris Rodgers and Bilirakis,

The Consumer Technology Association (CTA)® commends your efforts and leadership in seeking to reach a bipartisan, bicameral comprehensive privacy bill.

As the Committee convenes its June 14th legislative hearing to discuss the American Data Privacy and Protection Act, CTA welcomes the opportunity to provide feedback based on the core principles for federal privacy legislation we articulated during the 116th Congress.

Thanks to a legislative and regulatory philosophy that has emphasized flexible but clear rules of the road, U.S. technology companies have flourished, becoming the envy of the world. Federal privacy legislation that enables innovators to continue building new and creative products without fear of frivolous lawsuits or compliance with complex regulatory schemes is key to American innovation and entrepreneurship.

As CTA outlined in 2019, this foundation begins by having a clear national privacy standard. By exempting a wide range of state and local laws, the discussion draft provides what could be perceived as 'preemption' in name only. Small companies, (80% of CTA's membership) will struggle to balance rapid growth and job creation with compliance and complex regulatory burdens, under the many exempted conflicting and ambiguous state and local laws. Indeed, creating a new federal framework while largely maintaining liability for state and local mandates could create a "worst of both worlds" scenario.

Similarly, we ask you not burden industry and federal courts with a new private right of action. We appreciate the process and notice to state AGs and opportunity to cure, and the four-year delayed effective date, but this simply postpones the inevitable: a rush of lawsuits that will slow the pace of innovation and embolden trial lawyers seeking to take advantage of a litigious environment under the guise of helping consumers. We have seen this scenario before in the patent context, where so-called "patent troll" trial lawyers barrage small businesses and startups with costly and non-meritorious shakedown lawsuits. CTA asks that any privacy legislation exclude a private right of action provision. Our businesses and economy already pay the world's highest lawyer tax and creating a new private federal cause of action would further disadvantage American businesses.

With the draft just having been publicly circulated, we find several provisions that would benefit from further review by industry and advocates alike. Our trading partners will also assess the bill against US international commitments. Particularly, definitions within the baseline text should be reviewed and understood before moving forward. Further, certain provisions would impose broad new regulatory mandates on developers and users of artificial intelligence systems and tools. Apart from the imposition of potential new liability for claims, the bill requires developers and users of such systems to undertake annual impact assessments and design evaluations, and to disclose the results to the FTC and Congress. The impact of these mandates on this dynamic new sector of the tech industry should be carefully scrutinized and evaluated before any final Committee action.

CTA members' initial feedback includes concerns about mandating changes in corporate reporting structure to elevate the role of chief privacy officers; the expanding FTC rulemaking authority; and ambiguous privacy-by-design requirement. Additionally, the lack of a risk-based framework results in mandated impact assessments and evaluations on all systems, even low (or no) risk systems; and the duty to file these assessments is also overbroad and can be narrowed to apply only where a violation of law has occurred.

Ultimately, CTA understands that consumer trust must be a central tenet of the products and services developed by our industry. It is earned when companies are good stewards of their consumers' data. We believe a well-informed, balanced approach will ensure consumer data is protected and enable businesses to grow and innovate.

These are complex issues, and we recognize that Congress has been grappling for years with how to effectively structure a federal privacy law. It is an important and critical undertaking, and we appreciate the opportunity to help improve upon the current draft to ensure that it does not harm small businesses and innovators and protects consumers.

A strong privacy bill focused on a federal approach would clarify consumer expectations and rights and affect almost all American businesses. It should not burden new market entrants and require new bureaucracies. It should value consumer privacy and encourage economic growth. We stand ready and willing to provide our continued feedback to the Committee.

Thank you,

Gary Shapiro
President and CEO
Consumer Technology Association

Cc: Members of the House Energy and Commerce Committee
Ranking Member Roger Wicker, Senate Commerce Committee

June 14, 2022

Representative Frank Pallone, Jr., Chairman
Representative Jan Schakowsky, Subcommittee Chair
Representative Gus Bilirakis, Ranking Member
Representative Cathy McMorris Rodgers, Ranking Member
U.S. House Committee on Energy and Commerce
Subcommittee on Consumer Protection and Commerce of the Committee on Energy and Commerce

Re: Hearing on "Protecting America's Consumers: Bipartisan Legislation to Strengthen Data Privacy and Security"

Dear Chairman Pallone, Subcommittee Chair Schakowsky, Ranking Member Bilirakis, and Ranking Member McMorris Rodgers:

We the undersigned members of the Disinfo Defense League respectfully request that you accept this letter for the record of your June 14, 2022, hearing on "Protecting America's Consumers: Bipartisan Legislation to Strengthen Data Privacy and Security."

The Disinfo Defense League, or DDL, is a distributed national network of over 230 grassroots, community-based organizations that are building a collective defense against disinformation campaigns that deliberately target Black, Latinx, Asian American, and other communities of color.

We are deeply concerned by systemic problems posed by the complex set of digital tactics, extractive data practices, and manipulative designs that undermine confidence in our democracy, sow distrust among Americans in our public health institutions, disenfranchise voters, and chill engagement for our communities. Extractive data practices contribute to the weaponization of online narratives that target our communities.

We are encouraged by this Subcommittee's efforts to provide guardrails around the use of people's personal data and prevent digital civil rights violations. The American Data Privacy and Protection Act would prohibit data collection, use, selling and sharing in any way that violates civil rights. It would stop collection or use of sensitive data — like Social Security numbers, genetic information, biometric information and precise geolocation information — without individuals' express, informed and unambiguous consent to such practices. This is a strong start to blunting extractive data practices.

The draft bill would also take a meaningful step by requiring companies to make privacy policies and notices available in each language in which they provide a product or service. This is a welcome attempt to eliminate the gross disparity between what tech companies do and disclose in English versus what they convey in other languages. While the bill strengthens FTC enforcement and guidance by adding agency staff and providing rulemaking authority for the Commission to implement these new protections, the legislation also sets up an eventual private right of action for individuals to go to court.

While there's more work to be done on the discussion draft of the American Data Privacy and Protection Act, we write today to urge your continued consideration of principles codified in our Disinfo Defense League Policy Platform.[177] Those principles are designed to rein in technology companies' extractive data practices and to safeguard privacy and civil rights on social media platforms with comprehensive digital-privacy measures that protect digital civil rights by:

- Limiting Big Tech's collection and use of our personal information.
- Establishing individuals' rights to control our own data.
- Enhancing data transparency.
- Preventing discrimination by algorithms.
- Enhancing platform transparency about the impacts of their business models.
- Protecting whistleblowers & external researchers.
- Setting a floor for consumer protection, not a ceiling.
- Enlisting the assistance of other federal agencies that protect the public with specialized expertise.
- Expanding Federal Trade Commission oversight.

The bipartisan legislation before you today is a promising start to fulfilling these goals. We look forward to continued dialogue on these issues to ensure the inclusion of robust civil rights protections against abusive data practices as the bill advances through the legislative process.

Respectfully submitted,

Access Humboldt
Access Now
Asian Americans Advancing Justice -AAJC

[177] Disinfo Defense League, Policy Platform (Dec. 7, 2021), https://www.disinfodefenseleague.org/policy-platform.

Common Cause
Equality Labs
Free Press Action
Friends of the Earth
Kairos Action
MediaJustice
Muslim Advocates
New Georgia Project Action Fund
ReFrame Action
United Church of Christ Media
Justice Ministry

Disinfo Defense League Policy Platform, December 2021

The Disinfo Defense League is a distributed network of grassroots, community- based organizations that are building a collective defense against disinformation and surveillance campaigns that deliberately target Black, Latinx, Asian Americans and I ndigenous people, along with other communities of color.

Over the past year, disinformation campaigns built on the system of surveillance capitalism have disrupted the ability to organize and disseminate accurate information — leading to real-world harms such as voter suppression, an insufficient public- health response to the pandemic, hate crimes, violence, harassment and a deadly insurrection at the U.S. Capitol.

Weaponized narratives targeting our communities are amplified through the toxic business models of Big Tech and Big Media.

Online platforms, cable channels and broadcasters alike have all shirked responsibility and accountability for their roles in spreading dangerous disinformation. Policymakers must examine how the corporate media ecosystem distorts facts and spreads lies — and move swiftly to redress the harms.

We are calling for policymakers to enact a strategic set of solutions to quell disinformation and build a media ecosystem that serves the public interest by promoting accurate news and information, protecting civil and human rights, and fostering an informed, equitable electorate across all languages.

Legislative Action

Congress should adopt comprehensive digital-privacy legislation that protects digital civil rights by:

1. Limiting Big Tech's Collection and Use of Our Personal Information
   Users should be able to control how apps use our data. We may want to share our data to receive services we sign up for, but apps should be prohibited from collecting more information than they need from us and from surreptitiously tracking us across the web. For example, the information we hand over for one reason — like providing a

phone number for security purposes — shouldn't be shared or sold to third party companies.

2. Establishing Individuals' Rights to Control Our Own Data
   We should have rights to easily access, correct, delete or download our personal information and take it with us when we leave an online service. Making data portable by law would let people free themselves from a corporate walled garden and easily use other services. These rights should apply equally to users across languages.
3. Enhancing Data Transparency
   We deserve to know what kinds of information companies and data brokers are collecting about us and there need to be strict safeguards on what is off limits. Data brokers gather incredibly private details like individuals' sex, age and gender, geolocation, health information; they can also collect internetsearch histories that can reveal even more sensitive information like a visit to a mental-health facility or religious site. Companies need to disclose not just what information they collect, but where they get the information; who shares data with them, and with whom they share data; how they analyze data to profile us; how they use our information; how they make decisions about what content, goods or services to offer us; and how they secure our data.
   Congress should close loopholes in existing privacy law by banning law enforcement from purchasing information from data brokers without a warrant and companies must conduct routine audits for bias, including an opportunity for independent analysis of algorithmic bias, as well as privacy assessments to determine the risks of this collection. And companies should be required to convey all of this information in two different ways: in an easyto-understand format proactively notifying users, and in an exhaustive and detailed format for regulators, advocates and researchers for regular review.
4. Preventing Discrimination by Algorithms
   Everything we do online generates data and every bit of that data can be tracked and used — no matter how innocuous it may appear in isolation — to create dangerous and invasive online profiles. Data feeds powerful algorithms to deliver personalized ads, recommendations and other services. There are some beneficial and harmless uses of these mechanisms when robust transparency and user control are present. But Congress should ban algorithms that profile users and target content to them in ways that constitute age, racial and sex discrimination in employment, housing, lending, and e-commerce. Congress should investigate voting and other civil rights violations that flow from abusive data practices.
5. Enhancing Platform Transparency about the Impacts of Their Business Models
   Reporting over the past several years has demonstrated that — just as the tobacco companies knew that their products were killing people long before the public was made aware — social-media companies knew about how their business models were harming people and communities long before the details came to light. Companies should be required to provide access to researchers and to immediately disclose when they learn their platform algorithms are being used to discriminate against or otherwise harm people; and the companies should actively and in an ongoing manner mitigate those harms and be held accountable for any persisting harms.
6. Protecting Whistleblowers and External Researchers

We must protect whistleblowers who come forward to expose unethical, immoral and discriminatory behaviors, algorithms and practices inside of tech companies. Protection from retaliation, labor violations, baseless lawsuits, and targeted harassment are critical to guaranteeing the rights of whistleblowers. We must also set out explicit protections for external researcher access to platform data.

7. Expanding Federal Trade Commission Oversight
   The FTC should have the power and resources to conduct rulemakings and effectively enforce against and prevent data abuses and other unfair or deceptive practices. Congress cannot anticipate and legislate against all future uses and abuses of data that companies may engage in, so lawmakers should enable the FTC to oversee and respond to future violations. For instance, users shouldn't have to waive our privacy, quality of service, or other rights just to access a given service when there's no need for that data to deliver the promised goods.
8. Enlisting the Assistance of Other Federal Agencies That Protect the Public with Specialized Expertise.
   Federal agencies such as the Consumer Financial Protection Bureau, Department of Education, Department of Labor, Department of Justice and Department of Veterans Affairs, among others, should study how personal information is used in their fields, identify disparities and risks for discrimination, and issue public reports to Congress on a regular basis with special focus on the discriminatory effects on communities of color and non-English speaking groups.
9. Setting a Floor for Consumer Protection, Not a Ceiling.
   A federal law must refrain from preempting the work that states are doing to build their own consumerprotection or privacy regimes. Many state consumer-protection laws are used to protect marginalized communities. A federal data-privacy law that broadly preempts state laws and weakens these kinds of protections would jeopardize civil rights.

Congress should pass legislation to tax digital advertising and direct those monies to support high-quality noncommercial and local journalism.

- Local news can be a powerful antidote to the spread of disinformation. To fully combat the problems of disinformation, hate and other malign practices online, we must fund high-quality, local journalism and urge Congress to create a small percentage tax on the online advertising revenues of the largest online platforms.
- For example, a 2% tax, could yield more than $2 billion for a national endowment to support local news and information, including journalism by and serving people of color, non-English speakers, and other minority groups.*

Executive Action

- The Biden administration should leverage existing authorities to rein in disinformation.
- The administration should appoint a White House official to coordinate interagency study and action on tech companies' civil-rights violations and other harmful data practices

- The FCC should issue guidance pursuant to the broadcast-hoax rule warning broadcasters to refrain from airing inaccurate claims about the pandemic, a public-health emergency. The FCC's broadcast-hoax rule prohibits broadcasters from knowingly airing false information about a catastrophe if it's foreseeable that doing so would cause substantial harm.
- The FCC should use this authority to stop the spread of deadly health disinformation. Before renewing broadcasters' licenses, the agency should evaluate whether licensees are adhering to their public-interest mandates.
- The Federal Trade Commission should initiate a rulemaking on harmful data and algorithmic practices and prosecute discriminatory data practices and data-related abuses
- The Justice Department, FTC and other federal and state enforcement agencies should apply antitrust law to stop tech giants' never-ending acquisition of new firms.
- Agencies should stop the dominant platforms' monopoly abuses, collusion and other anticompetitive practices when and where they happen. Congress should ensure that the agencies are well funded.

International Action

The United Nations should document and analyze the harms that disinformation has caused to historically-oppressed populations around the world, and set in place the building blocks for repair.

The U.N. should investigate the harms of disinformation across the world and the unique harms to Black, Indigenous, and brown people. Building on the 2021 report on disinformation by the Special Rapporteur on the promotion and protection of the right to freedom of opinion and expression made to the U.N. Human Rights Office of the High Commissioner, the U.N. should issue a full report on the harms caused by disinformation, with particular focus on the harms to Black, Indigenous, immigrant, and brown communities around the world.

In consultation with expert organizations, the full report should be accompanied by a set of recommended state policies for governments to consider adopting to stop the spread of disinformation. It should also suggest remedies for the harms people have already experienced.

Policy Platform Signatories

The following organizations have signed on to the Disinfo Defense League policy platform:

Access Humboldt
Access Now
Arab American Institute
Asian Americans Advancing Justice - AAJC
Asian Pacific American Labor Alliance, AFL-CIO
Common Cause
Cybersecurity for Democracy

Demos
Detroit Community Technology Project
Equality Labs
Facebook Users Union
Fight for the Future
Free Press Action
Global Exchange
Greenlining Institute
Indian American Impact
Instituto di Geopolitica Digitale
Japanese American Citizens League
Kairos
Media Alliance
MediaJustice
Miami Workers Center
Mijente
National Council of Asian Pacific Americans (NCAPA)
New Georgia Project
Noticias Para Inmigrantes
OpenMIC
People's Action
ProgressNow New Mexico
Public Good Projects
ReFrame
Rural Organizing Project
Ultraviolet
United We Dream
Women's March

The Disinfo Defense League (DDL) is a distributed national network of organizers, researchers and disinformation experts disrupting online racialized disinformation infrastructure and campaigns that deliberately target Black, Latinx, Asian American / Pacific Islander and other communities of color. DDL was created by and for these communities and is supported by services and insight provided by expert partners and organization.

Launched in June 2020, DDL uses coordinated strategy, disinformation training, and research to support member organizations with resources to fortify and scale current inoculation efforts and increase cohesion and collaboration in targeted communities.

DDL features over 230 organizational members who work across geography, generation, and gender to equip communities with tools, training, and tactics needed to combat racialized disinformation and win.

June 10, 2022

Honorable Frank Pallone
Chair
House Energy & Commerce Committee

Honorable Jan Schakowsky
Chair
House Energy & Commerce Committee
Consumer Protection &
Commerce Subcommittee

Honorable Cathy McMorris Rodgers
Ranking Member
House Energy & Commerce Committee

Honorable Gus Bilirakis
Ranking Member
House Energy & Commerce Committee
Consumer Protection &
Commerce Subcommittee

Chairman Pallone and Ranking Member McMorris Rodgers:

On behalf of Illinois employer associations that represent millions of employees from various sectors across Illinois, thank you for the opportunity to comment on the American Data Privacy and Protection Act that was released last week. We appreciate your bipartisan efforts to create a national standard on how and when data may be collected from individuals and used. This would create one standard while eliminating a patchwork of regulations across the nation.

Unfortunately, we have issues with a number of provisions in the draft bill, but are writing today to register our strong concerns about one provision in particular that would grandfather an Illinois law. If this provision remains intact in the federal legislation, Illinois will continue to be an outlier as one of very few states in the nation that do not fall fully under this new federal legislation. As a result, Illinois employers will continue operating under a different set of rules than the overwhelming majority of employers in the United States. It would violate the spirit of the federal law to create one uniform standard.

The Illinois BIPA law has spawned more than 1,400 lawsuits in the past few years. Employers are unable, as a practical matter, to use technologically advanced equipment that utilizes biometric identifiers for security purposes and biometric time clocks for example. Hospitals and medical facilities have faced lawsuits for utilizing biometric information to control access to prescription pharmaceuticals. The Illinois law even allows lawsuits when there has been no data breach or any harm for an employee.

We strongly encourage you to revise the current legislation to create one uniform standard that applies evenly to all states rather than continuing the patchwork by exempting certain laws and regulations in a small handful of states.

Thank you for your consideration.

Donovan Griffith
Illinois Manufacturers' Association

Jack Lavin
Chicagoland Chamber of Commerce

Matt Hart
Illinois Trucking Association

Mark Biel
Chemical Industry Council of Illinois

Jim Watson
American Petroleum Institute

Don Erickson
Security Industry Association

AJ Wilhelmi
Illinois Health and Hospital Association

Rob Karr
Illinois Retail Merchants Association

Todd Maisch
Illinois Chamber of Commerce

Michael Jacobson
Illinois Hotel & Lodging Association

Jim Kaitschuk
Illinois Sheriffs' Association

Matt Pickering
Health Care Council of Illinois

Thomas A. Thanas
Illinois Casino Gaming Association

cc: U.S. Senator Dick Durbin
U.S. Senator Tammy Duckworth
Illinois Congressional Delegation
House Energy & Commerce Committee

* * *

June 13, 2022
The Honorable Frank Pallone
The Honorable Cathy McMorris Rodgers
House Energy & Commerce Committee

The Honorable Roger Wicker
Senate Commerce Committee

RE: draft 3-corners privacy bill, the American Data Privacy and Protection Act

Dear Chair Pallone, Ranking Member McMorris Rodgers and Ranking Member Wicker,

The Insights Association (IA), the leading nonprofit trade association for the market research and data analytics industry (also known as the insights industry), writes to provide urgent comment on your new draft comprehensive privacy legislation, the American Data Privacy and Protection Act, prior to hearing and markup in the House, and some recommended amendments (pages 2-7).

Our more than 7,200 members are the world's leading producers of intelligence, analytics and insights defining the needs, attitudes and behaviors of consumers, organizations and their employees, students and citizens. With that essential understanding, leaders can make intelligent decisions and deploy strategies and tactics to build trust, inspire innovation, realize the full potential of individuals and teams, and successfully create and promote products, services and ideas.

IA supports comprehensive federal privacy legislation and we welcome your efforts. A recent study[178] conducted by IA member companies Research Narrative and Innovate MR, on behalf of Privacy for America, revealed that nearly all Americans surveyed (92 percent) believe it is important for Congress to pass new legislation to protect consumers' personal data, and a majority (62 percent) prefer federal regulation over individual state regulations. Four out of five voters (81 percent) support a national standard that outright prohibits harmful ways of collecting, using, and sharing personal data. So do we.

However, details in such a bill, particularly the draft ADPPA, matter dearly to the insights industry.

Like most industries, we are quite concerned by the state preemption and private right of action, but there are other details upon which we wish to focus our recommendations, in priority order, below.

1. Sensitive Covered Data – Online Activities and Media Viewership – and Independent Audience Measurement

Sensitive covered data would require an opt in for its collection, processing, or sharing with third parties, which makes sense. However, as drafted, the definition's clause (xi), covering online activities, and clause (xiv), covering media viewership, would not allow for independent audience measurement, an essential underpinning to valuation of content and advertising (online and offline), which responsibly collects and shares covered data about individuals for the purpose of understanding groups. IA urges you to protect independent audience

[178] New Study Shows Overwhelming Bipartisan Support for U.S. Federal Privacy Legislation. DECEMBER 1, 2021. https://www.insightsassociation.org/Information-Updates/Industry-News/View/ArticleId/16553/New-Study-Shows-Overwhelming-Bipartisan-Support-for-U-S-Federal-Privacy-Legislation.

measurement in Sec. 2 (22)(A) as follows, based on language used in Florida H.B. 9 earlier this year[179]:

Sec. 2 ... (22) SENSITIVE COVERED DATA.— (A) IN GENERAL.—The term "sensitive covered data" means the following forms of covered data:

.... (xi) Information identifying an individual's online activities over time or across third party websites or online services, except when processed for the purpose of independently measuring or reporting advertising or content performance, reach, or frequency.

.... (xiv) Information identifying or revealing the extent or content of any individual's access or viewing or other use of any television service, cable service, or streaming media service, except when processed for the purpose of independently measuring or reporting advertising or content performance, reach, or frequency.

In concert with that definitional clarification, we recommend that the definition of targeted advertising be amended to also clarify such measurement in Sec. 2(26) as follows:

Sec. 2 ... (26) TARGETED ADVERTISING.—The term "targeted advertising," notwithstanding Sec. 2(22)(xi) and Sec. 2(22)(xiv)—

(A) means displaying to an individual or unique identifier an online advertisement that is selected based on known or predicted preferences, characteristics, or interests derived from covered data collected over time or across third party websites or online services about the individual or unique identifier; and

(B) does not include—

(i) advertising or marketing to an individual in response to the individual's specific request for information or feedback;

(ii) first-party advertising based on an individual's visit into and purchase of a product or service from a brick-and-mortar store, or visit to or use of a website or online service that offers a product or service that is the subject of the advertisement;

(iii) contextual advertising when an advertisement is displayed online [that is related to/based on] the content of the webpage or online service on which the advertisement appears; or

(iv) processing covered data solely for measuring or reporting advertising or content performance, reach, or frequency, including independent audience measurement.

2. Loyalty/Pricing Provisions and Market Research Participation

Participant incentives are an important tool in the insights industry toolkit to encourage research subjects' involvement in market research involving their covered data, as response rates have declined. Participant incentives are particularly key to research in which the research subject has affirmatively consented to participate. Adding a new clause in Sec. 104(b) would help clarify the continued legality of participant incentives for research subjects in face of the draft bill's pricing discrimination provisions, as follows:

---

179 "Personal data processed solely for the purpose of independently measuring or reporting advertising or content performance, reach, or frequency pursuant to a contract with a controller that collected personal information in accordance with this act. Such information may not be sold or shared unless otherwise authorized under this act." https://www.flsenate.gov/Session/Bill/2022/9/

SEC. 104. LOYALTY TO INDIVIDUALS WITH RESPECT TO PRICING.

... (b) RULES OF CONSTRUCTION.—Nothing in subsection (a) shall be construed to prohibit—

(1) the relation of the price of a service or the level of service provided to an individual to the provision, by the individual, of financial information that is necessarily collected and used only for the purpose of initiating, rendering, billing for, or collecting payment for a service or product requested by the individual; ~~*or*~~

(2) a covered entity from offering a loyalty program that provides discounted or free products or services, or other consideration, in exchange for an individual's continued business with the covered entity, provided that such program otherwise complies with the requirements of this Act and any regulations promulgated under this Act.;

(3) a covered entity from offering a financial incentive or other consideration to an individual for participation in market research.

Along with it should come a definition of the term "market research" as follows in Sec. 2:

( ) MARKET RESEARCH.—The term "market research"—

means the collection, processing or transferring of covered data as reasonably necessary to investigate the market for or marketing of products, services, or ideas, where the information is not:

(i) integrated into any product or service; (ii) otherwise used to contact any particular individual or device; or (iii) used to advertise or market to any particular individual or device."[180]

3. Third Parties and Legitimate Access to Data

The draft bill would unreasonably limit the data that the digital economy requires to enable commerce, understand consumers' and citizens' needs and desires, and maintain a functioning Internet for consumers. Access to data by and from third parties is vital to the U.S. economy and the functioning of government programs. Imposing burdensome and ambiguous requirements would thwart access to legitimate data by businesses, federal agencies, and local governments that rely on such data for day-to-day operations, and short-term and long-term planning and decision-making. IA urges you to amend Section 302(b) as follows:

Sec 302. (b) Third Parties.—A third party—

(1) shall not process third party data for a processing purpose inconsistent with the notice provided to individuals;

(2) for purposes of paragraph (1), may reasonably rely on representations made by the covered entity that transferred the third party data regarding the notice provided to individuals and

---

[180] This definition for market research is based on one used by the model federal privacy legislation put forward by Privacy for America in Part I, Section 1, R: https://www.privacyforamerica.com/overview/principles-for-privacy-legislation/

(3) shall be exempt from the requirements of section 204 with respect to third party data, but shall otherwise have the same responsibilities and obligations as a covered entity with respect to such data under all other provisions of this Act.

4. Market Research Needs a General Exception

Critical product development and market research involving covered data should be permitted to function. The draft should not prevent companies and organizations from using data to better the products and services they offer to consumers or conduct research on the markets for their offerings. Innovation and developments in products and services work to benefit consumers. The bill should not unnecessarily restrict companies and organizations from using covered data to better their offerings (and public policies) for the general public (and for governments). Therefore, IA urges the amendment of Section 209(a) as follows:

SEC. 209. GENERAL EXCEPTIONS. ...
(a) GENERAL EXCEPTIONS.—
A covered entity may collect, process, or transfer covered data for any of the following purposes, provided that the collection, processing, or transfer is reasonably necessary, proportionate, and limited to such purpose:
.... (2) With respect to covered data previously collected in accordance with this Act, notwithstanding this exception, to perform system maintenance, diagnostics, maintain a product or service for which such covered data was collected, conduct internal research or analytics to improve products, and services, and ideas or to develop new products, services or ideas, perform inventory management or network management, or debug or repair errors that impair the functionality of a service or product for which such covered data was collected by the covered entity,
... (10) To process or transfer covered data as reasonably necessary to investigate the market for or marketing of products, services, or ideas, where the information is not—
(A) integrated into any product or service;
(B) otherwise used to contact any particular individual or device; or
(C) used to advertise or market to any particular individual or device.

5. Civil Rights – Discrimination and Market Research Participation

Sec. 207(a) would prohibit covered entities from collecting, processing or transferring "covered data in a manner that discriminates or otherwise makes unavailable the equal enjoyment of goods or services on the basis of race, color, religion, national origin, gender, sexual orientation, or disability." IA is concerned that choosing research subjects for participation in market research, when it involves a participant incentive, could be misconstrued as discrimination, despite the bill specifying that the prohibition doesn't apply to "diversifying an applicant, participant, or customer pool" (Sec. 207 (a)(2)(A)(ii)).

Research subjects are sought in certain segments and numbers for market research studies, with the samples varying depending on the needs and scope of the study. For example, a study may oversample or focus entirely on black homosexual women in their 30s and 40s – if a participant incentive is involved, would other potential research subjects disqualified from participation potentially have been discriminated against? The situation is different from Sec. 207 (a)(2)(A)(ii), since "diversity" is not explicitly the goal of every study; statistical or otherwise representation of a population (or populations) is more often the goal. Moreover, while participation in market research should not be considered a "good" or "service" to the research subject participating, if a participant incentive is involved, this could get misconstrued.

To preserve the ability to conduct market research and to adequately include necessary populations, IA requests an additional exception in Sec. 207(a)(2)(A):

Sec. 207 ... (a) CIVIL RIGHTS PROTECTIONS.—

(1) IN GENERAL.—A covered entity may not collect, process, or transfer covered data in a manner that discriminates or otherwise makes unavailable the equal enjoyment of goods or services on the basis of race, color, religion, national origin, gender, sexual orientation, or disability.

(2) EXCEPTIONS.—This subsection shall not apply to—

(A) the collection, processing, or transfer of covered data for the purpose of—

(i) a covered entity's self-testing to prevent discrimination; or

(ii) diversifying an applicant, participant, or customer pool; or

(iii) solely for purposes of determining participation of an individual in market research; or

(B) any private club or group not open to the public, as described in section 201(e) of the Civil Rights Act of 1964 (42 U.S.C. 2000a(e)).

Along with it should come a definition of "market research" as follows in Sec. 2:

( ) MARKET RESEARCH.—The term "market research"—

means the collection, processing or transferring of covered data as reasonably necessary to investigate the market for or marketing of products, services, or ideas, where the information is not: (i) integrated into any product or service; (ii) otherwise used to contact any particular individual or device; or (iii) used to advertise or market to any particular individual or device.[181]

Alternatively, IA recommends that you amend Sec. 207(a)(1) to make clear that it prohibits the processing of covered data in ways that discriminate against individuals for housing, education, employment, healthcare, insurance, or credit opportunities (none of which would apply to participation in market research) as follows:

SEC. 207. CIVIL RIGHTS AND ALGORITHMS.

(a) CIVIL RIGHTS PROTECTIONS.—

(1) IN GENERAL.—A covered entity may not collect, process, or transfer covered data in a manner that discriminates or otherwise makes unavailable the equal enjoyment of goods or services for housing, education, employment, healthcare, insurance, or credit opportunities on the basis of race, color, religion, national origin, gender, sexual orientation, or disability.

---

[181] As used in Part I, Section 1, R of the Privacy for America model federal privacy bill.

6. Third Parties and Data Sharing between Affiliates

The draft bill would prevent covered data transfers between affiliates of large data holders. There is no consumer benefit or other principled reason for this restriction on intra-company data transfers. IA urges you to amend the definition of third party in Section 2(27) as follows:

Sec. 2 ... (27) THIRD PARTY.—The term "third party"—

(A) means any person or entity that—

(i) collects, processes, or transfers third party data; and

(ii) is not a service provider with respect to such data; and

(B) does not include a person or entity that collects or transfers covered data from or to another entity if the 2 entities are related by common ownership or corporate control and share common branding,

7. Civil Rights - Impact Assessments on Algorithms

Requiring impact assessments for every processing activity or algorithm used by an insights company or organization would be exceedingly onerous and costly. Algorithm assessments and privacy impact assessments should be appropriately scoped to high risk data processing activities or processing activities involving sensitive covered data, not routine algorithm and processing functions, such as random sampling of research subjects for segments in a survey. IA recommends amending Sec. 207(c) and 301(d) as follows:

SEC. 207. CIVIL RIGHTS AND ALGORITHMS. ... (c) ALGORITHM IMPACT AND EVALUATION.— (1) ALGORITHM IMPACT ASSESSMENT.—

(A) IMPACT ASSESSMENT.—Notwithstanding any other provision of law, not later than [4 years] after the date of enactment of this Act, and annually thereafter, a large data holder that uses an algorithm that may cause potential harm to a consumer, and uses such algorithm solely or in part, to collect, process or transfer sensitive covered data, must conduct an impact assessment of such algorithm.

... SEC. 301. EXECUTIVE RESPONSIBILITY.

... (d) LARGE DATA HOLDER PRIVACY IMPACT ASSESSMENTS.—

(1) IN GENERAL.—Not later than 1 year after the date of enactment of this Act or 1 year after the date that a covered entity first meets the definition of large data holder, whichever is earlier, and biennially thereafter, each large data holder shall conduct a privacy impact assessment that weighs the benefits of the large data holder's sensitive covered data collecting, processing, and transfer practices against the potential adverse consequences of such practices to individual privacy.

8. Data Protections for Children and Minors – Actual Knowledge Standard

The draft bill should retain the "actual knowledge" standard, with which companies are familiar due to the Children's Online Privacy Protection Act (COPPA), for restrictions on targeted advertising and data transfers regarding minors. (Even companies and organizations not specifically covered by COPPA look to the law/regulation as guidance on how to protect minors.) The "actual knowledge" standard sets a clear rule for companies and organizations to follow and should remain in the draft. The bill should also cap its requirements to individuals under age 16, which has become the common age range in state legislation and policy discussions. IA urges changes to Sec. 205 as follows:

SEC. 205. DATA PROTECTIONS FOR CHILDREN AND MINORS.

(a) PROHIBITION ON TARGETED ADVERTISING TO CHILDREN AND MINORS.—A covered entity shall not engage in targeted advertising to any individual under the age of 16 if the covered entity has [actual knowledge] that the individual is under the age of 16.

(b) DATA TRANSFER REQUIREMENTS RELATED TO MINORS.—A covered entity shall not transfer the covered data of an individual to a third party without affirmative express consent from the individual or the individual's parent or guardian if the covered entity [has actual knowledge] that the individual is at least 13 years of age and under the age of 16 years of age.

9. Sensitive Covered Data – Health Data

Sensitive covered data would require an opt in for its collection, processing, or sharing with third parties, which makes sense. While IA would ordinarily oppose the inclusion of race/ethnicity data in the definition of sensitive covered data, because it is such common demographic data in market research that it is even in the decennial census, clause (ix) adds a common-sense limitation: "in a manner inconsistent with the individual's reasonable expectation regarding disclosure of such information." A similar limitation is applied to clause (x), covering sexual orientation or behavior. Clause (ii) of the definition, however, includes various health data so broadly drawn as to potentially cover anything as simple as how a research subject feels today.

Therefore, IA requests similar language in an amendment to Sec. 2 (22) as follows:

Sec. 2 ... (22) SENSITIVE COVERED DATA.—

(A) IN GENERAL.—

The term "sensitive covered data" means the following forms of covered data:

.... (ii) Any information that describes or reveals the past, present, or future physical health, mental health, disability, diagnosis, or healthcare treatment of an individual, in a manner inconsistent with the individual's reasonable expectation regarding disclosure of such information.

Next Steps

The Insights Association and our members support consumer privacy protections, as we've discussed, and we look forward to talking with you, your staff, and your fellow legislators, and providing further information regarding these priorities and related issues with the American Data Privacy and Protection Act.

Sincerely,
Howard Fienberg
Senior VP, Advocacy
Insights Association

CC: House Energy & Commerce Committee members

* * *

June 13, 2022

The Honorable Frank Pallone
Chairman
U.S. House Committee on Energy and Commerce
Washington, DC 20515

The Honorable Jan Schakowsky
Chair
U.S. House Subcommittee Consumer Protection & Commerce
Washington, DC 20515

The Honorable Cathy McMorris Rodgers
Ranking Member
U.S. House Committee on Energy and Commerce
Washington, DC 20515

The Honorable Gus Bilirakis
Ranking Member
U.S. House Subcommittee on Consumer Protection & Commerce
Washington, DC 20515

RE: Hearing on "Protecting America's Consumers: Bipartisan Legislation to Strengthen Data Privacy and Security" (June 14, 2022)

Dear Representatives Pallone, Rodgers, Schakowsky and Bilirakis:

The Main Street Privacy Coalition (MSPC), a coalition of 19 national trade associations representing more than a million American businesses,[182] appreciates your focus on the need for federal data privacy protections and offers this statement for the hearing record. MSPC is comprised of a broad array of national trade associations representing businesses that line America's Main Streets. From retailers to REALTORS®, hotels to home builders, grocery stores to restaurants, gas stations to travel plazas, self-storage to convenience stores, including franchise establishments, MSPC member companies interact with consumers day in and day

[182] The Main Street Privacy Coalition website and member list may be accessed at: https://mainstreetprivacy.com.

out. Our members' businesses can be found in every town, city and state, providing jobs, supporting our economy and serving Americans as a vital part of their communities.

Collectively, the industries that MSPC member associations represent directly employ approximately 34 million Americans and constitute over one-fifth of the U.S. economy by contributing $4.5 trillion (or 21.8%) to the U.S. gross domestic product (GDP). Our success depends on maintaining trusted relationships with our customers and clients: trust that goods and services we provide are high quality and offered at competitive prices; and trust that information customers provide to us is kept secure and used responsibly. For these reasons, our associations are actively engaged in the discussions surrounding data privacy and continue to work together to support Congress's enactment of a comprehensive and uniform federal data privacy law.

MSPC is dedicated to the enactment of a uniform, national federal data privacy law that creates privacy obligations for all businesses handling consumers' personal information, and we appreciate the Committee's efforts to develop the American Data Privacy and Protection Act (ADPPA), a bipartisan bill to achieve this goal. In this statement, we examine several provisions of the ADPPA on which we recommend the Committee continue its work to improve the bill:

1. Preemption of State Law

We appreciate the bipartisan effort to develop a uniform, preemptive federal privacy bill that would set a national standard for consumer privacy protections. If enacted, such a privacy law would aid consumers and businesses alike by ensuring consumer privacy protections are the same regardless of the State in which a consumer resides or a business is located. This is necessary because the increasing patchwork of newly enacted state privacy laws threatens the ability to provide comprehensive and uniform privacy protections to Americans. For this reason, MSPC has long supported federal privacy bills that would establish a uniform national privacy framework to cover all businesses handling consumers' personal data. Despite the drafters best intentions to achieve this goal, we are concerned that the ADPPA's current preemption provision is unlikely to withstand legal challenges to its intended effect, potentially leaving States free to maintain or adopt different privacy laws that leave consumers with different rights depending on where they live and saddle Main Street businesses with compliance burdens going beyond the federal standard. We therefore urge you to examine the key Supreme Court rulings on federal preemption of state laws and adopt the type of preemption provision in the ADPPA that the Court has consistently found sufficient for Congress to establish a preemptive federal law. Improving the ADPPA to clarify Congressional intent to preempt state laws by using the language the Supreme Court upholds would make it much more likely to achieve its primary goal of creating a uniform, national privacy law for Americans.

2. Private Rights of Action

We understand the current bipartisan agreement regarding private rights of action is one the sponsors believe is necessary to advance a privacy bill that can pass Congress. Many businesses, however, are wary of allowing individuals to file lawsuits to enforce a privacy law.

Our members share those concerns, which predominantly stem from the technical complexity involved in achieving mistake-free compliance with data privacy laws and from Main Street's experience with large volumes of questionable legal claims that proliferated under other areas of the law. Additionally, we urge Committee members to consider that, taking into account the Act's many exemptions (discussed further in point 3 below), private rights of action will be disproportionately used against, and significantly impact, Main Street businesses compared to other businesses. All too often, potential litigants are able to exploit the Main Street businesses' realization that obtaining legal representation and defending against an alleged claim under a complex federal law is expensive. Those costs can lead Main Street businesses to agree to settlements of even non-meritorious claims simply to avoid litigation, which has the compounding effects of making it more difficult for them to cover their expenses and consequently costing Americans their jobs. In addition, due to the complexity of achieving compliance, our preference would be for the Committee to adopt an enforcement approach similar to what state privacy laws have adopted as the most effective way to drive compliance with privacy laws: exclusive government agency enforcement against businesses after a 30- or 60-day cure period following agency notice of non-compliance.

3. Exemptions for Service Providers and Financial Services Companies

We appreciate that the Committee has not resorted to reliance on private contracts to create legal obligations between parties because businesses vary greatly in size and bargaining power. However, we remain concerned that nationwide and global service providers, as defined and covered in the ADPPA, do not have equivalent privacy requirements to those applying to even the smallest of Main Street businesses. To protect Americans' privacy comprehensively, federal data privacy legislation, including the ADPPA, should ensure that all industry sectors are covered by the bill's requirements in order to avoid privacy loopholes that can leave consumers unprotected when their personal data is handled by a range of businesses. However, service providers remain exempt from providing consumers some aspects of the privacy rights all other covered entities must provide under sections 203 and 204, and financial services companies are deemed in compliance with all provisions despite not having equivalent ones under federal banking law. For example, section 203 requires covered entities to provide consumers' with privacy rights to access, correct or delete their personal information, and section 204 requires them to first obtain consumers' affirmative consent before transferring their sensitive personal data. These are privacy requirements that exist nowhere else in federal privacy law and should be required of all businesses in the ADPPA.

These exemptions for service providers predominantly extend to businesses in the telecommunications, cable and technology sectors, and we believe the ADPPA could be improved in this regard to better protect Americans' privacy. For example, the ADPPA should be modified to meet the principle that each business handling consumers' personal data should have statutory requirements to do what is in that business's control to protect consumers' data privacy as required in the legislation. This would avoid making consumer-facing businesses responsible for the privacy violations by businesses that "serve" them – many of which are larger businesses they cannot control – including nationwide and global service providers. If the ADPPA adopts this approach, it would more effectively secure the consumer rights it establishes and would treat industry sectors fairly by making them responsible for their own conduct, not exposing them to liability for privacy violations by their business partners, including contractors, franchises and other businesses – a key MSPC principle.

MSPC members are also concerned with the exemption for financial institutions and other entities subject to the Gramm-Leach-Bliley Act (GLBA) from the consumer privacy protections in the ADPPA. We urge the Committee to recognize that GLBA is a 1999 federal law that is significantly outdated in its extremely narrow privacy protections, which do not provide anything close to the privacy protections that the ADPPA would impose on non-exempt "covered entities." For instance, GLBA only requires that an entity sharing consumer financial data with unaffiliated third parties for marketing purposes provides an annual opt-out notice in writing, which most consumers likely never read. GLBA does not, however, require any access, correction or deletion of consumers' financial data upon request, as the ADPPA would require of every other consumer-facing business on Main Street. GLBA also does not require affirmative opt-in consent of customers before transferring sensitive financial information to unaffiliated third parties. The ADPPA's exemptions for financial institutions and other entities subject to GLBA permit these select consumer-facing businesses – ones with the most sensitive financial information – to avoid the bills' privacy requirements and, unless amended, the bill will leave consumers' financial information unprotected while providing a false sense of security that consumers are fully covered.

4. Preserving Customer Loyalty Rewards and Benefits

It is clear that Americans overwhelmingly want customer loyalty programs that provide rewards, discounts and other benefits to remain legal.[183] Generally, the four States that have enacted privacy laws of general application since California's 2018 law have all found ways to sufficiently preserve these programs that consumers desire by protecting the ability of businesses to continue to offer better prices and services to customers who voluntarily participate in bona fide customer loyalty, club or rewards programs. It is unclear, however, that the current language of the ADPPA will preserve loyalty plans. For example, section 104 of the Act requires "loyalty…with respect to pricing." This is a concept that does not exist today. If a sales price only applies to customers who have signed up for a rewards program, does that fulfill "loyalty" to the customers who decline to give their consent to enter the rewards program? The section's rule of construction regarding loyalty programs is also conditioned on the program complying with all of the other requirements in the Act and any regulations. That language is unnecessary and further raises an interpretive question as to whether requirements in the ADPPA that would not otherwise apply to rewards programs should now apply.

Getting this section right will be important to American consumers who wish to maintain their earned points, rewards and discounts, and is a critical need for Main Street businesses under a federal privacy law. We urge the Committee to consider an approach to privacy law that is well understood in the European Union. The principle embodied in EU privacy law is that consumers should not face retaliation for exercising a privacy right. This is consistent with the purposes of this Act and privacy laws in general. The continued operation of loyalty or

183 According to a survey by Bond Brand Loyalty Inc., 79% of consumers say loyalty programs make them more likely to continue doing business with brands that offer them, and 32% of consumers strongly agree that a loyalty program makes their brand experience better. Bond Brand Loyalty Inc., The Loyalty Report (2019).

rewards programs that consumers may voluntarily participate in would not be a retaliatory act against another consumer who exercises a privacy right. We believe this may be the best way to restructure section 104 so that it would not undermine this vitally important aspect of the American customer experience on which consumers and Main Street businesses rely.

We appreciate your continued consideration of the views of Main Street businesses on the ADPPA given that Main Street represents the backbone of the United States economy. Main Street businesses – many of whom have struggled to remain open to serve consumers during the COVID-19 pandemic and are now facing historic pressures from the confluence of inflation, supply chain constraints, and labor shortages – will bear the full burden of complying with the regulatory obligations under the ADPPA that the Committee is examining today. As you consider ways to improve and advance the ADPPA in the legislative process, the members of the MSPC urge you to consider and address the issues raised above. We look forward to continuing our constructive dialogue with you on these matters as you craft federal data privacy legislation going forward.

Sincerely,

The Main Street Privacy Coalition

cc: Members of the Committee on Energy and Commerce

* * *

November 21, 2019

The Honorable Mitch McConnell
Majority Leader
United States Senate
S-230, The Capitol
Washington, D.C. 20510

The Honorable Nancy Pelosi
Speaker of the House
U.S. House of Representatives
H-232, The Capitol
Washington, D.C. 20515

The Honorable Charles Schumer
Minority Leader
United States Senate
S-221, The Capitol
Washington, D.C. 20510

The Honorable Kevin McCarthy
Minority Leader
U.S. House of Representatives
H-204, The Capitol
Washington, D.C. 20515

Dear Majority Leader McConnell, Minority Leader Schumer, Speaker Pelosi and Minority Leader McCarthy:

We understand the relevant committees in both the Senate and House are continuing their important reviews of the nation's consumer privacy laws and we are encouraged by reports of a possible legislative hearing in the Senate Commerce Committee next month. Given how tightly the Internet is now woven into every aspect of our lives and the American economy, we applaud this crucial effort that you and your colleagues have undertaken.

At the state level, the sweeping California Consumer Privacy Act (CCPA) is slated to take effect in January, marking a significant development in the privacy debate. As our member companies work to comply with the CCPA, including efforts to clarify key elements of the bill, other states have enacted or proposed additional legislation, including Nevada that recently passed privacy legislation with provisions that are inconsistent with the CCPA. These efforts have already begun to create a patchwork of conflicting new restrictions on data collection and use along with other onerous obligations on businesses. Indeed, as businesses are awaiting final rules implementing the law, the CCPA's chief proponent has proposed new rules as part of a planned ballot initiative to bypass the legislative process and create yet another new law in 2020. In addition, Europe's General Data Protection Regulation (GDPR) has been adopted by some large multinational companies, while others have discontinued European operations as a result of the regulatory costs and uncertainty.

Data underlies the basic functions of virtually every component of the consumer economy, from new product development to supply chain management to billing and reconciliation; in the absence of Congressional action, policy affecting the entire consumer economy and consumers nationwide is being been shaped by Europe and a single state. This fragmented regulatory environment is untenable, creating a disparate set of privacy protections for American consumers depending on where they live, as well as significant disruption, costs and uncertainty for American businesses. The California Attorney General's office has published a detailed economic analysis that estimates compliance costs for businesses in that state alone of more than $80 billion.

This environment underscores the need for a federal privacy law that applies equally to all Americans – and one that fundamentally rethinks how we provide consumers with real protections. Congress has the opportunity to adopt strong legislation that improves on the approaches being considered in the states and establishes consumer protections nationwide for the first time, backed by a strong federal regulator while preserving state enforcement authority. The time is right for Congress to step in to adopt a new comprehensive data privacy law that protects consumers and establishes clear, enforceable standards that apply to all consumers and businesses nationwide.

The Internet of today needs a legislative framework that does not put the onus on consumers to sort through myriad onerous privacy notices in an effort to protect their privacy. Rather, consumers deserve a law that creates clear and enforceable requirements for businesses to collect and use data responsibly, to better inform consumers how their data is being used, and to outlaw harmful data practices. As founding members of the Privacy for America coalition, our organizations have joined with others to support such an approach.

This legislative approach should make plain what data uses are forbidden. For example, companies should not be allowed to use someone's personal information, unless specifically permitted by federal or state law, to deny them a job, credit, insurance or health care. Similarly, the practice of digital redlining – using data about a person's race, color or religion in setting prices for products or services – should be outlawed.

The law must also make clear that the most sensitive types of personal information – data like medical, financial or biometric information – must not be used or collected unless a company has a person's explicit permission. And companies should be barred from sharing someone's personal information with third parties, unless they have enforceable contracts ensuring that the other party will secure the data and use it lawfully.

This more comprehensive approach to protecting consumers privacy will only be effective, however, if regulators have the necessary resources and power to actually investigate and punish bad actors. For this reason, privacy reform legislation should enhance the Federal Trade Commission's (FTC) longstanding expertise in overseeing privacy issues and strengthen privacy oversight and enforcement by creating a new Data Protection Bureau at the FTC. The FTC should also be provided with additional privacy staff and resources, as well as privacy jurisdiction over common carriers and nonprofits. Recognizing that new data practices will arise over time, a new law should set forth specific criteria for the FTC to identify and prohibit additional data practices through rulemaking.

We urge you to continue prioritizing this important issue and call on both chambers to consider and pass privacy legislation in this Congress. Thank you for your steadfast work toward creating a world in which Americans can feel safer and more comfortable online.

Sincerely,

Marla Kaplowitz
President and CEO
American Association of Advertising
Agencies (4A's)

Randall Rothenberg
CEO
Interactive Advertising Bureau (IAB)

Steve Pacheco
President and CEO
American Advertising Federation (AAF)

Bob Liodice
CEO
Association of National Advertisers (ANA)

Leigh Freund
President and CEO
Network Advertising Initiative (NAI)

David W. Almy
CEO
The Insights Association

cc: All Members of Congress

* * *

July 11, 2019

The Honorable Roger Wicker
United States Senate
Washington, DC 20510

The Honorable Frank Pallone
United States House of Representatives
Washington, DC 20515

The Honorable Maria Cantwell
United States Senate
Washington, DC 20510

The Honorable Greg Walden
United States House of Representatives
Washington, DC 20515

Dear Sens. Wicker and Cantwell, and Reps. Pallone and Walden,

On behalf of a diverse group of businesses across the economy, we write to urge your support for a comprehensive federal privacy law that establishes a single technology and industry-neutral framework for our economy. While our organizations do not typically work together, we believe the importance of passing a consumer privacy law warrants cross-sector support. Our associations, and the companies we represent, are united on the need for Congress to act quickly to adopt a robust and meaningful national consumer privacy bill to provide uniform privacy protections for all Americans. Although we use data in different ways and may have different views about the details of a final bill, we all agree that the time has come for Congress to pass a consumer privacy law that will provide consumers and businesses alike with the certainty and trust to power our digital economy and ensure our competitiveness in the global marketplace.

The potential benefits of our digitally-driven economy are limitless. Innovative uses of data have already greatly improved the lives of Americans and enhanced our well-being in countless ways, from safety and security, to consumer conveniences and business efficiency in delivering goods and services to customers. We have gotten better and smarter at using data over the past century to improve Americans' standard of living and provide social and economic benefits across our nation. But in this increasingly connected world, consumers and businesses deserve clear and consistent rules for how businesses can use, collect, and share data. Our data privacy laws must embrace past ingenuity while encouraging future innovation.

Individuals expect that companies accessing their data will use it responsibly. This expectation extends to all companies. Consumers should not need to worry about determining what privacy laws apply to their data based on the technology or platform they use, or with whom the data is shared, whether they are online or in a physical location, or in what state they may reside across the country. To that end, we encourage Congress to ensure a national law is technologically and industry neutral and applies across all sectors of the economy. In addition, consumers' privacy protections should not vary state by state – a uniform federal framework should be put in place to provide certainty for businesses and consumers alike.

We are encouraged that many in Congress have been actively engaged in this important policy discussion and see the need for a federal privacy law. As our economy's reliance on data continues to grow and evolve, we need Congress to act now more than ever. We urge you to pass a federal consumer privacy bill this Congress.

Sincerely,

ACT | The App Association
Alliance of Automobile Manufacturers
American Pizza Community
Association of Global Automakers, Inc.
Computer & Communications Industry Association (CCIA)
Computing Technology Industry Association (CompTIA)
Consumer Technology Association (CTA)
CTIA
International Franchise Association (IFA)
Internet Association (IA)
National Association of Convenience Stores (NACS)
Nation Association of Tower Erectors (NATE)
National Association of Realtors
National Association of Wholesaler-Distributors
National Council of Chain Restaurants (NCCR)
National Grocers Association (NGA)
National Restaurant Association
National Retail Federation (NRF)
NCTA – The Internet & Television Association
NTCA – The Rural Broadband Association
Petroleum Marketers Association of America (PMAA)
Retail Industry Leaders Association (RILA)
Security Industry Association (SIA)
Society of Independent Gasoline Marketers of America (SIGMA)
Software & Information Industry Association (SIIA)
Travel Technology Association
USTelecom – The Broadband Association

Public Comment to the Energy and Commerce Committee Hearing on "Protecting America's Consumers: Bipartisan Legislation to Strengthen Data Privacy and Security," Submitted to the Subcommittee on Consumer Protection and Commerce of the Committee on Energy and Commerce, June 14th, 2022

Good morning, Chair Schakowsky, Ranking Member Bilarakis, and Members of the Consumer Protection and Commerce Subcommittee. I commend you for holding this important hearing on "Protecting America's Consumers: Bipartisan Legislation to Strengthen Data Privacy and Security" and I respectfully submit these comments for your consideration.

There are three devices that cause the collection of the massive amount of personal data the American Data Privacy and Protection Act seeks to protect and regulate: computers, smartphones, and vehicles. The first two are often discussed (and I am sure will be mentioned multiple times during this hearing). Vehicles however collect terabytes of sensitive personal information… but too often remain in the shadows of data privacy and security discussions.

I founded Privacy4Cars to give businesses in the automotive industry a simple, reliable, and auditable solution to delete the personal data vehicles routinely collect from drivers and passengers in order to prevent harms to consumers' privacy, security, and safety. This is an issue that affects over 100 million Americans every year and something the Federal Trade Commission warned about multiple times. We have also, from the very beginning of our company, offered free tools to consumers to help them reduce their vehicle data footprint.

I am writing to you to share my firsthand experience with what safeguards are put in place (or not) when it comes to the electronic Nonpublic Personal Information collected by and stored in vehicles and how different companies treat this consumer data which includes sensitive GPS locations, phone records, garage door codes, connected services, and more. This data can, and has, in turn be used to re-identify consumers, collect intel on them, profile them, contact them, harass them, stalk them, and invade their private homes.

It is important for this commission to realize that modern vehicles are like web browsers…. but in the physical world, and your "browsing history" is being collected, sold, and shared at accelerating and concerning pace. Just like with laptops and smartphones, focusing on the manufacturers of those devices alone is vastly insufficient to protect the privacy and security of consumers, because the data generated by those devices fuels an entire ecosystem. At Privacy4Cars we track hundreds of companies that engage in the brokerage of vehicle data. Unfortunately, we are just at the beginning of the vehicle data revolution: according to consulting company McKinsey the market for vehicle data will be worth between $400 and $750 billions by 2030. Fortunately, we are just at the beginning of the vehicle data revolution: there are no decades-long entrenched interests or large established economies relying on this data. Setting clear rules now can allow for this market to ethically develop in a manner that enables innovation, fosters safety, but balances that with the need to protect the interest of the public at the same time. This is why solutions to address vehicle privacy and security must go well beyond the companies who manufacture vehicles. Protecting consumers requires action from auto insurers, auto finance companies, business and rental fleets, dealerships, repairers, and the many other verticals within the broader auto industry who collect, use, share, and sell this data.

We are already seeing some early encouraging signs that setting reasonable protections for consumers is possible. A growing cohort of auto finance players, including vehicle manufacturers' captive auto finance companies, national banks, large subprime institutions, all the way to regional lenders and credit unions have adopted the practice to remove the electronic personal information left behind by consumers in vehicles that are repossessed or at the end of a lease so they are not breached and disclosed to unauthorized third parties, including dealership personnel and future owners. Similarly, most major fleet management operators (who supply and help manage many corporate and government fleets) have put similar measures in place. Dealerships are starting to take steps as well to protect the Nonpublic Personal Information captured by vehicles on their lot and give their customers the peace of mind they deserve that their data (including their home address and garage codes) does not fall into the hands of somebody else. These companies are supported in this privacy and security protection effort by a vast network of entities that process their vehicles from the time the vehicle stops being under the control of a consumer and until it is resold including auto auctions, vehicle inspection companies, and recovery agents. Those companies have collectively determined and agreed that clearing this data is a reasonable safeguard standard that needs to be in place every time a vehicle is handed off from a consumer to another.

Many of these entities are regulated under the Gramm Leach Bliley Act (GLBA). Given the upcoming December 9th change to GLBA's Safeguards Rule we hope to continue to see businesses pay more attention to the Nonpublic Personal Information vehicles collect, store, and share – and on how to safeguard this data.

Yet, most auto finance companies are still not taking action. Several companies are delaying putting in place much-needed protections due to the lack of clear guidance from Congress, the Federal Trade Commission and the Consumer Financial Protection Bureau on the necessity to protect the electronic personal data consumers captured by vehicles. This is wrong for a number of reasons, including:

- Many vehicle manufacturers' privacy policies attempt to place the burden on consumers to delete any personal data collected by or stored in the vehicle, but our surveys show most consumers are unaware of this data collection, and so are dealership personnel because of the endemic lack of transparency and no investment in educating either business partners and final users of automobiles.
- Conversely, auto finance companies who repossess a vehicle or at the end of a lease, insurance companies after a total loss accident, and dealerships who purchase vehicles to resell them, all have the financial ownership and, directly or through their service providers, the physical access and sufficient time required to clear consumer data from a vehicle before putting it back into the stream of commerce: an activity that usually takes a couple of minutes or less.
- There is a clear parallel and precedent with the many state-by-state requirements to protect personal information left in vehicles that are repossessed, most states have data security, data minimization, and data breach laws, and most states have Model 670 privacy laws and model 673 data security laws for insurance companies. Those hundreds of local statutes by and large require companies to protect personal information of consumers from being accessed by unauthorized third parties and to dispose of personal records that are no longer required for business reasons.[184] It is unclear to us what reasonable business motivation companies in the broader automotive ecosystem may advocate for not disposing of personal consumer records stored in the assets they financed, insured, resold, or rented before transacting on those assets, and for leaving this data available to anybody that will have future physical access to the vehicle.
- NIST published a guideline[185] that provides clear guidance to companies: clearing personal data is the practical sanitization decision and the minimum standard that needs to be in place for any media-storing device, including vehicles. The computer

---

[184] https://privacy4cars.com/legal-resources/laws-by-geography/.

[185] https://www.nist.gov/publications/nist-special-publication-800-88-revision-1-guidelines-media-sanitization.

and mobile phone industries self- regulated themselves and created nationwide standards for the ethical reselling and recycling of used laptops, hard drives, smartphones, and other media-storing devices. Those standards require clearing data before reselling any of those devices that may contain Personal Information. Automobiles remain the only mass data capture and storage device for which those standards are not being followed, despite the fact that every year over 40 million used vehicles are resold and over 150 million vehicles are rented.

- Auto industry groups have been actively warning during the Right-To-Repair debate that giving vehicle data access to a third party is a significant risk for consumers.[186] However, the same companies insist that neither they, their auto finance, their franchised dealership, and their service providers and partners have any responsibility in protecting and safeguarding consumers' Personal Information. That's not right.
- We have demonstrated over and over how easy it can be for a person with physical access to a vehicle (which may include the personnel of a dealership or the future buyers and users of the vehicle) to see and extract Personal Information of the former owner and family members, possibly including minors. New owners, for instance, could enter the home of the consumer whose vehicle was resold with just two clicks ("go home" on the navigation system, pressing the garage opener): just as shown in those anti Right-To-Repair ads ran by the auto industry.
- Last but not least, the recent FTC amendment to the Safeguards Rule[187] which comes into full effect on December 9th 2022, seems to clearly apply to the case of personal information stored in vehicles. The new Rule requires regulated entities, including auto finance companies and dealerships who repossess vehicles, to meet a prescriptive list of requirements, and not doing so would constitute an Unfair or Deceptive Act or Practice. Based on our expertise on how vehicle embedded systems work (for instance, data in vehicles is often unencrypted, the only factor of authentication is the highly shared key, etc.), the only way for companies to comply with the revised Rule is to dispose of the personal information of previous occupants by clearing it prior to the sale of the asset.

We are glad to see that many provisions included in the American Data Privacy and Protection Act clearly highlight how vehicles collect Sensitive Personal Information as defined in the law, and that passing this Act would result in substantial protections being created for vehicle drivers and passengers (including minors) who see their data collected, brokered, and left behind unprotected every day. Based on out audits, last year oved 4 out of 5 vehicles have been resold while still containing the sensitive personal data of the previous owner(s) and their family member(s). This implies that every year the personal information of millions of Americans is being breached and leaked on a day-by-day basis through cars. This massive, silent data breach keeps happening despite the local laws, despite the NIST guidelines, and despite the upcoming changes to the Safeguards Rule because too many auto companies have taken the position that they should not take care of clearing their customers' electronic personal information stored in the infotainment and other systems of the vehicles they control and profit

[186] See for instance this TV advertisement that ran in advance of the vote on Proposition 1 about the risk of a home invasion: https://youtu.be/_FEeGhS7Ac0.

[187] https://www.govinfo.gov/content/pkg/FR-2021-12-09/pdf/2021-25736.pdf.

from. This anachronism is astonishing considering that those same companies have clear policies requiring them to remove and destroy data from their computers, servers, storage media, and smartphones used by their employees.

Your Committee has the power and ability to end this opaque and large scale breach of trust and breach of consumer data. My hope is that this Committee will recognize that vehicles are "the third screen," and that vehicles should be subject to exactly the same rules the American Data Privacy and Protection Act would establish for all other consumer personal information.

Thank you for considering these concerns. I'm available for further discussion or additional information as needed.

Sincerely,

Andrea Amico
Founder and CEO
Privacy4Cars
https://privacy4cars.com
andrea@privacy4cars.com

* * *

June 13, 2022

The Honorable Frank Pallone (D-NJ)
Chair
House Committee on Energy and Commerce
2107 Rayburn House Office Building
Washington, D.C. 20515

The Honorable Cathy McMorris Rodgers (R-WA)
Ranking Member
House Committee on Energy and Commerce
1035 Longworth House Office Building
Washington, D.C. 20515

Dear Chairman Pallone and Ranking Member McMorris Rodgers:

The need to pass a federal privacy law has never been greater. The global nature of data impacts every industry across our economy and demands a federal approach. Instead, we're seeing a growing patchwork of state laws that are confusing consumers and hurting businesses, especially small businesses. As more states pass their own privacy laws, failure by Congress to take action will cost our economy more than $1 trillion over 10 years, with more than $200 billion being paid by small businesses.

TechNet is the national, bipartisan network of technology CEOs and senior executives that promotes the growth of the innovation economy by advocating a targeted policy agenda at the federal and 50- state level. Our membership includes dynamic American businesses ranging from startups to the most iconic companies on the planet and represents over 4.7 million employees and countless customers in the fields of information technology, e-commerce, the sharing and gig economies, advanced energy, cybersecurity, venture capital, and finance.

Tomorrow's hearing in the Consumer Protection and Commerce Subcommittee to examine the *American Data Privacy and Protection Act* is an indication that leaders from both parties are committed to action and willing to compromise on key issues like a private right of action and preemption. While the bill still needs improvements, we are more hopeful than we have been in years that a bipartisan privacy bill can make its way to the President's desk. Enactment of a federal data privacy law would also be a much-needed bipartisan achievement in the face of increasing polarization among voters. Polls overwhelmingly show that Americans across the ideological spectrum want Congress to come together to act on privacy legislation, with four in five Democrats and Republicans saying Congress should make passing privacy legislation a priority.

We stand ready to assist Congress in protecting American consumers, helping small businesses, and propelling our economy forward. We thank you for your commitment to advancing a federal data privacy law and look forward to working with you on this important issue. Please don't hesitate to reach out if we can be a resource on this issue or if you have any questions. I can be reached at cholshouser@technet.org or (202) 372-7000.

Sincerely,
Carl Holshouser
Senior Vice President; June 13, 2022

Urgent Concerns with Privacy Legislation and the Legislative Process

National Political Advocacy Department
915 15th Street, NW, 6th Floor
Washington, DC
20005-2112 aclu.org
Kary Moss
Acting National Political Director

Anthony D. Romero
Executive Director

Deborah N. Archer
President

Dear Representatives:

The American Civil Liberties Union writes to you today with considerable concern and urgency about congressional consideration of consumer privacy legislation. While we greatly appreciate the work and leadership of the chairs and ranking members of the Senate Commerce Committee and House Energy and Commerce Committee in developing legislative proposals, we strongly urge the committees of jurisdiction, including the House Judiciary Committee, to take the time necessary to conduct thorough hearings and full and informed markups of legislation before sending legislation to the House or Senate floor. While the two draft discussion proposals, one sponsored by the chairman of Senate Commerce and the other by the chairman of House Energy and Commerce, each contain important advances, they also each have very problematic provisions. We urge the committees to take the time to consider both proposals, perfect them into a single bill that provides the most protection for individuals, and do so without undermining other protections.

Our concern about the possibility of legislation being rushed towards enactment without taking the time to ensure that it provides the most protection possible for individuals is based on the experiences of several of our ACLU state affiliates who have been unable to stop harmful or effectively useless state privacy bills from being pushed quickly to enactment with the enormous lobbying and advertising support of sectors of the technology industry that resist changing a business model that depends on consumers not having protections against privacy invasions and discrimination. The result is that several states now have "privacy" laws that were rushed through legislatures, and have little or no effect on privacy. Congress should not make the same mistake.

To be clear, Americans need a strong federal privacy law, as well as laws that provide more robust civil rights protections against tech-driven harms—and mechanisms to better enforce existing civil rights protections. Right now, due to a lack of federal consumer privacy protections, Americans risk being tracked and surveilled every time we open an app, walk into a store carrying a phone, or do an online search for a new doctor. And too often, access to critical opportunities such as a new home or a new job is blocked through online or data-driven discrimination. That is not acceptable, and federal legislation is long overdue.

But neither proposal, based on reports of current drafts, meets the nation's needs without very significant revisions. Congress must take the time now, working off of both proposals, to make the protections stronger, make sure the legislation can survive judicial review against any First Amendment claims, bolster enforcement provisions, including providing a strong private right of action, and allow the states to continue to respond to new technologies and new privacy challenges with state privacy laws.

While it is urgent for Congress to enact legislation to protect the rights of Americans to privacy and nondiscrimination, it is critical that Congress learn from the mistakes of state legislatures that rushed "privacy" laws to enactment at the urging of segments of industry, only to realize later that they failed to deliver protections to residents of their states. We are very interested to work with you to get it right. Thank you for your attention to this issue, and please reach out with any questions to Nate Wessler at nwessler@aclu.org.

Sincerely,

Christopher Anders
Federal Policy Director

Nathan Freed Wessler
Deputy Director
Speech, Privacy and Technology Project

* * *

June 13, 2022

The Honorable Janice D. Schakowsky
Chairwoman
Subcommittee on Consumer Protection and Commerce
Committee on Energy and Commerce
U.S. House of Representatives
Washington, DC 20515

The Honorable Gus M. Bilirakis
Ranking Member
Subcommittee on Consumer Protection and Commerce
Committee on Energy and Commerce
U.S. House of Representatives
Washington, DC 20515

Dear Chairwoman Schakowsky and Ranking Member Bilirakis,

On behalf of the Credit Union National Association (CUNA), I am writing regarding the hearing entitled, "Protecting America's Consumers: Bipartisan Legislation to Strengthen Data Privacy and Security." CUNA represents America's credit unions and their 130 million members.

We appreciate the Committee bringing data security and privacy to the forefront. Credit unions strongly support the enactment of a national data security and data privacy law that includes robust security standards that apply to all who collect or hold personal data and is preemptive of state laws. We firmly believe that there can be no data privacy until there is strong data security. With that in mind, credit unions strongly support the approach of the bicameral, bipartisan proposal discussed today that would cover all entities that collect consumer information and hold those who jeopardize that data accountable through regulatory enforcement.

Securing and protecting consumer data is important not only for their individual financial health but as a further safeguard against rogue international agents and interference by foreign governments.

Data privacy and data security are major concerns for Americans given the frequency of reports of misuse of personally identifiable information (PII) data by businesses and breaches by criminal actors, some of which are state sponsored. Since 2005, there have been more than 10,000 data breaches, exposing nearly 12 billion consumer records. These breaches have cost credit unions, banks, and the consumers they serve hundreds of millions of dollars, and they have compromised the consumers' privacy, jeopardizing their financial security.

Stringent information security and privacy practices have long been part of the financial services industries' business practices and are necessary as financial institutions are entrusted with consumers' personal information. This responsibility is reflected in the strong information security and privacy laws that govern data practices for the financial services industry as set forth in the Gramm Leach Bliley Act ("GLBA"). GLBA's protection requirements are strengthened by federal and state regulators' examinations for compliance with the GLBA's requirements and robust enforcement for violations.

Although protecting members' data is of paramount importance to credit unions, credit unions and their members are adversely impacted by lax data security standards at other businesses. For example, CUNA members have reported a massive increase in fraud against state unemployment insurance programs. These reports have been confirmed by the United States Secret Service. The fraud appears to be mainly coming from an international fraud ring that has the capacity to exploit many states' unemployment programs.

According to the Secret Service, the criminals are likely in possession of a vast amount of PII, which they are using to apply for unemployment insurance. It is almost certain that this PII was stolen in a data breach, or many data breaches, and it is now being used to exploit state unemployment insurance programs. This is clearly an example of how the multiple data breaches where PII has been stolen are causing harm to Americans and costing everyone money.

With that in mind, credit unions applaud the bill's agreement with our data security and privacy principles as outlined in previous communications to the Committee:

- *New Privacy and Data Security Laws Should Keep GLBA Intact:* We appreciate the acknowledgement of the efficacy of the GLBA standard and the protection and security it has provided to consumer data over the last two decades. The rules and regulations surrounding GLBA have been developed to respond to not only the needs of consumers but also to the size and resources of the financial institution. The requirements contained in this bill are especially onerous for institutions already complying with a strong data security and privacy framework. Compounding the regulatory burden on financial institutions, especially small institutions, would be especially onerous. We ask that the "related requirements" language of § 404 be removed and compliance with the strong security and privacy standards of GLBA and its implementing regulations be deemed compliant with the American Data Privacy and Protection Act.
- *Data Privacy and Data Security Are Hand in Glove:* We are extremely supportive of the bill's comprehensive data privacy and data security framework. Credit unions feel strongly that data cannot be kept private unless it is also secured.
- *Every Business Not Already Subject to Federal Law Should Follow the Same Rules:* The broad inclusion of all entities under Federal Trade Commission (FTC) jurisdiction, nonprofits, and telecommunications common carriers is vital to the protection of consumers because any company that collects, uses, or shares personal data or information can misuse the data or lose the data through breach. Credit unions strongly support this broad inclusion of entities.
- *There Should Be One Rule for the Road:* The national standard established by this bill is crucial to ensuring data privacy and security, and credit unions champion this approach. The current patchwork of state laws perpetuates a security system littered with weak links and leaves entities and consumers on unequal footing in protecting data. While we recognize the bill's intent to preserve existing laws and regulations unrelated to the data security and privacy aims of this legislation, we do have concerns about potential loopholes in the preemption coverage of § 404(b)(2). The exclusion of laws governing the privacy rights of employees (§ 404(b)(2)(C)) as well as the exclusion of laws addressing "banking records, financial records, tax records, Social

Security numbers, credit cards..." (§ 404(b)(2)(J)) provides for loopholes that states can exploit to disrupt the national standard established by this bill.

- *Hold Entities that Jeopardize Consumer Privacy and Security Accountable Through Regulatory Enforcement:* We applaud the enforcement measures created in this legislation, and their ability to address the harms that result from privacy and security violations. Particularly the treatment of rights of action and the provision of a 45-day cure period for potential violations of the bill. We ask that the 45-day cure period be extended to cases brought by the FTC and state attorneys general. There will be a learning curve for implementation of this comprehensive national standard, and unintentional violations may occur. Allowing entities to cure these violations in good faith will aid compliance with this Act.

Additionally, we would like to express concern for the feasibility and financial burden of § 301's requirement that all covered entities designate a privacy officer and data security officer. There is currently a shortage of qualified employees in the data security and privacy space, and the addition of all covered entities filling these roles would quickly exhaust the system. Small institutions would be most severely impacted by this provision because the shortage of available applicants would quickly drive up the market rate for these positions, pricing out small institutions. We recognize the importance of establishing the infrastructure within entities to ensure compliance with the provisions of this Act; however, that implementation must be feasible.

On behalf of America's credit unions and their 130 million members, thank you for your consideration of our views and for holding this important hearing.

Sincerely,

Jim Nussle
President & CEO

* * *

June 14, 2022
The Honorable Jan Schakowsky
Chair
Subcommittee on Consumer Protection & Commerce
Washington, DC 20510

The Honorable Gus Bilirakis
Ranking Member
Subcommittee on Consumer Protection & Commerce
Washington, DC 20510

Dear Chair Schakowsky and Ranking Member Bilirakis:

On behalf of the Electronic Transactions Association (ETA), I appreciate the opportunity to submit this statement for the record before the Subcommittee's hearing, "Protecting America's Consumers: Bipartisan Legislation to Strengthen Data Privacy and Security."

ETA is the world's leading advocacy and trade association for the payments industry. Our members span the breadth of significant payments and fintech companies, from the largest incumbent players to the emerging disruptors in the U.S and in more than a dozen countries around the world. ETA members make commerce possible by processing more than $21 trillion in purchases worldwide and deploying payments innovation to merchants and consumers.

ETA and its members support U.S. and international efforts to strengthen privacy laws in ways that help the industry combat fraud and help consumers understand how their data is being used. As lawmakers and regulators explore additional ways to protect consumers, it is critical that the government coordinates with the payments industry to combat fraud and cybercrime so that all consumers have access to safe, convenient, and affordable payment options and other financial services.

A robust financial system is integral to the economy because it enables the fundamental functions of economic activity, including connecting borrowers with savers, facilitating investments, processing payments, and safekeeping financial assets. For the U.S. financial system to remain competitive in the global economy, the U.S. must continue to prioritize consumer protection, safety, and reliability, while also continuing to lead in innovation.

ETA looks forward to encouraging a collaborative approach and believes a framework should include the following principles:

- National Standard
  By providing consumers and businesses with consistent protections through an established, uniform law, consumers and businesses will benefit. Enacting a federal uniform national standard will provide certainty and consistency to businesses and consumers alike without requiring them to navigate the patchwork of state laws. A uniform national standard — that is the ceiling — would also reduce the complexity and costs associated with the compliance and enforcement issues resulting from a patchwork of laws.
- Permissible Uses
  The payments industry has a long history of fighting fraud and is constantly developing and deploying new technology to detect, deter, and eliminate fraud. New and enhanced technologies have amplified the payments industry's ability to offer new fraud solutions and strengthen our ongoing efforts. Any privacy or data protection standard should include provisions for permissible uses of data to prevent fraud and protect consumers.
- Maximize Transparency
  Businesses must promote transparency with their customers as well as when engaging with regulators or other appropriate authorities. Regulators and government officials should be appropriately transparent about their objectives.
  With respect to personal data, consumers should have reasonable access to clear and understandable statements about businesses practices and policies. Businesses should be transparent about the types of personal data collected, how the personal data will be used, and whether personal data may be disclosed or shared. Businesses should also provide clear privacy notices to consumers as well as appropriate procedures for individual control, including the opportunity to control data sharing.

- Access to Data
  Individuals must have a reasonable right to access the personal information they have provided to a company and, where practical, the right to have that information corrected. Individuals should also have the ability to request the deletion of personally identifiable information provided to companies, unless there is a legitimate or legal obligation to retain that information.
- Enforcement
  To protect consumer rights and provide responsibility, enforcement needs to be consistent and coordinated between the federal government and the state's regulatory body.
  Congress should encourage collaboration between the Federal Trade Commission (FTC) and state attorneys general to enforce a national consumer privacy law. Strict coordination should be followed to avoid duplicate or conflicting enforcement actions. ETA believes the FTC should be granted targeted rulemaking authority and have civil penalty authority. However, a federal privacy law should not provide monetary relief in the form of a private right of action for privacy enforcement.
- Maintaining Flexibility
  Technology that is involved in data processing evolves rapidly. A baseline law can provide clarity on achieving specific privacy principles; however, laws and regulations should undergo reviews and be flexible. A government should not mandate a specific technological solution or other instrument to implement consumer protections. Including a safe harbor within a federal privacy law would promote the development of adaptable, consumer-friendly privacy programs.
- Global Leadership
  Congress should adopt policies that facilitate international electronic commerce and promote consumer privacy — both of which benefit consumers, economic growth, and trade. Burdensome international regulations hamper the growth of new businesses and create conflict of law between jurisdictions. Although the U.S. is uniquely positioned to benefit from the experience and regulatory proposals being adopted or considered by its international counterparts, having the U.S. establish a national privacy framework will facilitate an international data framework and reinforce U.S. leadership worldwide.

The payments industry never rests — we are working tirelessly to fight fraud and protect consumers by developing new tools to prevent or identify fraud data analysis as well as by frequently introducing new fraud-fighting solutions. Privacy laws should continue to recognize these goals and the important role the payments industry plays in combating fraud. By working together, lawmakers, regulators, and industry participants can protect consumers while providing them with access to the safest and most convenient payments system in the world.

ETA would like to thank the Subcommittee for this opportunity to provide this statement for the record on this important topic. We appreciate your leadership on this important issue. If you have any questions, please feel free to contact me or ETA's Senior Vice President of Government Affairs, Scott Talbott, at stalbott@electran.org.

Sincerely,

Jeff Patchen
Director of Government Affairs
Electronic Transactions Association

* * *

June 14, 2022

The Honorable Frank Pallone
Chairman
House Committee on Energy and Commerce
Washington, DC 20515

The Honorable Janice Schakowsky
Chairman
Subcommittee on Consumer Protection and Commerce
House Committee on Energy and Commerce
Washington, DC 20515

The Honorable Cathy McMorris Rodgers
Ranking Member
House Committee on Energy and Commerce
Washington, DC 20515

The Honorable Gus Bilirakis
Ranking Member
Subcommittee on Consumer Protection and Commerce
House Committee on Energy and Commerce
Washington, DC 20515

Dear Chairman Pallone, Ranking Member McMorris Rodgers, Chairman Schakowsky, and Ranking Member Bilirakis,

On behalf of The Leadership Conference on Civil and Human Rights, a coalition charged by its diverse membership of more than 230 national organizations to promote and protect the rights of all persons in the United States, we thank you for the opportunity to submit our views on the discussion draft of "The American Data Privacy and Protection Act." The measure is intended to hold companies accountable for the data they collect and use through establishing long overdue privacy and civil rights protections. We ask that this statement be entered into the record of the subcommittee hearing entitled "Protecting America's Consumers: Bipartisan Legislation to Strengthen Data Privacy and Security" on June 14, 2022.

The Leadership Conference is encouraged by the bipartisan discussion draft of privacy legislation, "The American Data Privacy and Protection Act," which was released earlier this month. Last month, more than 70 civil rights and privacy organizations signed a letter calling on Congress to pass a strong law to protect all American's privacy and civil rights.

At that time, we stated that "privacy rights are civil rights."[188] We also noted the importance of enacting a strong law, recognizing that privacy legislation can empower communities of color and open doors for marginalized populations. Simply put, well drafted comprehensive federal consumer privacy legislation will protect civil and human rights.

We have been clear on what needs to be included in privacy legislation:

- *Civil right protections:* With data-driven AI systems becoming more ubiquitous, those systems should not result in discriminatory outcomes or exacerbate existing biases.
- *Privacy protections:* The law should require companies to minimize the data they collect; define permissible and impermissible purposes for collecting, sharing, and using personal data; prohibit discriminatory uses of personal data; and provide for algorithmic transparency and fairness in decision-making.
- *Enforcement:* Protections are only meaningful if they can be enforced, including by the Federal Trade Commission (FTC), state attorneys general, and individuals.

The civil rights protections in the discussion draft are strong and will protect communities by:

- *Applying protections to the digital age:* The bill prohibits the use of personal data to discriminate based on protected characteristics. This will address data practices and automated decision-making systems that have led to discrimination in housing, employment, credit, education, finance, and other economic opportunities, which has negatively impacted communities of color.
- *Prohibiting algorithmic bias:* This bill will prohibit algorithms from reproducing patterns of discrimination in recruiting, housing, education, finance, mortgage lending, credit scoring, healthcare, vacation rentals, ridesharing, and other services.
- *Requiring companies to perform impact assessments:* The bill's impact assessment provisions require companies to identify biases and mitigate harms; large companies like Google and Facebook will be required to assess their algorithms annually and submit annual algorithmic impact assessments to the FTC. Impact assessments must seek to mitigate harms related to: (1) advertising for housing, education, employment, healthcare, insurance, or credit; and (2) access to or restrictions on places of public accommodation, and any disparate impact on the basis of an individual's race, color, religion, national origin, gender, sexual orientation, or disability status. The FTC is granted rulemaking authority to adopt rules establishing processes for submitting algorithmic impact assessments.
- *Requiring algorithms to be audited for bias:* The bill requires companies to evaluate their algorithms at the design phase, which will help identify potential discriminatory impacts before they are deployed. Training data, which can be a cause of bias in AI systems, must be included in the evaluation. Companies are also required to engage in independent audits during their algorithmic evaluations.

---

188 https://civilrights.org/resource/support-a-comprehensive-consumer-privacy-law-that-safeguards-civil-rights-online/.

In addition to the civil rights provisions, the discussion draft addresses the remaining elements we believe should be included in privacy legislation:

- *Empowers enforcement* by the FTC and state attorneys general and includes a private right of action.
- *Preserves state civil rights laws* and other types of state laws that are important for the protection of consumers and marginalized communities.
- *Requires companies to minimize the data they collect* and give clarity on permissible and impermissible data uses.
- *Provides individuals rights,* including to access, correct, and delete their personal data.
- *Addresses the data broker industry.*
- *Creates transparency mechanisms* that are helpful to consumers and enable robust oversight, research, language accessibility, and accountability.

While the discussion draft includes a solid framework, it is imperative that the protections in the provisions are resilient and robust. That means ensuring there are no loopholes that will allow covered entities to avoid compliance and appropriate recourse mechanisms.

The need for a privacy law is more urgent than ever. Americans want their data protected. A recent study concluded "just about everyone wants government to play a bigger role in data security with 87 percent of the people in the US and 76 percent of business leaders agreeing that there should be more rules and regulations around data collection and management.[189] Another recent survey echoed those results, finding 86 percent of consumers "care about data privacy" and want more control. The survey noted that "many consumers don't trust private companies to follow their own policies and treat data responsibility, so they look to the government to provide enforcement and protection."[190]

Industry agrees that Congress should pass a national law to protect people's privacy rights. Fifty-one companies, including IBM, Amazon, Dell, General Motors, and Salesforce have called for a comprehensive consumer data privacy law, noting it would enable continued innovation and growth.[191] They joined companies like Microsoft[192] and Apple,[193] who have also advocated for a federal privacy law.

We look forward to working with the Chairman, Ranking Member, other Committee members, and stakeholders on improving the draft's provisions to ensure that the bill that is introduced is as strong as possible and includes the strongest possible civil rights protections and enforcement mechanisms.

Congress has a unique opportunity to pass a landmark law, hold companies accountable, and protect the American public.

---

[189] Corporate Data Responsibility: Bridging the Trust Chasm (kpmg.us) (August, 2021).

[190] Cisco 2021 Consumer Privacy Survey.

[191] US business leaders voice strong support for federal privacy laws, Letter from the Business Roundtable to Congressional Leaders (Dec. 12, 2019). brt-ceoletteronprivacy-2.pdf (privacylaws.com).

[192] Written Testimony of Julie Brill, Corporate Vice President and Chief Privacy Officer, Microsoft Corporation, before the US Senate Committee on Commerce, Science, & Transportation on Examining Legislative Proposals to Protect Consumer Data Privacy (Dec. 4, 2019). A01E3A8C-0BC4-4B84-A425-8AFDB0F08F2F (senate.gov).

[193] Tim Cook Delivers Keynote Speech to Privacy Group - MacStories (April 12, 2022).

Thank you for the consideration of our views. If you have any questions about the issues raised in this letter, please contact Anita Banerji, Senior Program Director, Media & Tech, at banerji@civilrights.org, or Frank Torres, Civil Rights and Technology Fellow, at torres@civilrights.org.

Sincerely,

Maya Wiley
President and CEO

Jesselyn McCurdy
Executive Vice President of Government Affairs

* * *

May 25, 2022

Support a Comprehensive Consumer Privacy Law that Safeguards Civil Rights Online

Dear Speaker Pelosi, Minority Leader McCarthy, Majority Leader Schumer, and Minority Leader McConnell,

On behalf of The Leadership Conference on Civil and Human Rights, the Lawyers' Committee for Civil Rights Under Law, and the 57 undersigned civil rights, civil liberties, and consumer protection organizations, we write to urge Congress to pass comprehensive consumer privacy legislation during this session that prohibits data-driven discrimination and ensures that everyone has the right to equal opportunity on the internet. As advocates, industry, and stakeholders on all sides of the debate have made clear, now is the time to take up this critical issue.

Privacy rights are civil rights. Protecting privacy can help ensure that people's identities and characteristics cannot be used against them unfairly. Strong legislation can secure for everyone the "inviolability of privacy" that is "indispensable to preservation of freedom of association."[194] Privacy legislation can empower communities of color and open doors for marginalized populations. It can also provide clarity to businesses and level the playing field for entrepreneurs.

There are many avenues to enacting comprehensive data protections. We believe that successful legislation would accomplish the following:

- Prohibit using personal data to discriminate on the basis of protected characteristics.
- Ensure that automated decision-making systems are tested for bias and other risks, especially in matters concerning housing, employment, education, credit, and public accommodations.

---

[194] *NAACP v. Alabama*, 357 U.S. 449, 462 (1958).

- Empower enforcement by the Federal Trade Commission and state attorneys general and include a private right of action.
- Preserve state civil rights laws and other types of state laws that are important for the protection of consumers and marginalized communities.
- Require companies to minimize the data they collect and give clarity on permissible and impermissible data uses.
- Provide individuals the right to access, correct, and delete their personal data.
- Regulate the data broker industry.
- Create transparency mechanisms that are helpful to consumers and enable robust oversight, research, language accessibility, and accountability.

The time has come to enact a comprehensive consumer privacy law that safeguards civil rights online. We look forward to working with Congress on this essential task to protect everyone's rights and create a more just and equitable society. Should you have any questions, please contact David Brody, managing attorney of the Digital Justice Initiative at the Lawyers' Committee for Civil Rights Under Law, at dbrody@lawyerscommittee.org, or Anita Banerji, senior program director of media & tech at The Leadership Conference on Civil and Human Rights, at banerji@civilrights.org.

Sincerely,

The Leadership Conference on Civil and Human Rights
The Lawyers' Committee for Civil Rights Under Law
Access Now
African American Ministers In Action
Alphabet Workers Union - CWA Local 1400
American Atheists
Arab American Institute
Asian American Legal Defense and Education Fund (AALDEF)
Asian Americans Advancing Justice - AAJC
Autistic Self Advocacy Network
Brennan Center for Justice
Center for American Progress
Center for Democracy & Technology
Center for Digital Democracy
Center on Privacy & Technology at Georgetown Law
Color Of Change
Common Cause
Common Sense Media
Communications Workers of America
Consumer Action
Consumer Federation of America
Demand Progress
Democracy Fund Voice
Electronic Privacy Information Center (EPIC)

Equal Rights Advocates
Equality California
Fairplay
Fight for the Future
Free Press Action
Human Rights Watch
Impact Fund
Japanese American Citizens League
Media Alliance
Muslim Advocates
NAACP Legal Defense and Educational Fund, Inc. (LDF)
National Association of Consumer Advocates
National Association of Social Workers
National CAPACD- National Coalition for Asian Pacific American Community Development
National Consumer Law Center
National Consumers League
National Fair Housing Alliance
National Urban League
National Women's Law Center
New America's Open Technology Institute
Oakland Privacy
Open MIC (Open Media and Information Companies Initiative)
Public Citizen
Public Justice
Public Knowledge
Ranking Digital Rights
Reproaction
Sikh American Legal Defense and Education Fund
Stop Online Violence Against Women Inc.
The Greenlining Institute
United Church of Christ Media Justice Ministry
Wikimedia Foundation
X-Lab

* * *

June 13, 2022
The Honorable Janice D. Schakowsky
Chairwoman
Committee on Energy and Commerce
Subcommittee on Consumer Protection
and Commerce
U.S. House of Representatives
Washington, DC 20515

The Honorable Gus M. Bilirakis
Ranking Member
Committee on Energy and Commerce
Subcommittee on Consumer Protection and Commerce
U.S. House of Representatives
Washington, DC 20515

Re: Tomorrow's Hearing, "Protecting America's Consumers: Bipartisan Legislation to Strengthen Data Privacy and Data Security"

Dear Chairwoman Schakowsky and Ranking Member Bilirakis:

I write to you today on behalf of the National Association of Federally-Insured Credit Unions (NAFCU) ahead of tomorrow's hearing, "Protecting America's Consumers: Bipartisan Legislation to strengthen Data Privacy and Data Security." NAFCU advocates for all federally-insured not-for-profit credit unions that, in turn, serve over 130 million consumers with personal and small business financial service products. NAFCU and our members welcome the Subcommittee's review of this important issue.

As NAFCU has previously communicated to Congress, we believe there is an urgent need for comprehensive federal data privacy legislation that protects consumer data, establishes data safeguards, and recognizes the standards that have been in place for over two decades with the *Gramm-Leach-Bliley Act* (GLBA). In 2019, recognizing the importance of data privacy and the ongoing privacy debate, NAFCU issued a series of data privacy principles that calls for a comprehensive federal cybersecurity standard, the harmonization of existing federal data privacy laws, and the preemption of state privacy laws. As the Subcommittee works to develop much-needed comprehensive federal data privacy legislation, NAFCU recommends you include the following elements as key aspects in any such proposal:

- *A comprehensive federal cybersecurity standard covering all entities that collect and store consumer information.* Uniformly strong cybersecurity is necessary to ensure Americans' data is adequately protected across the economy. Existing strong federal cybersecurity standards, like that contained in the GLBA, should be extended to the activities of all data collectors and processors exceeding certain reasonable thresholds.
- *Harmonization of existing federal laws and preemption of any state privacy law related to the privacy or security of personal information.* The current patchwork of federal and state data privacy laws generates incredible consumer confusion and significant compliance burdens while failing to address the most significant data privacy risks to Americans—those risks posed by unregulated or inconsistently regulated entities that collect, control, and process vast amounts of our data. Comprehensive federal data privacy legislation should responsibly build on the successes of robust, time-tested federal laws by extending the same high data privacy standards across the economy and ensuring that already well-regulated entities, like credit unions, may confidently operate within their existing federal frameworks without fear of being subject to more than 50 different data privacy and security standards.

- *Delegation of enforcement authority to the appropriate sectoral regulator.* The National Credit Union Administration (NCUA) should be federal credit unions' sole data privacy and cybersecurity regulator. Allowing the NCUA, which is well-versed in the unique nature of federal credit unions and their operations, to continue to examine and enforce any privacy and cybersecurity requirements is the most efficient option for both credit unions and American taxpayers. Exposing credit unions and other already well- regulated entities to suits by states' attorneys general and private rights of action will dramatically increase compliance costs without providing a corresponding increase in consumer protection.
- *A safe harbor for businesses that take reasonable measures to comply with the privacy standards.* Comprehensive federal data privacy legislation should adopt principles-based requirements based on an organization's specific operations and risk profile and include a safe harbor for organizations that design and implement appropriate measures.
- *Notice and disclosure requirements that are easily accessible to consumers and do not unduly burden regulated entities.* Providing multiple data privacy disclosures and opt-out mechanisms across multiple channels creates consumer confusion and unreasonable burdens for subject entities. A new privacy law should avoid conflicting or duplicative disclosure requirements by incorporating easy to understand language, like that consistent with the GLBA's disclosure requirements.
- *Scalable civil penalties for noncompliance imposed by the sectoral regulator that seek to prevent and remedy consumer injury.* Actual damages to consumers are too difficult to establish by evidence, and statutory damages for violations are incredibly ripe for frivolous lawsuits. Sectoral regulators alone should have the power to assess scalable civil penalties, which can then be used to remedy and prevent consumer harms in a meaningful way.

NAFCU looks forward to working with the Subcommittee and those in industry to address these concerns with consumer privacy. In particular, any federal privacy legislation must be operationally workable for small- and medium-sized businesses like credit unions. We would urge you to work collaboratively with other interested Committees in the House to find a package that can advance and receive bipartisan support.

On behalf of our nation's credit unions and their more than 130 million members, we thank you for your attention to this important matter. Should you have any questions or require any additional information, please contact me or Janelle Relfe, NAFCU's Associate Director of Legislative Affairs, at 703-842-2836 or jrelfe@nafcu.org.

Sincerely,
Brad Thaler
Vice President of Legislative Affairs

cc: Members of the Subcommittee on Consumer Protection and Commerce

* * *

June 13, 2022

Representative Janice Schakowsky
Chair
Subcommittee on Consumer Protection and Commerce
Committee on Energy and Commerce
Washington, DC 20515

Representative Gus Bilirakis
Ranking Member
Subcommittee on Consumer Protection and Commerce
Committee on Energy and Commerce
Washington, DC 20515

Dear Chair Schakowsky and Ranking Member Bilirakis:

The National Association of Manufacturers welcomes the Subcommittee's attention to the topic of data privacy with the hearing "Protecting America's Consumers: Bipartisan Legislation to Strengthen Data Privacy and Security." We appreciate the opportunity to share our perspective on this important issue. While manufacturers resoundingly support a federal data privacy standard, manufacturers are seeking to avoid a patchwork of state privacy laws and expect a legislative outcome that provides legal clarity, not additional confusion. We urge the Subcommittee to continue refining the bipartisan discussion draft, "American Data Privacy and Protection Act."

The NAM is the largest manufacturing association in the United States representing manufacturers in every industrial sector and in all 50 states. Manufacturing employs more than 12.8 million men and women, contributes nearly $2.71 trillion to the U.S. economy annually, has the largest economic impact of any major sector and accounts for 58 percent of all private-sector research and development in the nation.[195] The NAM is the powerful voice of the manufacturing community and the leading advocate for a policy agenda that helps manufacturers compete in the global economy and create jobs across the United States.

Manufacturers are developing innovative products and transforming the manufacturing process with the latest technologies. Data continues to be a critical source and biproduct of these breakthroughs and developments as modern manufacturing evolves. The Internet of Things (IoT) is continuing to transform manufacturing through billions of connected devices and advanced wireless infrastructure that allow for the transmission of vast amounts of data.

Connected shop floors are creating data that industry is harnessing to improve efficiency, manage production activities, streamline repairs and safeguard plant security. Additionally, connected products utilize data to transform the customers' experience in countless ways.

Our nation's manufacturers support ongoing efforts to craft federal data privacy legislation that advances individuals' privacy while promoting U.S. innovation and industrial competitiveness. Without clarity from federal law, uncertainty will continue for our industry, causing manufacturers to sort through conflicting state privacy laws across the country.

However, federal privacy legislation should pre-empt state privacy regulations to resolve conflicting requirements in different states. A national approach to data privacy will strengthen

[195] https://www.nam.org/facts-about-manufacturing/.

businesses while supporting consumers. The "American Data Privacy and Protection Act" falls short of that goal.

Patchwork state privacy laws and unpredictable regulatory changes on data privacy are currently undermining the ability of organizations to manage privacy risks, protect consumers and make business decisions with the certainty they need. State-by-state privacy requirements create conflicts for manufacturers, their operations and their processes due to the interstate nature of data flows. They stall innovation by creating a regulatory burden that distracts from the development of next generation technologies and products. Manufacturers design and build security and privacy into their systems and products, and it is often an extensive process to adjust those systems and products in the face of evolving data regulations.

Ongoing innovation requires flexibility, and any federal action on data privacy must be carefully balanced and thoughtfully implemented without sacrificing opportunities for economic leadership and progress. Additionally, the inclusion of a private right of action encourages a legal dynamic that could encourage excessive legal challenges and will take full advantage of current definitions that are vague, conflicting or unclear in the legislation. Rather than innovating, companies could be focusing resources on unending legal challenges that the legislation unintentionally encourages.

Our companies are entrusted with vast amounts of data through diverse business interactions with customers, vendors, suppliers and governments. They understand that safeguarding privacy, protecting information and building consumer trust is a critical responsibility. Manufacturers support a data privacy policy that provides flexibility for innovation and advances U.S. economic growth and technological leadership. The NAM appreciates the work of the Subcommittee but believes more time must be devoted to crafting a federal privacy standard that will work for manufacturers. We look forward to engaging with you on this issue.

Sincerely,

Robyn M. Boerstling

cc: Chair Frank Pallone
U.S. House of Representatives
Committee on Energy and Commerce

Ranking Member Cathy McMorris Rogers
U.S. House of Representatives
Committee on Energy and Commerce

Ranking Member Roger Wicker
U.S. Senate
Commerce Committee

* * *

June 14, 2022

The Honorable Janice Schakowsky
Chair
House Energy & Commerce Subcommittee on
Consumer Protection and Commerce
United States House of Representatives
2367 Rayburn House Office Building
Washington, D.C. 20515

The Honorable Gus Bilirakis
Ranking Member
House Energy & Commerce Subcommittee on
Consumer Protection and Commerce
United States House of Representatives
2354 Rayburn House Office Building
Washington, D.C. 20515

Re: House Energy & Commerce Subcommittee on Consumer Protection and Commerce Hearing, "Protecting America's Consumers: Bipartisan Legislation to Strengthen Data Privacy and Security"

Dear Chair Schakowsky and Ranking Member Bilirakis:

On behalf of the National Restaurant Association, we thank you for the opportunity to submit our views regarding the draft bipartisan bill, "American Data Privacy and Protection Act" (ADPPA). We ask that this letter be entered into the record of the June 14, 2022, hearing, "Bipartisan Legislation to Strengthen Data Privacy and Security."

Founded in 1919, the National Restaurant Association ("The Association") is the leading business association for the restaurant and foodservice industry, representing national and small restaurant businesses. As the nation's second-largest private sector employer, with nearly one million locations across the country, the restaurant industry is a vital driver of the U.S. economy.

While 90% of restaurants across the country have less than 50 total staff, restaurants of all cuisines and sizes routinely safeguard their most valuable assets. Whether it is putting cash and receipts in a register or safe, maintaining the highest standards when selecting, storing, and preparing food, or providing a safe environment for customers and employees alike, security is a priority for restaurant operators. Securing our customers' personal information is no different—as the backbone of communities throughout America, restaurant operators build their business on trusted relationships with their guests, and they rely on robust data privacy and security practices to strengthen that trust in today's digital economy.

Our industry firmly believes that consumers across the country should be empowered to control their data. We are therefore strong advocates for a preemptive federal data privacy law that creates a single, uniform standard as opposed to a patchwork of state laws that are confusing and burdensome for businesses and consumers alike. While we appreciate the ADPPA's attempt to establish a federally preemptive framework, the Association is concerned that the bill as drafted includes far too many carveouts for other relevant state- level privacy laws, consumer protection laws, and laws that govern both employee and biometric data, among others. These carveouts essentially nullify the bill's preemption provision and would require businesses to continue complying with the multitude of federal and state laws that already exist today.

In addition to its problematic preemption language, the Association is disappointed to see a private right of action included in the ADPPA. In its current form, the bill would allow persons or classes of persons to bring a civil action in federal court seeking compensatory damages, injunctive relief, declaratory relief, and reasonable attorney's fees and litigation costs. While this provision has been couched as a "limited" private right of action, we have significant concerns that this language would enable trial lawyers to act as privacy "trolls" that create class action lawsuits for alleged violations that may not have actually occurred. We have experienced this trolling practice in other spaces like patents and ADA-related lawsuits. These actions do not improve consumer protection but do often penalize the operations targeted. In these cases, larger restaurant chains are generally forced to settle, and smaller operations are often put out of business. While the bill includes a 4-year delayed implementation for the private right of action and a 45-day notice and cure period, the Association fears that a federal data privacy law enforced by a private right of action to any degree will only result in restaurants and other consumer-facing businesses being forced to fight never-ending lawsuits.

In a world where business is supported and grown through technology, virtually every industry sector— whether consumer-facing or business-to-business—handles significant volumes of consumer information. The Association believes that any federal data privacy legislation should include statutory obligations for all players within the digital ecosystem so that no consumer is left unprotected. Restaurants are often a first point of collection for consumer data based on agreements where consumers are aware they are providing data to improve convenience and their dining experience. However, restaurants should not be held liable for potential data privacy violations committed by their downstream business partners. Therefore, the Association urges the Committee to better align the ADPPA's service provider and third-party requirements with those found in data privacy laws enacted in Virginia, Colorado, and Connecticut. Doing so would not only help small businesses across the country by requiring service providers and third parties to meet their obligations or otherwise be in violation of the law; more importantly, it would ensure that there are no privacy loopholes that leave consumers unprotected when their personal data is handled by any business, regardless of where they live.

Finally, the Association appreciates the ADPPA's intent to preserve customer loyalty programs, but we feel that the legislation in its current form does not adequately achieve this goal. Loyalty programs are a critical and ever-growing facet of the restaurant business model. As such, the industry is already "privacy protective" by establishing and maintaining these loyalty programs on an opt-in basis. We agree with the Committee that customers should not be discriminated against for choosing to exercise one of their privacy rights, but as drafted, this provision would inhibit the ability of consumers and businesses to voluntarily establish mutually beneficial business-customer relationships and set the terms of those relationships. Therefore, we once again encourage the Committee to consider aligning the ADPPA's loyalty program provision with the language and framing found in the Virginia, Colorado, and Connecticut data privacy laws. Otherwise, restaurants and other entities may be forced to significantly modify or altogether get rid of their loyalty programs, which would prevent our customers from enjoying the discounts and other benefits they already and expressly choose to enjoy today.

In sum, the Association appreciates the Committee's leadership on data privacy legislation but urge that our significant concerns enumerated above be addressed before the ADPPA is formally introduced. Restaurants stand ready to work collaboratively with Members of this Committee to establish a federal data privacy framework that will protect consumers and hold all businesses accountable for safeguarding personal information.

Sincerely,

Brennan Duckett
Director, Technology & Innovation Policy

* * *

June 13, 2022

The Honorable Maria Cantwell
Chair
Senate Committee on Science, Commerce & Transportation
Washington, DC 20510

The Honorable Roger Wicker
Ranking Member
Senate Committee on Science, Commerce & Transportation
Washington, DC 20510

The Honorable Frank Pallone
Chair
House Committee on Energy and Commerce
Washington, DC 20515

The Honorable Cathy McMorris Rodgers
Ranking Member
House Committee on Energy and Commerce
Washington, DC 20515

Subject: The American Data Privacy and Protection Act

Dear Chair Cantwell, Ranking Member Wicker, Chair Pallone, and Ranking Member McMorris Rodgers:

As trade associations representing hundreds of companies across the information and technology sectors at all stages of development – from the startup to the household-name multinational – we believe that a uniform federal privacy law is essential for consumer protection, to sustain a favorable innovation environment in the United States, and to promote global trade. For years, our organizations, individually and as part of coalitions, have urged Congress to pass comprehensive, bipartisan privacy legislation. The draft privacy bills, including the American Data Privacy and Protection Act (ADPPA), represent a promising step toward achieving that goal.

We are encouraged by the bipartisan and bicameral support behind the ADPPA. Indeed, while federal privacy legislation has long had support from both sides of the aisle, the release of the ADPPA by members of both parties in the House and the Senate is remarkable. Although the bill still needs further improvements, we believe the ADPPA provides a workable framework to build on, and we are optimistic that an effective compromise can be achieved in the near term.

The legislation contains several provisions that concern our member companies and need further refinement, among them an attempt to restrict the dissemination of information "derived" from publicly available information, a novel "duty of loyalty" and its attendant obligations, and an untailored, burdensome requirement to submit assessments of virtually all computer-based activities involving algorithms.

The bill's inclusion of a private right of action has the potential to compound the problems created by these and other novel obligations. The ADPPA represents the regulation of a massive, rapidly developing, and highly technical interstate information ecosystem. Every state that has considered and enacted a consumer privacy statute has eschewed a private right of action for good reason: the Federal Reporter is replete with instances of litigation abuse, a risk compounded by the bill's provisions allowing for recovery of attorneys' fees. The health of that system is properly delegated to competent and empowered regulators (in this case the FTC and state Attorneys General), and not a host of private lawyers for hire.

In addition, Congress's consideration of this novel legislation occurs against a backdrop of a rapidly growing patchwork of state laws, each containing slightly different and sometimes contradictory obligations. The language of the bill's preemption provisions appears to allow those laws to continue to remain in effect so long as the complaint does not allege violations of the ADPPA. In addition, the bill expressly preserves Section 1798.150 of the California Civil Code, which created a private right of action with recovery for statutory damages and led to a wave of costly litigation.

We believe that there is a path forward to resolve these issues. That path involves Congress stating clearly that its federal privacy law will be the uniform standard and that state laws creating qualitatively equivalent rights or duties are preempted. If that path must involve a private right of action, such a right must prevent class action abuse and be narrowly tailored to remedy substantial privacy harms that are specific, individualized, and tangible. Such an approach enables consumers to have clearly defined rights and businesses to have streamlined and scalable compliance. It also provides redress for individual consumers that are truly injured while enabling the federal government to create uniform rules of the road.

As you are no doubt aware, the window to enact this legislation is closing. Although we cannot support the legislation in its current form, we stand ready to work together with Congress to build on bipartisan and bicameral legislation that protects consumers, provides predictability to businesses of all sizes, and promotes innovation.

Respectfully submitted,

Computer & Communications Industry Association (CCIA)
Software & Information Industry Association (SIIA)
TechNet

* * *

Rep. Frank Pallone
Chair
House Energy and Commerce Committee
2107 Rayburn House Office Building
Washington, DC 20515

Rep. Cathy McMorris Rodgers
Ranking Member
House Energy and Commerce Committee
1035 Longworth House Office Building
Washington, DC 20515

Dear Chair Pallone and Ranking Member McMorris Rodgers:

The Wikimedia Foundation writes to strongly support the House Energy and Commerce Committee's bipartisan and bicameral efforts to enact consumer privacy protections for everyone in the United States. The American Data Privacy and Protection Act (ADPP Act) represents a good first step toward achieving a long-sought goal of ensuring privacy protections and reducing harmful uses of data that can amplify disinformation, increase risks of economic and even physical harm, fuel spam and other fraudulent schemes, and deter the free exchange of knowledge that is essential to the growth and development of the projects the Wikimedia Foundation hosts, including Wikipedia.

The goal of the Wikimedia projects is to provide access to freely reusable, objective, and verifiable content that everyone can edit and improve. As an organization dedicated to a vision of the web as an inclusive space shaped by people from around the world, Wikimedia is committed to actively promoting wide and equitable participation in knowledge. Privacy is essential to this effort. Many people, particularly members of marginalized groups or people who are located in regions with authoritarian governments, may be deterred from contributing to our projects if their contributions can be surveilled. The logic for our privacy-protective policy is therefore simple: storing personally identifying information imperils the privacy of contributors and can discourage some individuals from contributing in the first place. Based on this principle, Wikimedia collects very little information about both readers and contributors to Wikimedia projects and also facilitates pseudonymous and anonymous contributions. Wikimedia also does not engage in online advertising, allow the placement of any advertisements on its projects, or have a commercial focus. Moreover, Wikimedia does not use algorithms powered by a trove of personal data to target users of its projects with suggested content.

Because of Wikimedia's deep commitment to privacy, and our strong belief that privacy protections will advance the goals of creating an internet that is free, open, secure, and available to everyone, we were pleased to see many of the protections the ADPP Act would create. In particular, the bill would create new protections for civil rights that will help protect many from harmful discrimination. The bill would also meaningfully restrict some of the most harmful uses of biometric information, location data, and other kinds of sensitive personal information, create strong protections for sensitive covered data, and grant people the ability to opt-out of targeted advertising. The Wikimedia Foundation further supports the ADPP's efforts to empower people by giving them more control over their personally identifiable information. With these provisions, the ADPP makes significant strides toward putting individuals in charge of which entities can collect their data and how it can be used and toward restricting some of the most insidious and unreasonable uses of data that can harm human rights and undermine some of our most cherished freedoms.

Of course, no legislation is perfect. The Wikimedia Foundation looks forward to working with the Committee to improve the bill as it moves through the legislative process. In particular, we urge the Committee to consider amendments to places in the bill that would inadvertently require covered entities to collect and use more covered data than they already do in order to comply with certain provisions, including the provision requiring individual notice of material changes to policies. It could also be beneficial to define specifically what an "advertisement" covered by the bill is and to consider stronger enforcement mechanisms to ensure large covered entities comply with new requirements and will not treat penalties for violations as a mere cost of doing business. We further recommend specific examination of potential impacts on non-profit entities that have an affiliated structure and consideration of ways in which small non-profit entities could be helped to comply with the legislation's new requirements.

Thank you for considering our views and for your work to enact such important legislation to protect digital and human rights for everyone. The Wikimedia Foundation looks forward to continuing this conversation. If you have further questions, please contact Kate Ruane, Lead US Policy Specialist for the Wikimedia Foundation, kruane@wikimedia.org.

Sincerely,

Kate Ruane
Lead US Policy Specialist
Wikimedia Foundation

* * *

*Mrs. Rodgers. Ms. Ohlhausen, one of my priorities serving as Republican leader of this committee is to promote innovation in a level playing field; and as you are aware, the discussion draft moves a numbers of FCC authorities to the FTC, so there is parity when it comes to online services; however, it stops short on other categories such as video and phone services. I don't believe such a dual regulatory regime between the FTC and the FCC makes much sense.

Can you speak to the consequences of such a regime addressing phone services different than Google Voice or video programming different than a service like Netflix?

*Ms. Ohlhausen. Certainly. For consumers, they are not paying attention to these regulatory legacy regulations. They don't see a difference between traditional voice services or over-the-top services when they are collecting essentially the same types of information. So I think, it's important to have the same protections in place and have the same regulator, the FTC, overseeing that.

On video, as I mentioned briefly in the testimony, there are good strong and balanced protections in the Cable Act and in the Satellite Act or preceding Communications Act that should be transferred over to the FTC to preserve what consumers – the protections they have and the benefits that they enjoy already from these providers which with whom they have had a long relationship, and I think, understand the benefits of what they are getting.

*Mrs. Rodgers. Thank you. On a related note, Mr. Kantor raises an example in his testimony of a internet service provider tracking someone's online traffic and is concerned that a small business using their broadband service could face responsibility under this legislation for such a practice. What would you say to him?

*Ms. Ohlhausen. What I would say is that no one should be liable for someone else's violation of this Act, so each player has certain obligations under this Act; and if they engage in behavior that is a violation, that entity should be liable.

*Mrs. Rodgers. Okay. Thank you. I appreciate that.

Mr. Dufault, in the United States of America, a big part of our success and our advancement has been around innovation and entrepreneurship. It is what makes the United States unique and has done more to lift people out of poverty, raise the standard of living. There is no country in the world that values startups like the way that we do.

I think, it is important that we learn from some of the mistakes of GDPR and CCPA and its impact on small businesses. How does this legislation compare to GDPR in terms of encouraging a competitive environment for startups?

*Mr. Dufault. Well, thank you, Ranking Member McMorris Rodgers. I would agree. I think, the United States can improve upon what we have learned from GDPR. I think, there are two ways in which I think this draft that we are considering here today is a little bit more thoughtful when it comes to younger companies and small companies.

The first I would point to is that, GDPR includes sort of a blanket ban on processing unless you can point to a specific lawful basis for processing; and if you are a startup, and you are just getting your company off the ground, and you are going through the first couple of stages of growth, you are looking at that legitimate basis, and you know that your business is going to have to be a little bit nimble and respond to consumer demand and changes in the market, and you are wondering whether or not you are going to have to shift.

I think, the difficulty with the GDPR approach is that, if you start with a presumption of it is illegal to process data, that presents some uncertainties, especially for companies that are trying to figure out exactly what their business is going to be and what it is going to do and how it is going to benefit people.

And the second thing I would point to is, the way that the draft provides for compliance programs, it doesn't completely blanket accept small companies, I think, appropriately so. I think, we have been calling for this subcommittee and others to ensure that there are ways that small companies can comply because our member companies want to do that, and they compete with much bigger companies.

And so the compliance program provides resources for small companies to do so.

*Mrs. Rodgers. Thank you. I appreciate that, and I have more questions, but I am running out of time. I want to thank all the witnesses for being here, and I want to note, it has taken us over 20 years to reach this moment because there is difficult issues that require tradeoffs.

Our goal is to continue to get both member and stakeholder feedback to ensure that this bill is in the best position possible while preserving the compromise that we struck in ensuring these strong protections. And that is why your constructive feedback is so important to find the right balance, and I just appreciate the leadership and the commitment to getting to a place where we can pass a bill, and I yield back.

*Ms. Schakowsky. The gentlelady yields back.

And now, I recognize remotely my colleague from Illinois, Bobby Rush, for his five minutes of questions.

*Mr. Rush. I want to thank you, [audio malfunction] Schakowsky for holding this important hearing today. I would also like thank the full committee Chair Pallone, and the ranking member Rodgers for their important work in conducing this discussion [] and also subcommittee Chairman Bilirakis.

As many have heard me discuss before, I am a small component [inaudible]. In simple terms, these are companies that make a profit from buying, compiling, and selling information about individuals like you and I. They do this in an environment where the individual has no control over who possesses information about them or what is done with that same information.

So our data [inaudible] reaches the consumers suffer, and that is why I am so pleased to see that this discussion draft includes regulations of their [inaudible] referred to as third-party collecting entities in the legislation language that would turn control of consumers' information back to the [inaudible] consumer.

Furthermore, this discussion draft empowers consumers by requiring in the FTC create a [inaudible] a sensible registry of third parties collecting entities that allow individuals to look up information, including their contact information, and creates a necessary mechanism similar to the Do Not Call List by which consumers may submit a single request to all these third-party collecting entities to have all current data about them [inaudible] within 30 days.

Ms. Fitzgerald, can you please discuss why reigning in these nationally third-party collecting agent entities better known as "data brokers" is so very important for the average consumer? Can you, please, also discuss the impact the creating of a central registry of third-party collecting entities would have on the self [inaudible] consumers?

*Ms. Fitzgerald. Thank you, Congressman Rush.

As you know, data brokers are some of the worst offenders in the online space, particularly, because they don't have a direct relationship with the individuals whose data they are harvesting. You know, users don't expect that their online activity will be sent to these parties who then combine it with other data and make decisions about us and sell it to the highest bidder.

So EPIC strongly supports the substantive limits in the bill that we think will curtail a lot of the data broker industry, but the creation of a registry is an important step because it just – it shines light on who these companies are. We have seen that in Vermont, California, states that have data broker registries.

So I think, it is an important piece of the bill.

*Mr. Rush. Thank you very much.

Mr. Brody, in previous hearings, I have repeatedly brought up businesses of tech companies abusing our current system to [inaudible] the protections afforded by decades old civil rights laws. We have given them ample opportunity to write these laws over and over and over again, and they have failed to do so at this moment.

In many ways, the terrible practice of redlining when the original form of discrimination using algorithms. The civil rights community seem to recognize this and has repeatedly said that privacy rights are civil rights. Can you, please, elaborate on that, specifically, what is more important than civil rights [audio malfunction]?

*Mr. Brody. Thank you, Congressman.

As you mentioned, algorithmic discrimination is nothing new. Redlining was a form of a discriminatory algorithm, and we are still reckoning with the consequences of that today.

So we have a society where there are people who live in certain places, have certain levels of education, have certain job and credit opportunities as a result of past segregation and redlining, and this systemic inequity creates the data that is now fed into algorithms used by companies to make decisions.

As I said earlier, algorithms aren't magic. They are built by people, people that have biases, and they are trained on data that comes from society; and if that societal data is itself infected with bias, it is going to produce discriminatory effects as well, and that is why the algorithmic assessment provisions in this bill are so important.

*Mr. Rush. Thank you. And I yield –

*Ms. Schakowsky. Thank you. The gentleman's –

*Mr. Rush. – back.

*Ms. Schakowsky. Yeah. The gentleman's time has expired.

And now, Mr. Latta, you are recognized for five minutes.

*Mr. Latta. Well, thank you, Madam Chair, and thanks to our witnesses for being with us today. Thanks for your testimony today, and I also want to thank our leadership on both sides for their hard work on this legislation so thanks very much.

A preemptive national privacy and data security bill clearly is a priority for consumers, for economy, and to maintain U.S. competitiveness. I believe that we can continue to work in a bipartisan manner in this committee to ensure that this legislation will protect consumer data, provide certainty for businesses, small and large, and continue to foster technological innovation.

[inaudible] so my questioning is with you, acting chair, welcome back to the E and C Committee. It is nice to see you again. In your testimony, you mention how the bill does not preempt the Federal Communications Commission's privacy and data security authority related to voice services.

In section 222 of the 1996 Act exclusive – is the section 222 of the 1996 Act exclusive of privacy regulation?

*Ms. Ohlhausen. Yes, Congressman. That is what I was referring to. There is privacy regulation in the Communications Act for voice and the coalition believes that, that privacy oversight should be transferred to the FTC for voice services for the reasons that I gave about giving consistent approach to consumers.

*Mr. Latta. Let me follow up. Is it clearly being used for any other purposes by the FCC?

*Ms. Ohlhausen. I am not aware of that, but we can certainly get back to you on that issue.

*Mr. Latta. Okay. I appreciate that. Also, based on your experience at the FTC, would you speak to how completing rulemakings works versus issuing guidance?

*Ms. Ohlhausen. Yes. So if Congress has given the FTC authority under a bill like COPPA to engage in APA rulemaking, the commission puts rules out for comment, gets public comment, enacts a rule, and then, it can enforce it and get penalties for the violation.

The FTC also issues guidance which is merely the FTC's interpretation of its organic unfair and deceptive acts or practices authority. Violating guidance is not subject to a fine. It would have to be prosecuted by the FTC as a violation of the FTC Act which gives it much more limited redress authority or fining authority.

*Mr. Latta. Well, thank you very much.

Mr. Miller, I believe that we must treat sensitive data such as health information and government-issued identifiers with the utmost protection. I appreciate this bill makes that distinction. From consumers' points of view, this data is what they hold most dear and are the most uncomfortable with being transferred or sold.

In your testimony, you raised concerns about some of the sections of the sensitive covered data, in particular, the term "individual's online activities over time or across third-party websites or online services," I really thought were fairly broad.

Would you expand on why you believe that definition should be narrowed and what should be the practical implications of how it currently reads?

*Mr. Miller. Thank you, Congressman Latta, for the question.

Yeah. As I explained in my testimony, that provision can be read extremely broadly because, again, you know, it is under the sensitive data definition as you point out, and online tracking activity, I mean, it is possible that the drafters intended to get at things like search histories, but the way that the provision functions, it would actually prevent lots of very ordinary activities because information related to search activity would include things like IP addresses, and you know, other identifiers that are related to that activity the way that, that is broadly drafted.

So I mean, it is something that we think is critical to fix in the bill and just to narrow the provisions [crosstalk]

*Mr. Latta. What would happen?

*Mr. Miller. Well, one of the things that could happen is that it would actually make it very difficult for an individual to use a search engine for instance. You know, the individual would have to give their consent every time it appears that they are just typing a search into, you know, any common search engine, and that would, you know, potentially be problematic.

I think, even more problematic would be the potential impacts on security, you know, for security prevention which is not exempted in the bill. You know, there is all types of data telemetry and analytics that security companies do to process data that does relate to online activity, in that they would not be able to do that.

So even though the bill has robust data security protections, there are other provisions that potentially could undermine security.

*Mr. Latta. Well, thank you very much.

Madam Chair, my time has expired, and I yield back.

*Ms. Schakowsky. The gentleman yields back.

And now, I recognize Representative Castor for five minutes.

*Ms. Castor. Well, thank you, Madam Chair and thank you for the great bipartisan work by Chairman Pallone and Ranking Member McMorris Rodgers, and the staff. Thank you to the witnesses for being here.

This is very important for us to be working on a comprehensive data privacy bill. I mean, everything we do in our lives these days is tracked online. We are surveilled.

Every internet search, everything we buy, where we go, we are all surveilled, and it is time to kind of – for a reset, and it is particularly important for children.

We have learned here through our hearings the extent of harm to the wellbeing of kids driven by online platforms. There has been an extensive expose in The Wall Street Journal. We have the Facebook Whistleblower here, Frances Haugen. There is a study that comes out just about every week on the extensive data that has been collected on our kids even though we have had a Children's Online Privacy Protection Act.

So I am very excited that the important provisions from my kids privacy act and the KIDS Act were incorporated, but I know that many of you said it's a starting point, and we can make some improvements.

Ms. Cuaresma, for Common Sense, you have also provided us with a list of key sections that must be strengthened. Can you go through a couple of those? You say, maybe, the age at 17 or under is not the right one. Maybe, it is for all minors 18 and under?

*Ms. Cuaresma. Sure. Thank you for the question.

First, let me be clear. On day one, we will be able to ban companies from processing, from collecting, and sharing data about children under the age of 17 because section 204 clearly prohibits any company from doing that unless a parent provides affirmative express consent. So I think, that is fantastic.

As to other provisions about under 17, I think, it, from a compliance standpoint, makes a lot of sense to just cover anyone under the age of 18. It just is easier. I would hate for small businesses to have to figure out: "What should I do for somebody who is under 17? What should I have to do for someone under 18? And what should I have to do for someone under 13?"

So at the end of the day, let's make it all minors, especially if we are going to talk about knowledge standards, right? It is really easy right now to get confused about whether somebody is 14 or if somebody is 17, right? My daughter has a pretty mature voice, and she can often pass for me.

And so I would like to make sure that we are not creating burdens for small companies in having all of these different ages within a bill.

*Ms. Castor. And it is important also in your testimony you say the new Youth Division at the Federal Trade Commission so that, over time, they can keep up with the innovations regarding our youth and protecting kids online.

But I am so glad that my colleague, Mr. Bilirakis, raised that the actual standard versus constructive knowledge standard, because under the current COPPA, Children's Online Privacy Protection Act, that actual knowledge – requiring actual knowledge has been a huge loophole for Big Tech companies to claim ignorance, that they didn't know they were kids online. They just assumed they were adults.

And it is appropriate, as you said, that it is being addressed in part, but this clearly is an area that there is room for improvement in the draft if we are serious about protecting kids online.

Can you give us some examples of how some of the Big Tech companies are using it to claim ignorance. They know kids are there, but they say, "No. This is really for an adult."

*Ms. Cuaresma. Sure. Here is the thing. The FTC has incredibly limited resources. On top of that, Congress has already asked them to enforce 82 statutes. That is crazy. So the youth division can better do its job if we ensure that there is appropriate funding and staffing for it.

As somebody who has co-taught law school students and MIT computer science students, I understand how important it is that we have experts on staff providing explanations to the lawyers. I have watched the students think that they each understand one another, and that is not the case at all, especially given that we are about to enter the metaverse. It's incredibly important that our youth division understands exactly the technology that is driving what we are dealing with on a day-to-day basis.

*Ms. Castor. My time is up, but you highlighted a very important point on virtual reality and what meta proposes to do. I know they have recently rolled out "Well, we are going to propose some privacy protections for kids." That is not totally inadequate, and that is why we need a strong privacy law to protect our kids and everyone online.

So I look forward to working in the coming days. Thank you. I yield back.

*Ms. Cuaresma. Thank you.

*Ms. Schakowsky. The gentlewoman yields back.

And now, I recognize Mr. Guthrie for five minutes.

*Mr. Guthrie. Thank you, Madam Chair. I appreciate it.

Mr. Default, when we look at – are thinking about this – we often think about Big Tech and so forth, but this bill will effect businesses, small retailers, Mr. Kantor, in our districts as well.

And so kind of in that context, would you talk about how the limited private right of action in the underlying legislation impacts these kind of businesses, and can you talk about how a more expansive private right of action that includes statuary (sic) or punitive damages would impact small businesses in this country? And then, if Mr. Kantor would like to comment on that as well.

*Mr. Dufault. Absolutely. I think one of the things that we are worried about is that a private right of action, in the process of trying to better protect consumers and better enable them to seek the redress that they should be getting for privacy harms, that we don't create a sort of a sue-and-settle business model that we have seen crop up in other contexts like with patent trolls in other situations.

Those kinds of activities – and I am not speaking about broadly folks that need redress; I'm talking about folks that are sort of taking advantage of what the law provides – tend to target small businesses because small businesses, they don't have legal departments, and it costs a lot of money to hire an attorney.

And so they are, in many cases, more willing to just settle and make the issue go away even if it is a violation that may be inadvertent and not necessarily result in harm to a large class of folks.

So that is why we think it is really important for some safeguards to be in place, and that the redress be sort of calibrated to what the kinds of harms that we are dealing with here with data security and privacy.

*Mr. Guthrie. Okay. Thank you.

Mr. Kantor?

*Mr. Kantor. Thank you, Congressman, for that question.

We are concerned. Look, this is a complex area, and complying with everything in this bill is going to be difficult. It is going to be new for everyone across the country, and so the idea that there can be litigation without some additional safeguards here is worrisome.

And I would note in particular, one piece of this. In the private right of action, it provides for compensatory damages. Now, that concept in the law is actually different than what it sounds like in just common parlance. Compensatory damages includes, not just actual damages, which is another standard that could be set, but things like mental anguish, inconvenience, loss of enjoyment of life, loss of opportunity.

There is a lot of things that lawyers can jam into that concept to make dollar values get pretty high. In addition too, there is also attorneys' fees here. So there is a lot of motivation for these lawsuits, and so we worry that plays into all aspects of this bill in trying to really be careful that we get things right because folks are going to be on the line.

*Mr. Guthrie. [Inaudible] point out where it is absolutely necessary to protect data and the American consumers, but also the small businesses in our district are going to have to do the same thing that the big mega companies have to do. So we need to – I just want to point that out.

Mr. Miller, you talked about, in your testimony, about the importance of digital advertising, and your testimony highlights some concerns with the current definition in the draft. Can you talk about preserving digital advertising and opt-out impacts – how preserving digital advertising and opt-out impacts – effects small businesses, and then, specifically, I think, you cited some states that had definitions better that would be more appropriate, and if you would talk about that.

*Mr. Miller. Thank you very much for the question, Congressman Guthrie.

Yes. You know, as I pointed out in the testimony, the definition of targeted advertising when combined with the sensitive data definitions and some of the other definitions in the bill here, in particular, is very restrictive, you know, I think we have heard testimony from other witnesses about very various different players in the online ecosystem, dictative brokers and others.

But as written, it would really appear to restrict targeted advertising even from a company through its own digital customers, if you will, and consumers that are interacting with its websites without express opting consent, I think, you know, every time because of that definition I was discussing with Congressman Latta, online activity, you know, and so on.

So – yeah. I mean, in the privacy laws passed by Virginia, Colorado, Utah, and Connecticut, there is a different balance in those laws that does provide the ability for companies to reasonably advertise to users on their own sites and the specific – yeah.

And so I'll just leave it there, but again, it is important to note that effects companies of all sizes.

*Mr. Guthrie. Okay. Thank you. My time has expired.

I yield back.

*Ms. Schakowsky. The gentleman yields back.

And now, I recognize Congresswoman Trahan for five minutes.

*Mrs. Trahan. Well, thank you, Madam Chair, and I would like to thank my colleagues on both sides of the aisle for reminding Americans that when it comes to protecting consumers, thoughtful compromise is still possible.

To say that we need a comprehensive policy privacy legislation now is an understatement. Today, when a consumer makes a purchase, types their symptoms into a browser, or applies for a job, they check "I agree" next to an unreadable privacy policy and hope that their personal data and sensitive information is only being used for the services they expect.

But as we all know, that is often not the case. Opaque and often discriminatory data practices have resulted in a loss of human autonomy needed in a healthy democracy.

This draft text represents a strong first step towards a data protection model in which consumers can trust that their data is being used in the ways they expect. I am particularly, happy to see provisions in line with ideas in the bipartisan TLDR Act, the DELETE Act, and my office's Tech Oversight staff draft released last summer.

You know, as a mother of two elementary school-age daughters, I want to echo Representative Kastor's call for strong enforcement of the child protection provisions in the text. Today, when parents send their children to school, or as experienced during the pandemic, sit them in front of a screen, they not only put their trust in educators, but increasingly in software.

I have spoken to several educators and parents who speak highly of many of these tools, and I am certainly grateful that children are becoming familiar with technology.

But absent guard rails, student data rights are under threat. For example, researchers with Human Rights Watch and the Signal Network analyzed 164 educational apps and Websites and found that nearly 90 percent of the educational tools were designed to send the information they collected to ad technology companies.

Purchases are not the only things that student data is used to predict. Some ed tech companies attempt to process facial expressions, bodily gestures, and keystrokes to predict cheating or student engagement.

AI researchers emphasize that this technology is susceptible to faulty predictions and puts children in a state of constant surveillance.

Ms. Fitzgerald, can you speak to why the Family Educational Rights and Privacy Act, or FERPA, has proven insufficient to protect students from this kind of software?

*Ms. Fitzgerald. So I thank you for the question, Congressman Trahan.

This gets back to the central problem with the state of privacy law in the United States right now. It only gets to be in certain spheres. So FERPA covers educational records, which are, you know, grades, attendance records, discipline records.

But it does not cover at all the data collected from the new Website and that my second graders use in the classroom now.

*Mrs. Trahan. That is right. Thank you for that.

And I wonder if you can speak to how provisions in the draft text, such as the Office of Youth Privacy and Marketing Division, privacy by design, algorithm impact assessments, could support the FTC in their efforts to protect student data rights?

*Ms. Fitzgerald. So yes. So oversight and enforcement are just so critical when it comes to privacy, and the fact that those algorithm impact assessments will have to be submitted to the FTC will help them conduct that oversight.

They will be able to look at the assessments, make sure that these tools, you know, being used in the educational setting are fair.

I did note in my testimony I think that those should bea little more prescriptive than what is included in those impact assessments, and I think that is important to strengthen FTC oversight, and I look forward to working with the committee on that.

*Mrs. Trahan. I could not agree more.

Can you lastly speak to additional actions this division may be able to take, such as offering clarity and guidance to ed tech companies or other provisions, such as those proposed in the U.K.'s age-appropriate design code?

*Ms. Fitzgerald. Yes. I would hope that withconcentrating experts on youth privacy in a division in the FTC, they will be able to offer guidance to ed tech companies and maybe even to school districts.

You know, I have seen it in my own school district. It is overloaded and they have to sign these contracts, and I am not sure even the district understands the amount of student data we are seeing funneled to these companies and how it is being used.

*Mrs. Trahan. Thank you.

With my remaining 40 seconds I just want to zero in on the Youth Division. Ms. Cuaresma, you spoke a little bit about the resources that would be needed, but in your testimony, you highlighted that the formal division's authority may not be clear or withstand judicial scrutiny under non-delegation.

Can you just speak that a bit more?

*Ms. Cuaresma. Sure. Thank you.

Under the non-delegation doctrine, Congress members would have to write extremely detailed statutes for anything to get done, right? So we trust our administrative agencies to fill in the details.

In order to be able for the FTC to fill in the details of what the statutory program is, they need resources, not even additional resources. They needed resources yesterday.

And so without actually providing additional resources to the Youth Division, it is completely powerless. So I strongly recommend that we provide resource for it or else this is just one more thing that is going to go on some enforcement attorney's list of things to do.

Thank you.

*Mrs. Trahan. Thank you, Madam Chair. I yield back.

*Ms. Schakowsky. The gentlewoman yields back.

And, Mr. Dunn, you are recognized for five minutes.

*Mr. Dunn. Thank you very much, Madam Chair. I appreciate the opportunity to discuss the importance of enacting a bipartisan, bicameral national privacy and security bill.

You know, a national standard is necessary to get consumers the certainty that their data is protected from abuses and to provide clear regulatory guidance for industry to follow without stifling American innovation and competition.

But it must be carefully crafted because this is wickedly complex stuff. Mr. Miller, to begin my questioning, I want to speak to the opportunity we have in Congress to protect the American people.

We know the Communist Party and other state actors are intent on attacking our digital system specifically to steal intellectual property and collect Americans' personal sensitive data, which can advance their agendas on several fronts, including military capabilities.

So even data that we think, we tend to believe is not sensitive can become sensitive when aggregated in the individualized.

So currently there is no requirement for big tech companies to tell Americans if they're transferring or storing their personal data in China, Russia, Iran, and North Korea, and even Chinese companies in America can be coerced into sharing sensitive data with the Chinese government.

So my question is small and medium businesses are often the only retail outlet. I am sorry. I skipped one.

How important is it to you that the national data privacy law mandates transparency and requires a covered entity to report to users if their data is transferred to one of these state bad actors?

*Mr. Miller. Thank you for the question, Congressman Dunn.

You know, I think that the provision you are referring to speaks to a very important national security issue that I think has been, you know, front and center in a variety of different policy measures even beyond the scope of this bill, and that involves, you know, potential access to data including sensitive data of Americans by foreign governments.

So I mean, I think that the provision here and also I should add that the principle of transparency and letting consumers know what is happening with their data is certainly one that I agree with as well.

We have not really heard too much feedback from members on that particular provision, but you know, I must say that it does seem like a reasonable provision.

*Mr. Dunn. We hear about it a lot up here, I promise you. Thank you for that answer.

I want to move on to the effects of small business, Mr. Kantor.

Small and medium businesses are often the only retail outlets that provide groceries, consumer goods, pharmaceuticals in rural areas of my district. These businesses are often family owned, may not have resources to comply with complicated privacy regulations.

So given the differing sizes and sophistications of these companies if this legislation is passed, how important is it to small businesses that data privacy law is clear and consistent through all 50 States?

*Mr. Kantor. So we do think it is really important because not only does the law apply to them, but these businesses have to deal with these much larger technology companies and others that are in the category of service providers or banking institutions, et cetera, in order to conduct business.

And so having them on a level playing field where those legal responsibilities are clear and you cannot have contracts that put the liability back onto the small and medium size business is really important here.

*Mr. Dunn. So specifically, this financial transaction exclusion for small businesses which you referenced in your written testimony, but they could end up being categorized as a large data holder simply because their business model depends on having a large amount of small dollar transactions.

If you can, expand on that a little. How long would it take and what would the burden be for a convenience store to collect the sensitive data of, say, 100,000 individuals through that practice?

*Mr. Kantor. Yes, that does concern us because a corner gas station on a pretty good corner can have 100,000 customers in a year, and so without having payment due to exclude it there, we expect a huge number of our members will be considered large data holders.

Interestingly, there is the small data exception in the bill which does take into account that payment data should be treated differently, and so we actually think unless we work these things out, we will have a lot of members who are both in the small data exception and large data holders under the bill.

*Mr. Dunn. My time has expired, but I want to encourage all of the panel members to give us your suggestions as we are drafting this because this is, as I said earlier, complex stuff.

Thank you, Madam Chair. I yield back.

*Ms. Schakowsky. The gentleman yields back.

And, Mr. McNerney, you are recognized for five minutes.

*Mr. McNerney. I thank the chair.

I thank the witnesses.

You all seem to say it is about time we are doing this, but there are a lot of things that you need to improve. So I appreciate your insights, and on both sides of the aisle, we are going to take that into consideration.

My first question regards the security. Ms. Ohlhausen, would this bill ensure that the covered entities adequately protect personal data, and would it be possible for the Federal Trade Commission to define effective encryption standards if it has the resources?

*Ms. Ohlhausen. The bill has security protections built into it. The FTC has not traditionally been a technical agency. So for it to actually define data encryption standards, I think it would have to draw on outside expertise for that.

*Mr. McNerney. Thank you for that answer.

Ms. Fitzgerald, Section 203 gives the FTC the rulemaking authority to establish provisions for individual data ownership and controls, including not keeping data indefinitely.

Do you think it would be helpful to have data deletion standards?

*Ms. Fitzgerald. A very good question. There is actually a pretty good standard for data deletion. It does not say "deletion.'' It says in the data security section that deleting data must mean permanently erasing it or modifying it to make it permanently unreadable.

But, of course, you know, I think technology changes after (inaudible) – *Mr. McNerney. With the cloud and all, it is really hard to know if the data is really deleted.

*Ms. Ohlhausen. Right.

*Mr. McNerney. There must be some standards that can define that.

Thank you.

As chair of the Artificial Intelligence Caucus, I want to see continuing development of artificial intelligence to help address some of our biggest challenges and issues. But I want to ensure that the companies that conduct impact assessments examine how the AI may be harming people at the same time.

Mr. Lee, would the algorithm impact assessments outlined in this bill capture those effects of artificial intelligence?

*Mr. Lee. Thank you, Congressman, for the question.

And I think it would. And I also think it is important to keep in mind that with the E.U. AI Act and the algorithmic assessments that have been highlighted in this bill, what we have are really global standards and global acknowledgement that we do need to understand the impact that AI can have, particularly on individuals and hybrid systems and also on protected opportunities.

So we have done an analysis at Privacy Forum that shows kind of there is a broad overlay of protected characteristics that are in the E.U. of Convention on Human Rights and also with U.S. civil rights law and also a lot of the high-risk categories with the E.U. AI Act and a lot of the protected classes and protected categories of AI use that we have seen with respect to protected opportunities like housing, employment, education, so on and so forth. There is broad overlap.

And so between pre-deployment E.U. AI Act and post deployment with the ADPPA, you have broad coverage of an algorithm's lifecycle and a better understanding of how algorithms and particularly artificial intelligence are impacting our lives.

*Mr. McNerney. Thank you for that.

Mr. Kantor, you mentioned more than once really that we need more distinction between the covered entities, more definition there. Given that the large companies are having difficulty protecting data, how can we assure that smaller businesses will be able to implement effective, sufficient data security practices?

*Mr. Kantor. This is where I really think, you know, the FTC is instructed in the bill to take into account the size of the entity, but then there are a series of mandatory requirements that have to be part of data security, and that we worry might not be appropriate to size.

We think it is better left with a reasonable standard, a reasonable missed standard that is set in the bill for data security rather than setting those specifics because, frankly, the specifics can be too difficult for small and medium size businesses, but also likely laughably fall short of what the big, sophisticated businesses should do.

So we do not think that they are doing the proper work that, I know, confuses the FTC's job here in setting that reasonableness standard and taking into account how large the businesses are and what kind of data they handle, too.

*Mr. McNerney. Thank you.

I have a lot of really great questions, but I am out of time. So I am going to yield back to the chair.

Thank you.

*Ms. Schakowsky. The gentleman yields back.

Mrs. Lesko, you are recognized for five minutes.

*Mrs. Lesko. Thank you, Madam Chair.

And I want to thank both the Republicans and Democrats on this committee for working on this legislation. I think it is a bipartisan issue. I do not care if it is Republicans or Democrats. People are concerned about the misuse of their private information.

My first question is for Ms. Cuaresma, and it is on Section 205, and I am going to read the section that I am talking about. It is Section 205(b).

"Data transfer requirements related to minors. The covered entities shall not transfer the covered data of an individual to a third party without affirmative expressed consent from the individual or the individual's parent or guardian if the covered entity has actual knowledge that the individual is between 13 and 17 years of age.''

I think that that may need clarification just because you could read it, and I think some of the staff that I have talked to has read it, that the individual, meaning the minor, could give consent to opt out.

And so I was wondering if you share my concern or had any concerns.

*Ms. Cuaresma. Thank you for the question.

I do have concern about how that could be read. I definitely would not want my child to be able to affirmatively consent, given the definition here.

I will note that the definition of individual and minor is not provided in the statute. However, I do think there is widespread recognition in the law that individuals under 18 cannot contract.

And so I think it is okay, but this is something that would end up having to be litigated. We would not want to tie up court resources litigating something as easy as just defining and clarifying this section.

*Mrs. Lesko. Thank you.

My next question is for both Mr. Lee and Ms. Ohlhausen, and it is on Section 207, and I am just going to read part of the summary instead of the bill itself.

It says, "This section also requires large data holders that use algorithms to assess their algorithms annually and submit annual algorithms' impact requirements to the FTC.

These assessments must describe steps the entity has taken or will take to initiate potential harms from the algorithms, including any harms specifically related to individuals under 17. These assessments must also seek to mitigate algorithmic harms related to advertising for housing, education, employment, health care, insurance, and credit, access to or restrictions on places of public accommodation and any disparate impact on the basis of an individual's race, color, religion, national origin, gender, sexual orientation, or disability status.''

I have many constituents on the conservative side that are concerned that algorithms are used against people with certain political viewpoints. Do you think that political viewpoints should be added to this?

Mr. Lee.

*Mr. Lee. Thank you for the question, Congresswoman.

I think there may, from what I understand, and I am not an expert in kind of First Amendment speech with respect to this, but there may be First Amendment concerns with respect to including political class as a protected category, maybe.

But I am not particularly sure, but we would love to get back with your office about that.

*Mrs. Lesko. Ms. Ohlhausen.

*Ms. Ohlhausen. Thank you, Congresswoman.

I think that is an area outside the FTC's expertise, you know, political viewpoint discrimination. So we would need to get back to you.

But I would mention the definition of algorithm is also rather broad, and so the Coalition has some concerns about the sweeping and very routine kinds of business activities.

*Mrs. Lesko. Well, good. I want to thank all of the people that are here testifying today. I think this is very important legislation that needs to be done, and I hope we can come to a consensus.

And with that, I yield back.

*Ms. Schakowsky. The gentlewoman yields back.

And now I recognize Ms. Clarke for five minutes.

*Ms. Clarke. Thank you, Chairwoman Schakowsky and Ranking Member Bilirakis, for convening this important hearing on data privacy.

Thank you also to our very distinguished panel of witnesses for your testimony here today.

To put it simply, our Nation desperately needs comprehensive Federal privacy protections. Our personal data is currently collected and sold under a patchwork of regulations that do little to actually protect the consumer.

And these impacts are felt most acutely by vulnerable populations, including communities of color who are frequently targeted and preyed upon.

That is why I am thrilled to be discussing the draft of this bipartisan, bicameral American Data Privacy and Protection Act.

I am also very pleased to see that this draft includes large pieces of my Algorithmic Accountability Act, which I reintroduced this Congress, along with Senators Ron Wyden and Cory Booker.

These crucial pieces of my legislation, now part of this larger privacy package, will direct companies to perform impact assessments on their algorithms, including those derived from machine learning, to catch and eliminate potentially dangerous flaws that often lead to biased and discriminatory outcomes in the real world.

In the absence of common-sense oversight and regulations, these automated systems will continue to perpetuate systemic injustices by operating off algorithms that reinforce broader societal discrimination against women and people of color.

So under the American Data Privacy and Protection Act, covered entities are required to submit annual algorithmic impact assessments that describe what steps they have taken or will take to mitigate potential harm from algorithms that are already being used to make critical decisions about people's lives.

Ms. Fitzgerald, could you please elaborate on why impact assessments of algorithmic discrimination are a critical part of the comprehensive consumer data privacy legislation?

*Ms. Fitzgerald. Thank you for the question, Congresswoman, and thank you for your longtime leadership on this issue.

It could be algorithms can change over time. You learn from more and more data. It is important to do those regular checks to make sure that the inputs and outputs are thorough, equitable, and effective.

*Ms. Clarke. Thank you.

Under this draft privacy legislation, covered entities would also be required to evaluate algorithms during their initial design phase for potential harmful impacts as well as consult with independent auditors or researchers.

Mr. Lee, why are algorithms design evaluations at the front end not crucial for protecting the public against discriminatory uses of data, especially for marginalized individuals?

*Mr. Lee. Thank you for the question, Congresswoman.

And algorithmic I would say design principles are really important to keep in mind, particularly when we are thinking about data. As Mr. Brody and Ms. Fitzgerald have said both in their testimony and in front of us today, a lot of the systems and the data sets that we use are based on the historical concept of discrimination.

And so in a lot of contexts and in a lot of cases, whether it is like a resume trolling machine or whether it is kind of like who is more likely to be able to get a business loan, the historical data behind that is not necessarily representative of where America is in its full diversity and full capacity.

This is a way in which to think about that from an algorithmic perspective. Using that and looking at that data for potential impacts that it might have on marginalized communities and how can we potentially avoid those in the data and design space.

Similarly, why are external, independent auditors and researchers essential for the process of algorithmic impact assessments and design evaluations as opposed to internal company auditors?

I think one way to think about independent assessments and independent auditors is that there has been a lot said already about what kind of algorithmic harms have already happened to marginalized communities over at least the past decade.

A way in which to think about how to prevent that is to think about using independent auditors as a means by which to do so. Well, there are pros and cons to both.

The inclusion of both, there is an argument to be said that some may think that it would be too intrusive, but also, there has to be a way for us to be able to check and ensure that businesses are actually doing the checks that this bill requires and making sure that compliance exists.

And one way to do that is through the independent auditing systems.

*Ms. Clarke. I thank you for your response.

And I thank all of you for testifying here today.

I yield back, Madam Chair.

*Ms. Schakowsky. The gentlewoman yields back.

And now I recognize Mr. Pence for five minutes.

*Mr. Pence. Thank you, Chairwoman Schakowsky and Ranking Member Bilirakis.

And thank you, all the witnesses, for being here today.

I am encouraged by the bipartisan recognition of a problem that exists with opaque data collection practices. As our committee continues improving the bill through our legislative process, I urge my colleagues on both sides of the aisle to remain focused on allowing the consumer to rightfully control their data.

Like my colleagues have discussed today, our increasingly digital world leaves Hoosiers and all Americans in the dark about who has access to their information. It is striking how little consumers know about how personal details of their lives are collected, shared with third parties, and monetized without their informed consent.

Just as truth in lending and banking was enacted to protect consumers from bad actors manipulating a complex financial industry, Congress needs similar protections for Internet platforms that are becoming all but required to participate in modern society and here in Congress as well.

Consumers deserve to be informed in plain English as to how their information is collected, used, and shared. Provisions in this legislation like clear, conspicuous notice of privacy rights and express consent requirements will begin to empower consumers to control their own data and the data of their children.

We should make sure that these requirements are explicit enough to inform consumers exactly how platforms or third-party data brokers are using their information, whether it is being monetized or used for marketing activities and whether their collection practice is materially related to the services they are providing and what is the value of this information.

Ms. Fitzgerald, I brought up in past hearings the extent to which big tech is manipulating the addictive qualities of their platforms. Unfortunately, this growth at any cost mindset has led to more divisive interactions online, as we have all experienced over and over.

There is nothing wrong with making money. I am a businessman, spent most of my career making money, but it seems to me that user information has become the bedrock of their business model and excuses are everywhere as to covering that that fact exists.

In my view users ought to be compensated for the value that they choose to bring to these big tent platforms.

Ma'am, do you believe that it is feasible to consider opportunities, compensate individual users in exchange for the data they provide to platforms, and create a contractual relationship between a user and the platform?

*Ms. Fitzgerald. Thank you, Congressman Pence.

I think it is a concrete concept because we do not want to set up a system where only the rich can afford privacy. We do not want to set up incentives where, you know, lower income folks accept the terms and accept –

*Mr. Pence. Maybe I was not clear. Is there a way for me to be compensated for the data that is being collected by big tech on the platforms?

Do you foresee a possibility of that?

*Ms. Fitzgerald. I just think it might set up a system where folks with needs say, "I can do without it.'' And then it would go for –

*Mr. Pence. That is certainly a choice.

Mr. Kantor, the retailers or the data collectors that you represent, do they get compensated for the data they collect and then are sent on to platforms or are processed by platforms, which are then sold to others?

*Mr. Kantor. So there are a lot of roads data gets exchanged. Some of it is just somebody pays for something. Like you send that data along.

There are times when there are compensation arrangements, and there are lots of times when data is used for advertising, and there is a lot of that.

Look. While a lot of us get annoyed about advertising, might not like it, it is really important to our economy. It is important to –

*Mr. Pence. So just in the interest of time here, so you do have a contractual, in some cases, relationship where you are compensated for the data that is being garnered from you or you are providing through the transactions at your location, correct?

*Mr. Kantor. There are times.

*Mr. Pence. Why, as a user, do I not have that choice in this system?

And with that, Madam Chair, I yield back.

*Ms. Schakowsky. The gentleman yields back.

And now I recognize Representative Kelly for five minutes.

[No response.]

*Ms. Schakowsky. I understand that Ms. Kelly is not there. So I recognize Representative Soto for five minutes.

*Mr. Soto. Thank you so much, Madam Chair.

And what an exciting and historic day today when I think about how we as Americans value our privacy in our daily lives and then how the Internet has become such an integral part of them.

The calls for privacy have reached a fever pitch across the Nation.

I am really excited about the bipartisan nature of the bill before us and looking forward to many more opinions from you all.

But I want to share with a lot of folks back in Florida's Ninth Congressional District a little bit of the scope. So first of all, we are narrowing what companies can use with your data.

There is a duty of loyalty, something that has been needed for a long time, that companies can only collect and use data as reasonably necessary, that is proportionate.

So they cannot take data from one thing and sell it across the universe when it only needs to be collected for what they need to use and for the product and service request within the scope of the products that so many people already have assumed is the way it goes.

But the point I want to bring to the greatest attention is the sensitive data, the sensitive covered data section. While it is a modest name, it is nothing short of an Internet bill of privacy rights that we are establishing.

Can you imagine some of these things getting public? We are going to take a stand for it, such as protecting your Social Security numbers, passport numbers, and driver's licenses.

Protecting past, present, and future physical health, mental health, disability, health care treatment.

Protecting the financial account numbers of your debit cards, credit cards, and other security items.

Protecting biometric information, something I know so many people are worried about, along with genetic information so that people cannot just sell this throughout the Internet.

Protecting our geolocation information to reveal where we have been and where we are.

Protecting our individual private communications, like our voice mails, our emails, our texts, our direct messages, mail, and other things identifying our communications Account and device login credentials.

Information related to American's race, ethnicity, national origin, religion, and union membership, or non-union status.

Information identifying sexual orientation or sexual behavior of an individual. This is actually being added to a long list that is already prohibited from discrimination, like race, color, religion, origin, gender, age, disability, and veteran status. We are adding sexual orientation to that to make the discrimination statutes, the anti-discrimination statutes stronger.

Individual's ability to identify their activities on third party Websites.

Your calendar information that is online, like address book information, phone and text logs, photos, audio recordings, videos.

Photography and film depicting folks who are sadly in the nude. That obviously has been a big issue, as well as other information identifying and revealing the extent of an individual's ability to review or access television service.

And lastly and as importantly as all, banning information outright for folks under the age of 17, and changing that to constructive knowledge technology standard.

So when we look at what we are doing here today, any of these things getting out on the Internet would be catastrophic for a constituent, and in Florida, two years in a row the Florida legislature has failed to pass privacy laws.

So you have some States that have very aggressive privacy laws, but you have others that really have not even gotten started yet. So when we look at how Floridians are vulnerable, it is really important.

I wanted to briefly ask a question to Ms. Ohlhausen and Ms. Cuaresma about are we missing any rights there or should there be other specific privacy rights added there.

We will start with you, Ms. Ohlhausen.

*Ms. Ohlhausen. The bill is extremely comprehensive. As we heard, it puts together a number of other proposals, and it is then iterated over time. So nothing comes to my mind right now that is not covered.

*Mr. Pence. Okay. Thanks.

*Ms. Cuaresma. So those two things I would hope gets clarified that there is, in fact, a ban on all third-party advertising to children, given the way the section details what is not considered third party advertising, and so I would want those things clarified in the bill.

*Mr. Pence. Thanks so much, and I yield back.

*Ms. Schakowsky. The gentleman yields back.

And now I recognize Mr. Upton for five minutes.

*Mr. Upton. Well, thank you, Madam Chair. Sorry I had to step away for a little while. So I hope that the questions that I am going to ask have not been asked, but if so, tell me.

I want to thank Chair Pallone and Leader Rodgers for bringing a bipartisan bill to the subcommittee. It is very important. Internet privacy and data security issues have been around, yes, forever. There are probably only a couple of us on the committee who were here when it was not an issue.

The full House actually passed data security legislation not once but twice over a decade ago on a bipartisan basis, and I obviously had to grapple with privacy and security for my six years as full committee chair.

So I hope that we can get this right. I appreciate the testimony that all of you provided as well.

Mr. Kantor, your testimony is that NACS is in favor of the subcommittee moving forward on privacy legislation, but it did not seem like you were quite there yet with this bill. You talked a little bit about the preemptive States in your testimony. I wondered if you might expand on that perhaps a little bit and whatever suggestions you might have for us.

*Mr. Kantor. Thank you, Congressman.

Yes, we think there are changes that ought to be made here. Preemption is just one of them where because of the way the courts have viewed preemption, we do not think the language in the bill will actually meet the drafters' intention of preempting all privacy legislation in the States, in part, because there are so many exceptions.

And I have cited a number of cases, the Geier case and others, where that has been found to be a reason to move to a different preemption analysis.

But there are a bunch of other areas. The private right of action has some things that really concern us, in particular, as it relates to a pricing and loyalty programs. The pricing provisions in the bill, and we had testimony about this today, raise the specter that, in fact, we are going to have broad pricing regulation unless we deal with that.

*Mr. Upton. Is that because of the reward program? When you buy so many cups of coffee, you get a free one after ten? I mean, it is –

*Mr. Kantor. That is only one part of it. It is not only that, but Mr. Brody pointed to the possibility of redlining. Let's say I have two stores. One is in a more minority-heavy community than the other.

The problem he has brought up is that if I have a sale on different items in the one store than the other, am I discriminating? Is that why I am doing it?

That is a real concern where lots of retailers today, just to keep up with the competition, do use pricing software to know how to best price their products, and a lot of that is just based on where certain things are selling versus other items and how you want to pick up your sales. But if those neighborhoods are different and suddenly it is a discrimination issue, that is a real concern.

*Mr. Upton. Thank you.

Mr. Dufault, it is nice to see you again, for sure.

Small and developing businesses in my district in Michigan rely on data from third party sources to grow their businesses, reach new customers. The pandemic showed just how valuable that data was as they shifted their businesses online.

Section 302 of the bill changes the way that third party data can be collected, processed, and used. What steps can small businesses take to access the data that they need to operate, given the changes in this bill?

*Mr. Dufault. Thank you, Congressman. It is good to see you, too.

There are a few things that small businesses can do to make sure that they are accessing data that they need to continue to access in order to have the market intelligence and to evolve.

I think one area I would point to is Section 304, which provides the ability for the FTC to certify, authorize compliance programs, and these compliance programs, I think, are going to be very helpful for small companies that meet certain thresholds to find ways to access data in a manner that is compliant with the law.

And so it is not just how do I respond to the consumer request. It is not just how do I take these steps to secure data. It is also aspects like how do I source data in a way that is responsible and that meets sort of the spirit of the law as well.

So I think not relying too heavily on these compliance programs, but I think they are going to be very valuable beyond just pure compliance.

*Mr. Upton. Thank you.

I want to say my time is expiring. I really appreciated, Ms. Cuaresma, your thrust on children and the impact on children, and I look forward to trying to make sure that this bill accomplishes many of those same things.

And with that, Madam Chair, I yield back.

*Ms. Schakowsky. The gentleman yields back.

And now I recognize Miss Rice for five minutes.

*Miss Rice. Thank you, Madam Chair.

And I want to echo the sentiments of all of my colleagues in thanking the full committee chairs, co-chair, and also Mr. Bilirakis and Ms. Schakowsky for bringing this incredibly important piece of legislation.

I mean, this is what we all come here to do, to actually pass laws that impact in a positive way people's lives, and there has been no business that I can think of that has more of a negative impact, along with positive, but particularly negative impact on people in this country.

The social media companies which we hope are going to be, you know, more honest with how they deal with consumers, their consumers.

Mr. Brody, the American Data Privacy and Protection Act includes important provisions that would institute a new course of responsibility and authorities for the FTC and State AGs, including the ability to obtain civil penalties and relief for consumers who have been harmed by abusive data practices.

The D.C. Attorney General recently brought a suit against Facebook seeking to hold their CEO, Mark Zuckerberg, liable for data abuses and for misleading users about their privacy protections.

Can you speak to any other examples of cases where State AGs have sought penalties against companies for offenses, under existing privacy laws?

And what challenges do AGs face for suing these types of cases without a comprehensive Federal privacy standard?

*Mr. Brody. Thank you for that question. It is a great one.

So State Attorneys General play a very important role here in enforcing this bill and augmenting the authority of the FTC in private rights of action.

For example, the Attorney General of New York has brought cases against data apps that leaked information that resulted in really sensitive information being released and used to harm people, and that is just one example.

What often holds State AGs back though is a lack of transparency into how companies are using data, and so the provisions in this bill around transparency, around access, correction, deletion, around algorithmic assessments, that should provide State Attorneys General with a lot more information about what companies are doing and how to address it.

And the reason that State AGs are so important here is because they have a really close connection to the communities they serve and can really connect at a local level to address harms that might not be national in scope.

*Miss Rice. All right. So can you tell us what additional resources this bill provides State Attorneys General to empower them to prosecute cases involving data abuses or violation of privacy protection?

*Mr. Brody. Under this bill, State Attorneys General would have full enforcement authority to bring actions for any type of violation of the Act and to seek injunctive relief, to seek civil penalties or compensatory damages or what have you to ensure that citizens are protected and compensated.

*Miss Rice. Thank you, Mr. Brody.

Mr. Kantor, protecting our Nation's small businesses and ensuring that they have the tools and resources they need to compete against large companies is a major priority that many of us on this committee share.

The ADPPA aims to ensure that more focus and responsibility are placed on large data holders and includes certain exemptions for small businesses. For example, the bill contains exemptions for small and medium size covered entities that do not meet specified thresholds related to their revenue derived from transferring, collecting, or processing covered data.

How would a Federal privacy law help small businesses in particular?

Would this legislation help to level the playing field with the larger businesses that small businesses work and compete with?

*Mr. Kantor. Thank you, Congresswoman, for that question.

Yes, there are some key things this bill does do and some things we think it still needs to do to get to that.

The thing it does do is set statutory requirements for covered entities and service providers to lay out their different responsibilities, and that is key so that the larger business cannot just impose things by contract.

One concept that I think is important and Ms. Ohlhausen spoke to this earlier is that they should make sure these entities are not liable for the others' activities. They should both have the responsibilities, whether that is covered entity, a service provider, and have to follow through on them, and they need to rely on each other but should not be liable for the other one's acts of commission or omission.

And that is especially important for small business. So having a national standard matters so that these small businesses cannot be taken advantage of by the big technology companies.

And as we said, we think there is still more work to do to get to that point, but the concepts and the way it was laid out here is a really good starting point to move from.

*Miss Rice. Thank you so much.

Madam Chair, my time is up and I yield back.

*Ms. Schakowsky. The gentlelady yields back.

The chair now recognizes Mr. Bucshon for five minutes.

*Mr. Bucshon. Thank you, Mr. [sic] Chair. Thank you for calling today's – I want to thank Madam Chair for calling today's legislative hearing on what I think is one of the most significant and pressing needs within our committee's jurisdiction, modernizing the protections and acceptable uses of American citizens' data.

Today it is difficult for Americans to go about their daily lives without some form of data about them being collected, stored, and used for businesses or government entities around the world.

Like many of my colleagues, I am glad that this committee is approaching this issue with the seriousness it deserves and demands and is considering the American Data Privacy and Protection Act draft legislation.

I know that Ranking Member Rodgers, Chairman Pallone, and Ranking Member Wicker and their staffs put together this legislation using years of experience as well as industry and user feedback on how we can form safe and appropriate guidelines for data privacy in the 21st century.

I am pleased that we are following up that work by debating this draft in a regular order process that ensures users and industry are able to express their thoughts and help make this committee take a huge step forward for privacy.

Over the last ten years we have seen too many instances of controllers of my constituents' data not having adequate internal systems and protections for data they use, which is why I am glad that the draft includes privacy by design guidelines that account for things such as size of the company, the types of data, and the risks associated.

Mr. Miller, aspects of privacy by design procedures have already been implemented across the globe, such as data protection by design in Europe's GDPR. In your opinion, have these measures been well received and are they working for consumers?

*Mr. Miller. Thanks very much for the question, Congressman.

I think I would answer that question two ways. I mean, I do think generally speaking that privacy by design concepts have been very well received by both business and advocates. You know, many, I think, in industry have been supportive of the concepts for a very long time.

And I mean, I think the concept as it appears in the GDPR has also been welcome.

You know, I do think that one question that folks reasonably have about it is, you know, there is a question about privacy. I mean, you can have a requirement about privacy by design, but it does not necessarily explain how to do privacy by design if you are a company.

So, I mean, I think in the case of – and we have seen that in other laws. So you know, the development of standards, for instance, on that, you know, one of the things that NIST in the U.S. is doing is they have developed a privacy framework which has many different standards, including in that area.

It is something that is very important, and perhaps that is something that could also be, you know, worked out as the bill would be implemented, but positively received from my perspective, but the devil is in the details.

*Mr. Bucshon. Understood. Mr. Dufault, this draft also includes protections for data users age 13 through 17. As a father of four, I have seen firsthand how critical it is that people I represent in this age group use and become more familiar with the Internet and how to use it.

When done safely, it can lead to them taking a greater interest in technology, as was the case for my daughter, who recently graduated from Cornell and began working as a computer science engineer.

But it should not be the Wild West when it comes to handling their data, which is why I am glad that the draft legislation includes new regimes for these young people who are inevitably exposed to the good, the bad, and the ugly of the online world.

Do you anticipate your members being willing to work with the new Youth Privacy and Marketing Division at the FTC?

*Mr. Dufault. Yes, definitely. I think Congress is right to be focusing on these issues, and I think these are provisions that we can work with.

*Mr. Bucshon. Great. Are there any additional guardrails that this committee should consider as part of this draft to ensure that the division can accomplish its stated goals?

*Mr. Dufault. Well, that is a good question. I think a lot of questions have been raised around, you know, what should be the right age to protect kids.

*Mr. Bucshon. Right.

*Mr. Dufault. I think as you consider further updatesto COPPA, for example, one thing to think about, and it was brought up earlier, is actual knowledge, a workable standard, or should we look at something more like constructive knowledge to protect kids?

And I think one of the things I will point out is that early in the early 2010s, the ACT Association was encouraging the FTC to more rigorously enforce COPPA, and we thought that there were instances where actors out there in online services were not exactly in compliance with the law even under the actual knowledge standard.

But we also recognized the FTC had had a lot of difficulty gathering the right evidence to enforce the actual knowledge standard, and so one thing I want to point out is that we have some work to do before we can best enforce the actual knowledge standard, before we move to broaden that concept because I know that is in brackets in the draft right now.

*Mr. Bucshon. Okay. Thank you very much.

I yield back.

*Mr. Soto. [Presiding.] The gentleman yields back.

The chair now recognizes Ms. Kelly for five minutes to ask questions.

*Ms. Kelly. Thank you, Mr. Chair.

And thank you, Chair Schakowsky and Ranking Member Bilirakis, for holding this hearing today. It has been a long time coming.

I am very encouraged by the progress that has been made for the bill that can pass both chambers and truly strengthen privacy protections for all Americans.

One issue I have been focused on for a long time is ensuring that consumers know what they are agreeing to. No one reads the long privacy policies of today, and neither do I.

Mr. Lee, can you please explain how the short-form privacy notices will help consumers better understand how their data is being used?

*Mr. Lee. Thank you for the question, Congresswoman.

So for too many people, long form privacy notices are difficult to read. They are even difficult to read for privacy lawyers in certain circumstances.

The short-form privacy notices give the agency back to consumers to allow the consumer to better understand how their data is being used and in what context.

*Ms. Kelly. In this legislation we also take steps to make sure our processes are more inclusive. In addition to the discrimination the American Data Privacy and Protection Act also ensures information is accessible in different languages when a covered entity is operating in different languages.

Mr. Brody, can you tell us more about how making privacy policies available to users in the language they speak when the services are offered in that language is key to making services more protective for everyone?

*Mr. Brody. Absolutely. Thank you for that question.

This is a very big country. We have a lot of people that speak a lot of different languages, and if they are expected to understand their rights under this Act and how to effect their rights and enforce their rights, they should be able to see privacy policies and other important materials in the language in which they primarily use the service.

I think this is also an area where the new Office of Business Mentorship at the FTC could play a big role both by assisting businesses with ensuring language accessibility, but also by ensuring that the policies, guidelines, and regulations which the Commission issues to help small businesses are also available in multiple languages to assist immigrants, small business owners and others who need help complying with the Act.

*Ms. Kelly. Thank you for that.

I also think this draft does a lot to protect users, and even for opt-in choices it protects some manipulation beyond the strong data minimization protection that stops certain collection processing and transfer. There is a robust opt-in requirement for sensitive data that also includes protections to stop companies from using dark patterns to manipulate users.

Increasingly, these dark patterns will be in the system with AI to be more effective and creative in their manipulation.

Ms. Fitzgerald, why is it so important that we address dark patterns to ensure deceptive design elements do not undermine consumer opt-in rights under the bill?

*Ms. Fitzgerald. Thank you for the question, Congresswoman.

We have all seen these dark patterns, right? The pop-up shows up, has a big "accept'' button and then has a tiny, you know, or "click here'' to confirm your choices and then a big window comes up with a million choices you have to go through and folks get about halfway through.

So it is important because it makes the rights meaningful that are in the bill.

*Ms. Kelly. Thank you.

When I testified before the European Parliament on transatlantic cooperation or artificial intelligence, I spoke about the importance of the U.S. and E.U. strengthening privacy and ensuring AI is a tool that positively benefits society.

It is my great hope that this bill together with the E.U.'s efforts will be complementary and create a new paradigm for trustworthy AI. I look forward to working with the committee to advance this important legislation.

And with that, I yield back. Thank you.

*Ms. Schakowsky. [Presiding.] The gentlelady yields back.

And now I recognize Mr. Armstrong for five minutes.

*Mr. Armstrong. Thank you, Madam Chair.

For as long as I have been in Congress, which is not quite that long yet, we have been talking about a national privacy group. Big business has come in and said we cannot do a patchwork of 50 States. Small businesses have said the same thing, banks, health care, big tech, small tech, advocacy groups.

And the reason we have not gotten there yet is because it is really hard, and everybody recognizes we need to compromise, but we cannot compromise on whichever particular issue you want to compromise on because platforms will tell you it breaks the Internet. Small businesses will say you are passing too much of that cost onto the credit card machine on a counter.

And you will create censorship. It will be anti-competitive. We will give too much power to the FTC. We are not giving enough power to the FTC.

And then users are bombarded with ads on whatever platform they are in that Congress is trying to break the Internet as we know it.

And last Congress we get almost to the point, and I was not on the committee yet and I am not sure I would have been helpful, and we get stuck on two things, preemption and private right of action.

So today we are here, and we have a compromise on preemption and private right of action, and this is more of a message to everybody who is watching it. It is a neat trick to go back and tell all of your members, all of your constituents, all of your consumers that we are working really, really hard for a privacy bill, but any framework that comes out we hate.

Be a part of the conversation. That is what this conversation is about. So guess what I want to talk about preemption because we are trying to compromise, but I think our number one job as we are moving through this should be to provide clarity and decrease litigation.

And as we are dealing in this space, it is always going to be an evolving field.

So Section 404(b) details the general and specific statutes that are not preempted by this bill. Specifically identifying laws that are not subject to express preemption in a Federal bill is sometimes referred to as anti-preemption.

An anti-preemption doctrine is actually relatively undeveloped in Federal court, and notwithstanding any unsettled questions of law surrounding attempts to remove State law actions to Federal court, anti-preemption leaves a number of substantial questions.

And without further clarity, I am worried this is going to evolve into substantial further litigation and, more importantly, potentially lack of action by State governments.

For example, the bill specifically did not preempt Illinois Biometric Information Privacy Act. What happens to the anti-preemption status provided to that State law if Illinois subsequently amends it?

What happens if Illinois enacts a minor technical change, but the date on the legislation changes in Illinois code?

If the State law is significantly altered, will itsanti-preemption status be subject to a conflicting preemption challenge?

Will these uncertainties disincentivize Illinois from considering rational amendments to the law, particularly in a field that is evolving rapidly and could actually do a lot of good for the citizens of Illinois?

The same applies to Illinois's Genetic Information Privacy Act. Will State lawyers in Illinois risk anti-preemption status granted by this law?

And I understand the compromise because we had to get here, and several of my colleagues have repeatedly stated that California's privacy law must be protected, but I wonder if we are going to extend that protection to subsequent changes to that State law.

And without guardrails, we leave these issues to certain States and Federal courts that will one day have to decide the preemption challenge.

Mr. Miller, do you have any insight on the status of the preservation of these State laws if they are subsequently amended?

*Mr. Miller. Thank you for the question, Congressman Armstrong.

You know, I think you raise a very good point. You know, one of the things that I recommended in my written testimony and that is often discussed in this context is, you know, whether to simply preempt laws that are covered by the provisions of the Act or all laws relating to the subject matter covered by the Act.

I mean, with respect to your example and the Illinois biometric privacy law, I mean, clearly, biometric privacy seems covered by the provisions of the Act, but yet, you know, it is preempted, but other State laws like Texas' biometric law are not.

You know, I think one concern perhaps or at least I would submit that the bill does seem to freeze these laws in place, right? So I do not think we have the answer to your questions, and it actually may just end up leading to more litigation ultimately.

*Mr. Armstrong. Well, I am going to ask the same question of Mr. Kantor. I actually am not going to get to it because I am out of time.

But I want to be clear. I think we have to have these conversations about enforcement because I think we have to do the best we can to get the clarity and to decrease that litigation, and I think it also exists in private right of action, and that does not mean we should not try because we should because our constituents are demanding this. Our business groups are demanding this.

Everybody who is involved in this space is, you know, in the 21st century that is demanding that.

And with that, I yield back.

*Ms. Schakowsky. The gentleman yields back.

And now I recognize Congresswoman Fletcher for five minutes.

*Mrs. Fletcher. Thank you so much, Chairwoman Schakowsky. And thanks to you and Ranking Member Bilirakis for convening this hearing to discuss the American Data Privacy and Protection Act.

You know, as we have heard throughout the day, we have an opportunity to advance privacy rights for Americans through bicameral and bipartisan collaboration. That is certainly what my constituents would like to see more of in Washington, and I am really glad to hear you all want to move this bill forward and have this hearing today and to hear from our witnesses.

I really want to thank all of you for taking the time to testify and provide your insight and be a part of these important conversations.

Just listening to Mr. Armstrong talk about the enforcement provisions with you and understanding there are still so many important parts that we need to work through and really do all we can to protect the privacy of our fellow Americans, I know this is something that is important in many, many contexts, and it is certainly important here when we talk about our data.

And one of the places I just want to focus with the time I have right now is on the heightened protection for sensitive data. It is a lot of data that, frankly, a lot of people may not realize is being shared and certainly would want to protect.

So this sensitive data, which includes biometric and genetic information, Social Security numbers certainly, bank account and credit card numbers, health diagnosis, disability, treatment information.

Kind of on a separate track, I have a lot of concerns about how much of this data is actually available for sale and the detail that you can find, and I think we have a lot of work to do in that area.

But I think what I want to do is ask Ms. Fitzgerald if you can talk a little bit about the health data, which I know is so important to so many of my constituents, and why that should be considered sensitive data and why it is not sufficiently protected by HIPAA in an online ecosystem.

If you could share that with us, then I have another question for you as well on geolocation data.

*Ms. Fitzgerald. Yes, thank you, Congresswoman.

People feel that their health data is sensitive. They assume it is covered by HIPAA because it is alarming that it is not, right? HIPAA goes back to, like I said before, the problem with having these sectoral laws. HIPAA only covers interactions you have with your doctor's office, with your health insurer and the health exchanges that they use.

It does not cover the health data that we put into ACT. So that is why we need a comprehensive privacy law, so that that health data is covered no matter who is collecting it.

*Mrs. Fletcher. Thank you for that.

And I could not agree more, especially now where we see tracking of a lot of our own personal data. I am really concerned about access to women's reproductive health data, and it is something that we will be working on more in the coming days.

But I do want to ask you in the time I have left, just under two minutes, kind of connected to this, you have probably seen, as a lot of folks have, I am sure, that people are able to get geolocation data.

And, in particular, there is an article that we were just looking at about people being able to purchase geolocation data that would show where people have been, for example, to particular health clinics or searching online for particular services.

But geolocation data is also considered sensitive data, and can you just talk a little bit about why it is important to place heightened restrictions on this type of data, especially with regard to how it can be used by these data brokers who are looking to profit from this geolocation data and why we need to protect that?

*Ms. Fitzgerald. Yes. So this goes back to people's expectations. You expect that your weather app is going to collect your location data to give you the weather. You do not expect that they are then going to sell it to data brokers so it can be used to build profiles about you.

But unfortunately, for a few thousand dollars a month, you can get access to two years of raw location data from millions of phones.

And the fact that it is anonymized is a lie. It can be linked back to an individual. That is what happened, you know, with the Catholic priest I noted in my opening statement where they tied his location data back to him and outed him.

So that is why this data is particularly sensitive. There is a huge market for it because it can be reidentified, and we need to stop that.

*Mrs. Fletcher. Well, thank you so much for sharing that.

I could not agree with you more. There are times that I think it is best to have a right to privacy in [audio malfunction] as well as others, but certainly in their data.

And we come together now. As I said, at least we have with this bill to take steps to protect the privacy of Americans.

So with that, I am out of time, but I thank you all very much for being here today.

And, Madam Chair, I yield back.

*Ms. Schakowsky. The gentlelady yields back.

And now I want to welcome as a waive-on to this committee someone who has been very involved in these issues and to close us out, I recognize you for five minutes, Mr. Walberg.

*Mr. Walberg. Thank you, Madam Chair.

Are you saying this is the last word?

*Ms. Schakowsky. This is the last word.

*Mr. Walberg. Well, thank you.

And thanks to the panel for sitting here for a long time today.

After years of negotiating, it has been said I am glad that we are holding a hearing on one of our country's most pressing needs, the comprehensive national privacy and data network security framework.

It is amazing that we have such a tool. The technology is unbelievable. The abilities that are in tech are so important to us, but I continue as an adult feeling more and more violated all the time as I use the resources, almost the same feeling I get when I am in a Beijing hotel at times, knowing that I am probably being overwatched.

We need to keep the platforms but figure some way to deal with the privacy.

And so, Ms. Ohlhausen, earlier this year I reintroduced the bipartisan PROTECT Kids Act with my friend, Representative Rush, which would update and modify COPPA.

This has been a longstanding issue for me and many members of the committee, and while the draft does not directly amend COPPA, it does provide broad new protections for minors under the age of 17.

It also requires the FTC to update their COPPA rules to reference additional requirements for covered entities under Section 406.

Can you briefly explain how this increases protections for children?

*Ms. Ohlhausen. Yes. Thank you, Congressman.

The Children's Online Privacy Protection Act is now more than 20 years old, and it was kind of a watershed moment early on in the consumer-focused Internet, but it needs to catch up to new technologies, new risks, new ways of doing business.

So I believe taking a look at what COPPA tests and how it can be strengthened and additional protections that may be necessary is a very good step forward.

*Mr. Walberg. As you know, COPPA uses an actual knowledge standard for companies that determine the age of a child. Do you think this standard works well?

And why is it important as opposed to a constructive knowledge standard, especially if the age is raised to under 17?

*Ms. Ohlhausen. When COPPA was enacted, my understanding of why the actual knowledge standard was adopted was the fact that there are large – whether at the time it was Websites; now it could be a whole host of things that attracted a very broad audience, and you could presume that there were probably children in that audience.

And there were concerns about essentially putting obligations on based on the fact that you might have some children in the audience.

So what the FTC did was focus on things that were particularly targeted towards children, things that had like cartoon characters and things like that, and they have actually brought an enforcement case also where a company's contracting and proposals made it clear that they did have actual knowledge of the children in the audience. So that is the way the FTC has tried to address it.

There was a law called COPA, C-O-P-A, that was actually struck down on First Amendment grounds as being over-inclusive in sweeping in too many adults. So that may also have been one of the areas of concern that the actual knowledge standard was trying to address.

*Mr. Walberg. Okay. Mr. Dufault, what type of obligations would small app developers have if the knowledge standard was changed to constructive?

*Mr. Dufault. Well, one of the concerns that we have is that they would have to potentially collect more data if they do not already have all kinds of metadata or direct data associated with an individual. Then they might have to collect more to figure out whether or not, you know, they put together a picture of constructive knowledge.

So that would be potentially an issue, and then there is just sort of a broader universe of services that might be swept in by constructive knowledge, and even in services that maybe we do not intend to include.

So that would be a couple of concerns that we would have.

*Mr. Walberg. Okay. Ms. Fitzgerald, I believe there are benefits to certain targeted advertisements. They allow small companies and start-ups easier entry into the marketplace, often dominated by household names.

Section 205 of this legislation would prohibit targeted advertising to any individual under 17. How do you think this prohibition will impact the mental health of our Nation's children?

*Ms. Fitzgerald. Thank you for the question, Congressman.

It is so important because kids are still developing critical thinking skills. They often cannot distinguish advertisements from non-commercial content. So that ban is necessary to protect them as they develop those skills.

*Mr. Walberg. Okay. Well, I see my time has ended, and I yield back.

*Ms. Schakowsky. Thank you, Mr. Walberg.

I spoke too soon. Congressman Cardenas has come online, and so I want to yield five minutes to him.

Mr. Cardenas.

*Mr. Cardenas. Thank you, Madam Chairwoman. And also, I would like to thank the ranking member.

I thank the witnesses very, very much for helping to clarify before the people of our great country as to what is going on and what would be some good things that we should be doing as Congress to protect and create a balanced environment, especially when it comes to these apps that are being used by tens and tens and tens of millions of people in our country.

Americans are very concerned about how the data is being collected and spread online, and it is clear that an overwhelming majority of the public agrees that individuals should have control over their personal information and how it is used on the Internet.

It is important that we have this hearing today not only to discuss the sections that this bill brings to the table, but to shine a light on ways that our personal information is spread, monetized, and in some cases abused by many of the organizations, corporations, and applications that Americans are handling every single day.

Mr. Brody, there are countless examples of mobile phone applications collecting more data about consumers than they need to function on the app. Facebook Messenger, for example, an app designed for messaging and video calls, collects health and fitness information, financial information, and location data, none of which are necessary to facilitate communication with your friends or your family.

Can you explain why these apps and Websites collect so much data on it and what they do with that data if they do not need it to function on the app?

And how would this legislation address this situation?

*Mr. Brody. Thank you for that question.

Put simply, the apps collect that much data because they can and because they can monetize it by either using it themselves for advertising and other purposes or selling it to other companies who can find other ways to monetize it.

This bill has really strong data minimization provisions that would ensure that when you are using an app, that app is only collecting and using and transferring as much information as is reasonably necessary and proportionate to the services providing you and your expectations based on your engagement with that app.

This is incredibly important to ensure that there is not superfluous, extra information floating around that could be highly sensitive and that can be abused either by predatory actors or that could be leaked in a data breach.

And so the data minimization framework in this bill is extremely strong and central.

*Mr. Cardenas. Thank you. Thank you very, very much.

There are so many questions I want to ask you, but now I am going to go to Jolina Cuaresma.

Ms. Cuaresma, this bill rightfully focuses attention on enhancing protections for individuals 17 years of age and younger. Children and teens go through phases of development in which they gradually develop their critical thinking skills, those to distinguish ads from content.

How does this make children and teens uniquely vulnerable to privacy harm?

*Ms. Cuaresma. I am sorry. I think you cut out for about five seconds there, and I missed the question.

*Mr. Cardenas. When it comes to the bill would protect our teens, how is it that the way a young brain develops, how will this bill help make sure that teens, who are uniquely vulnerable, how would this bill help with their private data?

*Ms. Cuaresma. Thanks for the question.

So we have known for quite some time now that the human brain is not finished developing until perhaps around their mid-20s, and this means right now that my child, who is in high school, is still very susceptible to all sorts of images and online content that can influence her sense of self.

And so what I am really appreciative of about this Act is the Section 205 about targeted advertising. That is going to put a ban on advertising for children under 17, and it clearly co-bans third party advertising on its face, except under Section 226(b)(I) through (III). What happens is there is now an exclusion to what targeted advertising means.

So first part advertising, fine, that is well and good. That is going to be allowed, but in (I) and (III), advertising or marketing to an individual in response to any ask, that can include third party advertising.

So there is a loophole here in which third party targeted advertising can come in. And given what we all know about developing brains, we want to make sure that we close that loophole.

*Mr. Cardenas. Thank you very much.

My time has expired, Madam Chair.

*Ms. Schakowsky. The gentleman yields back.

And so at this point as we close this hearing, I want to really thank each and every one of our witnesses.

We do not usually have this many as we had today, eight witnesses, but this has been such a robust and useful conversation, and every one of you made such important contributions. I am so grateful to all of you.

I want to remind members, but also alert witnesses that pursuant to committee rules, that members have ten days to submit additional questions for the record, to be answered by the witnesses, the designated witness.

What we are asking for is not a particular date, but we ask each witness to respond promptly to any question that might come your way, and there probably will be more because there were so many important issues that were brought up.

So before I close, let me say that I request unanimous consent to enter into the record the 22 documents that have been reviewed by Democrats and Republican staff and enter those into the record.

*Mr. Bilirakis. Without objection; no objection

*Ms. Schakowsky. So let me just make one closing statement.

You know, Congresswoman Rice said this is why we are here, to actually get together in a bipartisan way and address issues that consumers, that businesses, that Americans really care about. And I just feel so happy today that we, I believe, have made such important steps forward.

We have introduced this bipartisan, bicameral legislation. There are some things that I think we can do better and make it even better, but we have taken such important steps in this journey.

I want to thank all of our witnesses for contributing to that, all of our members, and the leaders for bring us to this point.

And let me yield for just a closing statement to Mr. Bilirakis.

*Mr. Bilirakis. Thank you, Madam Chair.

I want to thank the chairman and the ranking member of the full committee and, of course, Madam Chair, yourself as well. This is how we legislate. This is regular order. That is what we want.

I think we have a good draft. We can improve the bill and move it forward.

So, again, I praise you, Madam Chair and the entire committee and, of course, especially the staff because they have done an outstanding job, and thank you to the presenters as well. We are going to make the bill even better.

Thank you. I yield back.

*Ms. Schakowsky. Thank you, Mr. Bilirakis.

And the committee is now adjourned.

[Whereupon, at 1:55 p.m., the subcommittee was adjourned.]

Subcommittee on Consumer Protection and Commerce, Hearing on "Protecting America's Consumers: Bipartisan Legislation to Strengthen Data Privacy and Security," June 14, 2022

Questions for the Record, Graham Dufault, Senior Director for Public Policy, ACT | The App Association

The Honorable Michael Burgess (R-TX)

1. Mr. Dufault, in the 114th Congress, I was chairman of this subcommittee and introduced a bill to combat patent trolls, called the Targeting Rogue and Opaque Letters – or TROL – Act. I am pleased to see this legislation includes a process to help prevent abusive demand letters. As written, this legislation requires a person seeking a private right of action to first notify the Federal Trade Commission and their State Attorney General with their intent to seek to action and to wait 60 days before proceeding with a private right of action should the FTC and State Attorney General choose not to pursue the case.

a. Do you believe this provides sufficient protection against abusive demand letters? If not, do you have suggestions to strengthen this part of the legislation?

Response

Similar to the Targeting Rogue and Opaque Letters (TROL) Act (H.R. 192), the American Data Privacy and Protection Act (ADPPA, H.R. 8152) preempts state laws directed at the same kind of conduct the Act prohibits. Both bills accompany preemption provisions with additional enforcement authorities beyond the Federal Trade Commission (FTC), empowering state attorneys general to enforce the bills' respective provisions. However, H.R. 8152 goes a step further by empowering individuals to sue for almost all violations of the Act's provisions. This additional capability is extraordinary, and experience has shown that private rights of action (PRAs) like this one can lead to serious abuse, which in turn can lead to higher costs and lower quality products and services for consumers[196]—unless there are safeguards in place to limit nuisance suits while optimizing remedies for aggrieved litigants.

During the hearing, I alluded to situations where small businesses receive abusive demand letters from patent trolls as examples of predatory sue-and-settle tactics that inappropriately leverage rights to sue for profit. Just as opportunists have converted the Telephone Consumer Protection Act (TCPA) and the Americans with Disabilities Act (ADA) into profit centers, patent trolls also induce small businesses to settle by enforcing their rights in situations the law never intended. Even where a patent owner makes a weak argument as to its patent's applicability to a small business's activities, hiring an attorney to fight that assertion is often too expensive for target companies without legal departments; for them, settling is often the only real option. Similarly, a private right of action encouraging trial attorneys to sue for a wide range of violations of a sweeping law could be an invitation for litigants to adopt the same sue-and-settle approach, including by alleging violations that are either insubstantial or unsupported by any facts. H.R. 8152 includes reasonable safeguards against this kind of opportunistic litigation and settlement seeking that lines attorneys' pockets without helping consumers. This Committee could strengthen these safeguards, however, including by requiring litigants to show some level of knowledge on the part of the target of an alleged violation; requiring litigants to show some level of harm to aggrieved consumers; and requiring federal or state enforcement agencies to verify the likelihood of success of a private claim before it can move forward.

b. How does this language provide necessary guardrails for businesses?

Response

The language provides guardrails that help prevent nuisance suits in two primary ways: 1) by giving state and federal enforcers right of first refusal, enabling them to consider whether the agency itself should bring the claim rather than an individual; and 2) by providing small businesses the right to "cure" an alleged violation to avoid unnecessary litigation. A similar right to cure appears in state privacy laws as well[197] and is a commonsense measure that enables small companies to demonstrate they have rectified any alleged violation of the law, saving courts time and precious resources and providing a remedy for consumers without imposing undue costs on small businesses. In my testimony, I pointed out that Sec. 403(c)(2), "Effect of Cure" should reflect earlier provisions, which we believe would merely correct a drafting issue. Specifically, Sec. 403(c)(1) provides that any claim brought against a small business is subject to the 45-day right to cure notice. However, we believe the effect of the cure (providing that if a business effectively cures the issue, liability does not attach) erroneously applies only to injunctions, whereas it should apply with respect to injunctions sought against businesses of any size; and *any* claim brought against a small business, including a claim for damages or other relief. This small change would help clarify what we think H.R. 8152 intends, that small businesses can rest assured that if they fix an alleged violation before a lawsuit is filed, that they will not nonetheless be dragged into court to fight the claim.

---

[196] *See* ALDA News, "How the Courts and Congress are Battling the ADA "Trolls,"" ASSOC. OF LATE – DEAFENED ADULTS (Jul. 27, 2021), *available at* https://alda.org/how-the-courts-and-congress-are-battling-the-ada- trolls/.

[197] *See* Co. Rev. Stat. Sec. 6-1-1311 (2021).

* * *

June 30, 2022

Mr. John Miller
Senior Vice President of Policy and General Counsel
Information Technology Industry Council (ITI)
700 K Street NW; Suite 600; Washington, DC 20001

Dear Mr. Miller:

Thank you for appearing before the Subcommittee on Consumer Protection and Commerce on Tuesday, June 14, 2022, at the hearing entitled "Protecting America's Consumers: Bipartisan Legislation to Strengthen Data Privacy and Security." I appreciate the time and effort you gave as a witness before the Committee on Energy and Commerce.

Pursuant to Rule 3 of the Committee on Energy and Commerce, members are permitted to submit additional questions to the witnesses for their responses, which will be included in the hearing record. Attached are questions directed to you from members of the Committee. In preparing your answers to these questions, please address your responses to the member who has submitted the question in the space provided.

To facilitate the printing of the hearing record, please submit your response to this question no later than the close of business on Thursday, July 15, 2022. As previously noted, this transmittal letter and your response, as well as the responses from the other witnesses appearing at the hearing, will all be included in the hearing record. Your written responses should be transmitted by e-mail in the Word document provided to Ed Kaczmarski, Policy Analyst, at ed.kaczmarski@mail.house.gov. To help in maintaining the proper format for hearing records, please use the document provided to complete your responses.

Thank you for your prompt attention to this request. If you need additional information or have other questions, please contact Ed Kaczmarski with the Committee staff at (202) 225-2927.

Sincerely,
Frank Pallone, Jr.
Chairman
Attachment

cc: The Honorable Cathy McMorris Rodgers
Ranking Member
Committee on Energy and Commerce

The Honorable Jan Schakowsky
Chair
Subcommittee on Consumer Protection and Commerce

The Honorable Gus Bilirakis
Ranking Member
Subcommittee on Consumer Protection and Commerce

Attachment—Additional Questions for the Record, Subcommittee on Consumer Protection and Commerce, Hearing on "Protecting America's Consumers: Bipartisan Legislation to Strengthen Data Privacy and Security," June 14, 2022

Mr. John Miller, Senior Vice President of Policy and General Counsel, Information Technology Industry Council (ITI)

The Honorable Kathleen Rice (D-NY)

1. Your testimony addresses the importance of digital advertising to the U.S. economy, noting that we can "protect the privacy of Americans while also preserving data innovation, including the business models that have helped the internet thrive and powered the growth of the global internet economy." In addressing the key role that digital advertising has to our economy, your testimony highlights some concerns with the current definition of "digital advertising" in the draft and that several states, including Virginia, Colorado, Utah, and Connecticut, seem to have struck the right balance here.

a. Can you speak more about ways we can improve our definition so that we don't end up with unintended consequences to the U.S. economy?

Response

Thank you for the question, which acknowledges the overarching point I made in my written testimony that the definition of targeted advertising as it appeared in the ADPPA discussion draft would in many ways not allow the ad-supported internet business model to continue, as, for instance, publishers would not be able to use their knowledge of the preferences and interests of their readers to show ads.

The good news is that the ADPPA Manager's Amendment remedied one of the central flaws in the Targeted Advertising definition that appeared in the draft by eliminating the language "derived from covered data collected over time *or* across third party websites or online services about the individual or unique identifier." (emphasis added). The problem in that original definition was the "or," which would have prevented first party publishers from being able to use the data that they collected from consumers viewing their content (as opposed to data provided by data brokers or other middlemen), which in turn would have prevented those entities from being able to show consumers ads that are relevant enough to generate the revenue needed to continue to support the content being provided. While simply replacing the "or" with an "and" to limit the definition to the use of data collected over time *and* across third party websites or online services would have been consistent with the approach taken in the states, the ADPPA Manager's Amendment eliminated the phrase entirely and thus also eliminated that problem.

However, the revised definition of "targeted advertising" in the ADPPA Manager's Amendment unfortunately added some new problematic language, the result of which is continuing confusion regarding how the ADPPA intends to address targeted advertising. For example, the targeted advertising definition's revised exception for contextual advertising is unnecessarily limiting. Contextual advertising should be allowed to take into account general trends known about the viewers of the applicable content. While ITI supports the prohibition of user profiles and related user data in contextual advertising, an allowance for the use of statistical, aggregate audience data and other non-covered data to inform a company's ad selection algorithms in these cases makes good sense, preserves user privacy, and performs well for advertisers.

Furthermore, the "targeted adverting" definition was expanded to include "content," which implicates all personalized content (paid and organic) across all services. It also brings into scope advertising based on first-party data. To the extent the rationale for this change was to not subject transfers of certain sensitive covered data to an opt-in requirement, there are more straightforward ways for the bill to address this issue without unnecessarily complicating and muddling the definition of "targeted advertising."

How the "targeted advertising" definition should be read relative to the revised duty of loyalty/data minimization section of the ADPPA is particularly confusing. On the one hand, the bill is now structured similarly to GDPR in that the data minimization section now expressly includes a list of permissible purposes (in other words what is not expressly allowed is prohibited), and the clear intention of this section appears to be to allow targeted advertising, subject to an opt out. However, while collecting sensitive data is now exempt from the opt in requirement if done for a permissible purpose specified in 101(b) (a broad exemption), transferring sensitive data is effectively prohibited and subjected to an opt in. This section, when coupled with the still broad definition of sensitive data, creates substantial confusion regarding whether opt-in or opt out applies in a variety of contexts, most notably regarding various forms of targeted advertising.

In particular, including sub. (xii) regarding video content or services in the "sensitive covered data definition" is creating significant confusion when juxtaposed with the bill's intent that targeted advertising should be "opt out" on relevant platforms, and sub (vii) regarding communications content would subject a wide swath of everyday communications to an opt in requirement. Those data categories should not be defined as sensitive covered data to avoid this confusion, or the list of permissible purposes should be expanded to eliminate this confusion regarding "targeted advertising."

The Honorable Michael Burgess (R-TX)

Mr. Miller, this bill divides data into that collected by "collectors" and that serviced by "processors."

As currently defined in this legislation, is there any chance that a processor could become, or be treated as, a collector?

Response

Thank you for the question. First, let me say that we appreciate the Manager's Amendment to ADPPA makes the effort to disentangle the term service provider (or processor) from covered entity (or controller as such entities are referred to in Europe's GDPR, or collector as framed in your question), making clearer the so-called "controller/processor distinction." The Manager's Amendment now defines covered entities or collectors much like an EU controller, as an entity "that alone or jointly with others determines the purposes and means of ...processing covered data." We also appreciate the intention to make the obligations attaching to collectors vs. processors clearer, as processors are now subject to only those provisions that expressly apply to processors. This is a major and welcome shift.

However – and I think your question alludes to this fact – while the ADPPA clearly intends there to be more stringent obligations on covered entities/collectors than service providers/processors, the reality is that many companies will indeed wear different hats (collector vs. processor) at different times – so I would not say one entity "becomes" another, but I would completely agree with the premise of your question that sometimes a processor could appropriately be treated as a collector in certain business contexts.

Unfortunately, there is still some confusion in the ADPPA Manager's Amendment regarding which obligations should attach to which entities and when. Since whether an entity is wearing a collector vs. processor hat carries different obligations, we recommend the bill include an accommodation for entities to reasonably determine which hat – collector or processor - they are wearing in which business use case. For example, delineating responsibilities when the entity is collecting directly from an individual versus analyzing or processing data on behalf of the collector.

One way to make sure this definitional distinction between covered entity/collector and service provider/processor is implemented effectively and clearly in the legislative text would be to insert "acting as a covered entity" or "acting as a service provider" throughout to further clarify which obligations are appropriate for CEs versus SPs with respect to each of the obligations enumerated in the bill. One reason this approach could be helpful in clearing up the confusion is because there are still a number of obligations imposed on service providers/processors that do not make sense given the context of how these entities typically interact with not only covered entities/collectors but data and customers, and as a result many of the obligations imposed on service providers/processors are unduly burdensome insofar as it will be difficult if not impossible for many of these entities to reasonably or practically comply with them, for instance because they lack visibility into or access to data or customers, or because the way SPs process data on behalf of CEs often varies by client.

To illustrate this point, obligations in ADPPA that currently apply to service providers/processors but which should be clarified as applying only to covered entities/collectors, or to "service providers/processors acting as covered entities/collectors," include: various "duty of loyalty" obligations that depend on the covered entity on whose behalf the service provider is processing data and that a service provider cannot possibly document at any one point in time. For example, categories of covered data collected or processed can change depending on the client, and the service provider often does not have visibility to the data it is processing on behalf of a covered entity/collector; the length of time a service provider intends to retain each category of covered data or the criteria for determining the retention time typically varies by client; and the description of data security practices employed may also differ from client to client.

Thank you again for the question and the opportunity to highlight the need to further clarify the obligations of collectors/covered entities vs. service providers/processors vs. service providers/processors acting as collectors/covered entities, as this is one of ITI's priority issues as the bill moves forward.

2. Mr. Miller, as a point of clarification, this legislation requires covered entities that engaged in targeted advertising to provide a clear way to opt-out of this targeted advertising.

a. If a person opts-out of targeted advertising, would they still receive generic advertisements?

Response

Thank you for the question. While I am not familiar with the term "generic advertising" my understanding is it typically refers to advertising related to a category or class of product rather than a particular brand. However, to the extent your question is asking is whether a person who opts-out of targeted advertising will nonetheless continue to receive some form of internet advertising, I think the answer likely depends on a variety of factors.

First, with respect to the premise of your question, while the ADPPA Manager's Amendment appears to intend to subject targeted advertising to a clear "opt-out" pursuant to the "targeted advertising" definition, when read in conjunction with various other provisions in the bill such as the definition of sensitive covered data, there actually exists quite a bit of confusion as to whether all targeted advertising is always subject to an opt-out, or whether some forms may sometimes be subject to an opt-in, and whether some species of targeted advertising may not be subject to even an opt-out.

To briefly illustrate some of the confusion that currently exists, the bill addresses at least three different meta-categories of targeted advertising: first-party targeted advertising, third-party targeted advertising, and contextual advertising. The restrictions in the bill vary from both meta-category to meta-category and sometimes within these categories, making it very difficult to answer your question in the abstract.

Examining how the ADPPA treats targeted advertising across these different meta-categories helps illustrate this confusion. For instance, it appears that first-party targeted advertising using data already collected for other permissible purposes may not be subject to either an opt in or opt out (sec. 101(b)(11), but first-party targeted advertising using data the covered entities did not collect for another permissible purpose and is not search/browsing history is opt out (101(b)(12)), but first-party targeted advertising using data covered entities did not collect for another permissible purpose, and is search/browsing history is opt in (sec. 201(a)(4)). Examining the different ways in which the bill appears to treat third party targeted advertising reveals similar variances and confusion. And while we believe the contextual advertising exception needs to be further amended/clarified, it appears that engaging in contextual advertising is not subject to an opt-out or opt-in requirement to the extent that such advertising does not use covered data.

The bottom line answer to your question as I understand it is that people who opt-out of "targeted advertising" will still receive some types of internet advertising, including even some forms of "targeted advertising" which appear to be permitted under the bill as currently drafted and as explained above.

* * *

June 30, 2022

The Honorable Maureen K. Ohlhausen
Former Acting-Chair, Federal Trade Commission
Co-Chair, 21st Century Privacy Coalition
700 K Street NW
Washington, DC 20001

Dear Ms. Ohlhausen:

Thank you for appearing before the Subcommittee on Consumer Protection and Commerce on Tuesday, June 14, 2022, at the hearing entitled "Protecting America's Consumers: Bipartisan Legislation to Strengthen Data Privacy and Security." I appreciate the time and effort you gave as a witness before the Committee on Energy and Commerce.

Pursuant to Rule 3 of the Committee on Energy and Commerce, members are permitted to submit additional questions to the witnesses for their responses, which will be included in the hearing record. Attached is a question directed to you from a member of the Committee. In preparing your answer to this question, please address your response to the member who has submitted the question in the space provided.

To facilitate the printing of the hearing record, please submit your response to this question no later than the close of business on Thursday, July 15, 2022. As previously noted, this transmittal letter and your response, as well as the responses from the other witnesses appearing at the hearing, will all be included in the hearing record. Your written responses should be transmitted by e-mail in the Word document provided to Ed Kaczmarski, Policy Analyst, at ed.kaczmarski@mail.house.gov. To help in maintaining the proper format for hearing records, please use the document provided to complete your responses.

Thank you for your prompt attention to this request. If you need additional information or have other questions, please contact Ed Kaczmarski with the Committee staff at (202) 225-2927.

Sincerely,
Frank Pallone, Jr.
Chairman

Attachment

cc: The Honorable Cathy McMorris Rodgers
Ranking Member
Committee on Energy and Commerce
The Honorable Jan Schakowsky
Chair
Subcommittee on Consumer Protection and Commerce

The Honorable Gus Bilirakis
Ranking Member
Subcommittee on Consumer Protection and Commerce

Attachment—Additional Questions for the Record, Subcommittee on Consumer Protection and Commerce, Hearing on "Protecting America's Consumers: Bipartisan Legislation to Strengthen Data Privacy and Security," June 14, 2022

The Honorable Maureen K. Ohlhausen, Former Acting Chair, Federal Trade Commission, Co-Chair 21st Century Privacy Coalition

The Honorable Michael Burgess (R-TX)

1. Mrs. Ohlhausen, in the 114th Congress, I was chairman of this subcommittee and introduced a bill to combat patent trolls, called the Targeting Rogue and Opaque Letters – or TROL – Act. I am pleased to see this legislation includes a process to help prevent abusive demand letters. As written, this legislation requires a person seeking a private right of action to first notify the Federal Trade Commission and their State Attorney General with their intent to seek to action and to wait 60 days before proceeding with a private right of action should the FTC and State Attorney General choose not to pursue the case.

a. Do you believe this provides sufficient protection against abusive demand letters? If not, do you have suggestions to strengthen this part of the legislation?

Response

Rep. Burgess, thank you for your questions and for your work on this urgently needed legislation. While I agree that any private right of action included in this legislation must be accompanied by strong guardrails, I believe this provision, while helpful, is unlikely on its own to prevent abusive, frivolous, and excessive litigation. In practice, a 60-day waiting period is unlikely to significantly deter abusive demand letters because many letters are likely to receive no response from the FTC or a State Attorney General. Instead, as outlined in my testimony, I believe further improvements to the private right of action are necessary before this Committee takes any further action.

b. How does this language provide necessary guardrails for businesses?

Response

As noted in my response to Question 1(a), I believe the language as currently drafted is unlikely to provide sufficient guardrails for businesses. For that reason, I believe covered entities should have an opportunity to cure any violations under the Act before individuals can avail themselves of a private right of action. Currently, Section 403(c) limits a right to cure only to actions for injunctive relief or pursuant to section 209 of the Act, and I am concerned that such a limitation opens the door to a broad variety of potentially abusive claims.

2. Mrs. Ohlhausen, this draft legislation provides for FTC rulemakings that correspond to specific sections of the bill rather than provide broad rulemaking authority. This legislation also authorizes the FTC to be appropriated such sums as may be necessary. I am generally opposed to an appropriation of "such sums…" because we can lose control over actions of the implementing agency.

a. Have there been any estimates or evaluations on the amount of funding the FTC will require to implement this legislation?

Response

Although I am not aware of any specific estimate or evaluations, it is vital that Congress appropriate adequate resources for the FTC to vigorously investigate and enforce violations of the law, efficiently implement the bill's required rulemaking, develop guidance for industry, and hire sufficient FTEs to fulfill the legislation's sweeping mandate. Currently, Section 401(a) of this legislation requires the FTC to create a new Bureau of Privacy, "comparable in structure, size, organization, and authority" to the existing Bureaus of Competition and Consumer Protection. In FY2022, for example, the Bureau of Consumer Protection operated on a budget of $191.4 million, while the Bureau of Competition had a budget of $159.5 million.[198] In light of the complexity of this legislation and its broad mandate, it is likely that a similar amount of funding will be necessary for the FTC to fulfill its statutory mission under this bill.

---

[198] FED. TRADE COMM'N, Fiscal Year 2023 Congressional Budget Justification – Bureau and Office Descriptions, at 51, https://www.ftc.gov/system/files/ftc_gov/pdf/P859900FY23CBJ.pdf.

Chapter 2

S. 3337. Digital Accountability and Transparency to Advance Privacy Act*

Committee on Commerce, Science, and Transportation

NOVEMBER 15, 2023

Ms. CORTEZ MASTO introduced the following bill; which was read twice and referred to the Committee on Commerce, Science, and Transportation

A Bill

To establish national data privacy standards in the United States, and for other purposes.

Be it enacted by the Senate and House of Representatives of the United States of America in Congress assembled,

Section 1. Short Title

This Act may be cited as the "Digital Accountability and Transparency to Advance Privacy Act" or the "DATA Privacy Act."

Sec. 2. Definitions

(a) IN GENERAL.—In this Act:

(1) COLLECT.—The term "collect" means taking any operation or set of operations to obtain covered data, including by automated means, including purchasing, leasing, assembling, recording, gathering, acquiring, or procuring.

(2) COMMISSION.—The term "Commission" means the Federal Trade Commission.

---

* This is an edited, reformatted and augmented version of 118th Congress; 1st Session; S. 3337; To establish national data privacy standards in the United States, and for other purposes, dated November 15, 2023.

In: Data Privacy and Security: Legislative Advances and Consumer Protection
Editor: Ricky K. Segura
ISBN: 979-8-89530-730-4

(3) COVERED DATA.—The term "covered data"—

(A) means any information that is—

(i) collected, processed, stored, or disclosed by a covered entity;

(ii) collected over the internet or other digital network; and

(iii)(I) linked to an individual or device associated with an individual; or

(II) practicably linkable to an individual or device associated with an individual, including by combination with separate information, by the covered entity or any potential recipient of the data; and

(B) does not include data that is—

(i) collected, processed, stored, or disclosed solely for the purpose of employment of an individual; or

(ii) lawfully made available to the public from Federal, State, or local government records.

(4) COVERED ENTITY.—The term "covered entity"—

(A) means any entity that collects, processes, stores, or discloses covered data; and

(B) does not include any entity that collects, processes, stores, or discloses covered data relating to fewer than 50,000 individuals and devices during any 12-month period.

(5) DISCLOSE.—The term "disclose" means taking any action with respect to covered data, including by automated means, to sell, share, provide, or otherwise transfer covered data to another entity, person, or the general public.

(6) PRIVACY ENHANCING TECHNOLOGY.—The term "privacy enhancing technology" means any—

(A) software solution, technical processes, or other technological means of enhancing the privacy and confidentiality of an individual's covered data in data or sets of data; or

(B) de-identification, anonymization, or pseudonymization technologies or techniques, filtering tools, anti-tracking technology, differential privacy tools, synthetic data generation tools, cryptographic techniques (such as secure multi-party computation and homomorphic encryption), or systems for federated learning.

(7) PRIVACY RISK.—The term "privacy risk" means potential harm to an individual resulting from the collection, processing, storage, or disclosure of covered data, including—

(A) direct or indirect financial loss;

(B) stigmatization or reputational harm;

(C) anxiety, embarrassment, fear, and other severe emotional trauma;

(D) loss of economic opportunity; or

(E) physical harm.

(8) PROCESS.—The term "process" means any operation or set of operations that is performed on covered data or on sets of covered data, including by automated means, including organizing, combining, adapting, altering, using, or transforming.

(9) PROTECTED CHARACTERISTIC.—The term "protected characteristic" means an individual's race, sex, gender, sexual orientation, nationality, religious belief, age, or disability status.

(10) PSEUDONYMOUS DATA.—The term "pseudonymous data" means covered data that may only be linked to the identity of an individual or the identity of a device associated with an individual if combined with separate information.

(11) REASONABLE INTEREST.—The term "reasonable interest" means—

(A) a compelling business, operational, administrative, legal, or educational justification for the collection, processing, storage, or disclosure of covered data exists; and (B) the interest does not subject the individual linked to the covered data to an unreasonable privacy risk.

(12) SENSITIVE DATA.—The term "sensitive data" means any covered data relating to—

(A) the health, biologic, physiologic, biometric, sexual life, or genetic information of an individual; or

(B) the precise geolocation information of a device associated with an individual.

(13) STORE.—The term "store" means any operation or set of operations to continue possession of covered data, including by automated means.

(14) THIRD PARTY SERVICE PROVIDER.—The term "third party service provider" means any covered entity that collects, processes, stores, or discloses covered data at the direction of, and for the sole benefit of, another covered entity under a contract.

(b) MODIFIED DEFINITION BY RULEMAKING.—If the Commission determines that a term defined in paragraph

(10) or (12) is not sufficient to protect an individual's data privacy, the Commission may promulgated regulations under section 553 of title 5, United States Code, to modify the definition as the Commission considers appropriate.

Sec. 3. Required Privacy Notice

(a) PRIVACY NOTICE.—Each covered entity shall post in an accessible location a notice that is concise, in context, in easily understandable language, accurate, clear, timely, updated, uses visualizations where appropriate, conspicuous, and free of charge regarding the covered entity's privacy practices.

(b) CONTENTS OF NOTICE.—The notice required bysubsection (a) shall include—

(1) a description of the covered data that theentity collects, processes, stores, and discloses, including the sources that provided the covered data if the covered entity did not collect the covered data from the individual;

(2) the purposes for and means by which the entity collects, processes, and stores the covereddata;

(3) the persons and entities to whom, and purposes for which, the covered entity discloses the covered data; and

(4) a conspicuous, clear, and understandable means for individuals to access the methods necessary to exercise their rights under sections 4 and 10 5.

Sec. 4. Required Data Practices

(a) REGULATIONS.—Not later than 1 year after the date of the enactment of this Act, the Commission shall promulgate regulations under section 553 of title 5, United States Code, that require covered entities to implement, practice, and maintain certain data procedures and processes that meet the following requirements:

(1) MINIMUM DATA PROCESSING REQUIREMENTS.—Except as provided in subsection (b), require covered entities to meet all of the following requirements regarding the means by and purposes for which covered data is collected, processed, stored,and disclosed:

(A) REASONABLE.—

(i) IN GENERAL.—Except as provided in paragraph (3), covered data collection, processing, storage, and disclosure practices must meet a reasonable interest of the covered entity, including—

(I) business, educational, and administrative operations that are relevant and appropriate to the context of the relationship between the covered entity and the individual linked to the covered data;

(II) relevant and appropriate product and service development and enhancement;

(III) preventing and detecting abuse, fraud, and other criminal activity;

(IV) reasonable communications and marketing practices that follow best practices, rules, and ethical standards;

(V) engaging in scientific, medical, or statistical research that follows commonly accepted ethical standards; or

(VI) any other purpose for which the Commission considers to be reasonable.

(ii) CONSIDERATIONS.—In promulgating regulations in accordance with this subparagraph, the Commission shall consider—

(I) the role of impact assessments in determining the privacy risk for high risk processing;

(II) the sensitivity of the covered data; and

(III) the impact of such regulations on small business.

(B) EQUITABLE.—

(i) IN GENERAL.—Covered data collection, processing, storage, and disclosure practices may not be for purposes that result in discrimination against a protected characteristic, including—

(I) discriminatory targeted advertising practices;

(II) price, service, or employment opportunity discrimination; or

(III) any other practice the Commission considers likely to result in discrimination against a protected characteristic.

(ii) CONSIDERATIONS.—In promulgating regulations in accordance with this subparagraph, the Commission shall consider—

(I) established civil rights laws, common law, and existing relevant consent decrees;

(II) the existing economic models and technology available in the digital advertising system;

(III) the role of algorithms and impact assessments; and

(IV) the impact of such regulations on small businesses.

(C) FORTHRIGHT.—

(i) IN GENERAL.—Covered data collection, processing, storage, and disclosure practices may not be accomplished with means or for purposes that are deceptive, including—

(I) the use of inconspicuous recording or tracking devices and methods;

(II) the disclosure of covered data that a reasonable individual believes to be the content of a private communication with another party or parties;

(III) notices, interfaces, or other representations likely to mislead consumers; or

(IV) any other practice that the Commission considers likely to mislead individuals regarding the purposes for and means by which covered data is collected, processed, stored, or disclosed.

(ii) CONSIDERATIONS.—In promulgating regulations in accordance with this subparagraph, the Commission shall consider—

(I) existing relevant consent decrees;

(II) the reasonable expectations of consumers;

(III) research on deceptive practices;

(IV) the role of deceptive user interfaces; and

(V) the impact of such regulations on small businesses.

(2) REQUIREMENTS FOR OPT-OUT CONSENT.— Except as provided in subsection (b), require covered entities to provide individuals with conspicuous access to a method that is in easily understandable language, concise, accurate, clear, to opt-out of any collection, processing, storage, or disclosure of covered data linked to the individual.

(3) REQUIREMENTS FOR AFFIRMATIVE CONSENT.—Except as provided in subsection (b), require covered entities to provide individuals with a notice that is concise, in easily understandable language, accurate, clear, timely, and conspicuous to express affirmative, opt in consent—

(A) before the covered entity collects or discloses sensitive data linked to the individual; or

(B) before the covered entity collects, processes, stores, or discloses data for purposes which are outside the context of the relationship of the covered entity with the individual linked to the data, including—

(i) the use of covered data beyond what is necessary to provide, improve, or market a good or service that the individual requests;

(ii) the processing or disclosure of covered data differs in material ways from the purposes described in the privacy policy that was in effect when the data was collected;

(iii) any other purpose that Commission considers outside of context.

(4) DATA MINIMIZATION REQUIREMENTS.—Except as provided in subsection (b), require covered entities to—

(A) take reasonable measures to limit the collection, processing, storage, and disclosure of covered data to the amount that is necessary to carry out the purposes for which the data is collected; and

(B) store covered data only as long as is reasonably necessary to carry out the purposes for which the data was collected.

(b) EXEMPTIONS.—Subsection (a) shall not apply if the limitations on the collection, processing, storage, or disclosure of covered data would—

(1) inhibit detection or prevention of a security risk or incident;

(2) risk the health, safety, or property of the covered entity or individual; or

(3) prevent compliance with an applicable law (including regulations) or legal process.

Sec. 5. Individual Control over Data Use

(a) REGULATIONS.—Not later than 1 year after the date of the enactment of this Act, the Commission shall promulgate regulations under section 553 of title 5, United States Code, to require covered entities to provide conspicuous, understandable, clear, and free of charge method to—

(1) upon the request of an individual, provide the individual with access to, or an accurate representation of, covered data linked to with the individual or the individual's device stored by the covered entity;

(2) upon the request of an individual, provide the individual with a means to dispute and resolve the accuracy or completeness of the covered data linked to the individual or the individual's device stored by the entity;

(3) upon the request of an individual, delete any covered data that the covered entity stores linked to the individual or the individual's device; and

(4) when technically feasible, upon the request of an individual, allow the individual to transmit or transfer covered data linked to the individual or the individual's device that is maintained by the entity to the individual in a format that is standardized and interoperable.

(b) PSEUDONYMOUS DATA.—If the covered data that an individual has requested processed under subsection (a) is pseudonymous data, a covered entity may decline the request if processing the request is not technically feasible.

(c) TIMELINESS OF REQUESTS.—In fulfilling any requests made by the individual under subsection (a) the covered entity shall act in as timely a manner as is reasonably possible.

(d) ACCESS TO SAME SERVICE.—A covered entity shall not discriminate against an individual because of any action the individual took under their rights described in subsection (a), including—

(1) denying goods or services to the individual;

(2) charging, or advertising, different prices or rates for goods or services; or

(3) providing different quality of goods or services.

(e) CONSIDERATION.—The Commission shall allow a covered entity, by contract, to provide relevant obligations to the individual under subsection (a) on behalf of a third party service provider that collects, processes, stores, or discloses covered data only on behalf of the covered entity.

Sec. 6. Information Security Standards

(a) REQUIRED DATA SECURITY PRACTICES.—

(1) REGULATIONS.—Not later than 1 year after the date of enactment of this Act, the Commission shall promulgate regulations under section 553 of title 5, United States Code, to require covered entities to establish and implement policies and procedures regarding information security practices for the treatment and protection of covered data taking into consideration—

(A) the level of identifiability of the covered data and the associated privacy risk;

(B) the sensitivity of the covered data collected, processed, and stored and the associated privacy risk; and

(C) the currently available and widely accepted technological, administrative, and physical means to protect covered data under the control of the covered entity;

(D) the cost associated with implementing, maintaining, and regularly reviewing the safeguards; and

(E) the impact of these requirements on small and medium sized businesses.

(2) LIMITATIONS.—In promulgating the regulations required under this section, the Commission shall consider a covered entity who is in compliance with existing information security laws that the Commission determines are sufficiently rigorous to be in compliance with this section with respect to particular types of covered data to the extent those types of covered data are covered by such law, including the following:

(A) Title V of the Gramm-Leach-Bliley Act 20 (15 U.S.C. 6801 et seq.).

(B) The Health Information Technology for Economic and Clinical Health Act (42 23 U.S.C. 17931).

(C) The Health Insurance Portability and Accountability Act of 1996 Security Rule (45 3 CFR 160.103 and part 164).

(D) Any other existing law requiring a covered entity to implement and maintain information security practices and procedures that the Commission determines to be sufficiently rigorous.

Sec. 7. Privacy Protection Officers

(a) APPOINTMENT OF A PRIVACY PROTECTION OFFICER.—Each covered entity with annual revenue in excess of $50,000,000 the prior year shall designate at least 1 appropriately qualified employee as a privacy protection officer who shall—

(1) educate employees about compliance requirements;

(2) train employees involved in data processing;

(3) conduct regular, comprehensive audits to ensure compliance and make records of the audits available to enforcement authorities upon request;

(4) maintain updated, clear, and understandable records of all data security practices undertaken by the covered entity;

(5) serve as the point of contact between the covered entity and enforcement authorities; and

(6) advocate for policies and practices within the covered entity that promote individual privacy.

(b) PROTECTIONS.—The privacy protection officer shall not be dismissed or otherwise penalized by the covered entity for performing any of the tasks assigned to the person under this section.

Sec. 8. Research into Privacy Enhancing Technology

(a) NATIONAL SCIENCE FOUNDATION SUPPORT OF RESEARCH ON PRIVACY ENHANCING TECHNOLOGY.—The Director of the National Science Foundation, in consultation with other relevant Federal agencies (as determined by the Director), shall support merit-reviewed and competitively awarded research on privacy enhancing technologies, which may include—

(1) fundamental research on technologies for de-identification, pseudonymization, anonymization, or obfuscation to protect individuals' privacy in data sets;

(2) fundamental research on algorithms, machine learning, and other computational processes or tools used to protect individual privacy when collecting, storing, sharing, aggregating, or analyzing data;

(3) fundamental research on technologies that promote data minimization principles in data collection, sharing, transfers, retention, and analytics;

(4) research awards on privacy enhancing technologies coordinated with other relevant Federal agencies and programs;

(5) research on barriers to, and opportunities for, the adoption of privacy enhancing technologies, including studies on effective business models for privacy enhancing technologies; and

(6) international cooperative research, awards, challenges, and pilot projects on privacy enhancing technologies with key allies and partners of the United States.

(b) INTEGRATION INTO THE COMPUTER AND NETWORK SECURITY PROGRAM.—Subparagraph (D) of section 4(a)(1) of the Cyber Security Research and Development Act (15 U.S.C. 7403(a)(1)(D)) is amended to read as follows:

"(D) privacy enhancing technologies and confidentiality."

(c) COORDINATION WITH THE NATIONAL INSTITUTE OF STANDARDS AND TECHNOLOGY AND OTHER STAKEHOLDERS.—

(1) IN GENERAL.—The Director of the Office of Science and Technology Policy, acting through the Networking and Information Technology Research and Development Program, shall coordinate with the Director of the National Science Foundation, the Director of the National Institute of Standards and Technology, and the Commission to accelerate the development and use of privacy enhancing technologies.

(2) OUTREACH.—The Director of the National Institute of Standards and Technology shall conduct outreach to—

(A) receive input from private, public, and academic stakeholders on the development and potential uses of privacy enhancing technologies; and

(B) develop ongoing public and private sector engagement to create and disseminate voluntary, consensus-based resources to increase the integration of privacy enhancing technologies in data collection, sharing, transfers, retention, and analytics by the public and private sectors.

(d) REPORT ON RESEARCH AND STANDARDS DEVELOPMENT.—Not later than 2 years after the date of enactment of this Act, the Director of the Office of Science and Technology Policy, acting through the Networking and Information Technology Research and Development Program, shall, in coordination with the Director of the National Science Foundation, the Director of the National Institute of Standards and Technology, and the Commission, submit to the Committee on Commerce, Science, and Transportation of the Senate, the Subcommittee on Commerce, Justice, Science, and Related Agencies of the Committee on Appropriations of the Senate, the Committee on Science, Space, and Technology of the House of Representatives, and the Subcommittee on Commerce, Justice, Science, and Related Agencies of the Committee on Appropriations of the House of Representatives, a report containing—

(1) the progress of research on privacy enhancing technologies;

(2) the progress of the development of voluntary resources described under subsection 20 (c)(2)(B); and

(3) any policy recommendations of the Directors and the Commission that could facilitate and improve communication and coordination between the private sector, the National Science Foundation, and relevant Federal agencies through the implementation of privacy enhancing technologies.

Sec. 9. Enforcement

(a) ENFORCEMENT BY THE COMMISSION.—

(1) IN GENERAL.—This Act and the regulations prescribed under this Act, other than the provisions of and amendments made by section 8, shall be enforced by the Commission under the Federal Trade Commission Act (15 U.S.C. 41 et seq.).

(2) UNFAIR OR DECEPTIVE ACTS OR PRACTICES.—A violation of this Act or a regulation prescribed under this Act shall be treated as a violation of a rule defining an unfair or deceptive act or practice prescribed under section 18(a)(1)(B) of the Federal Trade Commission Act (15 U.S.C. 16 57a(a)(1)(B)).

(3) ACTIONS BY THE COMMISSION.—Subject to paragraph (4), the Commission shall prevent any person from violating this Act or a regulation prescribed under this Act in the same manner, by the same means, and with the same jurisdiction, powers, and duties as though all applicable terms and provisions of the Federal Trade Commission Act (15 U.S.C. 41 et seq.) were incorporated into and made a part of this Act, and any person who violates this Act or such regulation shall be subject to the penalties and entitled to the privileges and immunities provided in the Federal Trade Commission Act (15 U.S.C. 41 et seq.).

(4) COMMON CARRIERS.—Notwithstanding section 4, 5(a)(2), or 6 of the Federal Trade Commission Act (15 U.S.C. 44, 45(a)(2), and 46) or any jurisdictional limitation of the Commission, the Commission shall also enforce this Act, in the same manner provided in paragraphs (1), (2), and (3) with respect to common carriers subject to the Communications Act of 1934 (47 U.S.C. 151 et seq.) and Acts amendatory thereof and supplementary thereto.

(b) ENFORCEMENT BY STATE ATTORNEYS GENERAL.—

(1) IN GENERAL.—

(A) CIVIL ACTIONS.—In any case in which the attorney general of a State has reason to believe that an interest of the residents of that State has been or is threatened or adversely affected by the engagement of any person in a practice that violates this Act or a regulation prescribed under this Act, the State, as parens patriae, may bring a civil action on behalf of the residents of the State in a district court of the United States of appropriate jurisdiction to—

(i) enjoin that practice;

(ii) enforce compliance with this Act or such regulation;

(iii) obtain damages, restitution, or other compensation on behalf of residents of the State;

(iv) impose a civil penalty in an amount that is not greater than the product of the number of individuals whose information was affected by a violation and 13 $40,000; or

(v) obtain such other relief as the court may consider to be appropriate.

(B) ADJUSTMENT FOR INFLATION.—Beginning on the date that the Consumer Price Index is first published by the Bureau of Labor Statistics that is after 1 year after the date of enactment of this Act, and each year thereafter, the amounts specified in subparagraph (A)(iv) shall be increased by the percentage increase in the Consumer Price Index published on that date from the Consumer Price Index published the previous year.

(C) NOTICE.—

(i) IN GENERAL.—Before filing an action under subparagraph (A), the attorney general of the State involved shall provide to the Commission—

(I) written notice of that action; and

(II) a copy of the complaint for that action.

(ii) EXEMPTION.—

(I) IN GENERAL.—Clause (i) shall not apply with respect to the filing of an action by an attorney general of a State under this paragraph if the attorney general determines that it is not feasible to provide the notice described in that clause before the filing of the action.

(II) NOTIFICATION.—In an action described in subclause (I), the attorney general of a State shall provide notice and a copy of the complaint to the Commission at the same time as the attorney general files the action.

(c) RIGHTS OF THE COMMISSION.—

(1) INTERVENTION BY THE COMMISSION.—The Commission may intervene in any civil action brought by the attorney general of a State under subsection (b) and upon intervening—

(A) be heard on all matters arising in the civil action; and

(B) file petitions for appeal of a decision in the civil action.

(2) POWERS.—Nothing in this subsection may be construed to prevent the attorney general of a State from exercising the powers conferred on the attorney general by the laws of the State to conduct investigations, to administer oaths or affirmations, or to compel the attendance of witnesses or the production of documentary or other evidence.

(3) ACTION BY THE COMMISSION.—If the Commission institutes a civil action for violation of this title or a regulation promulgated under this title, no attorney general of a State may bring a civil action under subsection (b) against any defendant named in the complaint of the Commission for violation of this Act or a regulation promulgated under this Act that is alleged in the complaint.

(d) VENUE AND SERVICE OF PROCESS.—

(1) VENUE.—Any action brought under subsection (b) may be brought in—

(A) the district court of the United States that meets applicable requirements relating to venue under section 1391 of title 28, United States Code; or

(B) another court of competent jurisdiction.

(2) SERVICE OF PROCESS.—In an action brought under subsection (b), process may be served in any district in which the defendant—

(A) is an inhabitant; or

(B) may be found.

(e) ACTION OF OTHER STATE OFFICIALS.—

(1) IN GENERAL.—In addition to civil actions brought by attorneys general under subsection (b), any other officer of a State who is authorized by the State to do so may bring a civil action under subsection (b), subject to the same requirements and limitations that apply under this subsection to civil actions brought by attorneys general.

(2) SAVINGS PROVISION.—Nothing in this subsection may be construed to prohibit an authorized official of a State from initiating or continuing any proceeding in a court of the State for a violation of any civil or criminal law of the State.

(f) PRESERVATION OF AUTHORITY.—Nothing in this Act shall be construed to limit the authority of the Federal Trade Commission under any other provision of law.

Sec. 10. Additional Enforcement Resources

(a) IN GENERAL.—Notwithstanding any other provision of law the Commission may, without regard to the civil service laws (including regulations), appoint not more than 300 additional personnel for the purposes of enforcing privacy and data security laws and regulations.

(b) AUTHORIZATION OF APPROPRIATIONS.—There is authorized to be appropriated to the Commission such sums as may be necessary to carry out this section.

Chapter 3

Generative Artificial Intelligence and Data Privacy: A Primer*

Kristen E. Busch

Overview

Since the public release of Open AI's ChatGPT, Google's Bard, and other similar systems, some Members of Congress have expressed interest in the risks associated with "generative artificial intelligence (AI)." Although exact definitions vary, generative AI is a type of AI that can generate new content—such as text, images, and videos—through learning patterns from pre-existing data. It is a broad term that may include various technologies and techniques from AI and machine learning (ML).[1]

Generative AI models have received significant attention and scrutiny due to their potential harms, such as risks involving privacy, misinformation, copyright, and non-consensual sexual imagery. This report focuses on privacy issues and relevant policy considerations for Congress. Some policymakers and stakeholders have raised privacy concerns about how individual data may be used to develop and deploy generative models. These concerns are not new or unique to generative AI, but the scale, scope, and capacity of such technologies may present new privacy challenges for Congress.

---

* This is an edited, reformatted and augmented version of Congressional Research Service, Publication No. R47569, dated May 23, 2023.

[1] There are various definitions of AI in statute and agency guidance. For example, the National Artificial Intelligence Initiative Act of 2020 (P.L. 116-283) defines AI as "a machine-based system that can, for a given set of human-defined objectives, make predictions, recommendations or decisions influencing real or virtual environments. Artificial intelligence systems use machine and human-based inputs to—(A) perceive real and virtual environments; (B) abstract such perceptions into models through analysis in an automated manner; and (C) use model inference to formulate options for information or action." Artificial intelligence and machine learning (ML) are often used interchangeably, but ML is a subfield of AI that focuses on systems that can "learn" and improve through experience and data. For more information on this distinction, see Columbia Engineering "Artificial Intelligence (AI) vs. Machine Learning," https://ai.engineering.columbia.edu/ai-vs-machine-learning/. For more information on artificial intelligence and machine learning, see CRS Report R46795, *Artificial Intelligence: Background, Selected Issues, and Policy Considerations*, by Laurie A. Harris.

In: Data Privacy and Security: Legislative Advances and Consumer Protection
Editor: Ricky K. Segura
ISBN: 979-8-89530-730-4

Generative AI at a Glance

Major Developers and Selected Products:[2]

- OpenAI (with partnerships and funding from Microsoft)—"ChatGPT" chatbot, "DALL-E" image generator
- Google—"Bard" chatbot
- Meta—"LLaMA" research tool, "Make-A-Video" video generator
- Anthropic (founded by former employees of OpenAI)—"Claude" chatbot
- Stability AI—"Stable Diffusion" image generator
- Hugging Face—BLOOM language model
- NVIDIA—"NeMo" chatbot, "Picasso" visual content generator

Types of Applications:

- Chatbots—systems that simulate human conversation, often in question-and-answer format
- Image generators—systems that generate images based on an input or "prompt"
- Video generators—systems that generate videos based on an input or "prompt," sometimes called deepfakes
- Voice clones—systems that generate speech and voice sounds, sometimes called audio deepfakes

What Is Generative AI?

Generative AI can generate new content—such as text, images, and videos—through learning patterns from data.[3] There are many types of generative AI models (see Figure 1), which can produce content based on different inputs or "prompts." For example, some models can produce images from text prompts (e.g., Midjourney, Stable Diffusion, DALL-E), while others create videos (e.g., Gen2 or Meta's Make-A-Video).

Some scholars and policymakers have recently coined the term "general-purpose models" (GPAI) to describe applications like ChatGPT that can complete various functions.[4] These GPAI models may have a wide range of down-stream applications compared to single-purpose

[2] Six of the seven listed companies were identified based on participation in White House initiatives to develop "public assessments" of existing generative AI systems. Meta was not included in the White House announcement. "Fact Sheet: Biden-Harris Administration Announces New Actions to Promote Responsible AI Innovation that Protects Americans' Rights and Safety," White House, May 4, 2023, https://www.whitehouse.gov/briefing-room/statements-releases/2023/05/04/fact-sheet-biden-harris-administration-announces-new-actions-to-promote-responsible-ai-innovation-that-protects-americans-rights-and-safety/.

[3] Generative AI models may use different technical approaches and techniques, such as generative adversarial networks (GANs) or generative pre-trained transformers (GPTs). The colloquial term "deep fakes," which refers to realistic machine-generated images, videos, and audio, may also fall under the umbrella term of "generative AI." Deepfakes are typically generated through GANs.

[4] European Parliament, "General-Purpose Artificial Intelligence," https://www.europarl.europa.eu/RegData/etudes/ATAG/2023/745708/EPRS_ATA(2023)745708_EN.pdf.

models designed for a specific task. Many general-purpose AI applications are built on top of large language models (LLMs) that can recognize, predict, translate, summarize, and generate language.[5] LLMs are a subset of generative AI and are characterized as "large" due, in part, to the massive amount of data necessary for training the model to learn the rules of language.

Image Generator

Prompt: *"The Library of Congress building in the style of Van Gogh."*

Response:

Chatbot

Prompt: *"Write a 4 sentence poem about the Library of Congress."*

Response:

"In the heart of D.C., there stands a place
A temple of knowledge, a palace of grace
The Library of Congress, a marvel to see
A monument to learning, for you and me

Rows upon rows of books, towering high
A treasury of history, never to die
Where stories and knowledge, together reside
A beacon of wisdom, that cannot be denied"

Source: Stable Diffusion and ChatGPT, via CRS. The image was generated by Stable Diffusion and the text response was generated by ChatGPT.

Figure 1. Examples of Generative AI Models.

How Do Generative AI Models Use Data?

Data is essential to train and fine-tune AI models. Generative AI models require especially large datasets for training and fine-tuning.

Definitions

- Training a model refers to providing a model with data to learn from, often called a training dataset. After a model is trained to recognize patterns from one dataset, some models can be provided with new data and still recognize patterns or predict results.
- Fine-tuning a model refers to training a previously trained model on new data, or otherwise adjusting an existing model.[6]

---

[5] Bender, Gebru, et al., "On the Dangers of Stochastic Parrots: Can Language Models Be Too Big?" March 2023, ACM Conference on Fairness, Accountability, and Transparency, https://doi.org/10.1145/3442188.3445922; Samuel Bowman, "Eight Things to Know About Large Language Models," April 2023, https://arxiv.org/pdf/2304.00612.pdf.

[6] For example, fine-tuning could include adjusting a pre-existing model's parameters.

Generative AI models, particularly LLMs, require massive amounts of data. For example, OpenAI's ChatGPT was built on a LLM that trained, in part, on over 45 terabytes of text data obtained (or "scraped") from the internet. The LLM was also trained on entries from Wikipedia and corpora of digitized books.[7] Open AI's GPT-3 models were trained on approximately 300 billion "tokens" (or pieces of words) scraped from the web and had over 175 billion parameters, which are variables that influence properties of the training and resulting model.[8]

Critics contend that such models rely on privacy-invasive methods for mass data collection, typically without the consent or compensation of the original user, creator, or owner.[9] Additionally, some models may be trained on sensitive data and reveal personal information to users. In a company blog post, Google AI researchers noted, "Because these datasets can be large (hundreds of gigabytes) and pull from a range of sources, they can sometimes contain sensitive data, including personally identifiable information (PII)—names, phone numbers, addresses, etc., even if trained on public data."[10] Academic and industry research has found that some existing LLMs may reveal sensitive data or personal information from their training datasets.[11]

Some models are used for commercial purposes or embedded in other downstream applications. For example, companies may purchase subscription versions of ChatGPT to embed in their various services or products. Khan Academy, Duolingo, Snapchat, and other companies have partnered with OpenAI to deploy ChatGPT in their services.[12] However, individuals may not know their data was used to train models that are monetized and deployed across such applications.

Some countries have taken action against AI developers for improper use of personal information. For example, the Italian Data Protection Authority issued a temporary ban preventing OpenAI from using Italian users' data.[13] After agreeing to certain changes—such as allowing users to submit removal requests for personal data under the EU's General Data Protection Regulation (GDPR)—OpenAI restored access to its service for users in Italy.[14]

---

[7] Brown, et al., "Language Models Are Few-Shot Learners," July 22, 2020, https://arxiv.org/abs/2005.14165.

[8] According to OpenAI, their models were trained on some datasets with a total of 300 billion tokens. A token is a piece of a word. One token is around ¾ of a word. Brown, et al., "Language Models Are Few-Shot Learners," July 22, 2020, https://arxiv.org/abs/2005.14165.

[9] Matt Burgess, "ChatGPT Has a Big Privacy Problem," *Wired*, April 4, 2023, https://www.wired.com/story/italy-ban- chatgpt-privacy-gdpr/.

[10] Nicholas Carlini, "Privacy Considerations in Large Language Models," December 15, 2020, Google Research Blog, https://ai.googleblog.com/2020/12/privacy-considerations-in-large.html.

[11] Nicholas Carlini et al., "Extracting Training Data from Large Language Models," Jun 15, 2021, https://arxiv.org/abs/ 2012.07805.

[12] Alex Heath, "Snapchat Is Releasing Its Own AI Chatbot Powered by ChatGPT," *The Verge*, February 27, 2023, https://www.theverge.com/2023/2/27/23614959/snapchat-my-ai-chatbot-chatgpt-openai-plus-subscription; "Introducing Duolingo Max, a Learning Experience Powered by GPT-4," March 14, 2023, Duolingo Blog, https://blog.duolingo.com/duolingo-max/; Sal Khan, "Harnessing GPT-4 So That All Students Benefit. A Nonprofit Approach for Equal Access," Khan Academy, March 14, 2023, https://blog.khanacademy.org/harnessing-ai-so-that-all-students-benefit-a-nonprofit-approach-for-equal-access/.

[13] Italian Data Protection Data Protection Authority (Garante per la protezione dei dati personali or GPDP), March 31, 2023, https://www.gpdp.it/web/guest/home/docweb/-/docweb-display/docweb/9870847#english.

[14] Adi Robertson, "ChatGPT Returns to Italy After Ban," April 28, 2023, *The Verge*, https://www.theverge.com/2023/4/28/23702883/chatgpt-italy-ban-lifted-gpdp-data-protection-age-verification.

Where Does the Data Come from?

Many AI developers do not disclose the exact details of their training datasets. For generative AI, most training data is "scraped" from publicly available web pages before it is repackaged and sold, or in some cases, made freely available to AI developers.

Some AI developers rely on popular large datasets such as "Colossal Clean Crawled Corpus" (C4) and "Common Crawl," which are amassed through web crawling (i.e., software that systematically browses public internet sites and collects information from each available web page). Similarly, AI image generators are commonly trained on a dataset called LAION, which contains billions of images scraped from internet sites and their text descriptions.[15] Some companies might also use proprietary datasets for training.

Generative AI datasets can include information posted on publicly available internet sites, including PII and sensitive and copyrighted content. They may also include publicly available content that is erroneous, pornographic, or potentially harmful. Since data may be scraped without the creator's consent, some artists, content creators, and others have begun to use new tools such as "HaveIBeenTrained" to identify and report their own content in such databases. In a 2023 investigation, the *Washington Post* and Allen Institute for AI analyzed the websites scraped for the C4 dataset, which is used by AI developers including Google, Facebook, and OpenAI.[16] The investigation found that the C4 dataset included websites with copyrighted content as well as potentially sensitive information, such as state voter registration records.

These forms of data collection may also raise questions about copyright ownership and fair use. For a discussion of copyright issues and generative AI, see CRS Legal Sidebar LSB10922, *Generative Artificial Intelligence and Copyright Law*, by Christopher T. Zirpoli.

What Happens to Data Shared with Generative AI Models?

Some critics have also raised concerns that user data shared with a generative AI application—such as a chatbot—may be misused or abused without the user's knowledge. For example, a user may reveal sensitive health information while conversing with a health care chatbot without realizing their information could be stored and used to re-train the models or for other commercial purposes. Many existing chatbots have terms of service that allow the company to re- use user data to "develop and improve their services."

These concerns may be particularly pertinent for generative models used in interactions or services that commonly result in the disclosure of sensitive information such as advising, therapy health care, legal, or financial services. In response, some critics have argued that chatbots and other generative AI models should require affirmative consent from users or provide clear disclosure of how user data is collected, used, and stored.

---

15 Marissa Newman and Aggi Cantrill, "The Future of AI Relies on a High School Teacher's Free Database," Bloomberg, April 23, 2023, https://www.bloomberg.com/news/features/2023-04-24/a-high-school-teacher-s-free- image-database-powers-ai-unicorns#xj4y7vzkg.

16 Kevin Schaul, Szu Yu Chen, and Nitasha Tiku, "Inside the Secret List of Websites That Make AI Like ChatGPT Sound Smart," April 19, 2023, *Washington Post*, https://www.washingtonpost.com/technology/interactive/2023/ai- chatbot-learning/.

Policy Considerations for Congress

Existing Data Privacy and Related Laws

The United States does not currently have a comprehensive data privacy law. Congress has enacted a number of laws that create data requirements for certain industries and subcategories of data, but these statutory protections are not comprehensive. For example, the Gramm-Leach-Bliley Act (P.L. 106-102) regulates financial institutions' use of nonpublic personal information, while the Health Insurance Portability and Accountability Act (HIPAA, P.L. 104-191) requires covered entities to protect certain health information. Under current U.S. law, generative AI may implicate certain privacy laws depending on the context, developer, type of data, and purpose of the model. For example, if a company offers a chatbot in a videogame or other online service directed at children, the company could be required to meet certain requirements under the Children's Online Privacy Protection Act (COPPA, P.L. 105-277).

Additionally, certain state laws on privacy, biometrics, and AI may have implications for generative AI applications. In many cases, the collection of personal information typically implicates certain state privacy laws that provide an individual a "right to know" what a business collects about them; how data is used and shared; the "right to access and delete" their data; or the "right to opt-out" of data transfers and sales.[17] However, some of these laws include exemptions for the collection of public data, which may raise questions about how and whether they apply to generative AI tools that use information scraped from the internet.

In the absence of a comprehensive federal data privacy law, some individuals and groups have turned to other legal frameworks (e.g., copyright, defamation, right of publicity) to address potential privacy violations from generative AI and other AI tools. For example, some companies have faced class action lawsuits for possible violations of right of publicity state laws, which protect against unauthorized use of an individual's likeness for commercial purposes.[18]

Congress may consider enacting comprehensive federal privacy legislation that specifically addresses generative AI tools and related concerns. In doing so, Congress may consider and evaluate similar state and international efforts. For example, the European Union's (EU) proposed AI Act includes various articles on data regulation, disclosures, and documentation, among other requirements. The EU AI Act recently added a category for general purpose AI systems and foundation models, another term used for AI models that train on large amounts of data and can be adapted for various tasks.[19]

---

[17] For example, the California Consumer Privacy Act (CCPA) and California Consumer Privacy Regulation (CPRA) provide certain privacy rights to California rights. California Office of the Attorney General, "California Consumer Privacy Act (CCPA)," May 10, 2023, https://oag.ca.gov/privacy/ccpa. For more information on the CCPA or data privacy laws, see CRS Legal Sidebar LSB10213, *California Dreamin' of Privacy Regulation: The California Consumer Privacy Act and Congress*, coordinated by Eric N. Holmes; and CRS Report R45631, *Data Protection Law: An Overview*, by Stephen P. Mulligan and Chris D. Linebaugh.

[18] Isaiah Poritz, "AI Celebrity 'Deepfakes' Clash with Web of State Publicity Laws," Bloomberg Law, April 14, 2023, https://news.bloomberglaw.com/ip-law/ai-celebrity-deepfakes-clash-with-web-of-state-publicity-laws.

[19] European Parliament, "AI Act: A Step Closer to the First Rules on Artificial Intelligence," press release, May 11, 2023, https://www.europarl.europa.eu/news/en/press-room/20230505IPR84904/ai-act-a-step-closer-to-the-first-rules- on-artificial-intelligence.

Proposed Privacy Legislation

Some Members of Congress have proposed various comprehensive or targeted privacy bills with requirements that could impact generative AI applications. These are three common mechanisms included in various privacy bills:

- *Notice and Disclosure Requirements.* Currently, most generative AI applications do not provide notice or acquire consent from individuals to collect and use their data for training purposes.
  Congress may consider requiring companies developing or deploying generative AI systems to (1) acquire consent from individuals before collecting or using their data, or (2) notify individuals that their data will be collected and used for certain purposes, such as training models. Some scholars dispute the efficacy of notice and consent requirements.[20]
- *Opt-out Requirements.* Congress may consider requiring companies to provide users an option to opt-out of data collection. Of note, opt-out systems may not necessarily protect data that is publicly-scraped from the web, and may be cumbersome for individuals to exercise.
- *Deletion and Minimization Requirements.* Congress may also consider requiring companies to provide mechanisms for users to delete their data from existing datasets or require maximum retention periods for personal data. Currently, most leading chatbots and other AI models do not provide options for users to delete their personal information.

In considering such proposals, Congress may also wish to consider practical challenges users may face exercising specific privacy rights as well as potential challenges for companies in complying with certain types of legal requirements and user requests.

Existing Agency Authorities

Various federal agencies may enforce laws relevant to AI and data privacy. The Federal Trade Commission (FTC) has been active in addressing data privacy issues and has taken various actions involving AI. The FTC has applied its broad authorities over "unfair or deceptive acts or practices in commerce" to cases related to data privacy and data security. In recent months, the commission reaffirmed that its authorities also apply to new AI tools.[21] Chairman Khan

---

[20] Claire Park, "How "Notice and Consent" Fails to Protect Our Privacy," New America Open Technology Institute, March 23, 2020, https://www.newamerica.org/oti/blog/how-notice-and-consent-fails-to-protect-our-privacy/.

[21] The Federal Trade Commission (FTC) released multiple blog posts to caution companies against using AI to deceive or mislead consumers. The FTC's recent blog post states that the FTC's "unfair or deceptive acts or practices" (UDAP) authorities could apply to companies that develop, sell, or use an AI system that is "effectively designed" to deceive consumers, "even if not the system's original purpose." Michael Atleson, "Keep Your AI Claims in Check," FTC Business Blog, February 27, 2023, https://www.ftc.gov/business-guidance/blog/2023/02/keep-your-ai-claims-check; Michael Atleson, "Chatbots, Deepfakes, and Voice Clones: AI Deception for Sale," FTC Business Blog, March 20, 2023, https://www.ftc.gov/business-guidance/blog/2023/03/chatbots-deepfakes-voice-clones-ai-deception-sale.

stated, "there is no AI exemption to the laws on the books, and the FTC will vigorously enforce the law to combat unfair or deceptive practices or unfair methods of competition."[22]

The data collection practices of AI companies may also raise competition concerns. At the 2023 Annual Antitrust Enforcers Summit, Chair Khan stated, "As you have machine learning that depends on huge amounts of data and also depends on huge amounts of storage, we need to be very vigilant to make sure that this is not just another site for the big companies becoming bigger and really squelching rivals."[23] The development of AI models may also require significant computational and financial resources, which may preclude new competitors and entrench incumbents.[24]

In evaluating existing agency authorities, Congress may consider updating or providing additional specific authorities to federal agencies to address AI and related privacy issues. Additionally, Congress could consider what resources federal agencies may require to conduct additional oversight of AI and privacy issues.

Regulation of Data-Scraping

There are currently no federal laws that ban the scraping of publicly available data from the internet. The Computer Fraud and Abuse Act (CFAA, 18 U.S.C. §1030) imposes liability when a person "intentionally accesses a computer without authorization or exceeds authorized access, and thereby obtains ... information from any protected computer."[25] Some court cases have held that this prohibition does not apply to public websites—meaning that scraping publicly accessible data from the internet does not violate the CFAA.[26]

Scraping publicly available information from the internet has privacy implications beyond generative AI models. The facial recognition company Clearview AI has scraped over 20 billion images from the web, including social-media profile photos, which have been used for software and databases provided to law enforcement and other entities.[27] Some technology companies have also scraped publicly available data to amass large data repositories. Web-scraping may raise competition concerns since larger companies may block competitors from scraping data.

Many researchers, journalists, and civil society groups, among others, rely on scraping to conduct research that may be in the public interest. If Congress were to consider broad legislation to limit or provide guardrails for scraping information from the internet, it might consider implications for a range of activities that it may find beneficial.

---

[22] Federal Trade Commission, "FTC Chair Khan and Officials from DOJ, CFPB and EEOC Release Joint Statement on AI," press release, April 25, 2023, https://www.ftc.gov/news-events/news/press-releases/2023/04/ftc-chair-khan- officials-doj-cfpb-eeoc-release-joint-statement-ai.

[23] Adi Robertson, "The US Government Is Gearing up for an AI Antitrust Fight," *The Verge*, March 28, 2023, https://www.theverge.com/2023/3/28/23660101/ai-competition-ftc-doj-lina-khan-jonathan-kanter-antitrust-summit.

[24] "ChatGPT and More: Large Scale AI Models Entrench Big Tech Power," AI Now Institute, April 11, 2023, https://ainowinstitute.org/publication/large-scale-ai-models.

[25] The Computer Fraud and Abuse Act is codified at Title 18, United States Code, §1030.

[26] Zack Whittaker, "Web Scraping Is Legal, US Appeals Court Reaffirms," TechCrunch, April 18, 2022, https://techcrunch.com/2022/04/18/web-scraping-legal-court/.

[27] Alex Hern, "TechScape: Clearview AI Was Fined £7.5m for Brazenly Harvesting Your Data—Does It Care?" *The Guardian*, May 25, 2022, https://www.theguardian.com/technology/2022/may/25/techscape-clearview-ai-facial- recognition-fine.

Research and Development for Alternative Technical Approaches

Congress may wish to consider providing funds to federal agencies for intramural and extramural research to examine the development of alternative AI models or related technologies that may preserve individual privacy, such as privacy-enhancing technologies.[28] There are benefits and tradeoffs to some AI models under development that may have privacy implications. For example, smaller models that use less data or avoid transmitting and analyzing data in the cloud may minimize some privacy concerns but may amplify other issues, such as bias, by training on smaller datasets and potentially limiting the representativeness of data being used to train models.[29] Congress may consider directing agencies to conduct and fund research to support privacy-by-design[30] for AI and ML applications in order to both foster greater privacy for individuals and support the development of AI technologies and the global competitiveness of U.S. AI companies.

---

[28] In a 2022 Request for Information, the White House Office of Science and Technology defined privacy-enhancing technologies as "a broad set of technologies that protect privacy." Examples could include "privacy-preserving data sharing and analytics technologies, which describes the set of techniques and approaches that enable data sharing and analysis among participating parties while maintaining disassociability and confidentiality. Such technologies include, but are not limited to, secure multiparty computation, homomorphic encryption, zero-knowledge proofs, federated learning, secure enclaves, differential privacy, and synthetic data generation tools." Office of Science and Technology Policy (OSTP), "Request for Information on Advancing Privacy-Enhancing Technologies," 87 *Federal Register* 35250- 35252, June 9, 2022.

[29] Kyle Wiggers, "The Emerging Types of Language Models and Why They Matter," TechCrunch, April 28, 2022, https://techcrunch.com/2022/04/28/the-emerging-types-of-language-models-and-why-they-matter/.

[30] James Coker, "#DataPrivacyWeek Interview: Overcoming Privacy Challenges in AI," *Infosecurity Magazine*, January 25, 2022, https://www.infosecurity-magazine.com/interviews/data-privacy-week-privacy-ai/.

Chapter 4

Banking, Data Privacy, and Cybersecurity Regulation*

Andrew P. Scott and Paul Tierno

Abstract

Financial data contains significant amounts of sensitive information, and ensuring the privacy of such data among financial institutions is a goal of many policymakers. In particular, Congress has demonstrated an interest in prioritizing data privacy standards in the financial system. Much of the legislative and regulatory data privacy framework established for banks and credit unions is constructed from a patchwork of cybersecurity provisions. Similarly, the implementation of cybersecurity supervisory programs among financial institution regulators is fragmented, and potential risks to the financial system have emerged as new technologies evolve.

Cybersecurity threats pose *operational risk*, *reputational risk*, and, potentially, *systemic risk*. Operational risk is the threat that an event such as a natural disaster, pandemic, or cyberattack limits or completely obstructs an institution's ability to do business. Reputational risk is the threat that customers will avoid future business with an institution due to such an event. Systemic risk is the threat that an event may trigger instability in an entire industry or the overall economy.

No single law provides a framework for regulating cybersecurity in the United States. Instead, several laws cover different industries, and numerous laws cover aspects of cybersecurity for the financial system. The Gramm-Leach-Bliley Act of 1999 (GLBA; P.L. 106-102) is the most comprehensive of these laws and directs financial regulators to implement disclosure requirements and security measures to safeguard private information. GLBA provides a cybersecurity framework built upon two pillars: (1) privacy standards that impose disclosure limitations or limit financial institutions concerning disclosure of consumers' information, and (2) security standards that require institutions to implement certain practices to safeguard the information from unauthorized access, use, and disclosure. The two major rules for implementing this framework are known as the Privacy Rule (Regulation P) and the Safeguards Rule, respectively. Other laws—such as the Sarbanes-Oxley Act of 2002 (P.L. 107-204), Fair and Accurate Credit Transactions Act (FACT Act; P.L. 108-159), Bank Protection Act (P.L. 90- 389), and Bank Service Company Act of 1962 (P.L. 87-856)—complete the general legislative framework for depository institution cybersecurity.

---

* This is an edited, reformatted and augmented version of Congressional Research Service, Publication No. R47434, dated March 13, 2023.

In: Data Privacy and Security: Legislative Advances and Consumer Protection
Editor: Ricky K. Segura
ISBN: 979-8-89530-730-4

Banking regulators implement the cybersecurity legislative framework through rulemaking, and then supervise institutions to ensure that banks are following regulations. Oversight of bank cybersecurity reflects a complex and sometimes overlapping array of state and federal laws, regulators, regulations, and guidance—many of which predate the emergence of cybersecurity risk. Congress is debating the extent to which it should unify or modernize the legislative framework for depository institutions. For example, one issue is how new technologies that facilitate financial data sharing should be treated under the existing cybersecurity framework. Another issue is how and whether the data privacy protections that exist for data sharing should also apply to data collection. The Data Privacy Act of 2023 (H.R. 1165), which the House Financial Services Committee ordered to be reported as amended in February 2023, examines several of these issues. Further, technology partnerships, particularly at smaller banks, with institutions such as cloud management companies, has led to new cybersecurity risks to the banking system. This has raised concerns among policymakers about the capacity of the existing framework to address new risks.

Introduction

Cybersecurity is a major concern of banks and banking regulators. Data breaches at large financial institutions and credit reporting agencies have increased concern about the privacy and security of the large amounts of consumer financial information that these companies gather, use, and store.[1] Many in Congress have demonstrated an interest in data privacy and cybersecurity, as evidenced by a number of hearings on large-scale data breaches in prior Congresses. In the 118th Congress, the Chair of the House Financial Services Committee identified data privacy as a legislative priority for the current session.[2] This report examines the existing legislative framework for financial cybersecurity, and provides some context for how regulators currently promulgate, supervise, and enforce various data privacy provisions.

The implementation of cybersecurity policy among banking regulators is fragmented, and potential risks to the financial system have emerged as new technologies evolve. This report focuses on the cybersecurity regulatory framework among the federal banking regulators—the Federal Deposit Insurance Corporation (FDIC), the Office of the Comptroller of the Currency (OCC), and the Federal Reserve—as well as the National Credit Union Administration (NCUA) and the Consumer Financial Protection Bureau (CFPB).

---

[1] For example, in spring and summer 2017, Equifax, one of the big three credit reporting agencies, announced that hackers had gained unauthorized access to the company's data, including that of 145 million customers. The data included Social Security numbers and drivers licenses. According to media reports, hackers were able to access the company's computer systems and consumer data for around two months before they realized it. See, for example, Tara Siegel Bernard, Tiffany Hsu, Nicole Perlroth, et al., " Equifax Says Cyberattack May Have Affected 143 Million in the U.S.," *The New York Times,* September 7, 2017, at https://www.nytimes.com/2017/09/07/business/equifax- cyberattack.html. For an overview of cyber incidents involving financial firms dating back to 2007, see *Timeline of Cyber Incidents Involving Financial Institutions*, Carnegie Endowment for International Peace, at https://carnegieendowment.org/specialprojects/protectingfinancialstability/timeline#click-hide.

[2] For example, on February 23, 2023, the House Committee on Financial Services scheduled a markup of several bills in February 2023, including the "Data Privacy Act of 2023." For more, see https://financialservices.house.gov/uploadedfiles/hmkp-118-ba00-20230228-sd002-u1.pdf.

Cybersecurity Risks to the Banking System

Cybersecurity means protecting systems, networks, devices, and data from digital attacks by criminals and other adversaries.[3] Cybersecurity threats pose *operational risk*, *reputational risk*, and, potentially, *systemic risk*.[4]

Operational risk is the threat that an event such as a natural disaster, pandemic, or cyberattack limits or completely obstructs an institution's ability to do business. Banks face risk from cyber threats, which could interrupt their daily operations.

Reputational risk is the threat that customers will avoid future business with an institution due to an event such as a cyberattack. The financial system depends on trust. For example, if a breach at a bank results in the release of personal data, customers may be reluctant to continue their relationship with the bank. They may choose to pull their deposits out from the bank and close their accounts. Without trust that customers' money and personal data are safe, the financial system cannot operate smoothly.

Systemic risk is the threat that a cyberattack may affect more than just the institution targeted and may jeopardize an industry or the entire economy. Banks, particularly large ones, can be highly interconnected, and many institutions depend on the same technological infrastructure. Thus, an attack on one information technology (IT) system could result in significant losses across the entire industry, both by costing the bank money to repair damages, and also the correlated risks that stem from consumers avoiding future business with the bank or other banks with similar exposure. Financial regulators consider the systemic risks to the entire industry. In doing so, they seek to ensure the safety and soundness not only of individual organizations but also their partners. The Financial Stability Oversight Council (FSOC) has identified three channels through which a cybersecurity event could threaten the stability of the U.S. financial system:[5]

1. Disrupting a key financial service or a financial market utility for which there are few substitutes (e.g., the central bank, securities and derivatives exchanges, and payment clearing and settlement institutions);
2. Causing a loss of confidence among a broad set of customers or market participants; and
3. Compromising the integrity of critical data (e.g., altering balance sheets), rendering information critical to financial firms either inaccurate or unusable.

Systemic risk from cybersecurity may have increased in 2020, as the pandemic has increased reliance on technology (e.g., remote payment systems, among others).

---

[3] See "Cybersecurity Awareness," Federal Financial Institution Examination Council, at https://www.ffiec.gov/cybersecurity.htm.

[4] For more on this landscape, see CRS Insight IN11621, *Cross-Cutting Issues in Cybersecurity: Financial Institutions*, by Chris Jaikaran and Andrew P. Scott; and CRS In Focus IF11717, *Introduction to Financial Services: Financial Cybersecurity*, by Andrew P. Scott and Paul Tierno.

[5] FSOC, Annual Report 2022, p. 66, at https://home.treasury.gov/system/files/261/FSOC2022AnnualReport.pdf.

Current Legislative Framework

No single law provides a framework for regulating cybersecurity in the United States. Instead, multiple laws cover different industries or cover aspects of cybersecurity for the broader financial system, while others apply more directly to banks. Some of these laws require financial regulators to establish cybersecurity standards for financial institutions, and provide regulators the authority to ensure compliance with such standards. Other laws provide broad authority to regulators to supervise some financial institutions for safety and soundness.

The *Gramm-Leach-Bliley Act of 1999* (GLBA; P.L. 106-102) is the most comprehensive of these laws and directs financial regulators to implement disclosure requirements and mandate security measures to safeguard private information. Specifically, Subtitle A of Title V of GLBA provides a framework for regulating data privacy and security practices for financial institutions.

The *Sarbanes-Oxley Act of 2002* (P.L. 107-204) requires certain corporations, including banks, to identify internal and external risks to their business and the ways that the company guards against those risks.

The *Fair and Accurate Credit Transactions Act of 2004* (FACT Act; P.L. 108-159) amended the Fair Credit Reporting Act to require regulatory agencies to develop identity theft guidelines, which outline "patterns, practices, and specific forms of activity that indicate the possible existence of identity theft" (15 U.S.C. §1681).

There are also two relevant laws specific to banks.

The *Bank Protection Act* (1968) (P.L. 90-389), as amended in 2010, directs the federal bank regulators to establish minimum security standards for banks and savings associations to "discourage robberies, burglaries, and larcenies" (12 U.S.C. §§1881-1884). Although the law does not mention cybersecurity specifically, the statutory language is broad enough to include protection against cyber threats.[6]

Other federal laws, such as the *Bank Service Company Act of 1962* (BSCA; P.L. 87-856) and the laws that establish the authorities for financial regulators to conduct safety and soundness examinations, allow regulators to supervise financial institution activities and partnerships (e.g., with technology service providers). Regulators rely on these broad authorities to shape and impose cybersecurity regulations on the institutions they regulate. For example, the banking regulators conduct on-site examinations under their authority to examine banks for safety and soundness and can require banks to take remedial action if their cybersecurity policies are deficient.

Recent Legislative Developments[7]

Division Y of the Consolidated Appropriations Act, 2022 (P.L. 117-103) requires that "covered entities" report a "covered cyber incident" to the Cybersecurity and Infrastructure Security

[6] For example, 12 C.F.R. §208.61 states that a bank must develop and maintain a security program and devices that ensure protection against robberies and other crimes.

[7] There are a number of legislative developments (e.g., H.R. 3912 and H.R. 3911) that pertain more broadly to cybersecurity policy and could impact the banking sector. The scope of this paper is limited to data privacy among banking regulators and depository institutions, and the legislation noted in this section reflects only bills that became law or bills in the current Congress that are being acted upon, which directly impact those entities.

Agency within 72 hours and a ransomware payment within 24 hours of occurrence, respectively.[8] Covered incidents include, at a minimum, any incident that leads "to substantial loss of confidentiality, integrity, or availability of such information system or network, or a serious impact on the safety and resiliency of operational systems and processes."

On February 8, the House Financial Services Committee held a hearing[9] on various efforts to update bank regulation, including a discussion draft on data privacy. On February 28, 2023, the committee held a markup of several bills, including the Data Privacy Act of 2023 (H.R. 1165), introduced by Chair McHenry.[10] The bill would amend GLBA, clarify the inclusion of data aggregators[11] under the scope of the law, and give consumers some added control over certain data, such as the ability to access and remove it from financial institution records. Also, the draft includes a national preemption measure, which would supersede state law.[12] During the markup, a number of amendments were introduced. While all eight amendments introduced by Democrats were rejected, the committee adopted a substitute amendment that would "allow exceptions for disclosures of personal information permitted under the Gramm-Leach-Bliley Act. The amendment also would specify that disclosure of data retention policies would include the period of time data is held and the criteria the institution uses to determine that time."[13] The bill was ordered to be reported to the full House, as amended, by a vote of 26-21.

Regulatory Framework

As mentioned earlier, this report focuses largely on the cybersecurity regulatory framework among the federal banking regulators—the FDIC, the OCC, and the Federal Reserve—as well as the NCUA and the CFPB. Together these agencies are responsible for implementing and ensuring compliance with banking laws.

Generally, banking institutions are regulated by a primary federal regulator (PFR). The PFR for each type of banking institution depends on its charter, as summarized in Table 1. In addition, the CFPB promulgates a number of consumer protection rules for a variety of financial institutions, including certain banks.

---

[8] The term "covered entity" applies to "an entity in a critical infrastructure sector, as defined in Presidential Policy Directive 21." The financial sector is included in the Policy Directive as a critical infrastructure sector. For more, see https://obamawhitehouse.archives.gov/the-press-office/2013/02/12/presidential-policy-directive-critical-infrastructure- security-and-resil.

[9] U.S. House Financial Services Committee, "Hearing Entitled: Revamping and Revitalizing Banking in the 21st Century, February 8, 2023, at https://financialservices.house.gov/calendar/eventsingle.aspx?EventID=408512.

[10] In this report, references to this bill are made to the amendment in the nature of a substitute, which can be found at https://docs.house.gov/meetings/BA/BA00/20230228/115381/BILLS-118-HR1165-M001156-Amdt-12.pdf.

[11] Data aggregators are entities that pull together various data to analyze and yield additional insights. This could be information that is public, such as names, geographical locations, and time, or more sensitive data such as account numbers.

[12] U.S. Congress, House Committee on Financial Services, *To Amend the Gramm-Leach-Bliley Act to [Modernize the Protection of the Nonpublic Personal Information of Consumers*, discussion draft.

[13] CQ Markup Report, H.R. 1165: Data Privacy Act, at https://plus.cq.com/bill/118/HR1165?3.

Table 1. Regulatory jurisdiction for different banking institutions

Bank Charter Type	Primary Federal Regulator
State charter, member of Federal Reserve	Federal Reserve
State charter, nonmember	Federal Deposit Insurance Corporation
Federal charter	Office of the Comptroller of the Currency
Credit unions	National Credit Union Administration

Source: CRS analysis.
Note: All national banks are also members of the Federal Reserve.

GLBA Data Privacy and Safeguards

As mentioned above, GLBA provides the most comprehensive framework for cybersecurity regulation among financial institutions. While this section largely focuses on the GLBA provisions for regulating data privacy and security practices for banks, GLBA applies to a broad range of financial institutions.[14] This framework is built upon two pillars: (1) privacy standards that impose disclosure limitations concerning consumers' information, and (2) security standards that require institutions to implement certain practices to safeguard the information from unauthorized access, use, and disclosure. The two major rules for implementing this framework are known as the Privacy Rule (Regulation P) and the Safeguards Rule, respectively. Each rule is summarized below in Table 2.

Table 2. Summary of privacy and safeguards rules requirements for financial institutions

Privacy Rule	Safeguards Rule
• provide initial, annual, and revised privacy policy notices to customers; and • set the conditions for when a financial institution may or may not disclose nonpublic personal information.	• design and implement a safeguards program; and • identify and assess the risks to customer information in each relevant area of the company's operation, including service providers and changes in the firm's operations.

Source: CRS analysis of relevant provisions of the Gramm-Leach-Bliley Act (P.L. 106-102).

These rules are promulgated by several government agencies, and the regulators generally have supervisory and enforcement authority over the entities in their jurisdiction. This is shown in Table 3 and Table 4.

GLBA Rulemaking Authorities

Rulemaking authority to implement the Privacy Rule through Regulation P is vested in four agencies. The CFPB promulgates the Privacy Rule for banks. The Federal Trade Commission (FTC) has the rulemaking authority for the Safeguards Rule. Table 4 provides an overview of federal agencies with GLBA rulemaking authority and which entities they regulate under each rule.

[14] Financial institutions are defined under P.L. 106-102 as any institution that engages in activities that are financial in nature. See 12 U.S.C. §6809.

Table 3. Relevant rulemaking authority for GLBA

Federal Regulator	Privacy Rule	Safeguards Rule
Consumer Financial Protection Bureau (CFPB)	Depository and nonbank financial institutions involving consumer financial products or services in the CFPB's jurisdiction	None
Federal Trade Commission (FTC)	n/a	Financial institutions significantly engaged in financial activities (e.g., bank and nonbank lenders, real estate appraisers, professional tax preparers, courier services, credit reporting agencies, and ATM operators)

Sources: 15. U.S.C. §6804; 12 C.F.R. §1016.1(b).

Recent Updates on Depository Regulation of GLBA Cybersecurity Provisions

Title X of the Dodd-Frank Wall Street Reform and Consumer Protection Act of 2010 (Dodd-Frank; P.L. 111-203) transferred rulemaking authority for most provisions of Subtitle A of Title V of GLBA to the CFPB. As can be seen in more detail in the following section, Dodd-Frank also granted authority to the CFPB to examine and enforce compliance with respect to entities, including banks, under its jurisdiction.[15] In December 2011, the CFPB effectively recodified Regulation P in Title 12, Part 1016, of the *Code of Federal Regulations*.[16] The most recent amendment to its rulemaking occurred in 2018, when a 2015 statutory amendment from the Fixing America's Surface Transportation (FAST Act; P.L. 114-94) provided an exception to the annual notice requirement for financial institutions that meet certain conditions.[17]

The FTC codified its implementation of the Safeguards Rule in 2002 in Title 16, Part 314, of the *Code of Federal Regulations*.[18] In 2016, the FTC sought public comments on the Safeguards Rule to assess the economic impact and benefits of the rule; possible conflict between the rule and state, local, or other federal laws or regulations; and the effect on the rule of any technological, economic, or other industry changes.[19]

On October 27, 2021, the FTC announced that it had issued a new final rulemaking[20] to specify safeguards financial institutions must implement as part of their information security programs— including limiting who can access consumer data and requiring encryption to secure the data.

Under the updated Safeguards Rule, institutions must also explain the administrative, technical, and physical safeguards used to "access, collect, distribute, process, protect, store, use, transmit, dispose of, or otherwise handle" customer information. Further, the definition of *financial institution* was expanded to include institutions that charge fees to connect consumers to potential lenders. In addition, the rule requires a financial institution to designate a single

---

[15] CFPB, *Laws and Regulations,* "GLBA Privacy," October 2016, at https://files.consumerfinance.gov/f/documents/102016_cfpb_GLBAExamManualUpdate.pdf.

[16] See CFPB, "Privacy of Consumer Financial Information (Regulation P)," 76 *Federal Register* 79025, December 21, 2011.

[17] CFPB, "Amendment to the Annual Privacy Notice Requirement Under the Gramm-Leach-Bliley Act (Regulation P)," 83 *Federal Register* 40945, August 17, 2018.

[18] See FTC, "Standards for Safeguarding Customer Information," 67 *Federal Register* 36484, May 23, 2002.

[19] See FTC, "Standards for Safeguarding Customer Information," 81 *Federal Register* 61632, September 7, 2016.

[20] See FTC, "Standards for Safeguarding Customer Information," 86 *Federal Register* 70272-70314, December 9, 2021.

qualified individual to oversee its information security program and provide periodic reports to the institution's board or information security officials. The FTC also announced that it is seeking comment in a supplemental notice of proposed rulemaking on an additional change to the Safeguards Rule to require financial institutions to report certain data breaches and other security events to the FTC.[21]

Other Regulatory Developments

In November 2021, the OCC, Federal Reserve, and FDIC announced a joint final rulemaking that imposed rapid notification requirements on banking organizations and bank service providers following "significant" computer-security incidents.[22] The rule requires a financial institution to notify its supervisor as soon as possible and no later than 36 hours after the banking organization believes in good faith that the incident occurred. This notification requirement is intended to serve as an early alert to a banking organization's primary federal regulator and is not meant to provide an assessment of the incident. Additionally, a bank service provider is required to notify each affected banking organization customer immediately after the provider experiences a computer security incident that has caused or is likely to cause a material service disruption for four or more hours.

Supervisory Process

In addition to writing rules to implement provisions of law, banking regulators have authority to conduct examinations or supervise institutions in their jurisdiction to ensure they are complying with the rules. As noted earlier, cybersecurity threats pose operational risk, reputational risk, and potentially systemic risk. Banking regulators together monitor these risks through the Federal Financial Institutions Examination Council (FFIEC).[23] FSOC monitors systemic risks to the financial system, including cyber threats. The FFIEC coordinates bank examinations for safety and soundness, as well as for compliance and information technology. Further, bank partnerships with third-party service providers are subject to the supervisory processes set forth in the BSCA.

GLBA Supervision

Agencies responsible for privacy and safeguard rulemaking are sometimes not the same agencies responsible for implementing and enforcing these rules for a particular entity. For instance, while the FTC has rulemaking authority for the Safeguards Rule, the banking and credit union regulators share supervisory authority for the rule. Further, most of the financial

---

[21] See FTC, "Standards for Safeguarding Customer Information," 86 *Federal Register* 70062-70067, December 9, 2021.

[22] OCC, Federal Reserve, and FDIC, "Computer-Security Incident Notification Requirements for Banking Organizations and Their Bank Service Providers," 86 *Federal Register* 66444, November 23, 2021 at https://www.federalregister.gov/documents/2021/11/23/2021-25510/computer-security-incident-notification-requirements-for-banking-organizations-and-their-bank.

[23] Federal Reserve, FDIC, NCUA, OCC, and the CFPB, along with representatives from state supervising organizations, comprise FFIEC.

regulators have some supervisory or enforcement authority to ensure that the institutions in their respective jurisdictions comply with the Privacy and Safeguards Rules (see Table 4).

Table 4. Supervision and enforcement authority for GLBA

Federal Regulator	Privacy Rule	Safeguards Rule
CFPB	Supervision and enforcement authority over depository and nonbank financial institutions involving consumer financial products or services in the CFPB's jurisdiction	None
Bank and Credit Union Regulators	Supervision and enforcement authority over banks or credit unions in their jurisdiction	Supervision and enforcement authority over banks or credit unions in their jurisdiction

Source: 15 U.S.C. §6805.

Note: The depository agencies include the Office of the Comptroller of the Currency, the Federal Deposit Insurance Corporation, the Federal Reserve, and the National Credit Union Administration.

Depository Institution Supervision

Bank and credit union regulators have dedicated teams of examiners who conduct both routine and special examinations of depository institutions to ensure that they are operating in a safe and sound manner, complying with relevant laws, and maintaining adequate information technology systems. Each of the regulators inform the financial institutions under their jurisdiction about their supervisory expectations.

Table 5. Depository supervision toolkit for cybersecurity

Agency	Supervisory Approaches & Resources	FFIEC Resources for Examinations
NCUA	Automated Cybersecurity Evaluation Toolbox Examinations (NCUA Examinations Guidebook and FFIEC Handbook) National Supervision Policy ManualGuidance Letters to Credit Unions Risk Alerts	
FDIC	Examinations for IT (IT Risk Management Program and FFIEC Handbook) Technical Assistance Video Series Supervisory Insights Journal Cyber Challenge for Community Banks Guidance (FDIC Financial Institution Letters)	IT Examination Handbook Cybersecurity Assessment Tool IT and Related Guidance
OCC	Examinations for IT (FFIEC Handbook and Comptroller's Handbook for Bank Supervision) Guidance (OCC Bulletins)	
Federal Reserve	Examinations for IT (Commercial Bank Examination Manual and FFIEC Handbook) Policy Letters (Supervision and Regulation Letters)	

Source: CRS analysis of each agency's cybersecurity, IT, and examination websites.

Notes: Intended for illustrative purposes only; not intended to capture all measures taken by an agency. Regulatory resources for information on these supervisory programs can be found at https://ithandbook.ffiec.gov/ it-booklets.aspx; https://www.fdic.gov/resources/bankers/information-technology/; and https://ncua.gov/regulation-supervision/regulatory-compliance-resources/cybersecurity-resources/ncuas-information-security-examination-and-cybersecurity-assessment.

In addition, while the regulatory framework for banks and credit unions is complex and fragmented among several agencies, the examination procedures among these agencies are largely coordinated through the FFIEC.

The depository regulators each approach cybersecurity examinations and supervision in different ways. Table 5 illustrates the general approaches and resources that each agency has established with respect to cybersecurity and information security. While each agency has developed its own approaches, tools, and resources, each agency relies on the FFIEC resources as well. The basic approaches include providing guidance to industry on how certain activities will be treated, policy manuals and handbooks that lay out the guidelines for examinations, and technical assistance.

Third-Party Service Providers

As banks facilitate more transactions through digital channels, financial institutions are increasingly relying on third-party vendors, specifically technology service providers (TSPs), to provide software and technical support. In light of this development, regulators are scrutinizing how banks manage their *operational risks*.[24] Rising operational risks—particularly cyber risks (e.g., data breaches, insufficient customer data backups, and operating system hijackings)—have compelled regulators to scrutinize banks' security programs. Regulators require an institution that uses a TSP to ensure that the TSP performs in a safe and sound manner, and activities performed by a TSP for a bank must meet the same regulatory requirements as if they were performed by the bank itself.

The BSCA gives regulators a broad set of authorities to supervise TSPs that have contractual relationships with banks. The BSCA directs the regulators to treat all activities performed by contract as if they were performed by the bank and grants them the authority to examine and regulate third-party vendors that provide services to banks, including check and deposit sorting and posting, statement preparation, notices, bookkeeping, and accounting.

The banking regulators issued interagency guidelines in 2001 regarding information security programs. The guidance requires banks to provide continuous oversight of third-party vendors such as TSPs. The regulators periodically update guidance and have since released additional guidance pertaining to third-party vendors.[25] For example, the Federal Reserve, FDIC, and OCC have each issued guidance addressing third-party relationships and appropriate risk management practices in 2008 and 2013, respectively.[26] In July 2021, the FDIC, Federal Reserve, and OCC issued joint proposed guidance on third-party relationships.[27] The proposed

---

[24] See Basel Committee on Banking Supervision, *Principles for the Sound Management of Operational Risk*, June 2011, at https://www.bis.org/publ/bcbs195.pdf.

[25] For example, see the following releases: NCUA, *Evaluating Third Party Relationships*, Letter No.: 07-CU-13, December 2007; FDIC, *Guidance for Managing Third-Party Risk*, FIL-44-2008, June 6, 2008; FFIEC, "Financial Regulators Release Guidance for the Supervision of Technology Service Providers," press release, October 31, 2012, at https://www.ffiec.gov/press/pr103112.htm; FDIC, *Technology Outsourcing: Informational Tools for Community Bankers*, FIL-13-2014, April 7, 2014; FDIC Office of Inspector General, *Technology Service Provider Contracts with FDIC-Supervised Institutions*, Office of Audits and Evaluations, Report No. EVAL-17-004, February 2017; and NCUA Office of Inspector General, *Audit of the NCUA Information Technology Examination Program's Oversight of Credit Union Cybersecurity Programs*, Report No OIG-17-08, September 28, 2017.

[26] For example, see FDIC, "Guidance for Managing Third-Party Risk," June 6, 2008, at https://www.fdic.gov/news/financial-institution-letters/2008/fil08044.html; Federal Reserve, "Guidance on Managing Outsourcing Risk," December 5, 2013 (revised February 26, 2021), at https://www.federalreserve.gov/supervisionreg/srletters/sr1319.htm; and OCC, "Third-Party Relationships: Risk Management Guidance," October 30, 2013, at https://www.occ.gov/news- issuances/bulletins/2013/bulletin-2013-29.html.

[27] Federal Reserve, FDIC, and OCC, "Proposed Interagency Guidance on Third-Party Relationships: Risk Management," July 13, 2021, at https://www.fdic.gov/news/financial-institution-letters/2021/fil21050.html.

guidance assists banking organizations in managing third-party relationships. Further, in August 2021, the OCC issued guidance on financial technology third-party relationships.[28]

Policy Issues for Congress

Oversight of financial services and bank cybersecurity reflects a complex and sometimes overlapping array of state and federal laws, regulators, regulations, and guidance—many of which predate the emergence of cybersecurity risk. Whether this framework provides adequate protection against cyberattacks without imposing undue cost burdens on banks is an open question. Successful hacks of banks and other financial institutions, in which large amounts of personal information were stolen or compromised, highlight arguments about the importance of ensuring bank cybersecurity.

That several regulators implement, supervise, and enforce federal provisions has also raised questions over the patchwork nature of regulatory standards for consumer privacy and security. With so many agencies involved with the cybersecurity of financial institutions, the Government Accountability Office (GAO) has raised concerns over interagency cooperation and tracking the success of agency efforts.[29] Some argue that a unified and modernized legislative framework could improve this patchwork approach.

As Congress continues to explore this issue, a few policy considerations, detailed below, may be informative.

Data Privacy

GLBA's financial data privacy provisions covers only nonpublic personal information held by financial institutions significantly engaged in financial activities. However, as the industry's data use has grown, some have debated whether the law covers all sensitive individual financial information. For example, data brokers can compile public and private data from different sources, many of which may not be subject to GLBA's provisions; combining these data might reveal financially sensitive information about a consumer. Further, consumers have a limited ability to know, control, or correct financial data, which can make it difficult to obtain redress for violations such as data breaches.

Technology Service Providers

Regulation aimed at banks' relationships with third-party vendors such as TSPs has benefits in mitigating operational risks but also imposes costs on banks. Some banks, particularly community banks and small credit unions, may find it difficult to comply with regulatory

---

[28] OCC, "OCC Bulletin 2021-40," August 27, 2021, at https://www.occ.gov/news-issuances/bulletins/2021/bulletin-2021-40.html.

[29] U.S. Government Accountability Office, *Critical Infrastructure Protection: Treasury Needs to Improve Tracking of Financial Sector Cybersecurity Risk Mitigation Efforts*, GAO-20-631, September 17, 2020, https://www.gao.gov/ products/gao-20-631.

standards applicable to their relationship with third-party vendors. For example, certain institutions may be unable to conduct appropriate due diligence when selecting TSPs or to structure contracts that adequately protect against potential TSPs-related risks. Some banks may also lack the resources to monitor whether the TSPs are adhering to GLBA and other regulatory or contract requirements. Regulatory compliance costs are sometimes cited as a factor in banking industry consolidation, because compliance costs may be subject to economies of scale that incentivize small banks to merge with larger ones or other small banks to combine their resources to meet their compliance obligations.[30]

Cloud Computing

Financial institutions may outsource the management of different controls over information assets and operations to cloud service providers (CSPs).[31] Banks pay CSPs to use their computing resources (e.g., servers and mainframes), rather than purchasing and maintaining their own. This relationship is referred to as a shared responsibility model, in which banks and CSPs are responsible for discrete tasks of a shared work stream. Failure to implement an effective risk management process could put sensitive information at risk.

The BSCA gives bank regulators supervisory authority over service providers.[32] Exercising this authority over CSPs, however, may raise challenges. Despite the integration of cloud services by the banking industry, different expectations from bank regulators and the cloud service industry,—such as what to expect during bank-like examinations—may persist.

Large, systemically important banks are reportedly moving significant portions of their operations onto cloud services, which could exacerbate the effects of a disruption at a CSP.[33] The cloud market is concentrated in three major CSPs—Amazon Web Services, Microsoft Azure, and Google Cloud—that collectively account for between 60%[34] and 70%[35] of market share and perhaps more among banks. In its 2022 annual report, FSOC identified "the financial sector's concentrated dependency on a limited number of service providers, such as cloud service providers, for critical information technology services as a potential risk to financial stability."[36] Traditional bank risks such as market and liquidity risks—not normally cloud computing concerns—can arise if the banks' abilities to transact are impeded by cloud-related disruptions. Banking regulators are concerned with risks to financial stability, so policymakers may choose to consider whether their authorities to regulate CSPs are appropriately calibrated.

---

[30] For more information on banking industry consolidation, see CRS In Focus IF11956, *Bank Mergers and Acquisitions*, by Marc Labonte and Andrew P. Scott.

[31] For more on bank use of cloud technology, see CRS In Focus IF11985, *Bank Use of Cloud Technology*, by Paul Tierno.

[32] 12 U.S.C. §1867(c).

[33] Ibid.

[34] Felix Richter, "Amazon Leads $150-Billion Cloud Market," *Statista*, July 5, 2021, at https://www.statista.com/chart/18819/worldwide-market-share-of-leading-cloud-infrastructure-service-providers/.

[35] Gartner, "Gartner Says Worldwide IaaS Public Cloud Services Market Grew 40.7% in 2020," press release, June 28, 2021, at https://www.gartner.com/en/newsroom/press-releases/2021-06-28-gartner-says-worldwide-iaas-public-cloud- services-market-grew-40-7-percent-in-2020.

[36] FSOC, *2022 Annual Report*, December 16, 2022, p. 70, at https://home.treasury.gov/system/files/261/FSOC2022AnnualReport.pdf.

Considering this close relationship, the scope of bank supervision may expand to CSPs. This may lead to technical resource mismatches, and regulators, like banks,[37] may find themselves with a shortage of cloud skills necessary to examine CSPs. CSPs may also not be familiar with or amenable to audits or bank-like examinations.[38] The Federal Reserve Bank of Richmond performed a formal exam of Amazon Web Services in April 2019, which reportedly exposed this culture clash.[39] Close integration between banks and CSPs may accelerate regulators' call for regular examination of CSPs to monitor aspects of their relationships with banks, including security and financial system stability risks.

Obstacles to data portability, such as proprietary technology and restrictive vendor contracts, may make switching CSPs difficult. Therefore, banks may adopt multi-cloud strategies—contracts with multiple CSPs—to avoid lock-in risk.[40] In addition to increasing costs, this introduces potentially two or more providers in the form of CSPs, and banks must manage these relationships effectively to ensure cybersecurity.

---

[37] Abbott, Michael, "Challenges and Opportunities in Banks' Cloud Migration," Accenture, January 27, 2021, at https://bankingblog.accenture.com/challenges-opportunities-banks-cloud-migration.

[38] Penny Crossman, "Timely Reminder About Who Bears Responsibility For Cloud Security," *American Banker*, May 4, 2020, at https://www.americanbanker.com/news/timely-reminder-about-who-bears-responsibility-for-cloud-security.

[39] Liz Hoffman, Dana Mattioli, and Ryan Tracy, "Fed Examined Amazon's Cloud in New Scrutiny for Tech," *The Wall Street Journal*, August 1, 2019, at https://www.wsj.com/articles/fed-examined-amazons-cloud-in-new-scrutiny-for- tech-11564693812.

[40] Matthew Leybold, Hrishi Hrishikesh, and Benjamin Rehberg, "Financial Institutions Need to Pursue Their Own Path to the Cloud," BCG, May 5, 2021, at https://www.bcg.com/publications/2021/strategies-for-financial-institutions- transitioning-to-the-cloud.

Index

A

B

C

T

V

Y